REACHING
FOR THE **STARS**

REACHING
FOR THE STARS

*A Celebration of Italian Americans
in Major League Baseball*

EDITED BY LARRY FREUNDLICH

BALLANTINE BOOKS • NEW YORK

A Ballantine Book
Published by The Random House Publishing Group

Copyright © 2003 by Freundlich Communications, Inc.

All rights reserved under International and Pan-American Copyright Conventions.
Published in the United States by The Random House Publishing Group, a division of
Random House, Inc., New York, and simultaneously in Canada by Random House of
Canada Limited, Toronto.

Ballantine and colophon are registered trademarks of Random House, Inc.

www.ballantinebooks.com

Book design by Joel Avirom and Jason Snyder

The Cataloging-in-Publication Data for this title is available from the Library of Congress.

ISBN 0-345-45706-4

Manufactured in the United States of America

First Edition: October 2003

10   9   8   7   6   5   4   3   2   1

CONTENTS

ACKNOWLEDGMENTS

Special thanks to Ira Berkow who, in addition to contributing the Ping Bodie essay to this volume, has given generously of his time and his major league baseball contact numbers. I received courteous, patient, and the most friendly treatment from world-class researchers Bill Francis and Bill Burdick of the National Baseball Hall of Fame in Cooperstown, New York. David Kaplan of the Yogi Berra Museum has been a staunch ally of this project, and it was he who first put this project in a good light with Yogi Berra. Above and beyond his contribution of his essay "A Special Breed," Donald Honig has been a treasury of baseball scholarship and an invaluable source of photo archive information. Jim Leary of Sports Media Enterprises, which is the publisher of the definitive *Total Baseball*, went out of his way to provide the digitized statistics with which *Reaching for the Stars* concludes. My debt to George Randazzo is acknowledged in my own essay for this volume, "Citizen of Baseball." Thanks to Tom Vallanti and Phil Dusenberry for their networking help. I want to thank Jim Schultz, media relations director of the Atlanta Braves, who gave me the wonderful news that John Smoltz's mother is Italian American (thereby giving us another all-time all-star pitcher). And, finally, a great big thanks to Yogi Berra, a man who always knows what he's talking about, especially when you listen carefully.

INTRODUCTION

It was a great day for me when Dave Kaplan, the director of the Yogi Berra Museum in Little Falls, New Jersey, told me that Yogi had agreed to make the final selections to the All-Time All–Italian American All-Star Team for this book. I submitted to Yogi a list of several candidates whom I had chosen at each position. For example, at first base I had listed Phil Cavarretta and Dolf Camilli and Jason Giambi. At second base the competition was among Tony Lazzeri, Billy Martin, and Craig Biggio. At third I had singled out Frank Crosetti, Frank Malzone, Ron Santo, and Cookie Lavagetto. Yogi's pal and teammate Phil Rizzuto was nominated at short, along with Rico Petrocelli. (Now that I have read Joe Veccione's essay in this volume, "Boys of the Golden West," I regret not having nominated Jim Fregosi or Rich Aurilia.)

At catcher the Italian Americans were really deep: Ernie Lombardi, Berra, Roy Campanella, and Mike Piazza, and I told Yogi that we didn't want to embarrass him by making him judge the position where he might have to pick himself. So we asked him to choose from among the three other guys. After talking to the essayists who contributed to this book and to the researchers who helped me out at the Hall of Fame in Cooperstown, we chose Yogi as our All-Time Italian American. (Yogi selected Roy Campanella.)

I submitted a list of pitchers to Yogi. It included Sal Maglie, Frank Viola, Johnny Antonelli, John Franco, Dave Righetti, Ralph Branca, Mike Mussina, Vic Raschi, Ernie Broglio, Tom Candiotti, Marius Russo, and young Barry Zito. (At the time, I did not know that John Smoltz's mother was Italian.) A mighty staff indeed, but among them, in my opinion, no superstars of the stature of Christy Mathewson, Bob Feller, Sandy Koufax, Bob Gibson, Randy Johnson, or Nolan Ryan.

In the outfield, after Joe DiMaggio the other candidates were not so easy to identify: Dom DiMaggio, Rocky Colavito, Carl Furillo, Tony Conigliaro, or Bart Giamatti's surprise candidate, Al Zarilla, were outstanding outfielders to be sure, but for all the admiration they deserved, they were dimmed by DiMaggio's incandescence.

Yogi also chose a manager, and the field was a strong one: Tom Lasorda, Bobby Valentine, Tony La Russa, Joe Amalfatano, Mike Scioscia, and Joe Torre.

I want to thank Yogi for his willingness to select this All-Time Italian American Team despite the fact that he was cautious about the assignment. In fact, he said, "I hate this kind of thing." I knew just what he meant. As much fun as it is to think in terms of "the best," it is controversial, and it sometimes leads you down the road to arguments you'd rather not have. But then again, it can lead you down the road to some terrific debates, which I am sure are a lot less sensitive if you aren't, like Yogi, an All-Star yourself.

Here is Yogi Berra's Italian American All-Star Team in Yogi's own words.

CATCHER: Campy (Roy Campanella), Ernie Lombardi, and Mike Piazza—that's not too shabby. Lombardi could hit pretty good, couldn't run, but boy he could hit. I think his last year, 1947, was my first. Campy was great. Great power, great guy. And great for only being half Italian. Piazza? He's a real good kid. He's going to break all the hitting records for a catcher. Guess I'm partial to Campy because he played when I did.

FIRST BASE: Phil Cavarretta and Dolf Camilli, they were pretty good. I like Jason Giambi though. He's a good kid. Good power, good numbers, and good that he's a Yankee.

SECOND BASE: Billy Martin was a scrapper, he helped us a lot. But Tony Lazzeri was the best. Frank Crosetti played with Tony and that's what Frank told me. Among the guys playing today, you've got to like Craig Biggio, but Lazzeri is the best ever.

SHORTSTOP: My buddy Phil Rizzuto. Rico Petrocelli was a good ballplayer, and he hit those forty homers in 1969, but Phil's a Hall-of-Famer.

THIRD BASE: Ron Santo was pretty good with the Cubs—probably the best. Frank Malzone was a real good ballplayer, too. Real bowlegged, but he could play.

OUTFIELD: Jeez. Well, you got Joe DiMaggio, that's easy. He did everything perfect. Carl Furillo and Rocky Colavito, they were both good right fielders, great arms. You sure Al Kaline wasn't Italian? Just kidding. Don't forget Dom DiMaggio on the Red Sox either—a superb player. Can you move one of these guys to left?

STARTING PITCHERS: Vic Raschi wasn't too bad, you know. He was a big reason we won five straight (1949–53) championships. I'd take him anytime. Sal Maglie was pretty strong. Only pitched ten years because he was in Mexico, but he was tough. You got to like Mike Mussina and Barry Zito of today's guys.

RELIEF PITCHERS: Dave Righetti and John Franco. Two lefties, but they're good. I was the one who made Rags a reliever, and he did pretty well. Great team player. Franco began as a starter, too, and he turned out good, too. Plus he's short, and I like short guys.

MANAGER: Joe Torre. He was a heck of a hitter and a pretty darn good manager. I always tell him he's the reason I got fired by the Mets as manager in 1975, because he hit into four double plays one game. And he tells me to blame Felix Millan, because he got on first every time Joe got up.

The desire to see an Italian everywhere and to make Italians of our favorites is one of the occupational hazards of working on a book such as this one. No wonder that when I first began thinking about the outfield that I dreamed of nominating the Bambino, whose greatness I speculated was in part magically imparted him by his nickname.

Along these lines, consider the case of Buttercup Dickerson, who in some scholarly circles is considered the first Italian American in the major leagues. Buttercup was born July 11, 1858 in Tyaskin, Maryland, and made his major league debut as a left fielder with the Cincinnati Red Stockings of the National League on July 15, 1878. He played his last game in the National League with Buffalo in 1885. Leading Italian American sports experts such as George Randazzo, the founder and chairman of the National Italian American Sports Hall of Fame in Chicago support Buttercup Dickerson's claim to the honor of being the first Italian American major-leaguer, and the argument seems plausible given the fact that Dickerson was baptized Lewis Pessano Dickerson. The "Pessano" in the middle of Buttercup's name does not, however, indicate Italian parentage, according to Charles Weaver of Ocean City, Maryland, who during assiduous research for a book on Dickerson has concluded that the "Pessano" in the newly born Lewis Dickerson's name may have been given him by his parents in honor of the Dr. Pessano who delivered baby Lewis, and that no documentary evidence exists that establishes either of Buttercup's parents as Italian. In fact, Buttercup's mother was born Mary Pricilla Larmore and his father William Porter Dickerson. The Dickersons arrived on the shores of Eastern Maryland in the seventeenth century from Scotland. Until Buttercup's Italian parentage can be proven, the present facts demand that Ed Abbaticchio, born in Latrobe, Pennsylvania, in 1877, who played nine years in the majors for Philadelphia, Boston, and Pittsburgh of the National League, be accorded the honor.

Ask a typical baseball fan who was the first man to hit sixty home

Tony Lazzeri, the first Italian American Major League superstar
(National Baseball Hall of Fame Library, Cooperstown, New York)

runs was, and he will wonder at the innocence of your question and tell you it was Babe Ruth. But ask a baseball fan who has spent perhaps a bit too much time researching the contribution of Italian Americans to baseball and he may put forth the sophistry that it was twenty-one-year-old Tony Lazzeri, even though Lazzeri hit his sixtieth for the Salt Lake Bees of the Pacific Coast League in 1925, the same year Ruth hit fifty-nine for the Yankees. (Ruth didn't hit his sixtieth until 1927, and by that time Lazzeri was the Bambino's teammate.)

And while we're on the subject of Tony Lazzeri and home runs, Lazzeri still holds the American League single-game record with eleven RBI against the Philadelphia Athletics on May 24, 1936, a game in which he became the first big-leaguer to hit two grand slams in one game. This offensive outburst contributed to two other records. He hit six home runs in three consecutive games and seven homers in four successive games. He also tied the big league record of five homers in two consecutive games.

Another of Babe Ruth's Herculean achievements (would Hercules' achievements be called "Ruthean"?) is challenged by an Italian American baseball hero, Phil Cavarretta, first baseman for the Chicago Cubs from 1934 to 1953. Cavarretta had a league-leading 197 hits in 1944 and his .345 batting average in 1945 made him the league's MVP. But, in the opinion of many baseball fans, including Ira Berkow, who has contributed an essay ("The

Phil Cavarretta, 1945 National League MVP of the Chicago Cubs (National Baseball Hall of Fame Library, Cooperstown, New York)

Extraordinary Life and Times of Ping Bodie") on Francesco Stefano Pezzolo, aka, Ping Bodie to this volume, a Cavarretta homer deserves consideration as the Greatest Home Run Ever Hit.

If you go along with Berkow on this, you are going to have to move aside Babe's dedicating his home run to a dying child by pointing his bat toward the center field bleachers in Yankee Stadium; the crippled Kirk Gibson's ninth-inning home run in the first game of the 1988 World Series off Oakland's Dennis Eckersley; and Carlton Fisk's soap-operatic finale off the left field foul pole at Fenway Park 1975 against Cincinnati in the twelfth inning of the sixth game of the World Series. Nonetheless, Cavarretta's home run stands up to this awesome company.

After a twenty-year career with the Cubs, the beloved but fading Cavarretta became player-manager of the Cubs. On July 29, 1951, against the Phillies, Cavarretta drove home three runs in a 5–4 first-game win, snapping the Cubs' ten-game home losing streak. His triple in the sixth ended the consecutive-scoreless-innings streak of the Phils' all-time-great pitcher Robin Roberts at 41. An exhausted Cavarretta discretely benched himself for game two of the doubleheader, but inserted himself as a pinch hitter in the seventh when Robin Roberts made his second appearance of the day, this time in relief. Having had the hubris to insert himself into the lineup against one of the greatest pitchers of all time, Cavarretta justified his wisdom as a manager and his greatness as a player by hitting a grand slam off Roberts as the Cubs swept, winning the nightcap 8–6.

Italian American major leaguers have contributed several candidates for inclusion among baseball's "Greatest" category. As Wilfrid Sheed so movingly argues in his essay "Joe DiMaggio: The Making of a King," the Italians have provided baseball with its greatest American icon. Sheed persuades us that DiMaggio's greatness was part of his gift of being Italian, a sense of personal power and style that the Italians have had for centuries. For these newly defined Italian Americans, DiMaggio's legendary stardom yoked them to America's national game and to the interests of their new country.

Joe DiMaggio
(National Baseball Hall of Fame Library, Cooperstown, New York)

Ralph Branca
(National Baseball Hall of Fame Library, Cooperstown, New York)

Donald Honig, in his essay "A Special Breed," argues convincingly that Cookie Lavagetto's hit with two outs in the ninth off Yankees starter Floyd Beven, who had been pitching a no-hitter, may have been baseball's greatest pinch hit, and that Brooklyn Dodger Al Gionfriddo's catch off the bat of Joe DiMaggio, also in the 1947 World Series, was the greatest clutch catch in the outfield.

"The greatest" for the Italian American major-leaguer has sometimes come in somber garb. Lawrence Baldassaro, in his essay on the great catcher Ernie Lombardi, recalls for us what must rank among the greatest of baseball injustices, short of the color barrier, when he recalls the infamy that unfairly hounded Lombardi after the sensationalist media distortion of Lombardi's so-called "snooze." Having been knocked senseless by a collision at home plate, Lombardi lay on his back as the winning run crossed the plate. The "snooze" haunted Lombardi for the rest of his life. And what for Bobby Thomson and all New York Giants fans must rank as the greatest home run of all time, for Brooklyn Dodgers fans and Ralph Branca, the Italian American right-hander who surrendered it, it must rank as the most tragic.

Of all the entrants into the category of greatest, the greatest rivalry ranks first. And, as the essays of Bob Leuci, George Vecsey, and Anthony Valerio imply, the greatest rivalry was between the Brooklyn Dodgers and the New York Giants in the days when its intense enmity was personified in the dark-hued visages of Brooklyn right-fielder Carl "The Reading Rifle" Furillo and Giants pitcher Sal "The Barber" Maglie. Unlike Joe DiMaggio, aka the Yankee Clipper, who emanated an effortless and fully realized grace that made him appear dispassionate, Furillo and Maglie evoked the dangerous worlds of vendetta and Cosa Nostra. Joe DiMaggio was light and the promise of the American future. Maglie and Furillo were dark and the memory of a tortured history. And while Furillo and Maglie stirred up smoldering passions, this was the place of ancient Italian pride.

Because of their central role in the greatest baseball rivalry, I have included two complementary essays that celebrate the days of Maglie and

Ralph Branca yields Bobby Thomson's pennant-winning home run.
(National Baseball Hall of Fame Library, Cooperstown, New York)

Furillo, George Vecsey's "The Barber and the Rifle" and Anthony Valerio's "Sal Maglie in Paradise."

Finally, among the Greatest, with admitted whimsy, I include what I think is the greatest Italian American baseball announcer's story. Ira Berkow told it to me, and he swears he heard it with his own ears.

In the days when Phil Rizzuto (Italian American) and Bill White (African American) were sidekicks in the Yankees broadcast booth, Rizzuto, as he often did, chatted away, not about the game but about the delicious Italian pastries and baked goods that had been sent to him by his Italian American fans who owned pastry shops. Phil was raving about the cannolis from Pietro's in Queens and the riccotta cheese cake from Marcello's in Paramus and the biscotti from Enrico's in the Bronx. White took some time from calling the action on the field to ask Rizuto why it was that all his friends' names ended in vowels. Rizzuto, not missing a beat, said, "Like yours, White?"

In order to compile the statistics of every Italian American ever to play in the major leagues, even if it was for a cup of coffee and even if he was only half Italian would have been an impossible feat of research were it not that the impossible had been accomplished by George Randazzo, the founder and chairman of the National Italian American Sports Hall of Fame in Chicago. Randazzo not only knows which major-leaguers have Italian ancestry lurking behind non–Italian sounding names (Jack Clark, the San Francisco power-hitting first baseman, for example), but also which are not Italian despite the way their names sound: for example, John Candelaria (Portuguese); Joe Rudi (Scandinavian); and most important—because he is singled out as being one of the first Italian names to appear in the baseball records by Jerre Mangione and Ben Morreale's in their scholarly *La Storia: Five Centuries of the Italian American Experience*— Tony DeFate. Not only was DeFate not Italian, he couldn't hit, batting .125 with the Detroit Tigers in 1917.

Once Randazzo and the National Italian American Sports Hall of Fame had given me their list, I could then ask Sports Media Publishing Inc., the publishers of the authoritative *Total Baseball,* for permission to

Phil Rizzuto, Yogi's All-Time Italian American shortstop
(National Baseball Hall of Fame Library, Cooperstown, New York)

use their cutting-edge statistical records for each and every Italian American major-leaguer. Because *Total Baseball* stores the statistics in digital form, they could provide me with exactly the categories I needed for this book.

The statistics section following the essay portion of this book is a uniquely valuable resource for those whose love of baseball is matched by their interest in the Italian Americans who have reached for the stars and found them within their grasp as they ascended to the major leagues.

REACHING
FOR THE STARS

CITIZEN OF BASEBALL

Larry Freundlich

Not surprisingly for a fan in his sixties, Maglie's Giants and Furillo's Dodgers form the bedrock of my baseball memory.

I was born and raised in the Flatbush section of Brooklyn in the 1940s and '50s. During the summers of my boyhood, my father and I would walk four miles down Bedford Avenue to Ebbets Field, into a swelling river of fans converging on Sullivan Place from other tributaries of the borough. It was one of the few times we held hands. On our twenty or so trips to the park each year, and as we sat together at the Formica-covered kitchen table of our family's two-bedroom apartment house on Kings Highway listening to Red Barber and Connie Desmond on the radio, I acquired my father's powerful emotional entanglement with the Brooklyn Dodgers, so that for me as well as for him, Bobby Thomson's home run off Ralph Branca in 1951 would remain an unhealed wound and the Dodgers' victory over the New York Yankees in the 1955 World Series a gift given for my faithfulness.

Neither he nor I felt any irony about our devotion to the Brooklyn Dodgers. My father, a dentist, whose office was in East New York, would not change his socks during a Dodgers winning streak. And for my part, when Leo Durocher left the Dodgers to manage the hated New York Giants, with hot tears in my eyes I tore his baseball card to pieces and burned it in the vacant lot across from our apartment house on Kings Highway.

Roy Campanella, Yogi's selection as All-Time Italian American catcher
(National Baseball Hall of Fame Library, Cooperstown, New York)

Roger Kahn's Boys of Summer were, indeed, my boys also—part of my family. I had an intense emotional attachment to and a scholarly vocation for the persons and careers of Pee Wee Reese, Jackie Robinson, Carl Erskine, Duke Snider, Johnny Podres, Clem Labine, Joe Black, Roy Campanella, Billy Cox, Andy Pafko, Gene Hermanski, Don Newcombe, and Gil Hodges. I knew their statistics cold. To this day, my personal banking card PIN number is a variant of the uniform numbers of the 1955 double play combination, Hodges, Robinson, and Reese. And because they were my family, I cared about its minor branches, even if their acquaintance with my team was brief and unremarkable. More than fifty years after they played for the Dodgers, Willie Ramsdell, Ed Head, Bobo Milliken, Stan Rojeck, Dixie Howell, Ed Roebuck, Bud Podbielan, Wayne Terwilliger, Don Wade, Cookie Lavagetto, Kirby Higbe, Marv Rackley, Al Gionfriddo, and George Shuba soften my heart and revivify my youthful innocence.

My love of the Dodgers, like atomic valences in organic chemistry, bonded me into an intricate compound with the most attractive players of the other franchise cities. Just say the name of a major league team to me, and my mind spontaneously downloaded its iconic star: Boston (Ted Williams), Detroit (Al Kaline), the Giants (Sal Maglie or Willie Mays), St. Louis (Stan Musial), Cincinnati (Ted Kluszewski or Ewell Blackwell), Chicago Cubs (Ernie Banks), Philadelphia Phillies (Robin Roberts), Chicago White Sox (Minnie Minoso or Nellie Fox), Cleveland (Bob Feller or Lou Boudreau), Boston-Milwaukee Braves (Warren Spahn), Milwaukee-Atlanta Braves (Hank Aaron), Pittsburgh (Ralph Kiner), and the New York Yankees (Joe DiMaggio).

Sometimes a team had no icon, and those teams proved to be moribund. For example, too much of a stretch was required for me to iconize Ned Garver of the St. Louis Browns, and Harmon Killebrew, who became a legitimate icon, was lost to the Washington Senators when they traded him to Minnesota. The Philadelphia Athletics hadn't had an icon since Jimmie Foxx in the 1930s. If the Senators and the Athletics had any iconic

*Billy Martin (half Italian) bowled over by Roy Campanella (half Italian)
as Gil Hodges looks on (Photofile)*

Dolf Camilli (Private Archive)

identity, it was through their executives: Calvin Griffith (nasty and cheap) and Connie Mack (ancient and moral).

Each one of these players (and others I might have mentioned: e.g., Luke Appling, Bob Gibson, Hal Newhouser) represented the interests of a baseball city-state, one in competition with my own baseball city-state: Brooklyn. Furillo was as redolent with patriotism for me as Medici was for a Renaissance Florentine; and Durocher triggered aggressive antagonism, as if he were the diabolical Duke Ludovico Sforza of Milan. DiMaggio and Musial, to this Florentine mind, might have summoned up the doges of Venice—entrusted with the affairs of a city so great (*Serenissima,* like Venice, the Lion City)—that it would be impossible to hate them, despite their competition with my city. When Brooklyn's dark tormentor Sal Maglie was set adrift from the Giants and shockingly found safe haven among his former victims, it was as if Rommel, at Patton's side, had led our khaki, white-starred Sherman tanks across the Rhine to defeat the Germans, clearing his name of infamy and earning him an honored place among our heroes.

This kind of passionate identification of one's city with individuals, whose names seemed as one with it, was, I believe, the strongest hold that baseball had on the fans before the era of free agency and television. In Bob Leuci's essay in this volume, "Hooks," Leuci recalls that as a kid growing up in Brooklyn, he assumed that all the Dodgers had been born in Brooklyn—no matter that Reese was from Louisville or Robinson from Cairo, Georgia, or Duke Snider from Los Angeles. That kind of instant call on the chauvinism of the fan was possible only because many of these iconic players were team lifers: Hodges, Furillo, Erskine, Reese, Robinson, Campanella, Ted Williams, Kaline, Bench, Banks, Robin Roberts, Brett, Clemente, DiMaggio, Whitey Ford, Berra, Rizzuto, Crosetti. If they did wander, it was only in their twilight years, and only because they could not yet give up the game (Mays and Spahn to the Mets, Hank Greenberg to Pittsburgh, Blackwell to the Yankees, Mize to the Yankees, Cavarretta to the White Sox).

In baseball today, such player-city identification becomes more rare

Frank Crosetti seated before a photo of his legendary Yankees teammates Lou Gehrig and Babe Ruth. (National Baseball Hall of Fame Library, Cooperstown, New York)

each year. Cal Ripkin is a Baltimore man forever, but Mussina and Giambi move to the Yankees, Schilling and Johnson to Phoenix, Griffey to Cincinnati, Manny Ramirez to Boston, Alex Rodriguez to Texas. These players are of surpassing excellence; staying to be venerated in their home cities, they would honor the place of their major league debut and mix their achievement with the civic pride of their baseball city-state—the player enriching the city, the city enshrining the player, the player becoming part of the imaginative life of the citizen-fan.

Instead the master players have become *condottiere*, willing to fight for the next city-state as long as they get paid enough. The player gets richer, the game becomes subservient to commerce, and the fan grows coarse. "Entertain me!" the fan demands of the oligarchic owners. "I'm buying the products that justify your television contracts. We know you're not doing this for love, and we know what to call it when you do it for money." As the historian Simon Schama points out in *Citizen,* his book about the French Revolution, when the citizens of Paris learned that the royals were as low-minded and venal as they themselves, Versailles was stripped of the illusion of sanctified privilege that protected its courtiers and potentates from the scorn and murderous hostility of the populace.

When the game of baseball becomes a subset of the entertainment business or communications industry, its aesthetic and ethical purity are compromised, and the game becomes subject to the exigencies of mundane life with all its relativity and design flaws. Whatever baseball's *condottiere* may gain personally or contribute to their current employer, their interchangeable alliances despiritualize baseball in the same way that disloyalty tears apart a family. We feel abandoned by those we trusted and loved, and this betrayal of our expectation of loyalty makes us resentful and angry. "Whatever happened to love of the game?" we ask. "What are these players and owners doing to deserve this money?" These are the kinds of emotions we feel when baseball loses its magic, and we see that behind the curtain the Wizard of Oz is either a cold-eyed, self-aggrandizing capitalist or a selfish brat.

When A. Bartlett Giamatti died in 1989, I planned someday to ini-

A. Bartlett Giamatti, seventh commissioner of Major League Baseball (Duomo)

tiate a book project that would celebrate the contribution that Italian Americans have made to major league baseball, because Giamatti better than anyone else understood the spiritual elements of baseball, which baseball was ignoring at its own peril.

In his philosophic and beautiful encomium *Take Time for Paradise,* Giamatti had expressed his belief that the geometric patterns and seasonal rhythms of baseball, solemnly recorded in each year's record book, resembled a divine plan, what in the Middle Ages and the Renaissance would have been seen as part of the great chain of being and in the eighteenth-century Enlightenment as the clockwork universe: a world with a purpose, built according to a perfect plan, adequate for all contingencies and capable of being learned and comprehended by the faithful. Each player's and fan's assent to the orthodoxies of baseball contributed to the perfect operation of the design. When we play by the rules, we are cared for and nourished, and, in turn, our devotion preserves the life force of the game. So when Pete Rose set himself above the rules by which he had achieved glory as a player, he broke the spiritual covenant between the game and the fan, between the church and the congregation. For Giamatti, Rose would be entitled to every honor except the one reserved for the great ones of the faith: the Hall of Fame, where only the faithful are entitled to holy ground. The commissioner of baseball banned Rose from the Hall not to demean Rose's genius as a player but to honor the game and preserve the level field of dreams on which it must be played. Rose thought it was all about him. Giamatti knew it was all about baseball. When given a chance to repent, Rose refused. Giamatti stood firm. Excommunication fit the crime.

For Giamatti the perfection of baseball was completed in the collaboration between player and fan. The fan was attracted to repetition and familiarity, and his continued faith depended on the maintenance of the rules and the slow evolution of its customs and paraphernalia. As the fan grew in knowledge and expertise, he felt himself empowered. He mastered the catechism in the daily sports pages and the encyclopedia of baseball and at his local bar. His opinion based on knowledge meant something. To love and understand baseball was self-esteeming. His city's team was his own team. He was a citizen of baseball and so were the players.

One thing the *condottiere* were not were partisans. The *condottiere* would fight for the highest bidder. One day they fought in the army of Florence, the next on the side of her enemy, Milan or Lucca. They had no primary allegiance except to their own careers. Because they considered themselves professional soldiers first, they identified with the interests of other professional soldiers whom they might oppose in today's battle and then partner in tomorrow's, depending on who was signing the checks. Battles between *condottiere* armies became, therefore, increasingly less lethal. With no altruistic commitment to the affairs of their employing city-state, why not cut their fellow *condottiere* some slack and get some mercy in return?—then no one in the soldiers's union will get hurt. War became an increasingly expensive and cynical fiasco, often involving a great deal of maneuvering but no deadly fighting. Anyone who has seen Rickey Henderson or Deion Sanders barely alert to his responsibilities in the field knows what a drain the play-for-pay mentality has on committed performance. And baseball's *condottiere* are everywhere you look.

The golden days of our fandom were the days when our heroes passionately served one master—one city's team. The 1950s rosters of the Yankees and Dodgers are the most glorious examples of long-lived commitment, and the Yankees, with DiMaggio on center stage, have the edge in mythological power. Weren't all the Yankees bombers from the Bronx and wouldn't they all want to buried in center field?

How well it would have served Bart Giamatti to have rooted for the Yankees, a team whose citizen players were in significant part Italian American. But Giamatti was fated to be a Red Sox fan whose deepest admiration was reserved for Red Sox lifer Bobby Doerr. Giamatti deserved a fuller plate.

If his heart had worn pinstripes, the citizens of his baseball city-state would have included Lazzeri, DiMaggio, Crosetti, Rizzuto, Berra, and Raschi—all of them in for the long term. He would have known that Billy Martin was half Italian, and in Joe Torre would have recognized a gentleman like himself.

We know that Giamatti cared particularly about Italian American baseball players. He once picked an All–Italian American All-Star team, which Don Freeman mentions in an interview with Giamatti for the *San Diego Union* of June 6, 1989:

> A. Bartlett Giamatti, commissioner of baseball, former president of Yale University, one-time professor of English, prize-winning author, and one of the most fervid fans the game of rounders has ever known, was sitting at his desk wearing a wool sweater with TIGERS emblazoned across the front.
>
> But this was out of synch, you thought, for Bart Giamatti grew up with his affection firmly affixed on the Red Sox.
>
> Why, then, this . . . apostasy?
>
> Was the commissioner no longer in thrall with the storied

Red Sox of Bobby Doerr and Mel Parnell and Ted Williams, the Red Sox that gave young Giamatti's boyhood its meaning and its purpose?

"Oh, no," he said with a smile (and it's a smile that gives light to a room), it was the air conditioning in this Park Avenue building that went on the fritz, and it got cold, and so he went down the hall to Baseball Properties and put on the first sweater he could find.

"Commissioner, your thoughts on Curt Gowdy," I began.

At the mention of the broadcaster's name, Bart Giamatti smiled again. His boyhood had returned and it was quite wonderful.

"It was Curt Gowdy's voice that I grew up hearing," Giamatti said. "This was when Curt was announcing the Red Sox games on the radio. It was the voice that introduced me to major league baseball. It was a voice that I shall never forget."

In that long-ago of memory, Bart Giamatti, the son of a professor of Italian at Mount Holyoke, was growing up in western Massachusetts. "We had no TV, no movies. But we had radio—and we had Curt Gowdy. And Curt had such enthusiasm. He loved that team, our Red Sox. And how obvious it was that he loved the game of baseball."

Giamatti went on to his own success, stirring the scholars at Yale in his literature classes, and in 1977 he wrote a yarn for *Harper's* on Tom Seaver, the Mets' sterling pitcher by way of USC.

With allusions befitting a classicist, this splendid piece of writing was honored as the best sports magazine article of the year. In it Giamatti referred to baseball as "a sport that touches of what is important in American life."

"Baseball," Giamatti was saying now, investing the word with a sense of familial warmth. "I love it. I enjoy it."

He is warmed by every aspect of the game—its history, its

lore, its language. "A box score, for instance, is quantified history, so factually complete and yet Hemingwayesque in its simplicity."

On the commissioner's desk was David Halberstam's *Summer of '49,* a corking good book (which he is reading with delight) on how it was in baseball that eventful year. In the book, Giamatti joyously picked his all-Italian team, derived, he says, from his boyhood.

Here, then, is Bart Giamatti's all-Italian team:

First base, Dolf Camilli; second base, Tony Lazzeri; shortstop, Phil Rizzuto; third base, Frank Crosetti; outfield—Joe DiMaggio, Dom DiMaggio, Sam Mele, Carl Furillo, Al Zarilla; catcher, Yogi Berra; pitchers, Sal Maglie, Vic Raschi, Ralph Branca.

But, I inquired of the commissioner, where's Joe Garagiola? And being overlooked would surely throw Tommy Lasorda off his feed. The commissioner nodded and declared: "Joe Garagiola, catcher and broadcaster, is hereby added to the Giamatti all-Italian team. And Tommy Lasorda is now my manager. Tommy may even pitch if he's as good as he keeps telling me he is."

Who sings the national anthem?

"Julius LaRosa," Giamatti said.

Not Frank Sinatra?

"All right, we'll have Sinatra there," the commissioner said, "and Tony Bennett

Al "Zeke" Zarilla,
St. Louis Browns outfielder
(National Baseball Hame of Fame
Library, Cooperstown, New York)

and Vic Damone and also Jerry Vale. They will sing together after Julius LaRosa's first chorus. It'll be beautiful."

It is something to look forward to. But in the meantime I was glancing at the picture of Bobby Doerr by the commissioner's desk.

"Bobby Doerr was the ballplayer I grew up wanting to emulate," he said. "Like Bobby on the Red Sox, I, too, played second base, but I was no Bobby Doerr. He played with grace and tremendous economy, with no ornamentation. He took competency and raised it to a high art. I was there, at Fenway Park, for Bobby Doerr Day, and I was thrilled to meet him."

Bart Giamatti paused in remembrance. "You're not supposed to meet your heroes—often they are mere mortals. But Bobby was that rarity. Bobby was exactly what I had hoped he would be."

How well Don Freeman captures the nostalgic playfulness and the serious emotion and intellect that mingle in Giamatti's love of baseball. Yes, Joe DiMaggio would have given Giamatti's love of the Red Sox Platonic perfection. Of all the Yankees and, indeed, of all the Italian Americans who have contributed to major league baseball, Giamatti would have recognized in Joe DiMaggio the most elegant manifestation of its severe grace.

For Italian Americans, DiMaggio became the iconic king of an oppressed people who in their political experience had never before united under a freely acknowledged sovereign. Like the great preponderance of early twentieth-century Italian immigrants, Joe's parents came from the South; in this case, Sicily. Southern Italians at the time when the mass emigration gained great power did not think of themselves as Italian. For the Southerner there was no Italy; there was only the name of his town or village. Sheed tells us that here in the Mezzogiorno, the people had no sense of an Italian nation despite the Northern Unification of 1861. Only between two and four percent of the population spoke "proper" Italian

Joe DiMaggio
(National Baseball Hall of Fame Library, Cooperstown, New York)

as opposed to local or regional dialect. As Sheed reminds us, it was only when the Southern immigrant arrived at Ellis Island and the customs officers filled in the mandatory nation-of-origin blank with the misleading approximation "Italian" that our men of Bari, Reggio di Calabria, Cosenza, Palermo, and Siracusa became Italian.

For these newly defined Italian Americans, DiMaggio's legendary stardom yoked them to America's national game and to the interests of their new country. When America went to war, as the song says, we wanted Joe DiMaggio on our side, because he was for all of us our greatest hero: Joe made Italians of us all.

A SPECIAL BREED

Donald Honig

Behind the plate," the exuberant fan was saying to his friends, "we have Piazza *and* Lombardi *and* Berra. Two Hall-of-Famers and a sure thing. *Behind the plate.*"

That array of catching talent is undeniably impressive, but even more worthy of note is that possessive pronoun: *"we* have . . ." No, it was not a statement of ownership; the "we" was in a familial sense and was meant to imply pride. Pride's reach is both near and far: If I can't do it, then let it be my brother, and if not he, my friend, and if not he, then one of my tribe. There are times when we are all one.

On our way along the sleek byways of a twenty-first century, we might think attaching ourselves to an athlete because of an ethnic identity unsophisticated; those allegiances seem to belong to a more primitive, rough-edged time, when Hank Greenberg was about all a Jewish boy had to cheer for, and the fact of Jackie Robinson's playing baseball for the Brooklyn Dodgers was a fraught "social experiment" that had blacks tense with anxiety and excitement. A mere two generations past. The world has since changed, in some places dramatically and beyond recognition. But people? Not so fast. They seem to prefer to stick to the pace of evolution.

No minority group is more established in the big leagues today than the Latin (see Rodriguez, Gonzalez, Martinez, Guerrero, et al.). Yet when Pedro—so gifted he needs only one name—pitches in Yankee Stadium, he empties New York's Dominican enclaves and the stands are patterned with the fluttering flags of his native land, as they are at Shea Stadium when Sammy Sosa steps to the plate. One senses that those vocal customers are not necessarily Red Sox or Cubs fans but, rather, the cultural ancestors of the Irish who yipped for the McGraws, Keelers, and Kellys in the waning decades of the nineteenth century and on into the twentieth.

That wave of Old Sod immigrants hit the beaches only to find NO IRISH NEED APPLY nailed to the workplace walls, and many of their boys turned instead to baseball's "Talent Only" ethos.

And so, too, the newly arrived German Americans raised their guttural exclamations for the Dutchman Wagner, who was not just good but the best. And there were even some self-disenfranchised, unreconstructed Americans who were drawn back to the mainstream by that "rebel-yell incarnate," the relentless Cobb. And then, of course, those lip-biting minorities who watched their Greenberg and their Robinson overcome more than pitched balls. And, lest we forget, those joyous Japanese flags whipping the air of the Pacific Northwest for their Ichiro (another single-name icon).

The Italian imprimatur was laid early but lightly upon the baseball scroll—twenty-year-old infielder Edward James Abbaticchio began his modest nine-year career with the Philadelphia Phillies in 1897, making him the first Italian player of prominence.

It took, however, three more decades before the Italian community got their Wagner, and when he arrived he was so baseball pure he became their talisman, a radiance so unique he was never allowed to depart, even long after his uniform was lockered for the last time and his plaque bolted to the Cooperstown wall.

Joe DiMaggio remains the most vivid and spectacular of Italian baseball heroes, rising from baseball nonpareil to revered national idol. As an American athlete, his renown is second only to Ruth's, and his impact on Yankee fortunes bears resemblance to that of his mighty predecessor. Where Ruth's unprecedented long-distance hitting brought customers by the droves through the Stadium turnstiles, DiMaggio's magical talents excited pride from Mulberry Street to the Bronx and attracted hitherto untapped reservoirs of fans to the Stadium where they sat and cheered their "Giuseppe." They may not initially have been conversant with baseball's subtleties, but it was enough to know that one of their own was the biggest man in that vast stadium.

Like DiMaggio's own father, a Sicilian fisherman who had migrated across an ocean and then a continent to San Francisco, immigrant parents sought opportunities for their progeny, and playing games was not considered one of them. Young Phil Cavarretta of Chicago, who was to go on to a twenty-two-year big league career, most of it with the Cubs, remembered facing the same parental resistance. Like every youngster with the gift, Cavarretta loved baseball and often played until it was too dark to see.

"Many was the time I walked into the house and found my father waiting for me," Cavarretta said. "He was from Italy and didn't understand baseball. 'Where've you been?' he would ask.

" 'Out playing baseball.'

" 'Baseball?' he would say, giving me this very quizzical look. 'You don't play baseball—you go to school and get an education.' "

This attitude was not unfamiliar, nor was it unreasonable; these men had, after all, worked hard and sacrificed much to establish themselves and provide opportunities for their children. But this was, again, after all, the New World, and a bat and a ball were as viable an opportunity as a union card or a college degree. One might presume that DiMaggio's electrifying success and the nationwide esteem in which he was held was cause for reevaluation in many an Italian household.

The idea of tapping into an ethnic group's pride to develop new gate attractions had occurred before DiMaggio's arrival. When the Yankees first scouted the boy, they were hoping the name Gehrig might be Jewish. (They settled for a "Larrupin' Lutheran.") The canny John McGraw, Giants' manager for thirty years until 1932, had long sought a Jewish drawing card. (Both clubs missed out on Bronx resident Henry Greenberg. The Giants didn't think the tall youngster had the talent, and

Tony Lazzeri hit sixty home runs for the Pacific Coast League Salt Lake Bees in 1925. (National Baseball Hall of Fame Library, Cooperstown, New York)

while the Yankees wanted to sign him, first baseman Greenberg was all too cognizant of the Lou Gehrig roadblock and pragmatically signed with Detroit.)

DiMaggio, of course, was not the first Italian American to break into the Yankee lineup with any degree of regularity. In 1918 a stocky outfielder named Ping Bodie began a four-year stint with the club. Bodie was better known to his family as Francesco Stefano Pezzolo, but like many other players of the time with conspicuous ethnic names, he morphed himself into another identity. This adoption spared him the catcalls that were common in those less decorous days (when players of German extraction were routinely called "Heinie," and so on). Aloysius Szymanski saw things the same way, and when he began his Hall of Fame career in 1924, he was an All-American boy named Al Simmons.

There are currently six Italian American players in the Hall of Fame: DiMaggio, Yogi Berra, Ernie Lombardi, Phil Rizzuto, Tommy Lasorda, and Tony Lazzeri (with Mike Piazza and Joe Torre on the fast track). The last of these, Lazzeri, was the first to reach the big leagues, joining the Yankees in 1926 and quickly becoming the first truly out-standing Italian star.

Like DiMaggio (as well as shortstop Frank Crosetti, who joined the club in 1932), Lazzeri was a native of San Francisco. With a face out of a Caravaggio canvas, the quiet, hard-hitting second baseman had a reputation for on-the-field intelligence, and it was he and not Ruth or Gehrig who was looked upon as the team leader.

Tony played with a smoldering competitive zeal and in six of his twelve Yankee seasons helped drive the club into the World Series, winning five championships. Like most Yankees, he took immense pride in his pinstripes; consequently, when the club let him go after the 1937 season (to make way for the gifted young Joe Gordon), Tony was deeply hurt. He played for the Chicago Cubs in 1939, was released by them, and in the spring of 1939 was trying to catch on with the Brooklyn Dodgers. The heartbreak of being discarded by the Yankees, however, had still not fully healed.

Early one morning Lazzeri commandeered Dodgers rookie Pete Reiser and the two got into Tony's car and drove to the Yankees' spring camp at St. Petersburg.

"He was pretty quiet the whole time," Reiser said, recalling the episode years later, "like he had something on his mind. There was a large suitcase on the back seat and every once in a while he'd glance back at it, scowl at me, and keep going."

The Yankees' camp was empty when they arrived, except for an old man sitting outside the clubhouse door. When asked what he was doing there, Lazzeri blithely replied that the Yankees had reacquired him.

"The old guy started to laugh and applaud," Reiser said, "saying he knew the Yankees had made a mistake in letting him go. Then Tony and me went into the clubhouse, Tony carrying the suitcase. Once we were inside he locked the door, opened the suitcase, and took out a couple of hammers and a lot of these big railroad spikes. Then he told me to start nailing spiked shoes into the floor."

Reiser, nineteen years old and pea green, did as ordered.

"Every so often," he said, "I looked over at Tony. He was going at it with a vengeance, muttering under his breath, still sore at the Yankees for letting him go."

These weren't just spiked shoes that were being nailed to the clubhouse floor. This was hallowed footwear, belonging to DiMaggio, Gehrig, Bill Dickey, manager Joe McCarthy, among others.

When they had finished their hammering, Reiser said, "Tony took a pair of scissors out of the suitcase and began cutting up uniforms, just going around snipping at sleeves and trousers and whatnot. When he was through he took a satisfied look around and said, 'Okay, let's get the hell out of here.' "

When they went back outside they found the old man watering down the infield.

"We're leaving," Lazzeri called to him.

"I'll tell them you were here," the old man said.

"I think they'll know," the old Yankee said, walking away, suitcase in hand. "But you tell them anyway. Tell them Tony Lazzeri was here."

"I guess," Reiser said later, "old Yankees die hard."

Despite a distinguished, Hall of Fame career, Lazzeri, ironically, is best remembered for having been struck out by an aging Grover Cleveland Alexander with the bases loaded in the seventh inning of the seventh game of the 1926 World Series. But twenty-one years later two other Italian American players were to etch their names heroically upon the scrolls of October glory.

If the World Series is a stage set and waiting for a hero, the 1947 edition supplied them; and as so often has been the case in Series history, it was the unheralded who orchestrated the thunder and the lightning. Their names were Harry "Cookie" Lavagetto and Al Gionfriddo.

The fourth game of the Series between the Brooklyn Dodgers and New York Yankees, with the Yankees up two games to one, was one out removed from becoming the first no-hitter ever thrown in Series competition. Yankees right-hander Bill Bevens, struggling with his control throughout, had labored through eight and two-thirds innings of no-hit

*Cookie Lavagetto beats Floyd Bevan and
ruins his bid for a World Series no-hitter.*

Cookie Lavagetto
(National Baseball Hall of Fame
Library, Cooperstown, New York)

ball, holding tenaciously to a 2–1 lead. With two out and two men on via walks (Bevens's ninth and tenth of the game), the Dodgers drew in their breath and sent the veteran Lavagetto to the plate to pinch hit. An immensely popular third baseman during his Dodger career, Cookie was at the end of the string, having drawn just sixty-nine at bats during the season. But if ever there were a career capper, this was it. Lavagetto tore into a pitch and drove it on a high line against Ebbets Field's right-field wall, sending the base runners off on the most jubilant homeward journeys in the history of Brooklyn baseball, collapsing Bevens's rainbow into wet confetti.

The first of the historic runs chased home by Lavagetto's heroic knock was scored by pinch-runner Al Gionfriddo, who no doubt believed that this above all would be the career memory he would treasure before his retirement fireside.

Even as an active player, Al Gionfriddo was little more than a faint mark in the box score. In 1947, his fourth and final year in the big leagues, the Dodgers spear-carrier appeared in just thirty-eight games, showing sixty-three at-bats and a .177 batting average. But it was his speed and his glove rather than his bat that would enshrine the 5´6" outfielder in World Series annals.

It was game six of that 1947 Series. In the bottom of the sixth inning the Dodgers held an 8–5 lead. Standing in left field for the Dodgers was Gionfriddo, just inserted into the game as a defensive replacement. There were two men on base, two out, and spread out at home plate, bat cocked, was the mighty DiMaggio. Joe ripped into one, and over seventy thousand people came to their feet as the ball shot away on a high, rising line to left field, on a trajectory that seemed sure to carry it into the bleachers for a game-tying three-run banger.

But there was Gionfriddo, swift as a bird out of a cage, tracking that scorched baseball, homing in on it as he raced toward the barrier, and finally snatching it from the air with his gloved hand before crashing into the barrier next to the 415 FT. sign. That dramatic, high-speed catch was to give Al Gionfriddo a permanent, flashing-neon moment in World Series history.

Gionfriddo's catch helped the Dodgers to their 8–6, Series-tying win, and while it is true the Yankees won it all the next day, the ballads are sung about two otherwise unspectacular Brooklyn Dodgers. (Interestingly, neither Lavagetto nor Gionfriddo, nor Bevens either, were to play in the big leagues after that October.)

Baseball, so it has been duly and endlessly noted, is a team game, designed as a collaborative effort by nine men. However, if one man ever dominated a World Series it was a twenty-five-year-old catcher with the colorful name of Fury Gene Tenace (born Fiore Gino Tennaci). What Gene Tenace did for the Oakland Athletics in their scintillating seven-game victory over the Cincinnati Reds in the 1972 World Series was as complete a one-man demolition as has ever been seen in baseball's fall festival.

Not quite as anonymous as Lavagetto and Gionfriddo, what Tenace did was nevertheless outlandishly startling. As Oakland's second-string catcher, he had batted just .225 for the season, hitting five home runs. In Oakland's five-game victory over Detroit in the League Championship

*Al Gionfriddo makes an epic home-run saving catch off the bat of Joe DiMaggio.
(National Baseball Hall of Fame Library, Cooperstown, New York)*

Series he had stroked just one hit in seventeen at bats, for a barely breathing .059 average. Referring to this dismal performance, Tenace remarked, "If anybody ever doubts what a strange and unpredictable game baseball is, all you have to do is take out the records of postseason play in 1972 and show it to them." Strange and unpredictable indeed. The 1972 Series was a closely played, low-scoring affair, with scores including 3–2, 2–1, 1–0, 3–2, 3–2. Most of Oakland's runs were Tenace runs—he drove in nine of the club's sixteen runs (no other Athletic had more than one) and hit four of the team's five home runs, tying a Series record.

Tenace's first two Series at bats were straight from the dream factory. He hit home runs. After the first one, he recalled, "I started around the bases, and when I was turning second base I thought I'd look for my folks in the crowd. I knew about where they were sitting, in the third base boxes. Sure enough, there was my father, jumping up and down and applauding and yelling."

Mr. Tenace jumped even higher the second time. "I thought they were gonna have to tie him down," his son reported. His father, Gene said, "was a baseball fan, and always wanted me to be a ballplayer." This was a little more than a generation removed from the fathers of Joe DiMaggio and Phil Cavarretta and others who had frowned upon their sons' desires to become part of America's game. The old "time wasting" sandlot activity had become a coveted and lucrative occupation.

But in addition to bestowing instant and lasting fame, a World Series can be cruel, its wardrobe consisting of shrouds of infamy as well as gowns of glory, as one of the game's great catchers and most feared hitters had the misfortune to find out: thus, Ernesto Natali Lombardi, another product of "DiMaggio country." Lombardi's rise from across the Bay in Oakland is etched most vividly in baseball memory for his infamous "snooze" at home plate in the tenth inning of the fourth and final game of the 1939 World Series. Knocked senseless, and unable to keep the winning run from scoring, he later was unjustly maligned for "snoozing" by a headline-driven and irresponsibly cruel press.

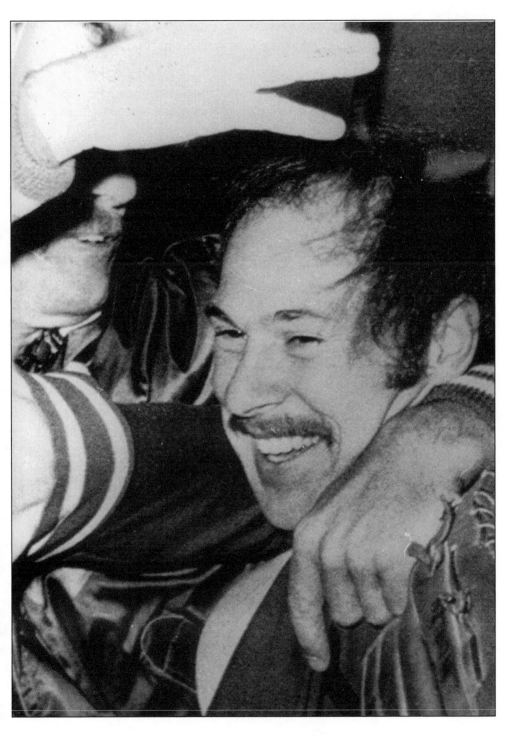

Gene Tenace (Private Archive)

Lombardi caught in the National League from 1931 through 1947, spending the majority of those seasons with the Cincinnati Reds. Nicknamed "Schnozz" in a less-sensitive era, for his most distinctive facial characteristic, Lombardi was a bear of a man, possessing enormous physical strength; he was also gentle and kindly, liked and respected by everyone.

Outfielder Tommy Holmes, a teammate of Lombardi's on the 1942 Boston Braves, recalled an example of Ernie's fine character.

"We were on the train making our first western trip," Holmes said. "We had a few rookies on the team and in those days they weren't making much money, maybe six hundred a month. They were pretty excited about making their first western trip. Well, Lombardi—bless him, I'll always remember him for this—went around to all the kids and said, 'Hey, kid, got enough money?' And without waiting for an answer he'd push a twenty on them. Just wanted them to make sure they had a few extra, to tip porters and waitresses, or buy themselves a beer, and so on. He wanted them to be able to feel like big-leaguers. That was the kind of guy Ernie Lombardi was."

As a player, Lombardi was known for two prominent distinctions. His bat was the most feared in the league, particularly by infielders, who automatically backed up when Ernie stepped into the box, for he could hit line drives like a man hammering rivets.

"His line drives had death written on them," Cubs third baseman Stan Hack said.

Lombardi himself said jokingly of Dodgers shortstop Pee Wee Reese, "He was in the league for a couple of years before I realized he wasn't an outfielder."

But it wasn't just instincts of self-preservation that put the infield in reverse, it was Ernie's other prominent distinction, a slowness afoot that was legendary—to the extent that his rare stolen bases (eight in seventeen years) often made headlines. Blistered shots that should have gone through for base hits were routinely scooped up on the outfield grass, the long pegs thwarting the achingly slow Lombardi at first base. Still, the big

Ernie Lombardi. They say no one hit the ball harder.
(National Baseball Hall of Fame Library, Cooperstown, New York)

man won two batting titles (one of only two catchers to win that crown) and left behind a .306 lifetime average.

Another facet of the Lombardi legend was the size of his hands. There is a picture of a shyly smiling Ernie holding seven baseballs in his right hand. Seven. And rather than shift his big body behind the plate, he was known to occasionally reach out with his bare hand and pluck an errant fastball out of the air (which must have been rather deflating for his pitcher).

But baseball memory will choose and select, often unjustly, and so with it all Lombardi is most remembered for that maliciously attributed "snooze," about which Larry Baldassaro's essay on Lombardi in this book gives the true story.

In baseball memory the man for all seasons is often no match for the man of the moment, so while the images of Hall-of-Famers Lazzeri and Lombardi are frozen in postures of mischance, the more marginal Lavagetto and Gionfriddo continue to spur tales of glory.

In 1941, the fraternity of Italian baseball fans had further reason to swell with pride when DiMaggio and Brooklyn's Dolf Camilli were voted Most Valuable Players in their respective leagues. There was, in fact, a postwar decade during which the Yankees' Italian contingent had a virtual arm lock on the MVP trophy, with DiMaggio winning in 1947, Phil Rizzuto in 1950, and Yogi Berra in 1951, '54, and '55. Other Italian winners of the coveted award were Lombardi in 1938, DiMaggio in 1939 and 1941, Cavarretta in 1945, Roy Campanella in 1951, 1953, and 1955, Joe Torre in 1971, and Ken Caminiti in 1995.

The Yankees remained the prime progenitors of the Italian star, for if Crosetti's days as the club's regular shortstop were coming to a close, it was because of the arrival of a diminutive, quick-handed New York City product named Phil Rizzuto, who began his long Yankee tenure in 1941.

Some years before, Rizzuto was one of a crowd of youngsters attending an open tryout at Ebbets Field. The Dodgers manager took one look at him and dismissed the 5'6" youngster as "too small." The crestfallen boy went home, but soon joined another band of hopefuls at a Yankee Stadium tryout.

"I seldom attended those things," Yankee skipper Joe McCarthy recalled years later. "It wasn't my department. But I guess I had nothing better to do that day and went over. I was sitting in a third base box watching them.

"I found I couldn't take my eyes off this kid at shortstop. He picked up everything in all directions and got rid of the ball in a real hurry. He had all the moves, all the instincts. You know, the things you can't teach a kid. Sign him, I told them."

Before entering the Navy after the 1942 season, Rizzuto helped McCarthy's Yankees win two pennants; but he did even better later for the former Brooklyn manager who had once turned him away, starring on Casey Stengel's five consecutive World Championship teams from 1949 through 1953, driving his "too small" frame to the MVP award in 1950.

Where DiMaggio was revered, Lawrence Peter Berra was looked upon with a warmth and affection accorded few ballplayers. Initially awkward and unsure behind the plate, hard work under the tutelage of predecessor Bill Dickey elevated him to the ranks of baseball's all-time catchers.

"You'd better listen to him," Stengel warned his pitchers, some of whom took the unlikely looking Berra and his grappling with the English language with a grain of salt. "He knows what he's talking about."

His old St. Louis sandlot buddy Joe Garagiola probably put it most succinctly when discussing Berra and his famous malapropisms.

"Listen to what he says," Garagiola said, "not how he says it."

What most enchanted the Yankees about their squat, unathletic-looking young prospect, however, was not his charm or affability but that flawless swing and his ability to perform under pressure.

When he was managing the Baltimore Orioles, Paul Richards recalled a New York sportswriter's "moaning about Berra's not hitting—Yogi was around .270 or so at the time. I told the guy to check back

Yogi Berra, All-Time Italian American All-Star catcher and one of the greatest clutch hitters (National Baseball Hall of Fame Library, Cooperstown, New York)

through his scorebook and see what Berra's hitting when the seventh inning starts. Well, he showed up the next day with a sheepish look on his face. 'Well, I give up,' he said. 'From the seventh inning on he's hitting .430.'

"That's right," Richards said. "From the seventh inning on. And in close games that's when they change the marbles, right there. Berra was a game-winner."

Berra had a reputation as a "bad-ball hitter," a man who would swing at "anything." That sounds like no foundation upon which to build a Hall of Fame career. But go inside of the game and hear another side of that. Former Milwaukee Braves pitcher Gene Conley recalled a conversation with the master of masters, Warren Spahn.

"He pitched to Yogi quite a bit over the years," Conley said of Spahn, "and he used to deflate the legend about Berra being a bad-ball hitter. 'He guesses with you,' Spahn said. 'That's what he does.' So if a guy is guessing on a pitch and he gets it, then it doesn't matter if he's hitting at a bad ball, because he's ready for that pitch, he's already timed it."

Vic Raschi, one of the greatest right-handers in Yankees history (Private Archive)

Spahn also said, Conley recalled, "That in a tight spot, when Berra was really bearing down at the plate, he wouldn't offer at pitches that were just off the corner, that you had to throw him strikes."

Berra was one half of what is probably the finest ever all-Italian battery, right-hander Vic Raschi, who joined the club in 1947, being the other. Away from the mound the heavyset Raschi was reserved and soft spoken; on the mound he was as resolute and formidable a competitor as any, the clutch man on Stengel's Raschi, Allie Reynolds, Eddie Lopat trio of aces. Given the situation—and the opposition—the game Raschi pitched at Yankee Stadium on the last day of the 1949 season was as clutch as any in club history.

After 153 games the Yankees and Red Sox had played themselves into a first-place tie. With all the eggs in the basket, Stengel gave the ball to Raschi.

"Everybody thinks a World Series is the most pressure-packed baseball there is," Eddie Lopat said. "Well, of course a Series is filled with pressure, but let me tell you, the real blood and guts of baseball is when you're playing for the pennant on the last day of the season and the team you're tied with is the team you're playing. You've got six months' sweat invested in that."

The Yankees scored a run in the bottom of the first and the tenacious Raschi protected the slim margin until the bottom of the eighth, when the Yankees broke it open with four runs. The Red Sox nicked Raschi for a too-little, too-late three spot in the top of the ninth.

"There's no way you can allow yourself to lose a game like that," Raschi said later. "You just don't let it happen."

Nor did he.

Teammate Tommy Henrich put it this way: "For guts, determination, and more guts, that's the textbook game."

There was another Italian ace right-hander plying his trade in New York during Raschi's heyday years: Salvatore Anthony Maglie of the New York Giants. These were the bitterest years of baseball's bitterest rivalry— Dodgers and Giants.

Of all the Giants, the one upon whom Brooklyn fans focused their most unbridled animosity was the veteran curveballer with the dour, five-o'clock-shadowed face. Not only did Maglie time and again turn the mighty Brooklyn bats to palm fronds with his sharply darting breaking pitches (he was known to throw his snake eighty percent of the time), but he would throw pitches that came close to restructuring some of the Dodgers' heroic profiles. Indeed, Sal's nickname for authoring these close shaves—"The Barber"—was well earned. (Dodger Carl Furillo, fed up with the target practice, once heaved his bat at Maglie. The two later became good friends when Sal joined the Dodgers near the end of his career.)

A young Dodgers fan of the time remembered the passions ignited by Maglie. "The hatred was real," he said. "It was visceral. The man had caused us so much misery. He was the incarnation of evil. We used to pray for his arm to fall off. Was this juvenile madness? No, Maglie haunted us; he was a nightmare. In 1950 he was 4–0 against us; in 1951 5–1, 1952 6–2. That's a lot of anguish, especially since we lost pennants by one game in 1950 and 1951. Believe me when I tell you that beating the Giants in a regular-season game meant as much to us as beating the Yankees in the World Series. Compared to Dodgers–Giants, Yankees–Red Sox is a family reunion."

A Dodgers–Maglie truce was declared when the veteran joined the Brooks early in the 1956 season and, ostensibly washed up, delivered some superb 13–5 pitching (including a no-hitter) that helped the club to a pennant on the last day of the season. In the World Series, Maglie went all the way to win the opener against the Yankees, then, again pitching well, fell victim to Don Larsen's 2–0 perfect game four days later.

"Sal pitched brilliantly for us," our unreconciled Dodgers fan said, "but we felt he owed us that."

But time, that methodically ongoing engine, not only heals, it has also been known to mature. Thus, some decades later, our grown and mellowed Dodgers fan, now a writer of modest repute, was to encounter the one-time arch villain in person.

"It was at an Old Timers Day at Shea Stadium," he said. "There was quite an impressive gathering of former stars, including a few former Brooklyn Dodgers and New York Giants, like Cookie Lavagetto, who I swear had the outline of a faint halo over him. I told him I had been waiting thirty years to shake his hand. I was unabashedly a boy again. Hell, that hit was like a living organism inside of me."

But the intimate memories of a player can never be as selective as those of the fan. For a Dodgers fan the World Series of 1947 ended with Game Four, but for Lavagetto, that hallowed member of the Little Man's Hall of Fame, it went further.

"You know," he said, "I pinch hit the next day, too. Nobody remembers that. But I'll never forget it. We were down 2–1 in the bottom of the ninth; there were two out and a man on second. Frank Shea was on the mound for the Yankees and pitching a hell of a game. Joe DiMaggio later said that when I came out to hit he started praying out in center field. Can you imagine that? Well, Shea got a strike on me. The next pitch he threw was right in my alley. But for some reason—I'll never know why—I let it go. I swear I could have driven that ball. It was strike two. Shea fanned me on the next pitch. But I can still see that strike two, sitting right there. I could have murdered that pitch."

"Cookie," the writer said, "it would have been too much."

"I can still see it," Lavagetto said.

The ache of the unseized moment versus the euphoria of glory at its very crest? A near tie, evidently.

Drifting through a crowded clubhouse, the writer's eye alit upon an elderly man sitting alone on a stool in front of his locker. Capless, he was wearing baseball pants and a white sweatshirt. Drawn irresistibly to this source of so much long-ago heartache, the Dodgers-fan-cum-writer, the detestation long melted from the marrow of his bones, pulled up a stool and sat alongside Sal Maglie and began a conversation.

"He was most cordial and soft spoken," the writer recalled. The face that had once glowered on otherwise serene summer evenings was lined and tired. "I asked him how he was, and he said he had just undergone some serious surgery but was doing well." The writer felt a quick flash of guilt for the calamities he had once wished upon this man, the hated "Barber," whose razor—that malignant curveball aimed at the chins of Pee Wee Reese and Duke Snider—had long since been packed away.

"I wasn't going to come down here for this," said Maglie, whose home was in Niagara Falls, "but I guess I was feeling sentimental."

"You miss it, do you?" the writer asked.

"I don't miss pitching," Maglie said, "but I do miss baseball."

It sounded strangely contradictory, but then the writer realized what Maglie was alluding to—the ageless and rhythmic things that bonded these men, these big-leaguers, as one: the clubhouse repartee, the camaraderie, the clack of spikes on a concrete floor, the smell of liniment, the endless travel. The shape and sound and fabric of a game that had drawn them all together: black, white, Italian, Pole, Jew, German, Irishman, Latin, boys from America's farms and cities, boys born in Europe, Asia, South and Central America, the Caribbean, Australia; boys like Marino Pieretti (Washington Senators, 1940s), born in Lucca, Italy, and Reno Bertoia (Detroit, 1950s), born in St. Vito Udine, Italy. The uniting nationality was baseball—talent your certificate of citizenship.

Before they parted with a handshake, the writer felt compelled to make his confession.

"I was a Dodger fan in those days, Sal," he said.

Maglie's sad, weathered face showed a wisp of smile. All in the past, it said.

"You gave us a hell of a lot of trouble," the writer said.

Maglie shrugged. "I was just an Italian kid from Niagara Falls, doing my job."

Just doing his job. That was how Sal Maglie saw it. And probably how all of them from Ed Abbaticchio on down to Joe Torre and Mike Piazza have seen and still do see it.

THE GREEN FIELDS OF THE MIND

A. Bartlett Giamatti

I t breaks your heart. It is designed to break your heart. The game begins in the spring, when everything else begins again, and it blossoms in the summer, filling the afternoons and evenings, and then as soon as the chill rains come, it stops and leaves you to face the fall alone. You count on it, rely on it to buffer the passage of time, to keep the memory of sunshine and high skies alive, and then just when the days are all twilight, when you need it most, it stops. Today, October 2, a Sunday of rain and broken branches and leaf-clogged drains and slick streets, it stopped, and summer was gone.

Somehow, the summer seemed to slip by faster this time. Maybe it wasn't this summer, but all the summers that, in this my fortieth summer, slipped by so fast. There comes a time when every summer will have something of autumn about it. Whatever the reason, it seemed to me that I was investing more and more in baseball, making the game do more of the work that keeps time fat and slow and lazy. I was counting on the game's deep patterns, three strikes, three outs, three times three innings, and its deepest impulse, to go out and back, to leave and to return home, to set the order of the day and to organize the daylight. I wrote a few things this last summer, this summer that did not last, nothing grand but some things, and yet that work was just camouflage. The real activity was done with the radio—not the all-seeing, all-falsifying television—and was the playing of the game in the only place it will last, the enclosed, green field of the mind. There, in that warm, bright place, what the old poets call Mutability does not so quickly come.

But out here on Sunday, October 2, where it rains all day, Dame Mutability never loses. She was in the crowd at Fenway yesterday, a gray day full of bluster and contradiction, when the Red Sox came up in the last of the ninth trailing Baltimore 8–5, while the Yankees, rain-delayed against Detroit, only needing to win one or have Boston lose one to win it all, sat in New York washing down cold cuts with beer and watching the Boston game. Boston had won two, the Yankees had lost two, and suddenly it seemed as if the whole season might go to the last day, or beyond, except here was Boston losing 8–5, while New York sat in its family room and put its feet up. Fred Lynn, both ankles hurting now as they had in July, hits a single down the right-field line. The crowd stirs. It is on its feet. Butch Hobson, third baseman, former Bear Bryant quarterback, strong, quiet, over 100 RBIs, goes for three breaking balls and is out. The goddess smiles and encourages her agent, a canny journeyman named Nelson Briles.

Now comes a pinch hitter, Bernie Carbo, one-time Rookie of the Year, erratic, quick, a shade too handsome, so laid back he is always, in his soul, stretched out in the tall grass, one arm under his head, watching the clouds and laughing, now he looks over some low stuff unworthy of him and then, uncoiling, sends one out, straight on a right line, over the center-field wall, no cheap Fenway shot, but all of it, the physics as elegant as the arc the ball describes.

New England is on its feet, roaring. The summer will not pass. Roaring, they recall the evening, late and cold, in 1975, the sixth game of the World Series, perhaps the greatest baseball game played in the last fifty years, when Carbo, loose and easy, had uncoiled to tie the game that Fisk would win. It is 8–7, one out, and school will never start, rain will never come, sun will warm the back of your neck forever. Now Bailey, picked up from the National League recently, big arms, heavy gut, experienced, new to the league and the club; he fouls off two and then, checking, tentative, a big man off balance, he pops a soft liner to the first base-man. It is suddenly darker and later, and the announcer doing the game coast to coast, a New Yorker who works for a New York television station, sounds relieved. His little world, well lit, hot combed, split-second timed, had no capacity to absorb this much gritty, grainy, contrary reality.

Cox swings a bat, stretches his long arms, bends his back, the rookie from Pawtucket, who broke in two weeks earlier with a record six straight hits, the kid drafted ahead of Fred Lynn, rangy, smooth, cool. The count runs two-and-two, Briles is cagey, nothing too good, and Cox swings, the ball beginning toward the mound and then, in a jaunty, wayward dance, skipping past Briles, feinting to the right, skimming the last of the grass, finding the dirt, moving now like some small, purposeful marine creature negotiating the green deep, easily avoiding the jagged rock of second base, traveling steady and straight now out into the dark, silent recesses of center field.

The aisles are jammed, the place is on its feet, the wrappers, the pro-grams, the Coke cups and peanut shells, the detritus of an afternoon; the anxieties, the things that have to be done tomorrow, the regrets about yes-terday, the accumulation of a summer: all forgotten, while hope, the an-chor, bites and takes hold where a moment before it seemed we would be swept out with the tide. Rice is up, Rice who Aaron had said was the only one he'd seen with the ability to break his records, Rice the best clutch hitter on the club, with the best slugging percentage in the league, Rice, so quick and strong he once checked his swing halfway through and snapped the bat in two, Rice the Hammer of God sent to scourge the Yankees, the sound was overwhelming, fathers pounded their sons on the back, cars pulled off the road, households froze, New England exulted in its blessedness, and roared its thanks for all good things, for Rice and for a summer stretching halfway through October. Briles threw, Rice swung, and it was over. One pitch, a fly to center, and it stopped. Summer died in New England and like rain sliding off a roof, the crowd slipped out of Fenway, quickly, with only a steady murmur of concern for the drive ahead remaining of the roar. Mutability had turned the seasons and translated hope to memory once again. And once again, she had used baseball, our best invention to stay change, to bring change on. That is why it breaks my heart, that game—not because in New York they could win because Boston lost; in that, there is a rough justice, and a reminder to the Yankees of how slight and fragile are the circumstances that exalt one group of human beings over another. It breaks my heart because it was meant to foster in me again the illusion that there was something abiding, some pattern and some impulse that could come together to make a reality that would resist the corrosion; and because after it had fostered again that most hungered-for illusion, the game was meant to stop, and betray precisely what it promised.

Of course, there are those who learn after the first few times. They grow out of sports. And there are others who were born with the wisdom to know that nothing lasts. These are the truly tough among us, the ones who can live without illusion, or without even the hope of illusion. I am not that grown up or up to date. I am a simpler creature, tied to more primitive patterns and cycles. I need to think something lasts forever, and it might as well be that state of being that is a game; it might as well be that, in a green field, in the sun.

I believe that A. Bartlett Giamatti, Sterling Professor of Italian and Renaissance Studies at Yale and seventh commissioner of Major League Baseball would have seen the nascent major league batting form in this statuette of Hercules by Francesco da Sant'Agata of Padua, dated 1520. (Reproduced by permission of the trustees of the Wallace Collection, London)

THE EXTRAORDINARY
LIFE AND TIMES
OF PING BODIE

Ira Berkow

*T*he question was posed to Joe Torre, the esteemed manager of the New York
Yankees: "Do you know who is believed to be the first Italian American to
play in the major leagues?"

"Before Ernie Lombardi?" he asked.

"Yes."

"Before Tony Lazzeri?"

"Yes."

He gave it more thought. Finally he said, "I don't know."

"Ping Bodie," came the reply.

"Who?" said Torre.

If Ping Bodie hadn't existed, someone would have had to invent
him. In fact, someone did. Two people, as it were: Franceto Sanguenitta
Pezzolo and Ring Lardner.

A 1961 obituary in the *Sporting News* told some of the story, under
the headline PING BODIE, COLORFUL PICKET AND OLD-ERA SLUGGER, DEAD:
"Frank S. 'Ping' Bodie, one of the most colorful characters the game ever
produced, died of cancer at Notre Dame Hospital in San Francisco,
December 17, at the age of 74."

It went on to say that Bodie, whose real name was Franceto

Ping Bodie, baseball player and fabulist
(National Baseball Hall of Fame Library, Cooperstown, New York)

Sanquenitta Pezzolo (sometimes Americanized, so to speak, to Francesco Stefano Pezzolo, or Pizzola) spent nine seasons as an outfielder with the White Sox, Athletics, and Yankees during a playing career that began in 1908 and ended in 1928.

"He compiled a .275 batting average in the majors, but no player ever had more confidence in himself than Bodie, who became a favorite of writers with tales of his power with the bat," continued the obituary notice. "In describing his home runs, Ping used such phrases as 'I whaled the onion,' 'I crashed the old apple,' 'I rammycackled the old persimmon' and 'I really hemstitched the spheroid.' He was the inspiration of some of the stories in Ring Lardner's *You Know Me Al* series, and it was an unsuccessful steal of a base by Bodie which prompted Bugs Baer to write his famous line, 'Ping had larceny in his heart, but his feet were honest.' "

When Bodie was with the Philadelphia Athletics, he held out for a larger salary than the owner-manager, the legendary baseball genius and tightwad Connie Mack, was willing to surrender. Bodie had led the Athletics in runs batted in the year before, and was thinking quite elevated thoughts about himself.

"I ain't bragging about myself or anything like that, but I got to admit I'm the only real ballplayer Connie's got," he told a reporter. "I and the Liberty Bell are the only attractions left in Philadelphia."

Shortly after, it was only the Liberty Bell, as Bob Creamer wrote in his biography, *Babe,* "for Mack sold the unsigned Ping to the Yankees."

It is often thought that the first Murderers Row in baseball was the Yankees of the late twenties led by Ruth, Lou Gehrig, and Bob Meusel. In fact, the Yankees of a few years earlier were first called Murderers Row, with Wally Pipp and Frank "Home Run" Baker and Ping Bodie.

Since the major leagues in the early part of the century were dominated by English, Irish, and German players, other ethnic groups found that the best way to assimilate, beyond pure talent, was to change one's name. One pertinent example was the Jewish players, such as Reuben Ewing of the Cardinals, Phil Cooney of the Yankees, Harry Kane of the

Phillies, and Sam Bohne of the Reds, to name but four. Each of them was born Cohn or Cohen. Another, the Polish Hall of Fame slugger, was born Aloysius Szymanski, and changed his name to Al Simmons.

Short but powerful and built like a beer keg at 5'8", 195 pounds, Bodie burst upon the scene in 1910 when he hit the then phenomenal number of thirty home runs for the San Francisco Seals of the Pacific Coast League. In the major leagues that season, no one belted more than ten homers. Of course, the Pacific Coast League wasn't the major leagues, but it was Triple-A, just a level below.

Bodie was front-page news. And his output was impressive enough to influence Jimmy Callahan, manager of the White Sox, to have the Chicago ballclub draft Bodie.

Bodie was now a member of the White Sox, but he started his rookie season, 1911, on the bench. After reading a complaint by Charles Comiskey, owner of the club, that his team couldn't hit, Bodie stalked into the boss's office.

"Put me in the lineup," Bodie said, "and I'll show you some hitting of the old apple." Comiskey ordered Callahan to play Bodie, and Bodie lived up to his boast.

He batted .289—only two other teammates hit for higher averages. He didn't get close to the thirty home runs of the season before, and hit but four. But he was productive in another way: his ninety-seven runs batted in were significantly better than any other White Sox player and were good for fourth in the league, behind three future Hall-of-Famers, Ty Cobb, "Wahoo" Sam Crawford, and Home Run Baker.

While Chicago had a substantial Italian population, Bodie's popularity transcended that ethnic connection. He was a drawing card because of his ebullient personality, as well as his considerable skills as a ballplayer. In his second season with the White Sox, Bodie batted .294 and hit five homers. His RBI production fell to a less impressive but still creditable seventy-two.

"Numerous funny stories were written with Bodie as the 'goat,'" the

Sporting News reported, "some of which were true, but the majority were new to Bodie until he saw them in print."

This one, however, was true: Bodie made an agreement with White Sox management not to drink liquor during the season. While Bodie seldom touched the hard stuff, he did like beer, and that put on weight, something the chunky Bodie could ill afford.

One day after a double-header in St. Louis against the Browns on a hot afternoon in which both games went into extra innings, Bodie found himself in a dilemma.

"When it was over," Bodie said, "I noticed a lot of dust had gathered in my throat. I went to Tony Faust's, a famous St. Louis restaurant, and asked a bartender to prescribe something for my condition. He prescribed a large stein of beer and I was prepared to lift the giant foaming mug to my lips when who should walk in but Manager Callahan.

"Callahan pointed to the stein and hollered: 'That will cost you exactly $500.' I told him: 'You're wrong. It's going to cost me $500.10. I've already paid a dime for this beer.'

"But it turned out that the beer didn't cost me anything. About two weeks before the close of the season, Comiskey called me to his office and gave me a check for $500.10. He not only refunded the fine but paid for the beer."

The story grew and grew, and changed in the telling, like some Homeric saga. Callahan apparently said that he rescinded the fine the next day—after Bodie had gotten three hits.

This was also the time when Ring Lardner was covering the White Sox for the *Chicago Tribune,* and with his exquisite eye and ear and sense of humor took in the language and behavioral patterns of this new sociological phenomenon known as the "modern" ballplayer, which included, to be sure, Ping Bodie, with whom Lardner was in almost daily contact for seven months of the year.

The first of Lardner's famous "Busher" stories was sold to the *Saturday Evening Post* in 1914, Bodie's fourth season with the White Sox.

He published five more, which became the contents of the bestseller and acclaimed classic *You Know Me Al*, which continues to be the best selling of Lardner's numerous books. They are stories of a faintly literate pitcher for the White Sox named Jack Keefe who writes letters to a friend named Al Blanchard. The outpouring of his trials and tribulations as a ballplayer, salary negotiator, and lover are depicted with slang, dialect, or baseball argot.

"Readers and baseball fans liked to speculate about who was the original Jack Keefe," wrote Donald Elder, in his biography *Ring Lardner*. "Ring's colleagues saw in him something of the braggadocio of Ping Bodie, the White Sox outfielder, and Frank Smith, the pitcher; his alibis reminded them of Ed Walsh." In addition, Hugh Fullerton, another star Chicago sports columnist of the day, saw in Keefe the traits of Solly Hofman, Jimmy Sheckard, Frank Schulte, and Lew Richie of the Cubs. "All of which indicates that there was no single original of Jack Keefe."

Lardner himself, in a preface to the first edition of *You Know Me Al*, wrote: "The writer has been asked frequently, or perhaps not very often at all . . . who is the original of Jack Keefe?" And added: "I have heretofore declined to reply to it, as a reply would have stopped the boys and girls from guessing . . . and I may as well give the correct answer. The original of Jack Keefe is not a ball player at all, but Jane Addams of Hull-House, a former Follies girl."

Whether Bodie luxuriated or recoiled from the possibility that he was a model, or one of the models, for Jack Keefe, the plain fact is that after his splendid start with the White Sox in the first two years, he trailed off.

He hit .264 in 1913 and a dismal .229 in 1914. It seems his outgoing personality and lack of production drove Callahan to sell Bodie back to the San Francisco Seals after the 1914 season.

Bodie vowed that he would do such good work that he would someday come back to the majors and "show up Callahan."

He returned to the San Francisco Seals of the Pacific Coast League, where he again hit with his former power and consistency. In his two seasons back in the Bay Area he hit nineteen homers and batted .325 in 1915, and walloped twenty homers and batted .303 in 1916.

Writing in the *New York Tribune*, Wood Ballard said, "Ping was such a demon with the ash that Connie Mack recalled him from the bushes and put him to work in the outfield for the Athletics."

Bodie was such a favorite with the fans because he "played to the gallery, which in baseball parlance means the bleachers," wrote Ballard. "And the gallery gods liked it and kidded Ping and Ping kidded them."

Ballard had a leaning toward description, and here is Ping Bodie illustrated:

> There is an apparent anthropoid stoop to Ping's broad shoulders, which seems to lengthen his long arms which dangle the more as he trots to and from his place in the outfield. . . . These characteristics may have been affected in his early baseball days to attract the attention of the gallery, for Ping is something of an actor. However they are a part of him now. . . .
>
> Bodie seldom strikes out. His batting average may fall, but it is because he stings the ball where some fielder can handle it. And Ping is usually good in the pinch. He grips his bat well down on the handle, puts all the strength of his powerful arms and shoulders into the blow and wades into the ball.
>
> Because of his apparent awkwardness he is faster than he really seems, and what he lacks as an outfielder of the first rank he makes up to a big extent with his bat.

In a time when ballplayers felt that a laugh was more important than a sectioned brief case, when any goofy shenanigan was more intriguing that an addition to his stock portfolio, Ping Bodie was game for any amusement. One of those came during spring training with the Yankees in Jacksonville in 1919.

"The contest for the heavyweight eating championship of the world between Percy the Ostrich and Ping Bodie of the Yankees drew a packed house to the South Side Pavilion last night," wrote W. O. McGeehan, in his column in the *New York Tribune*. "Percy the Ostrich quit on the eleventh platter, and Sheriff Donahue, the referee, declared Bodie the undisputed eating Champion of the world."

The match was promoted by the Jacksonville Chamber of Commerce, which had been advertising Percy as the world's greatest eater. Colonel T. L. Huston (who, wrote McGeehan, "foots the fodder bill for Bodie"—he was co-owner of the Yankees) "laughed at these pretensions, and the challenge followed."

Since Bodie was the challenger, he could choose the *cuisine de guerre*. He selected spaghetti. McGeehan described it as a boxing match, round for round. This was the conclusion:

> Round 11: The ostrich barely waddled from his corner. Percy's eyes were bloodshot and his sides were heaving as he toed the platter. He was a badly beaten ostrich. Bodie was almost

Ping roomed with Babe Ruth. (National Baseball Hall of Fame Library, Cooperstown, New York)

finished with his platter when Percy dropped to his knees. The timekeeper began to count. Bodie ferociously downed the first morsel and stepped back to survey his fallen antagonist. As the timekeeper muttered the final ten, the ostrich sank back to rise no more.

How Francito Sanguenitta Pezzolo, born October 8, 1887 in San Francisco, the son of Rose De Martini and Joseph Pezzolo, both born in Italy, became Frank S. "Ping" Bodie was explained by Bodie:

> "My folks bought a house when I was a youngster from a man named Dwyer," Bodie told a reporter in 1918. "The Dwyers had a boy, Jack, about my age, whose nickname was Ping. When we moved into the house and Jack moved out he left the Ping behind him and the neighbors hung it on me. As for the Bodie, I don't know. Some bloke must have wished it on me when I began playing ball. Anyway, by this time, it's mine. I couldn't get rid of it if I wanted to.

That's not how Ping's older brother, Dave, remembered the change of the last name. After the *Sporting Life* periodical had written a piece about Bodie, Dave wrote a letter to the editor saying that Ping's correct last name is Pizzola.

> He took the name of Bodie from our uncle—my mother's brother—when he started to play ball because he thought all the fans would josh him. Both Frank and I were born here in San Francisco at the old house on North Beach. Corner Vallejo and Pacific streets—what they call Telegraph Hill. Frank is here now, and we both wish you would correct what you said in next week's "Sporting Life."
>
> Yours truly, Dave Bodie (Pizzola).

The remark about the concern that fans might "josh" him for his name suggests that a purely ethnic Italian name was not what ball fans of that era were accustomed to.

Bodie also gave the impression that "Ping" came from the sound of his fifty-two-ounce bat striking the baseball in the Dead Ball Era. "You should have heard me crash the old apple," he said.

The mystery of the name thickens, however. Did the Pezzolos, or Pizzolas, like Dave Bodie, change their names to Bodie because Ping did, or was there yet another explanation?

And Bodie gave yet another version:

> All of the boys in our family of sixteen kids took the name of Bodie because it was the name of a California town where my father was a gold miner. A friend of the family named Jack Dwyer was nicknamed Ping and he didn't like it. Once, when I was two years old, he said, "That kid can't defend himself, so I hereby give him the name of 'Ping.' "
>
> So "Ping Bodie" became my legal name. My father didn't like the boys' adopting the name of Bodie, but he was more angry with me than the others, because I became a national figure, and the first player of Italian descent to reach the majors. He said I should have carried the name Pezzolo to fame.

Ping was, as one writer of the time termed it, "a swashbuckling youngster" growing up in his native San Francisco. McGeehan, who couldn't resist comical allusions to Bodie, said of him: "He's one of the rock-rollers of Telegraph Hill. They keep their territory free of invaders by pulling rocks out of the summit and rolling them down the streets."

Bodie, who was a product of the San Francisco sandlots and the Telegraph Hill section, San Francisco's "Little Italy," dropped out of high school after his first year and began his career as a professional infielder in 1906 in the California outlaw league. After one year he was transferred to the outfield and from 1908 through 1910 played for the San Francisco Seals of the Pacific Coast League.

In his four seasons with the White Sox (1911–14), he hit a total of twenty home runs. In his next to last season in Chicago his batting average sank to .264, though he slugged eight homers, and he hit .229 with three homers in 1914, playing in just 107 games (compared to 145 in his first season). He was sent back to the minor leagues, back to San Francisco.

Bodie complained that the decline in his hitting was all manager Callahan's fault. Bodie liked taking a whack at the first pitch, and Callahan had instructed him to be patient. Patience led to falling behind in the count. "I was always a first-ball hitter," explained Bodie, "and I always thought I had the advantage, because the pitcher would send up the first one mighty careful in attempting to make sure of the range and the groove. Callahan made me stop hitting the first one, and that gave the pitchers the percentage on me."

Baseball magazine sided with Bodie: "If a man has developed a batting style of his own, and has made his attack effective by cracking the first one, why try to make him change? . . . If a man is known to possess a keen lamp and a sharp swing, and is also famous as a first-ball hitter, the burden, the weight of trouble, all shift upon the pitcher."

The *New York Tribune* suggested another side to Bodie's plummet with the White Sox, referring to Bodie as "the 'comedian' who had fallen into evil ways around the gay life of Chicago's stockyard."

Bodie was described as possessing "an even temper that wins. He is congenial, a great mixer and likes to talk, and he can be entertaining in a baseball way." Perhaps at times he was too great a mixer.

Back with the Seals, for two seasons, he was hitting the ball with his one-time vigor. He batted .325 and hit nineteen homers in 1915, and hit .303 with twenty homers the following year.

He returned to the major leagues with the Athletics in 1917, when he batted .291 in 148 games, and was traded to the Yankees the following March for first baseman George Burns.

"The presence of Bodie in a Yankee uniform should furnish many

a merry quip for the metropolitan journalists who recount baseball anecdotes," wrote W. J. Macbeth in the *New York Tribune.* "Ping is a temperamental cuss, like most geniuses. . . .

"He proved one of the most dangerous hitters of the Mack clan,"
driving in seventy-four runs, to lead the last-place A's in that department,
and hit .291, second best among A's regulars. His seven homers tied for
third in the American League. "He was serious, at least, in his endeavors,"
continued Macbeth, "and campaigned through the year pounds lighter
than he had been as a member of the White Sox."

He hit .256, .278, and .295 in three full seasons with the Yankees,
and was with them in 1921 when they won the first of their pennants.
However, he didn't finish the season with them, and missed his chance to
play in a World Series. He was traded to the Red Sox in August of that
year. He didn't play a game with the Red Sox.

When Yankees officials turned down his demand for a one-half
World Series share, he refused to report to the Red Sox and returned
home and spent the next seven seasons with Vernon and San Francisco
(Pacific Coast League), Des Moines (Western League), and Wichita
Falls–San Antonio (Texas League).

When Babe Ruth joined the Yankees in 1920, he was assigned to
room with Ping Bodie and did so until Bodie was traded to the Red Sox
late in the 1921 season. Years later, Bodie recalled that period:

> Ruth, as I remember him, had a great personality. He was
> a perennial big kid. I guess he never really grew up. But that's
> one of the reasons we all loved him. He had an overpowering
> amount of energy, both on and off the field, and was always on
> the go. During one period, the Babe was hustling around so
> much after dark that when a reporter in Wichita Falls, Texas,
> asked me how I liked rooming with the Babe, I replied, "I'm
> rooming with a suitcase." I thought that was the best way I could
> describe the Babe's continual battle with manager Miller
> Huggins's curfew.

In 1925, Bodie, now a minor league player, was in the news again. This time for an odd twist on a divorce case. He filed suit for a divorce from Anna Bodie, to whom he was married in 1908. The Bodies had a son and a daughter but had not lived together since 1923. Bodie charged that in August 1922 his wife started a story among their acquaintances that he was a bootlegger and a "common drunk," and that she made the further false statement that he was crazy. However, his principal complaint was that five years earlier his wife had begun to send derogatory telegrams about him to Judge Kenesaw Mountain Landis, the commissioner of baseball; Miller Huggins, manager of the Yankees; E. Lee Keyser, manager of the Des Moines club of the Western League; and Eddie Maier, manager of the Vernon club of the Pacific Coast League. These messages, he said, attacked his character and conduct. Bodie was granted the divorce.

Bodie wound up his career in 1928 with the San Francisco Seals, hitting .347, at the age of forty. But he said he'd had enough. He bought a gas station, and then a diner, yet kept his hand in baseball by playing in semi-pro leagues.

One day he ran into Pat Monahan, a scout for the Boston Red Sox. Monahan was bemoaning the scarcity of good ballplayers and the terrible time a scout has in finding major league starters in minor league settings. He got no sympathy from Bodie.

"Why, you've got the softest job on earth," said Bodie.

"Soft huh, scouting seven years for a tail-end ball team?" Monahan replied with indignation.

"Soft is right," said the irrepressible Bodie. "You couldn't go wrong if you tried to. Any ballplayer you pick up is bound to go better than those the Red Sox are losing with."

When Bodie's filling station fell on hard times during the Depression, he tried a brief comeback in 1931 with Oakland. But his skills had eroded with age. He was now forty-three years old. He was recommended for a job in Hollywood as an electrician on movie sets. He held the job for the next thirty-one years. He was said to be a favorite of such screen stars as Charles Boyer and Carole Lombard.

"I ran across Bodie in a jungle on a Universal Pictures set recently, while the Giants were playing exhibitions around Hollywood," wrote Ken Smith, a sports reporter for the New York *Daily Mirror*, in 1948. "Lon Chaney Jr., stalking through the foliage, suddenly went into a trance that transformed him into a gorilla or something. The director yelled 'Cut' and a round man wearing a Yankees baseball cap stepped briskly and incongruously into the jungle, pulling a sound track wire from beneath a banana tree.

"It was Ping Bodie—and it is a pleasure to report that he can still go to his right or left when it comes to setting up movie stages, or grabbing baseballs."

Smith described Bodie as "one of the great colony of Italian ballplayers from the San Francisco hills—the DiMaggios, Tony Lazzeri, and Frank Crosetti." But added the ethnic description that Bodie "was one of New York's most famous spaghetti destroyers in his day." In a less politically correct atmosphere, such illustrations went virtually unnoticed—unless, of course, one was Italian and resented it.

When, in 1919, Bodie left the Yankees in spring training because he said he had personal and urgent business to attend to in New York, manager Miller Huggins did not give him permission to leave and a contretemps ensued, with Huggins saying he wanted to trade Bodie. The situation was described this way in the *New York Tribune:* "The temperamental Italian, in a word, is on the market." Another reference to Bodie stated: "Ping Bodie is his stage name. Ping needs a stage name. Pezzolo wouldn't look well in a box score."

In *Ethnicity and Sport in North American History and Culture,* Carmen Bazzano wrote that "the Depression years . . . proved to be a bonanza for Italian-American baseball players." He wrote that some have argued that the decline of Nativism—the practice or policy of favoring native-born citizens over immigrants—accompanied the economic hardship of the Depression, and proved instrumental in the acceptance of the new immigrants in baseball. "While it is difficult to substantiate (this) argument, the fact remains that during the 1930s many Italian players began finding their way to the major leagues. By the close of the fourth decade, so many of them were active in the majors that the National Italian American Civic League issued an 'All-Italian Team' for 1939."

On the set of Universal Pictures, Smith of the *Mirror* sat down with Bodie and reminisced. "Bodie is still stout, quick-actioned, happy and philosophical," wrote Smith. He proceeded to draw the old ballplayer out.

"I don't go to many games but I follow the scores," Bodie said. "I'd much prefer watching sandlot kids play. They have that will-to-win. The professionals go through their games as though it was a day's work. I don't mean all of them nor that they aren't giving their best. But there is that tendency to say: 'You do or you don't, a fellow can't do anything more.' But in my time there was more all-out determination to win."

Even at his retirement at age seventy-three, Bodie had not lost his confidence as a hitter.

Did he think he could still hit? a friend asked. "Give me a mace," Bodie shot back, "and I'll drive the pumpkin down Whitey Ford's throat."

HOOKS

Robert Leuci

My mother appears in the photograph immaculately dressed and groomed, she is wearing a suit, white shoes, and a cute little white hat. Her left hand is on a shapely hip and her right arm is around a baseball player. Stitched in script across the shirt of his uniform are the words S. M. FRANK, for S. M. Frank Medico smoking pipes.

In this photograph he is a young man, far too plain and homely to be my mother's boyfriend. The photo was taken on the day they met; she was seventeen, my father was twenty-two.

My mother's name was Lucy, and in my youth she would tell me time and again that she married my father because everyone said he was going to be a major-leaguer. Sports, like politics, were of no interest to my mother, but she had a passion for athletes.

"He had a great physique," she'd say, "I couldn't help myself, I loved athletes."

My father was an athlete, that's for sure, and for many years he was able to make a living from playing ball. He lived during Prohibition and the Depression and played ball during the thirties and forties. People who saw him play told me that he was better than anybody of his time.

My father hit left-handed and threw right. He had an arm like a cannon and hands that were huge. He was fast and strong. Men who had seen him play told me that he hit line drives that tore the gloves off the

Mom and Hooks (Robert Leuci and Family)

hands of infielders and that he was agile and ran like the wind. He was only a kid then, but right away he figured out that baseball would be a life for him.

My father had everybody believing that he would be a major-leaguer, but it never happened. Some said he threw out his arm, others said it was Lucy. It was always Lucy.

In this photograph he is lean and gawky, with large ears and a big Neapolitan nose. His socks are up to his knees; his pants are baggy and the baseball glove he carries has the palm worn out.

My mother does not look seventeen in this photograph. She seems mature and worldly to me, beyond her years, and she has the look of the troublemaker in those dimpled cheeks and dazzling eyes. There was always something sensual about Lucy, something she could not control; it was her nature, she'd say, she couldn't help it, that she was born that way.

When I was in grade school, one day each term my parents were required to be present at an evaluation session with my teachers. My father never attended. It was always my mother and she would be called back—often—and always greeted with faked disapproving smiles. I was having no more difficulty than anyone else; the teachers' concerns were only a pretext to see Lucy parade in her sweater and skirt and spiked high heels.

I remember my homeroom and science teacher, Mister Lynch, a tall, thin Irishman with a great mane of white hair who kept a bottle of Scotch in the upper drawer of his desk. He'd look sharply at me, telling me he'd been thinking that he should send a note to my mother, asking her to come to school to discuss my failings.

Throughout my youth my mother's beauty weighed on me like an unforgivable sin. I associated it only with harassment at school and the sly comments and private smiles of the male teachers. For my father it was so much worse.

I see him now, sitting at the head of the kitchen table, a great bowl of his favorite pasta in front of him, telling me his favorite Lucy story, his eyes sparkling with the memory of it, my mother standing at the stove,

*Mom, whose name became Lucy Leuci
when she married Hooks
(Robert Leuci and Family)*

her arms crossed over generous breasts, "Americans," she'd say, "they all thought who they were, you know, like they were big shots."

To my mother Americans were everyone who was not an Italian or a Jew. All people who spoke English without an accent were not to be trusted. Especially those persons in positions of power, a government official of any kind, a schoolteacher, a *policeman,* most doctors, bosses and landlords and train and trolley car conductors.

I have no memory of trolley cars, but my mother did, a savage memory of a nine-year-old brother named Mario who was thrown to his death from one by a conductor who spoke with a brogue. You could see it in her eyes, such unbelievable rage, such unabashed distrust and a readiness to believe only the worst of people outside her family.

Another brother, Joseph, when he was six years old, was carried to the hospital, suffering from whooping cough. My mother told me that Joseph was a remarkably beautiful boy, so beautiful that when he played in the street, strangers would stop and touch his face. The morning after Joseph was placed into the care of the "Americans" at the hospital, a man showed up at my grandparents' apartment. He returned Joseph's harmonica, telling the family that Joseph had died during the night from some unnamed, contagious disease. People at the hospital would care for the body.

"They stole that boy," my mother would repeat breathlessly, many years later, her voice conjuring up an abhorrent and reckless fear of strangers lurking in hallways and antiseptic rooms, outsiders scheming to do harm to her family.

"Remembering things that way makes your mother happy," my father told me. "Your mother," he said, "has no friends, only imagined enemies." He never believed the story about my mother's brother Joseph. But she did. You can bet she did.

I can see my father as he tells another Lucy story, the way the boss's kid asked Lucy for a date, how she turned him down and how that set free all sorts of havoc for two families.

"The guy was a foreman and Fuerbock's kid, the boss's son."

"I don't date Germans, is what I said."

"No Lucy, that's not what you said. You said I don't date strangers, especially German strangers."

"Well, something like that. The nerve, I hardly knew him. And, I was dating your father at the time. He knew that, the creep."

It seems that the boss's son was used to getting his way. "Stranger," he told my mother, "I'll show you stranger."

He fired her and two of her sisters, Louise and Rose. Then he fired two of my father's brothers, Tommy and Eddie.

"They had never met your mother, my brothers didn't even know her, and still they got laid off."

I asked my father why the boss's kid didn't fire him, too?

"Me, he wouldn't fire me. Hell, I was the captain of the baseball team and the best player they had. They weren't about to fire me."

"Did you do anything? I mean you were the captain of the baseball team."

"I did what I could. I went to see Mr. Silverman and he gave me a few words on workers' solidarity and told me I should be ashamed to play a *game* for a living.

"So, I guess the answer to your question is no."

"You called him 'Mister Silverman'?"

"That's right."

◆　　◆　　◆

Now, after all these years, I still don't know Silverman's first name. I saw him many times throughout my childhood. He'd sit and talk in the living room with my father. I'd see him at family weddings and wakes. Silverman was always there. It was Silverman or "Mister" Silverman. He had the habit of grabbing the hair at the top of my head and shaking me. "This kid's got some head of hair," he'd say.

My mother said Silverman was a communist.

My father said he was a great man.

Silverman gave my father books to read, talked to my father about evicted families and abused workers; he raised my father's social consciousness and turned him into a socialist and a union man, but all that would wait until he finished playing ball.

My father died in the middle of my troubled young adulthood and I'd regret not spending more time with him, forcing him to tell me more about his own childhood, more about his dreams.

Childhood and what his life was like back then were subjects my father had difficulty discussing. He hardly remembered his own parents; they died of diphtheria within weeks of each other when he was six or seven. Poor people's disease, he would say; my parents died from overcrowding and poverty. Raised by his twelve-years-older married sister Angelina, there had been little in his young life to make him happy, nothing other than playing ball.

When I'd insist that he tell me more about his childhood he would lean forward and fold his arms, stare at me a long time, and then a great smile would go across his face and he'd say, "I grew up during the

Depression; we had nothing, times were very rough, but I always had a rubber ball."

As a child my father lived to the cadence of a ball. It was a spaldeen, pink and lively, and the games he played with that magical pink ball were limited only by the players' imaginations. He'd play stickball, stoop ball, slap ball, and punch ball all day long.

When not in school he played on the sidewalks and streets of East New York, Hull Street and Hopkinson Avenue, a block from Fulton Street, the dividing line between his neighborhood and Brownsville. He'd tell you that he came from Brownsville. That's the way he chose to remember it, and he spoke of his neighborhood devotedly, proud of its socialist history.

"Hand and eye coordination," he'd say, "that's what kids learned on those Brooklyn streets. Stickball with a broom handle, hit it like a fungo or, if you had enough guys, pitched on one bounce. Slap ball was played curb to curb, in the middle of the street, two bases and home. Pitched on one bounce and slap the ball along the ground, in the air was an out. The pitcher could flick that spaldeen with two fingers and it would bounce and break any which way; you had to be quick to hit it with the palm of your hand, and you had to be fast to make it to first. Stoopball could be played with only two kids—one in the field, the other hitting. You throw that spaldeen off the edge of a stoop, you catch that stoop edge just right and that ball would sail over the head of your opponent and across the street for a home run. Catch it in the air and you're out.

"We played all day, see the ball, hit the ball. When I was old enough to play baseball that ball looked as big as a basketball and no matter who was throwing it, it would never break as much as a spaldeen, never."

My aunt Angie took good care of my father. I'm sure that there were more toys than just a ball, but that was how my father remembered childhood, a ball. When he got older my aunt would pack him lunch and he'd head off to Prospect Park and the Parade Grounds. It was on those great old Brooklyn fields that he discovered baseball.

"We were always together, Italians and Jews from East New York and Brownsville, all of us first-generation Americans. We were a people, a type, all of us neighborhood guys, most of whose parents didn't speak English."

They formed teams and soon those teams had sponsors, pizza parlors and saloons. They not only played baseball, they played fast-pitch softball too. And their sponsors, who were mostly gangsters, would bet on those games. Before long they were traveling throughout the city and playing teams from other neighborhoods: Irishmen from South Brooklyn, Sunset Park, and Bay Ridge; German clubs from Yorkville and Ridgewood; Polish teams from Greenpoint. Playing ball would be one long weekend, Friday, Saturday, and Sunday, baseball on a dirt field, and softball on a cement playground. Windmill, fast-pitch softball, was the money game, and my father would be paid to play.

The sponsors would bet among themselves, then put out beer and pizza and sandwiches in their saloons after the game. A good windmill pitcher could throw that softball ninety miles an hour, with a rise and a break from forty feet away. You had to have one fast bat.

My father played baseball at Dexter Park in Brooklyn and Sterling Oval in Queens and Dyckman Oval in the Bronx. When he was older he played against the Black Yankees on Randall's Island in Manhattan and told me that that team could beat *anybody*. He played against the convicts at Sing Sing prison. The other inmates would crowd the bleachers and root ferociously against their fellow prisoners.

Although my father was born in this country, his older brothers were born in Italy and their view of life was very different than his own. For my father there was a love of place, of Brooklyn in general, of Ebbets Field and ballplayers in particular. For his brothers it was the mountains and plains of *Italia*. They spoke no English and didn't care to learn. They had left a place where there was no work and little hope; they were hard people from a harsh and primitive land transplanted to a country they couldn't understand.

In that enclave on Hull Street, there was plenty of tension between my father and his brothers. These men were old enough to be his father, men who lived and led their families in the old way and believed that a life of playing a game for a living was less than manly.

My father would point to the DiMaggio brothers, Brooklyn-born Marius Russo, and his favorite, Tony Lazzeri, and later, Yogi Berra, Phil Rizzuto, Billy Martin, Ralph Branca, and Carl Furillo as examples of Italian American success in professional baseball. His brothers didn't want to hear it.

"Work," they'd say. "Get a trade," they'd say. "Be a man and help the family."

But my father's passion was baseball, only baseball. He told me, "I'd make more money on a Wednesday and Friday night and on Saturday and a Sunday than my brothers did swinging a *hammer,* using a pick and shovel all week."

The images of these men, of how hard they worked with their hands and backs, in pouring rain, in fierce sun and the freezing cold of winter, a battleground life day in day out was not for my father. He wanted to defy all that, and the only way he knew was to play ball.

"Immigrants were immigrants," he'd say, "Americans were Americans, and the gulf that existed between them was deep and wide. I was born here, and I wanted to be an American, and my bridge from here to there was baseball."

One day he told me that he almost did it.

"My star burned bright for a while," he said, "but then it vanished. Still, it was a great run and I loved it, every minute of every day."

I have a newspaper clipping from the *Long Island Press,* five columns from the Sunday sports section, a cartoonist's rendition of my father in his teens swinging a bat. Lee Benn, the illustrator, was brilliant. The caricature likeness of my father is absolutely amazing.

In the center of the page is a large drawing of my father finishing his swing. There is a sunburst, and in the center, right at the focal point, is written JAMES "HOOKS" LEUCI OF THE AUBURN CLUB.

In the upper left-hand corner of the clipping, a hitter is sketched smacking a ball. "Hooks," it says, "clouted four hits in five trips to the plate against the Glen Morris A.A. in its opening game recently."

In the upper right-hand corner a ballplayer sits on a bench sucking on a straw, drinking from a bottle of milk. In a balloon over his head it reads, "A home run in every bottle." Then, "Drinking milk, he will tell you, makes him the slugger that he is."

Then, an illustration of a fielder catching a ball and underneath: "One of the best third basemen in the Queens Baseball Alliance, he covers the hot corner like a big-leaguer."

Then, a sketch of a kid pitching a baseball to a cartoon of a man whose hat is flying off his head. The ball is doing loop-d-loops and the cartoon man shouts, "HOOKS!" And beneath, "He was the only kid on the block that could throw a curve, hence 'Hooks.'"

◆ ◆ ◆

In the mid-sixties when I was in my early twenties and a New York City police detective assigned to the Narcotics Division working in South Brooklyn, one of the street people came to me and told me that a man wanted to meet me—said the guy was night manager of the Bickfords cafeteria at Atlantic and Flatbush Avenues.

"He asked for me?"

"Yes, he did, and by name."

A few days later I went to see him. He was ageless, burly, and weary looking.

"The other night," he said, "one of the junkies mentioned your name and I wondered if you were related to Hooks."

"He's my father."

"A helluva ballplayer."

"I heard."

"No, he was one hell of a ballplayer," he said in a low voice. "I mean a real ballplayer."

"I know. Did you know him?"

"My brother better than me, but I met him a few times."

"What's your name?"

"Carlo Maione."

"And you manage this place."

"Night manager."

The name was not familiar to me, but he seemed like a decent enough guy, a hard worker. I knew that managing Bickfords late at night in that part of town was no day at the beach. It was a gathering point for scores of junkies, hookers, and pimps, a junkyard of troublemakers. I gave him my phone number and told him that if he ran into problems he should give me a call.

"They don't give me any problems. Junkies, you know, sick people, they're easy."

He said he'd been home six months and this was the only job he could find.

He asked about my father, my aunt Angie, and my uncle Tony. I told him that they were getting older, but they were fine.

I said, "You just got home, home from where?"

"Upstate."

"How long?"

"Twenty-five years."

"Jesus. For what?"

"Homicide."

With that he went quiet and smiled at me. "It was a long time ago," he said.

My father told me that he didn't remember Carlo Maione but he certainly remembered his brother, Happy. Happy and his crime partner, Dasher, worked for a guy named Mo Goldstein. Mo owned a string of pizza parlors in Brownsville, and in those pizza parlors he had slot machines that showed porn flicks. My father played ball for him.

When he spoke about Mo Goldstein, it seemed part admiration, part warning.

"He got me my first paying jobs," he'd say, "and I was paid to play ball. He was also a gangster, a boss, one of the top guys in Murder Inc. The truth is he did things for me, extraordinary things."

When my father was seventeen years old, it was Mo Goldstein who had sent him to the Bronx for a job at S. M. Frank Medico smoking pipes. They had a plant in the Bronx and it was there that my father began playing industrial league baseball. He didn't work in the plant so much as play ball for them, and soon he was captain of the team. Eventually S. M. Frank Medico moved to an enormous factory in Richmond Hill, Queens. A beautiful plant surrounded by trees and open spaces, it resembled a private boys' school more than a factory.

On the day he was to take his high school graduation photos my father went to see Mo Goldstein and told him that he didn't have a decent suit. Goldstein sent him to an apartment he kept across the street from one of his pizza parlors.

"Take whatever you need," he told him.

"I'd never seen anything like that. An entire four-room apartment, a closet for clothes. Hundreds of suits, shirts, ties, and shoes. I picked out a suit, Angie hemmed it and tucked it and I had the best suit of anybody.

"In one way, touching those beautiful suits, being around all those clothes, I was able to see what the gangster life could be like," he said. "But, there were other things, too."

For my father there was never a struggle on how to live in this world. He was a law-abiding and honest man his entire life. Baseball, my father told me, kept him away from all that.

"I was a baseball player, not a gangster; the gangster life was way too dangerous."

His family, his people, came from a part of Italy called the *Mezzogiorno*, "the land that time forgot." They were an oppressed people, peasants from a corrupt and medieval society. Over the centuries they had come to expect nothing from government or landowners or *stranieri* (foreigners). Their ancestors and their own experience of exploitation and violence had darkened and hardened and united them.

My father knew all the stories, the legends and myths. But he was born in America, and although he could talk at length about his new country's faults, he considered himself an American, and to him the country of his birth was a generous and wondrous place.

"They were so nice," my aunt Angie said to me, "they used to drive Tony home from the club. Tony always drank way too much wine and was always singing "Bella Sicilia." (Beautiful Sicily).

Her husband, Tony, came from Palermo and spoke practically no English at all. When he drank he had trouble walking, but he could sing songs of his *paese* and he had a beautiful voice. At night's end, if he was unable to get home on his own, young men from the Sons of Palermo club would drive him.

Happy and Dasher escorted him home on more than one occasion. They would carry him up three flights of stairs and my aunt Angie would express her gratitude by making them something to eat.

"They were killers," I told her. "I mean, serious, big-time killers." Happy Maione and Frank (the Dasher) Abbandando were part of the Brownsville gang known as Murder Inc. Between the two of them they killed about fifty people and both of them died in the electric chair.

"That's what they say, you know," she said.

Angelina went to their funeral after they had been electrocuted.

"They looked so beautiful, you wouldn't believe it. When I saw them, they looked like they were sleeping. Not a mark on their faces, you couldn't see that they had been burnt."

Aunt Angie told me that Dasher was electrocuted for a murder that Happy committed, and Happy was electrocuted for a murder that Dasher did.

"You see," she concluded, "they were innocent."

◆ ◆ ◆

It was no fun for me to be told repeatedly that I was only a shadow of my father.

"You couldn't carry his glove," someone once told me. "Your old man was a real ballplayer."

Growing up, I heard that a whole lot. But I wasn't chopped liver; I mean, when it came to neighborhood and high school ball, I could play. In 1956 and '57, when I was sixteen and seventeen, I pitched for the Richmond Hill Saxons, a team in the junior and senior division of the Queens, Nassau baseball league. The Saxons were arguably the best sandlot baseball team ever put together. One year our record was 26–1. I pitched the only game we lost, and we lost that game 1–0 and I pitched a one-hitter. Half that team got signed to play pro ball, the other half got college scholarships.

A bird dog for the Los Angeles Dodgers had watched me pitch that game, and he told me that he had seen me once before pitching for John Adams, my high school team. Adams was a team of great guys, terrific fielders who couldn't hit. I lost a lot of close games.

The bird dog took me aside and told me, "Leuci, you're good, but you're not nearly as good as your father was."

I got angry and told him that I was still young.

He said, "You're as good as you're going to get."

I shrugged and didn't answer.

He took ahold of my hands and examined them as if he were looking for stigmata. "You're not going to grow," he told me, "your hands are too small."

My father wasn't much bigger than I was, he stood about five feet, ten inches but had enormous hands and could easily put two baseballs between two adjoining sets of fingers. I remember thinking that I had Lucy's hands, and I was devastated.

That night, sitting at dinner with my father, we talked about the game, my loss, the bird dog, and my small hands. I didn't cry, but I sure as hell wanted to.

"What does that guy know," my father told me. "I played against him, and let me tell you, on his best day he couldn't hit you with a *tennis* racquet."

I loved the sound of that.

"He told me that I'm not half the ballplayer you were."

"He said that?"

"Yes."

"Well, he was a lousy ballplayer and he turned out to be a lousy guy. Remember," he said, "it's baseball and it's only a game."

But we both knew it was more than a game, for him and for me, too.

I remember it was only a few days later that I asked my father to come with me to a baseball field near where we lived. Maybe there was no potential for the major leagues in me, but I was having a banner year and I wanted to prove something to myself and maybe him, too.

That year I pitched for a number of all-star teams and on that day I was preparing myself to pitch at Yankee Stadium. It was an American Legion all-star game, a league that played at the Parade Grounds in Brooklyn, and I was to be the starting pitcher.

My catcher showed up with a dozen balls. I threw from the mound under the watchful eye of my father. I was young and I felt strong, felt as though I could throw the ball through the backstop.

My father watched me.

After a time he picked up a bat. I remember the way he stood there, smiling, saying, "So whadaya say, think you can get it past me?"

We had done this before, and in the past I'd thrown half speed, no breaking balls (my best pitch was a knuckle curve). Usually he'd pop one or two, but mostly he'd stand there and check my motion and delivery. On that day I was full of myself and a bit angry. Hell, that night I was going to pitch at Yankee Stadium. I'd show that Los Angeles Dodgers bird dog, that creep of a traitor.

"C'mon," I said, "get in there."

I called the catcher out to the mound, his name was Mario Rinari—a tough kid from an even tougher neighborhood, a place that was not all that far from where I lived, but really, a different world. Mario lived on 101st Avenue, a neighborhood that would gain notoriety years later as the stomping grounds for the Dapper Don, John Gotti.

"Listen Mario, one, fastball, two, curve. I'm gonna cut lose, no bull-shit, I'm gonna throw."

"Just don't hit him," Mario told me.

I did tend to go high and inside on anyone that I thought could hit.

"He's my father, I won't hit him."

I remember he took no practice swings, just walked into the box with the bat on his shoulder. He took a half swing and waited.

Mario called for a fastball, I waved it off. I'd throw a curve, my best pitch. My father was left-handed. The ball broke down and in and he ripped it. I don't mean a little line drive over second, I mean ripped it. It sounded like a rifle shot. He smiled.

A dozen balls: fastballs, curves, one high and inside, ripped, all of them. Ripped.

"Relax and concentrate. Do both things and you'll do better tonight," he said.

How do you relax and concentrate? How do you do both things?

"All the best do."

Right.

I don't remember if it was the third or fourth batter I faced that night, but only one other guy hit a ball off me harder than my father did. His name was Joe Torre, and the one he hit, it's still going.

I have seen fathers at Little League games deride their boys' talents. I coached a Little League team and once or twice got on my own son. All through sandlot and high school and later in the Queens Alliance, my father came to every single game I ever pitched and never once did he say more to me than "You did good. Keep your head up, you'll do better next time."

◆　　◆　　◆

By the time my father reached his late twenties he stopped playing base-ball. Major league scouts had tried to interest him. But he would make some excuse. Lucy would have thought his life with the "strangers" a catastrophe. He must have known that. My mother told me that he gave no explanation, no specific reason.

"One day," she said, "it came right out of the blue: 'That's it,' he said, 'no more ball playing for me.' He simply quit and went to work with the union. I don't know why."

My father was more complicated, a much more angry man than my mother wanted to see. She had none of his desire to become part of American society. Hunkered down in the certainties, prejudices, and fears of her Sicilian background, she probably felt threatened by his embrace of the democracy of baseball and the union movement. His attachment and attraction to her was so strong that he squelched the independence that choosing a career as a professional baseball player would have required. Finally he came to believe that he didn't have a future in baseball, a decision which fit in with Silverman's telling him from the shadows that it was time for him to stop playing at games and to become a responsible union man. It was Silverman, or maybe simply that his mind was filled with visions of change. He'd played ball for some real money while men that worked with their hands and backs in the same factories slaved for peanuts.

I remember sitting on the steps to the second floor of the house; my father was in the living room talking to workers from a factory that he was attempting to organize. He was laying it on thick and heavy, the plight of the working man, the callousness of the bosses.

One of the men said, "Hooks, hey Hooks, give us a break will ya. I know you thirty years and you never put in a hard day's work. Shit, you were a ballplayer and now you wear a suit and tie and organize unions."

I felt bad for him. I wanted him to say something, yell at that asshole, tell him that he worked twelve, fourteen hours a day, that he was never home. But he said nothing.

His silence lasted a long, long time, then the guy said, soft and easy, "It's okay Hooks, it's okay, tell us what you want us to do. How can we help here?"

"I want you to do what's right. I want you to stand up for yourselves.

If you need us, I promise the union will be there. I give you my word, and even if that word is only from an old, burnt-out ballplayer, let me tell you, it's for real."

I loved him so much. He was better than I could ever be, even back then I knew that.

And so my father gave up baseball and never complained. He never let me think that he had made a sacrifice of any kind. He devoted himself to the union. Then, in the 1950s, the ethos of the McCarthy era shook my father badly. There was nothing that he wanted more than to be considered a good American. What he read in newspapers and watched on television everyday during the fifties defined people who thought like him as traitors. He stopped reading the *Daily Worker,* dropped his allegiance to the Socialist Party and became a Democrat. Later, he would see the riots, assassinations, and drug culture of the sixties as frontal assaults on his family. His politics moderated, but never changed.

On one Saturday afternoon we were having a catch and my father told me that he'd thrown his arm out. He said that it was softball and warned me not to play softball.

I didn't believe him. I was in high school; he was in his early forties and could still throw BBs.

For years we had a framed photograph of Phil Rizzuto in our house. Rizzuto is standing on the mound at Yankee Stadium. It was signed to Hooks, "Hope to see you here real soon."

Rizzuto had tried out for a team my father had captained.

"At the time, Phil was in Richmond Hill High School," my father told me. "A bit light in the ass, a great fielder but couldn't handle big-time pitching."

"You're kidding?"

"I'm not kidding. Like I said, Rizzuto was a great fielder and even nicer guy, but too light. I told him that he should give it some time, he'd have to put on some weight, get stronger."

"Did you ever hear from him again?"

"Sure, he sent me that picture."

"If you knew Rizzuto and there were so many famous Italian Americans on the Yankees, like DiMaggio and Lazzeri, and Raschi and Berra, how come you never became a Yankee fan?"

"You're kidding me, right?"

"How come?"

"I was born in Brooklyn. I loved the Brooklyn Dodgers. They were my team, my people, my place. They were a workingman's team, always fighting to get ahead, almost there but never quite.

"The Yankees were from across the river, the other side of the tracks, suits and ties and limos, DiMaggio and Marilyn Monroe. C'mon, the Yankees?"

"You hated the Yankees."

"No, I hated the Giants. The Yankees were who they were. They were a breed apart. Not our real competition. They were irrelevant to us. We had no television, we'd never see them, wouldn't listen to them on the radio. And, they always won. Screw them. Look, money is power, okay. They had a great stadium and mountains of money to make things happen. They had all that and they had no heart, at least as far as I was concerned, they had no heart. There could be no connection between them and us. Rooting for the Yankees was like rooting for AT&T. They were some god of capitalism. You know, you can't hate AT&T but you can't love it either.

"The Giants were a whole other story. They were in our division and our kind of guys and they put a spear right into the heart of our dreams. The Giants put a gloom on Brooklyn we never recovered from. And, there was Leo Durocher and his wife Lorraine Day with her goddamned television show.

"Listen, even though he was an Italian it was easy to hate Sal Maglie—he threw at our heads. And, the perfect blond-haired Whitey Lockman; Alvin Dark and Bobby Thomson; you could really hate that whole crew.

"Then there was Leo 'The Lip' Durocher. You want to talk hate?"

"What about Willie Mays?" I asked.

The young bride
(Robert Leuci and Family)

A long moment of silence, then, "Willie Mays was the best baseball player I ever saw, period."

"Better than DiMaggio?"

I could tell that that subject made my father nervous.

"I think so," he said. "I think he was better than Joe D, I think so, then again, maybe I was prejudiced, DiMaggio, the Yankees and all that. . . ."

On that day I told him, "Pop, the Dodgers are gone. They're in L.A. It's the Los Angles Dodgers now. Remember when I used to believe that all the Dodgers were born in Brooklyn? Pee Wee and Duke and Roy and Billy Cox and Gil Hodges, and Newk and Erskine and Joe Black. All of them born in Brooklyn?"

He turned away from me and he smiled, turned back and said, "They're not gone, those Brooklyn Dodgers, the Duke's homers into Bedford Avenue, Furillo's rifle throws to third, Jackie's pigeon-toed run, those Dodgers will always be there and here."

He pointed to his heart.

"Screw O'Malley," he said. "Screw that capitalist bastard."

By the end of his life he continued to quote Vito Marcantonio, the socialist New York State Congressman from Greenwich Village, and my mother took to cursing Silverman for convincing him to quit baseball.

"He could have been a major-leaguer," she'd say. "That's what everyone said, your father could have played in the big leagues."

I remember telling her, "Mom, that's exactly where he played. Pop played in the big leagues all his life."

She grinned. "Yeah," she said. "He was a helluva athlete."

And one helluva man.

Lucy smiled, after all those years the dimples were still there, the face still beautiful.

JOE DIMAGGIO: THE MAKING OF A KING

Wilfrid Sheed

"Oh who owns Noo Yawk,
Oh who owns Noo Yawk?"

By the time I first hit the U.S., July 19, 1940, as a pint-size English refugee from Nazi bombs, the old Columbia football chant had long since drifted downtown to become a favorite battle cry of the city's small fry. And in those pre-switchblade days, it was not uncommon to see tots of all races squaring off and duking it out on street corners, hoping to settle the question once and for all or else get stuck with the humiliating punch line to the second verse, "Oh who sweeps the streets?" etc.

But turf battles (and bankers) aside, who really owned New York? Not the lease, of course, but the heart and soul, and the style of the place?

To these alien eyes, it was an open-and-shut case. The greatest mayor in New York history was called Fiorello LaGuardia, and the favorite comedian at my new school, and thus the greatest man, was Jimmy Durante, both by landslides.

Joe DiMaggio
(National Baseball Hall of Fame Library, Cooperstown, New York)

And if that wasn't enough for you, there was always Joe DiMaggio, a name so transcendent that I'd swear I heard it before I even knew what he was famous for or exactly what baseball was. Learning the words "Joe DiMaggio" seemed to be part of the Customs and Immigration process, with more information to follow immediately. Because I right afterwards learned that even before his famous hitting streak, Joe D loomed so high on the Magic Mountain that he had somehow managed to raise the status of his colleagues as well, so that you often heard people say, "Of course, Italians make the best ballplayers," an exaggeration that seemed to please them, and which would introduce me gradually to one of the basic mysteries of the Italian American phenomenon.

Whenever an Italian is really good at something, from Enrico Caruso at the beginning of the century to Luciano Pavarotti at the end, to such points in between as Valentino, Arturo Toscanini, Frank Sinatra, and, in sports, Vince Lombardi the football coach and Eddy Arcaro the jockey, a powerful impulse runs through Italians and barbarians alike to crown him the greatest at once and forever. And a matching impulse seems to stir in the great man himself to rise to the applause and deserve it. Thus, we always knew that Joe Montana would win the Super Bowl, and that Arcaro would take today's Derby, even if it was his only race of the season.

Perhaps we make these men kings because we sense that they really are anyway and will not let us down. Thus, a Tony Bennett, say, can cheerfully spend his best years toiling in Sinatra's shadow, and yet when Frank dies and fate taps Tony on the shoulder, he will be ready, like royalty in waiting, to become a totally satisfactory king himself, dignified but not stuffy, old-fashioned but not in any sense out of it, as if he had just stepped outside a minute and picked up every nuance he needed to know. Thus, just as each of Napoleon's soldiers carried a field marshal's baton in his gear, so Italians carry a crown along with instructions on how to wear it.

If they even need them. "You've either got or you haven't got class," as Sinatra and his *compadre* "Dino" Martin used to put it. "You've either got or you haven't got style." In which case there are no instructions, you either know or you don't know. Which brings us back to Joe DiMaggio with a bang. Because to a generation of New Yorkers Joe DiMaggio *was* style, from the moment he exploded gracefully from the dugout to lead his men into battle, to the moment he loped shyly back in—mission accomplished, no need for a fuss. No Englishman in the movies ever played these parts better, of either an officer or a gentleman, and Joe's classes in Class were open all summer long for the price of a bleacher seat or just a few minutes a day on the Lexington Avenue subway platform, before they chased you off. (As every fan knows, the Lexington Avenue line rises obligingly and quasimiraculously from the ground just in time to give you a sneak preview of tonight's game.)

It is seldom in life that one ever gets to see anything done perfectly, let alone, *everything*, from walking to crouching to picking up a bat. Even when Joe scratched his nose, we took notes. And possibly drew conclusions. My oldest and best friend, a Spanish–Puerto Rican with a premature taste for opera and fine buildings, had already decided at age twelve or so that the Italians were the real Master Race, and I had no trouble with this even though my own country, England, had allegedly just gone to war with Italy. In fact, to tomorrow's opinion-makers Joe DiMaggio alone seemed to supply all the answer to Mussolini that one needed: in one corner a comic-opera blowhard and master of the Empty Promise, and in the other, a quiet hero who promised nothing but delivered beyond our wildest dreams. "Joltin' Joe DiMaggio" was that year's song, "We want you on our side!" Nothing could have stopped us from laughing at *Signore Big Mouth* that year or at his make-believe army, but it was good-natured laughter. Nobody thought that Italians as such were a joke. Not after Joe DiMaggio's 56-game hitting streak.

Historically speaking, Joe's timing had as usual been exquisite. In that very summer of 1941, the U.S. had reluctantly begun drafting a serious, full-size wartime army, and it became clear that, any minute now, all kinds of Americans would find themselves not just meeting one another for the first time, but fighting and dying together; so the more stale ethnic jokes we could get rid of, the better. In this sense both Joe D and Joe

Louis might be said to have done their war service before hostilities even started, Louis by destroying the Aryan poster boy Max Schmelling and DiMaggio by decorating that last summer with the unbreakable record, the one that has been called a statistical impossibility and remains by any reckoning the height of lion-hearted, steel-nerved achievement in baseball.

Sports might not equal combat, but they're the closest we usually allow ourselves to come in this country, and with a pitcher throwing bullets, and three decks of fans roaring, and a year's work on the line, sports can get pretty damned convincing. But DiMaggio's hitting streak was even more convincing, for two other reasons, one being the eyes of the world and the other the horrors of waiting. The press corps might not have gotten quite as personal in those days as it does now, but it was even bigger and harder to get rid of. And it is worth noting that the intrepid Charles Lindbergh had cracked up badly under its attentions a couple of years earlier. And he didn't even have to hit the next day.

Anyhow, we didn't need to be told about the tension, because we felt it ourselves just picking up the newspaper. (At age ten your hands aren't supposed to shake like that are they?) And as DiMag rolled past the various landmarks—Rogers Hornsby, Willie Keeler, and the laws of probability themselves—the whole country seemed to break into a sweat, and haughty old ladies who usually didn't give you the time of day began to ask anxiously, "Did he do it? Did Joe get his hit today?"

Rarely if ever has one man held the whole nation's attention so long and so favorably. Yet years afterward one would still find articles saying in effect, "Have Italians finally arrived? Are we there yet?" as if nothing had happened, as if we had never wanted Joltin' Joe on our side, or as if Sinatra had never turned corn into pure gold by singing "That's America to Me" in the name of all of us.

So what is happening here? Is this some Rodney Dangerfield of ethnicity, tugging wretchedly at its collar as the good news rolls by? Or is Italy perhaps a land of a few kings and a lot of peasants? Certainly the kings have never stopped coming in all shapes and sizes, from Gian Carlo

Menotti to Madonna (according to tastes) to the brilliant Hollywood Cosa Nostra of Pacino, Coppola, De Niro, and Scorsese. And the style and class have never stopped coming either, from the day in 1940 when Mayor LaGuardia undertook to become Babysitter-in-Chief by reading the comics on the radio during a newspaper strike, making a whole tense city laugh with relief, to the day in 2001 when another Italian mayor seized the crown itself and became America's wartime leader for a day, our very own Winston Churchill simply because no one else knew how to wear it. Rudolph Giuliani was not, one could somehow tell, angling for the spotlight or posing for headlines. He was just doing what came naturally.

But was it just a coincidence that the actual crown that Rudy chose to wear at such times was a New York Yankees baseball cap? or that his all-time hero was and is this same star from an earlier time, Joe DiMaggio, the patron saint of Grace Under Pressure and the only man who ever made Giuliani nervous giving a speech? Since the occasion for this was actually Joe D's memorial service, Joe wasn't even present. But he made the mayor nervous anyway.

When Italian heroes die they don't just fade away, they go into stained glass, and enter the Tradition, to become part of one's moral education and inspiration. And just as one prays to St. Christopher on journeys, one's thoughts may turn to Joe D in the various ninth innings and seventh games of life. But was he really a saint? And did St. Christopher really exist? Never mind. Legends live or die by results, not by pinpoint accuracy.

The DiMaggio myth had worked like thunder from the start on at least a couple of other levels. For one thing, he was a genuine peasant king; which isn't that common even in this country (successful peasants yes, but not kings). The first obstacle for any immigrant is perennially his own family, which instinctively holds him so tight from falling that he can't rise either. Mario Puzo and others have simultaneously praised and cursed the great family love that always kept them going in the worst of times, but also kept them from going very far, what with the delivery job they had to take after school, and the nice Italian girl, and the great

Young Joe and his mother (Private Archive)

prospects with Uncle Vinny in the Parks Department. And what's keeping those grandchildren anyway? Your brother Frank already has three.

But in this respect history actually smiled crookedly on DiMaggio and the other ballplayers by sending the Great Depression, which made jobs of any kind so hard to get and real money so hard to make that baseball like show business moved up an inch or so on the chain of respectability. And unlike the other fine arts, you could master it without raising suspicion.

First-generation fathers must have had a terrible time deciding about baseball anyway. For one thing, it usually meant skipping school, which was OK unless you actually wanted your kids to learn English, but it also meant wasting their only asset, time, and it was hard to believe that people ever really got paid for that over here.

And then on the other hand a boy like DiMaggio was an ornament: Even neighbors who had no idea what he was doing out there could tell that he was doing it very well, and every so often rich-looking gents in neckties would come by to confirm it.

The San Francisco Bay area, with its Mediterranean overtones, teemed in those early 1930s with talent scouts and Italian ballplayers looking for each other, and before DiMaggio Senior could lay down any laws about working on the fishing boat or else, Joe was bringing home real money and obviously on his way to much more.

Success would, in fact, be the easy part. The only force on earth that could have kept Joe from becoming a great ballplayer was a career-ending injury of some kind; so sure enough, as if fate wanted to keep things interesting, it would send him several threats of this kind over the years. But all they did was to make him occasionally a great player with a limp, and leave the rest of us wondering how he would have done in a wheelchair (with his reflexes, center field might never have looked the same.)

But all the talent in the world does not quite make a king. John Madden, who is sort of a king himself among sports announcers, has also referred to another almost mystic quality, or K-factor, that tells you when a certain athlete has just entered the stadium, and from all accounts Joe

DiMaggio was born with this and died with it. The earliest witnesses and the latest all testify to Joe DiMaggio's singular aura, a pure presence that struck fear in the enemy's heart and reassured his friends. "We want you on our side." Yes indeed.

In later years, when someone asked Joe himself what he thought he still had to offer the kids who hung around him he said, of all things, "My gentleness," which suggests a subtle and surprising awareness of his role and his duties in retirement at any rate. But how much does any super-star ever know at the time?

Imagine this as a fable. A king is born into humble circumstances. (OK, a lot of us feel that way, but this time it's the real thing.) Naturally no one can tell him who he is, so all he has to go on is their reflexive re-action to him and his own innate sense of what to do next, some of it in this case crude and commonplace: Kings are successful (they win a lot) and kings are self-sufficient (they're rich), but some of it is extremely hard and demanding. (Kings never disappoint people; they are always at their best; they can establish their presence anywhere.)

It is with this last provision that DiMaggio stakes his crucial claim and lays down his challenge to the gods. It seems he won't settle for being the star of his neighborhood or even of the New York Yankees; in fact, he won't come to rest until he can hold his own in the quite different worlds of New York nightclubs and Hollywood premieres and celebrity wed-dings, not as a distinguished visitor or as a guest star but as one of them, a celebrity's celebrity, playing and winning by their rules. "If you can make it here, you'll make it anywhere." Fine. Cut the cards.

Fortunately a fourth provision of his vocation told him not to take anything for granted. To the naked eye DiMaggio might seem like the perfect ballplayer already, but that didn't mean he didn't have to work like hell on his fielding. Looking good was never enough until it rested on something more solid, and he clearly never imagined that he could sail into the Stork Club one day and expect to have the right words come to him. Broadway must have seemed a universe away from the broken vowels of home. So he'd better get started immediately.

Vince, Joe, and Dom (Private Archive)

When *Time* magazine began constructing a cover story of Joe in 1939, a researcher S.O.S.ed home to complain that the whole DiMaggio family gave him the creeps with their resolute refusal to connect with strangers. But by then Joe had already apprenticed himself to the team fop on the San Francisco Seals and was getting off phrases like "I've been nonchalantly meandering down the pike," worthy of Bing Crosby himself or some other fancy-talk comic of the period. And this is the element missing from most DiMaggio studies, namely his genuine streak of play-fulness. This was not just some solemn egomaniac, war-gaming the art of conversation, but a part-time cut-up who truly enjoyed the rhythms and exaggerations of humor, and hung out by choice with eccentric souls like Lefty O'Doul, the legendary "man in the pea-green suit," who cut short a magnificent big league career simply because he preferred living in San Francisco, and later with Lefty Gomez, the resident wit on the Yankees, and with George Solitaire, a Broadway character famous now only for his one-liners, which seemed to turn up in every edition of every newspaper in New York.

And perhaps the funny men liked him back because he instinctively knew a good joke from a bad one, as he knew a curve from a slider, and because, if he couldn't do something that well himself, he wholeheartedly enjoyed the people who could, without envy or reservation. Joe was at home with the First Rate in whatever form it took, but he seemed to be at his best and his most human among the wisecrackers, up to and in-cluding Woody Allen, his most surprising taste of all.

And this may be how and why he finally broke the glass ceiling that separates both snobs and working stiffs from nature's aristocrats. Any smart social climber can learn the manners and the clothes and how to act dignified, but how many *arrivistes* know that the top people also spend a lot of their time laughing and just horsing around?

Fortunately very few Italians need instructions in these particular arts, but only a green light. There has never been a funnier team than the boys from St. Louis—Joe Garagiola, the straight man and gag writer, and Yogi Berra, the solemn clown. And though DiMaggio was not funny in

Stylish Joe in 1946 (Private Archive)

that sense, ample proof of his natural high spirits can be found in his late blooming hobby of autograph collecting. The thought of Joe, the ultimate celebrity, hiding like a kid in a White House closet in hopes of catching a scribble from Mikhail Gorbachev might have brought a smile to Queen Victoria herself. And speaking of queens, there was the time in Baltimore when the real Elizabeth the Second thwarted him because her pen didn't work on baseballs: "I cahn't sign the bally thing," she said after the briefest of tussles, and Joe went home empty-handed but presumably tickled that Royalty had struck out with royalty. Ah well.

The point worth emphasizing is that this was not manufactured or calculated behavior on DiMaggio's part, done for money or publicity or anything but laughs. Joe had instinctively obeyed the first law of being a gentleman, which, incidentally is the first law of baseball and of much else: first learn the rules and then just be yourself and have some fun if you can.

To us pipsqueak connoisseurs, Joe played center field flawlessly but also joyfully, and any lessons we learned came to us the next time we played baseball ourselves, or the next time we tried to talk to a headwaiter or to squire a beautiful girl home. The course DiMaggio taught was baseball but the subject was doing things right, particularly in the big cities which were so far from DiMaggio's starting place. When Paul Simon sang "Where have you gone, Joe DiMaggio?" he could have added "And where have you gone Penn Station and Metropolitan Opera House and Algonquin Round Table?" and all the other monuments to style and sophistication that made New York the greatest of the world's great cities in the mid-twentieth century. That the son of a poor Italian fisherman still fits this lineup so perfectly, without need of asterisks, should be legend enough, but the fact that his family was first-generation Sicilian adds a footnote the size of another fable, and the short version goes like this.

As the great Italian journalist Ugo Stille used to say, "Of course there is no such thing as Italy. There are just cities which," he would add with a smile, "despise each other." Italy is in fact still a surprisingly young nation (less than 150 years old) full of extremely old cities, each of which has its own history and its own place in world history, which it guards diligently. For upwards of 2000 years, the Mediterranean was, as far as it knew, the center of the universe (except for Marco Polo, an Italian, who discovered that the Chinese thought that they were the center of the universe), and for much of that time the proudest claim you could make anywhere was not "I am the king of someplace or other," but simply "I am a Roman citizen."

But as more of the surrounding world came into play, several great cities to the north, such as Venice and Florence and Milan, picked up the spirit, and to this day anyone hailing from any of these or thereabouts—Sienna, Verona, Padua, etc. will do—will inherit enough pride of place to equip an emperor.

But of course the Statue of Liberty does not say, "Send me your aristocrats and your success stories" but "Bring me the bad news, your losers and your hard-luck cases." The bulk of the migration tended not to come from those great northern cities at all but from the scrawny southern part known collectively as the *Mezzogiorno,* or Sunbelt, which were too poor to afford enough history to go around, and where even the sundials had stopped a thousand years earlier in the feudal period.

And then there was Sicily, which was not only still feudal but in some sense alien. Sicily did in fact have a lot of history, but it tended to be of a bitter and shadowy kind, and the only outcome most people can see from it now is the Mafia with its rancid code of chivalry and its black parody of high style, which mainlanders prefer to think of as more Arabian in origin than Italian, although Bart Giamatti and others have pointed out that the Mafia's signature virtue of *omerta,* or knowing when to shut up, is a generic Italian ideal. Surely no one ever practiced it as grimly or assiduously as the Sicilians or produced so many cases of that strange anomaly, the Quiet Italian.

But finally, what and who was a typical Italian anyway, and who wasn't? Undoubtedly these fine regional distinctions would remain a matter of burning importance within the immigrant community itself for a very long time, and it's impossible to understand even so evolved a specimen as Frank Sinatra without knowing that a small piece of him was still a Milanese kid making his way in a world of Sicilian warlords and Calabrian, et al., enforcers.

Yet the quicker the immigrant learned English, the quicker he learned that it was all the same to the rest of us here and that they were all just Italians now, on their gradual way to becoming just Americans. Italy might not yet be one nation back home, but it might as well become one over here because the census didn't have room for two or more. And besides it is a triumphant paradox of the American experience that, having formed our notions of other countries in ritzy places like Paris and Rome, we then expect the hardscrabble survivors who actually get here to live up to these notions. And they do.

At least some of them do, some of the time. Which brings us one last time to Joe DiMaggio, who now fits into the regular, back-home Italian pantheon as smoothly as into the New York hall of fame, alongside the great doges of Venice and the Medici of Florence and even the dukes, not the *capos*, of Sicily. To my mind DiMag received his diploma—and in-

Joe and Dom (National Baseball Hall of Fame Library, Cooperstown, New York)

cidentally started me on this train of thought—back in 1969 when the sportswriters of America decided to overlook the likes of Willie Mays and Hank Aaron and Mickey Mantle long enough to vote Joe the greatest living ballplayer. Which by any statistical measure, he certainly wasn't. He was just Italian. And that was enough.

THE BARBER AND THE RIFLE

George Vecsey

The phone rang around midnight in Jack Lang's hotel room.

Lang was a baseball reporter covering the Brooklyn Dodgers for the *Long Island Press,* two institutions that in June of 1956 were both thriving and formidable.

The voice at the other end sounded familiar.

"Jackie," the voice rumbled.

There was only one person in the entire traveling party of the Brooklyn Dodgers who called Lang "Jackie."

"Jackie, you got any hooch?"

Likewise, there was only one member of the Dodgers who used that quaint word, with its conspiratorial Prohibition overtones.

Just by accident, Lang happened to have half a bottle of Scotch amidst his clothing and statistic sheets and battered portable typewriter.

"Bring it down," Carl Furillo commanded. So Lang put the bottle in a paper sack and took the elevator to another floor in the Chase Hotel in St. Louis.

Furillo was the right fielder for the Dodgers, ruggedly built and possessing one of the best arms in the major leagues. Because his home hamlet of Stony Creek Mills was not far from the larger town of Reading, Pennsylvania, Furillo had long since been nicknamed "The Reading Rifle," alliteration being very popular among sportswriters.

Carl Furillo
(National Baseball Hall of Fame Library, Cooperstown, New York)

He was also known as "Skoonj," the Anglicized version of *scungili,* the Italian delicacy, a form of shellfish, which some people equate to a snail. The "snail" part came from Furillo's being among the slowest runners on the team. Lang's pal Dick Young of the New York *Daily News* had tagged Furillo with the nickname Skoonj. The nickname was also a not particularly subtle reference to Furillo's Italian ancestry.

Now, there was another Italian American on the team. A few weeks earlier, the Dodgers had purchased the contract of Salvatore Anthony "The Barber" Maglie, a pitcher who was known to "shave" opposing batters—and was, as everybody knew, Carl Furillo's long-time enemy since Maglie toiled for the New York Capulets and tormented Furillo's Brooklyn Montagues.

Despite some pacific gestures upon Maglie's arrival, there were still some major questions about how this touchy arrangement was going to work out.

Lang tapped on Furillo's door. The player was alone, but there were a tub of ice and numerous bottles of beer. Lang enjoyed a beer on occasion, but he suspected there might be more beers in this room than the two of them could, or should, imbibe.

The writer began to wonder what the occasion was. Furillo was known to be somewhat of a loner, and was rooming by himself, a luxury in 1956.

Furillo also had a temper. One April afternoon in 1953, only the extremely muscular arms of Gil Hodges, the Dodgers' ex-Marine first baseman, had kept Furillo from reaching Maglie and committing violence. The Dodgers saw Furillo as a rock on offense and a rock on defense, but a smoldering rock, a Vesuvius, so to speak. Lang, a New Yorker, found Furillo well within normal range of the strong urban personalities he had grown up with, and liked him considerably.

This soiree went unexplained as the two men sipped a beer or a Scotch, or both. Then there was a knock on the door and a taxi driver entered, bearing a large and greasy paper sack. Furillo paid the man and opened the sack, which was full of pungent spare ribs. The right fielder arranged the ribs next to the bucket of beer, and the two of them helped themselves. Then there was another knock on the door, and in walked Sal "The Barber" Maglie, with his perennial five o'clock shadow and his dark eyes, which seemed to glower halfway between solemn and ominous.

Now these two ancient antagonists were alone in the Chase Hotel, with no Gil Hodges present to peel away any belligerents.

"This is going to be interesting," Lang thought to himself.

Nearly half a century later, Lang recalls the first words between the two old combatants.

"Hey, whaddaya say, Dago," Lang recalls Furillo saying.

"Hey, Dago," Maglie replied.

Thereupon, all three of them busied themselves for several hours with the ribs and the beer and the hooch. Lang cannot recall a single word or theme they discussed, except that it was strikingly similar to many other gatherings he had attended in hotel rooms around the league.

In those ancient days, it should be noted, ballplayers and sports-writers existed in somewhat the same economic universe, and were known to socialize and even trust one another, for better or worse. Lang was used to being in rooms full of beer and hooch and Dodgers, but certainly not alone with these two men.

As Lang recalls from those couple of hours, there was a lot of "we" and a lot of "us" as the two players discussed what had happened on the ball field earlier that evening in an 8–6 victory over the Cardinals. The men were now united in the common cause—winning the pennant, beating the Yankees in the World Series. The previous October, the Dodgers had captured the World Series for the first time, thereby ending their perennial lament of "Wait Till Next Year." Now they had purchased Maglie. In his first start as a Dodger, seven days earlier, Maglie had pitched a three-hit shutout over the up-and-coming Milwaukee Braves. Sheer pragmatism just may have motivated Furillo's little party. Maglie had proven he could still pitch, and that was surely worth a few beers and a few ribs.

"All I know is that I thought to myself, 'The war is over,' " Jack Lang recalls.

◆ ◆ ◆

These men were warriors, in the baseball sense. In his epic book on the Brooklyn Dodgers and what became of them, *The Boys of Summer,* Roger Kahn refers to the gruff right fielder as a "young indomitable centurion," a foot soldier in Caesar's legions. It is a stereotype, but a reasonable one. Kahn said he could see other Dodgers fulfilling other more prosaic roles in midcentury America, but he could see Furillo only as a ballplayer. There was something of the universal soldier in Furillo. One could sleep easier at night knowing that thousands of warriors like Furillo had been posted to far-off Wales or Romania or North Africa, guarding the empire.

Maglie, despite his hangman presence on the mound, was a more cerebral presence, owing to his surprisingly soft voice. It would not be hard to picture him in a field tent of the same Roman army, preparing his own specialty—crude field surgery, ad hoc military tactics, or perhaps grim prayers over the broken and the gutted.

In their post-Depression intensity, these two gritty Northern types were not all that different from Southerners like Enos "Country" Slaughter or Fred "Dixie" Walker, or city boys like Stan Musial from smog-bound Donora, Pennsylvania, or Westerners like Ted Williams from San Diego, and they surely began their lives ahead of the African American Dodgers, such as Jackie Robinson and Roy Campanella and Don Newcombe, who had come into manhood disenfranchised from the mainstream of the alleged national sport.

When the economics of the age put Maglie and Furillo into baseball uniforms in New York City, it made them members of opposing latter-day clans. Hardball was expected from every player, of course, but Sal Maglie and Carl Furillo brought their own bristling codes and attitudes to the Shakespearean rivalry between the Dodgers and the Giants.

"Basically, Italian Americans were regarded as second-class citizens," said Ralph Branca, a long-time Dodger and a friend of both. "There was a fierce competition to excel.

"I can't say I felt that way," added Branca, whose father's side hailed

Sal Maglie
(National Baseball Hall of Fame Library, Cooperstown, New York)

from Calabria and whose mother's family came from Hungary. He was raised in the Westchester suburbs and attended New York University and had a more secure sense of belonging than his two colleagues.

"But I do have that short fuse in my psyche"—particularly when he senses injustice, Branca added many years later.

Both Carl Furillo and Sal Maglie had struggled a long way through a lot of baseball wars to the point where Maglie was expected to buzz the ball under Furillo's chin and Furillo was expected to retaliate.

Furillo was born on March 8, 1922, in Pennsylvania Dutch country, the youngest of six children. His parents had emigrated from "just outside Naples," according to the player's son, Carl Jr., also known as Butch. This location takes in a lot of territory. Furillo did not demonstrate the devious ways of the *scugnizzi*, the ancient symbol of Naples, the street boys still very much in evidence today. More likely, he had the wary genes of the *paesani*—countrymen, peasants. Either way, being Italian was very important to Furillo, who carried a smoldering resentment of prejudice against his people.

"My father hated the word 'wop,' " Carl Jr. said recently. "I told him, 'Dad, it only comes from the words "without papers," you know, without all the documents. But he said, 'You think what you think, I think what I think.' " According to my dictionary, that slang word derives from the Italian *guappo,* a "dandy," one who preens, hardly Carl Furillo.

"My dad was very proud of his heritage," Butch said. "He would go to the Knights of Columbus and he loved going to the Italian festivals in the Village," that is, the feast of San Gennaro in Greenwich Village in Manhattan.

"My dad spoke fluent Italian," said Butch. "People said he had a slight Neapolitan accent. I know that when I was a kid, if my father wanted to say something, he'd say it in Italian. My mom didn't speak it but she understood it. They didn't want us to speak the language, so they never taught us."

Denial of the old language was very typical of Furillo's generation, which saw acclimation as a major step toward survival in this new world.

Furillo left school after the eighth grade, working at anything he could until he turned eighteen and was signed for $80 a month with Pocomoke City in the Eastern Shore League of Maryland. The next year he was sold to Reading, near his home, where he batted a robust .318.

In the fall of 1940 the general manager of the Dodgers, the brilliant if combustible Larry MacPhail, purchased the Reading club for $5,000. "This included the franchise, a set of uniforms, a broken-down bus, and three players, including Carl Furillo," recalled a Brooklyn assistant named Emil "Buzzie" Bavasi.

Bavasi and Furillo did not meet until after World War II, beginning a stormy relationship that would often involve money and pride and even a lawsuit. Bavasi was a college boy who had gotten into baseball administration. His father was from southern France and his mother from northern Italy, and given that his name ended in a vowel, he surely heard all the ethnic epithets as a young man. He was proud to be considered Italian, but fell somewhat short of sentimentality.

"Marching through Italy during the war put an end to any romantic notions," Bavasi said in 2002. (He did, he said with great pride, once spend four hours standing in the doorway in Florence where, according to legend, Dante observed his beloved Beatrice.)

Furillo also went away to war, reaching the major leagues in 1946 as the occasional center fielder between two folk heroes, Pete Reiser and Dixie Walker. He always felt that Leo Durocher, his first manager, did not care for him, but Durocher maintained to his final days that he loved Furillo as a player and as a human—unless they wore opposing uniforms.

Furillo soon became one of the building blocks of the Boys of Summer and their decade of excellence. Solidly built at six feet and 190 pounds ("strapping" was the adjective most often applied) he could hit with power and average, hitting 192 homers and batting .299 for his fifteen-year career (perhaps significantly, three hits short of being a .300 hitter.) He could only imagine what he would have hit with better than *scungilli*-like speed.

By 1947, Furillo was moved to right field, where he mastered the art of playing the eccentric combination of wall and screen in the irregular and funky Ebbets Field. He would have led the league in assists regularly except that runners learned not to run too far on that arm.

His Caesarian patrol included a rectangular advertisement, near ground level at the base of the scoreboard in right-center field. The sign for the haberdashery of Abe Stark said HIT SIGN, WIN SUIT.

The Starks were not eager to give away their merchandise. There is a classic post-war *New Yorker* cartoon by George Price in which the sign says HIT THIS SIGN AND ABE FELDMAN WILL GIVE YOU A SUIT ABSOLUTELY FREE. Backing up the right fielder is a lumpy little haberdasher in a suit, wearing a fielder's glove on each hand, obviously Abe Feldman himself.

Furillo insisted he never gave up a suit. In 1966, when Furillo was retired and Abe Stark was borough president of Brooklyn, Furillo told Stan Isaacs, the Brooklyn-born columnist for *Newsday*, "I asked the man for a pair of pants or something for guarding the sign but he never gave me anything. Dixie Walker, I think, wangled a few pair of slacks for his work out there."

But players did hit the sign, Furillo recalled: "Once Elmer Valo misjudged a line drive I hit to right center and the ball sailed over his head and off the sign. I remember that when I went to collect the suit they wanted to give me one of the cheap suits. I looked around and took one of the good ones."

Furillo's prowess in front of the sign figures in one of Bavasi's many delightful anecdotes. Decades later, Bavasi said, his son, Bob, bought a minor league team in Everett, Washington, and had a replica of the old Abe Stark sign painted on the outfield wall.

On opening day, a batter hit a screaming line drive that clanged directly onto the sign, putting Bavasi *figlio* out a couple of hundred dollars just innings into the season.

"Bob came screaming at me and thought I was not telling the truth about never giving a suit away," Bavasi Padre recalled.

"Bob!" the father blurted. "The guy playing right field for you is not Carl Furillo!"

As valuable as he was to Abe Stark, to say nothing of the Dodgers, Furillo was not in the mainstream of his team. The nucleus Dodgers, the Reeses and the Sniders, summered in the Bay Ridge section of Brooklyn, whereas Furillo tended to go his own way. He liked the jovial Campanella, who was of mixed Black and Italian heritage, but Furillo apparently was wary of Robinson, a college graduate, who was revered for his competitiveness but not necessarily loved for his opinions.

In recent years, there has been a rumor that Furillo was one of the Dodgers who signed a petition that they would not play with Robinson when he broke the major league color barrier in 1947. It is known that Durocher had held a meeting one night during spring training (a real dandy, Durocher was said to have been wearing silk pajamas and silk bathrobe), and he stridently warned all the players that he would use anybody who could help him win, white or black or green, and that Robinson most certainly fell into that spectrum.

The leader of the petition movement has always been identified as Dixie Walker, who came from Alabama. In all the years Furillo played in Brooklyn, his name was never connected to that abortive movement. And as long as he lived, Furillo raved about Robinson's skill and leadership, and he added how he had grown to admire him as a man. Were they friends? Well, Furillo chose his friends carefully.

"Our lockers were side by side," Branca recalled. "Out in the back, near the john."

There was no plot, no exclusion. "After the game, Carl used to stop in Tex's Pizzeria at the intersection of Eastern Parkway and Pennsylvania Avenue," Jack Lang recalls. The pizzeria, long since gone, was near the start of the old Interboro Parkway, a dangerously twisting and scenic route through the cemeteries and private homes and parks and apartment buildings of eastern Brooklyn and western Queens. The road has been rededicated as Jackie Robinson Parkway.

Furillo was hardly isolated in a city where Italian Americans were working the docks, the shops, the factories, and, without much notice, the schools and libraries and rectories, too.

"All our friends, we met from right field," recalls Carl Furillo Jr., who has the husky, earnest voice of his father. "People watched my dad play and we got to know them. My godfather, my brother's godfather, Uncle Jim, Uncle Vinnie, Aunt Jean, Aunt Grace, that's what I called them. I had two Uncle Petes and two Aunt Fannies. There were friendships you could not imagine today."

Fern Furillo, from Pennsylvania Dutch people, was not a mixer in the Dodgers social strata, but she was as solid with family and friends as her husband was protecting the wall in Ebbets Field. They had found their niche. In New York, there are many niches.

The Dodgers won the 1947 pennant, although Durocher was suspended for unspecified offenses. He came back in 1948 but promptly jumped across town to the Giants. One of his first orders was that Furillo (and Campanella, and others) hit less well when the ball was moving near their chins.

"Leo loved Carl," Bavasi said. "But when he moved over to the Giants, there was no room for any of that."

In 1949, Durocher and a crusty Italian American coach of his, Herman Franks, taunted Furillo with their intention to "stick it in your ear." Shortly thereafter, Furillo was beaned by the Giants' Sheldon Jones, whose nickname was "Available," because he would do whatever it took. Jones had the grace to visit Furillo in the hospital, where he was recovering from a concussion. The pitcher claimed he had thrown a curveball that got away, but Furillo scoffed, "First curveball that never bent." Nevertheless, Furillo absolved Available Jones, saying he knew Durocher had ordered it. (In his career, Furillo would be hit in the head six times, and he became the first Dodger to wear a plastic liner inside his cap, the forerunner to the mandatory helmet of today.)

In 1950, Furillo would confront his principal enemy on the field. Sal Maglie had just come back from the outlaw Mexican League and his subsequent ban from organized American baseball, giving off the somewhat foreign aura of a man who had been many places and was desperate to keep what he had.

"Nowadays it's called street smarts," said Maglie's nephew, Pascal Salvatore Grenga, the keeper of the flame of Sal Maglie. "These were people who managed to rise above what they started with."

The Maglie family came from a small village outside Lecce, on the heel of the Italian peninsula. (The name itself is the plural of *maglia,* which refers to knitting or stitchwork or a vest or even a coat of mail. In Italian the name is pronounced "MAHL-yeh" but in American it became anglicized to "MAGG-lee.")

Giuseppe Maglie grew figs and olives, and his first wife died giving birth to their first child, named Francesco, and then the farmer married a young neighbor named Immaculata Maria.

"My grandfather went to a seminary school, so he had some education, but my grandmother did not," said Pascal Grenga. "But she was as sharp as a whip, let me tell you."

Like so many other people, Giuseppe Maglie went to try his luck in the United States, first to Pittsburgh, then to the Niagara Falls area. Eventually, he sent for his wife, and they had three daughters—Santa, Pascal's mother, and Carmen—and then a son, Salvatore, born on April 26, 1917.

Salvatore was a star athlete as a child, but his immigrant parents did not see the immediate value of that.

"He had to sneak out to play ball," his nephew Pascal said years later. "He was pursuing his dream."

Ultimately, they reached a truce, in which Sal could play sports as long as he earned money in his spare time.

"He used to sweep out the barbershop for the Dominick Brothers, Frank and Andy," Grenga recalls. The shop was on East Falls Street, and part of the young man's job was cleaning spittoons.

"When they started to call him 'The Barber,' as a ballplayer, we thought that was funny because that's what people called him when he was a kid."

Maglie's basketball ability got him a scholarship offer from Niagara University, but he had no time for anything as frivolous as higher education, so he worked in factories like the Cataract Bottling Company. Mild in appearance, and without a raging fastball, Maglie was turned down by tryout camps of the Red Sox and Cardinals until, at the age of twenty-two, he was signed for $275 a month by Steve O'Neill, Bob Feller's old manager, then running Buffalo of the International League.

A chronic sinus problem kept Maglie out of military service, but he worked in defense plants in New York and Ontario, returning to baseball with Jersey City in 1945. It took him six years to hack his way out of the minor leagues, and he finally reached the Giants in 1945 when he was already twenty-eight years old.

Trying to make up for lost time and lost wages, Maglie then accepted an offer of $15,000 from the Pasquel brothers, Bernardo and Jorge, who were recruiting major-leaguers at extravagant salaries to play in the Mexican League. Maglie pitched in the mountain colonial city of Puebla de Los Angeles, learning to rely on his curve in humid sea-level ballparks like Tampico and his fastball in low-oxygen mountain cities like Mexico City.

"That was where he learned to pitch," said his nephew Pascal. "He had some good coaching down there."

One of his coaches was Adolfo Luque, an old Cuban pitcher who had been a star for eighteen years with the Reds and Giants and had been Maglie's pitching coach in Jersey City. Maglie also pitched for Luque in winter ball in Cienfuegos, Cuba, where he learned to speak Spanish to go along with his Italian.

Years later, Maglie would recall Luque's sermon on the curveball, delivered in English with a chewy Cuban accent.

"Learn thees, and you peetch like Mardy."

"Mardy? Who's that?"

"Mardy! Mardy! You never heard of Chreesty Mardyson?"

So Maglie learned to throw a curveball the way Christy Mathewson had taught Luque when Mathewson was manager of the Reds back in 1918.

The Mexican League folded in two years, and Maglie, now blackballed by baseball, bought a gas station at 56th and Pine Avenue in Niagara Falls. He had no heart for business and went barnstorming and later pitched for Drummondville, Quebec, in the outlaw Provincial League in 1949.

In 1950, following legal challenges by another player, Danny Gardella, Maglie was reinstated by the major leagues. The Giants were slow to accept him, feeling he was just on the roster by court order, but Durocher eventually had to use him.

All the wiles he had learned in Mexico now made Maglie a star. Although six-feet, two-inches tall and 180 pounds, quite substantial for the time, Maglie got most of his menace from his dark whiskers and baleful eyes and inside pitches.

"I threw at the head because I knew that a batter could see a pitch up around his face better than he could see a pitch to any other spot," Maglie admitted to the writer Dick Schaap for an article in *Cavalier* magazine after he retired.

With his Mexican League eminence, Maglie won fifty-nine games in the three years from 1950 through 1952. In 1951, the Giants erased a thirteen-and-a-half-game Dodgers lead and won the one-game playoff on Bobby Thomson's home run, perhaps the greatest single at-bat in baseball history. Maglie pitched the first eight innings that day. Furillo went oh-for-five batting leadoff.

"Furillo and Campanella weren't themselves against Sal," said the Giants' backup catcher, Sal Yvars, many years later. "He had them so rattled. One day, I remember Furillo was trying to dig a foothold in the batter's box before an at-bat. He was digging and digging and he couldn't seem to get a good hole to stand in.

"Well, it was a hot day, and Sal was standing out there on the mound watching, and eventually he walked down to the plate and said: 'Carl, you dig yourself a good hole because I'm going to bury you in it.'

"And he threw one right in on Carl. Almost started a brawl. He didn't hit Carl, though. Sal almost never hit a batter. He was 'The Barber,' he shaved them with that brushback."

This is exactly how Branca remembered Maglie. "He pitched inside to get guys out," Branca said. "That was part of the credo, we all did it. He didn't throw at guys."

Furillo was not convinced of that. In April of 1953, Furillo had to duck a Maglie pitch that soared over his head and landed on the screen behind home plate. Years later, Maglie clarified that he had been perturbed at one of his fielder's not being in the right position, so, "just in the spirit of the moment, I threw one up there on the screen behind home plate."

Furillo had his own spirit of the moment. On the next pitch, the bat flew out of his hands and skittered toward the pitching mound—a lost art, you could say. Maglie leaped over the bat and strode to meet Furillo, who was marching purposefully toward the mound. Fortunately, Gil Hodges could stop anybody in his tracks, and did.

Nearly half a century later, Dave Anderson, the Pulitzer Prize–winning columnist with the *New York Times,* can recall being a young reporter, just out of Holy Cross, and asking Furillo why he had headed toward the mound. "I was just going out there to get my bat," Furillo had said with a bland if not convincing look on his face.

After that game, Maglie had said: "I never threw at Carl in my life. I don't think I've ever hit him with a pitch. That's why I'm so surprised at him. I'll tell you one thing, though. If that bat had ever hit me, it would have been a different story."

The crisis was averted, but on September 6 of that year, Ruben Gomez of the Giants hit Furillo on the wrist. Furillo trudged to first base, which was close to the Giants' dugout, and he could hear Durocher taunting him. Furillo crooked his index finger at Durocher, inviting him out on the field.

"Leo in turn motioned Carl to come in," recalled Vin Scully, then a young Dodgers broadcaster out of Fordham University. "The two met halfway, and Carl got Leo around the forehead and put a lock on him like you wouldn't believe. If he'd got him around the throat, he would have killed him. And I'm not speaking figuratively. I mean actually killed him. Leo's bald head turned maroon before anybody could get to them."

In the brawl, somebody stepped on Furillo's left hand, breaking a bone and keeping him out for the rest of the regular season, and thereby preserving his .344 average, which would lead the league. He thought Durocher had stepped on his hand, but he also saw Maglie as the embodiment of Durocher's malicious will.

Did they truly hate each other? Or did they understand that they were both merely disposable warriors, used by club owners to sell tickets to a spectacle? Clearly, they took this Giants-Dodgers rivalry seriously. It was real life. It was what they knew. But both of them seemed to pick up on the other as the personification of the unworthiness of the other side. They brought something extra to the table. They had a seething ability to dislike and to not forget.

Or was there something else? It stuck in Buzzie Bavasi's mind that Furillo identified himself as a Southerner and so did Maglie, both of which made them feel like outsiders.

This may come off as Old World trivia to many Americans, who, after all, have their own North-South agendas. But many countries around the world have these North-South barriers, and none of them are more convoluted than the split among regions and people and dialects known as modern Italy.

Even today, when soccer teams from Naples or Palermo visit Florence or Milan, there are signs proclaiming BENVENUTO A L'ITALIA— Welcome to Italy. Some people place the "border" above Rome and others place it below Rome. There are politicians in northern Lombardy who want to secede from the South, while Neapolitans suspect they are treated as gauche outsiders in the North.

Were there any such feelings of being *stranieri*, foreigners, in Furillo and Maglie? Whatever it was, the two men learned to treat each other as the enemy.

"Dad took people at face value," Furillo Jr. said. "Sal was given orders to knock him down. Dad thought that wasn't right. You could end somebody's career. Dad did what he could do. He let the bat fly."

◆ ◆ ◆

Mine enemy grows older. Maglie won fourteen games in 1954 as the Giants swept Cleveland in the World Series, but the next year, having turned thirty-eight, he was promptly dispatched to Cleveland, which may have purchased him just to keep him from the Yankees.

With Maglie gone, the Dodgers won the World Series in 1955. The next year Maglie rarely pitched for a Cleveland club that had a strong pitching staff. But in mid-May he was showcased against the Dodgers in a charity exhibition in the Dodgers' home away from home, Jersey City.

The next day, Bavasi recalled, he received separate telephone calls from the two owners of the Indians, Bill Veeck and Hank Greenberg, both offering Maglie. Bavasi recalls Veeck's asking for $100,000 and Greenberg's asking for $10,000. This discrepancy implied to Bavasi that the owners did not want to release Maglie for nothing, so he offered $1,000—and they accepted it. In Bavasi's version, he told Walter O'Malley, the owner of the Dodgers, that the price was the rumored $100,000, just to see O'Malley's face turn a ghastly white. At that point, Bavasi explained Maglie cost only $1,000.

For all that, O'Malley's reaction was more measured than Furillo's.

"He came into the office, raising hell." Bavasi said. "He said he wanted to be traded because he didn't want to be associated with the 'damn Dago Maglie.' I explained that Carl himself was what he called Sal."

"Carl wanted to quit, until I explained it to him," Bavasi said. "I asked him what the object of our game was. He said, 'To win the damn pennant.' Well, I said, Maglie might help us to that."

Then Bavasi added, "I thought I understood them because they did things the Italian way."

And which way is that? "I hate you, I hate you forever," Bavasi explained.

It is a different age now. Sensibilities are different. One of the true Dodgers, a disciple of Branch Rickey named Al Campanis, whose mother came from the Greek island of Kos and whose father came from the northern Italian city of Modena, muttered a few dumb things—about black athletes not having the "necessities" to manage—into a live mike during an impromptu television interview in 1983, and paid the price with his job as general manager of the Los Angeles Dodgers. Campanis was a warm and generous and educated man with strong ties to Latino and black baseball people, yet he has become a convenient public stick figure for a bigot. Campanis never used ethnic or racial words, but they were common back then.

"It was a term of endearment," Branca said. "You hear black players using certain words to each other, but there's no way you use them. We'd call each other names, but if an Irish guy or a Polish guy used them, we'd get mad."

Anyway, Bavasi listened to Furillo's anger.

"Carl also thought that Sal threw at him because he didn't like him. I tried to explain that Carl also threw at Pee Wee and Jackie."

Furillo allegedly replied, "Yeah, but he throws at me every time I face him. With Jackie and Pee Wee it's only once a game."

Bavasi assured Furillo that it would all work out. The right fielder did not sound convinced.

Maglie drove his car from Cleveland to Brooklyn, but as soon as he arrived he was notified that his father had just died in Niagara Falls.

"The Dodgers had sent more flowers than you could believe," Pascal Grenga recalled. "My uncle told me that the Dodgers were more of a family organization than the Yankees or Giants."

After the funeral upstate, Maglie turned around and drove to Brooklyn. In the meantime, the clubhouse manager, the rotund and prankish "Senator" John Griffin, had placed Maglie's locker close to

Furillo's, who was still muttering to his teammates, "Maglie is a Giant Dago and doesn't belong here."

Nobody expected fisticuffs, but you never knew what kind of sullen or angry karma might be produced in a winning clubhouse.

The witnesses to the first encounter have mostly died. Branca, who was not with the Dodgers in May of 1956, has heard one version.

"Sal arrived early. There were a few players around, including Carl. Charlie DiGiovanni, the batboy, who had thick, black eyebrows, so they called him 'The Brow,' saw Sal coming in, and he saw Carl, and the Brow yelled, 'Hey, we're all *paesans* around here, let's get along.' "

Some versions have Furillo glancing up at Maglie in the cramped clubhouse and saying, "Hey, Dago." Some have him saying, "Hey, goombah." Others have him saying, "Hey, *paesan.*" In all versions Maglie responds in kind. There does not seem to have been a handshake or friendly words, just the overt acknowledgment that they were now officially teammates.

"You change uniforms, you don't harbor any grudges," Branca said.

Furillo was still working things over in his mind. Why was he in the same locker room with Leo's hatchet man? Plus, why bring in this reject?

Neither Furillo nor Maglie ever told the following story, but in his retirement in southern California, Buzzie Bavasi loves to tell how he ordered Furillo to take Maglie out to dinner at Toots Shor's, the popular midtown Manhattan hangout.

"I thought it would be nice if he took Sal to dinner, that they might get to know each other," Bavasi recalled.

"You got to be fucking nuts," is how Bavasi remembers Furillo's reaction, which sounds about right.

Bavasi claims he promptly peeled off $150 in cash.

"Carl quickly figured, hell, dinner at the most would be forty bucks. 'OK,' he said."

Bavasi claims he even arranged a free ride from his driver, to save Furillo the cab fare.

"In the meantime, I called Toots and told him that Sal and Carl would be there for dinner, and when Carl went to pay the check, I wanted Toots to make believe the meal was on him, and I would send Toots a check."

In those days, Shor's was the center of the universe for a certain raffish crowd of boxers, baritones, gamblers, and sports columnists who surely did not go there for the food but rather to prove they had arrived. There is no longer in these dispersed times any place quite like Shor's, when millionaire players live in mansions out in the suburbs, and the action is in Vegas, and some sportswriters stay home and share diaper duties with their wives. However, in those days, Shor's was big, with Joe DiMaggio as its greatest luminary. It is quite likely that neither Carl Furillo nor Sal Maglie had ever been there before. In Bavasi's version, Furillo never mentioned that Shor had comped the whole evening.

"My dad never told me about keeping the $150," said Carl Jr., who loves the story.

After this apparent evening at Shor's, Maglie and Furillo settled in as terse teammates.

"The first time I pitched for the Dodgers," Maglie once said, "I was about to warm up, when Buzzie called me over to the box seats. He told me I had to win; otherwise his wife wouldn't speak to him again. I won."

When Maglie beat the Braves in early June, Furillo decided that he could live with the guy, and set up the odd little ribs party for Maglie and Lang in his room. By all accounts, there were no handshakes and surely no hugs (men did not hug in those days), no touchy-feely going back over the old days. The two old warriors were in the same legion now.

"I went down to visit my uncle that summer," recalls Pascal Grenga. "We were in a parking lot outside Ebbets Field and he introduced me to Roy Campanella and Carl Furillo. It felt kind of funny because I had always thought of Furillo as a foe rather than a friend."

That wonderful late summer when he turned thirty-nine, Salvatore Anthony Maglie won thirteen games and lost only five. He was so rejuvenated that he asked the manager, Walter Alston, to pitch him every fourth day. On September 25, he even pitched the first no-hitter of his career, over the Phillies.

"The next to last day of the season in 1956, I was supposed to pitch the first game of a crucial doubleheader against Pittsburgh," Maglie recalled a few years later. "Before the game I walked into the locker room a little late. Furillo took one look at me and announced, 'Have no fear, the Barber's here.' "

They won both games and held off the Braves. And Bavasi recalled, "The next time I heard Carl use the word 'Dago' in referring to Sal was when he stopped by the office just before the season ended and said, 'Buzzie, getting that Dago was the best move you ever made.' "

In the World Series, Maglie beat the Yankees, and in his next start he lost to Don Larsen, who merely pitched a perfect game.

Maglie was now part of the Dodgers' wonderful ten-year run. He would sometimes join a room service breakfast with Furillo and his new roommate, a bonus-boy left-hander. Furillo sensed the Jewish kid from Brooklyn was being treated as an outsider, and became a lifelong friend of Sandy Koufax, and so did Maglie.

Maglie would also be part of the next generation, too. In 1956, the Dodgers brought up a lanky kid who could already throw hard and was not averse to pitching inside. Thus, in the glorious lineage of baseball, there is a direct link from Christy Mathewson to Dolf Luque to Sal Maglie to Donald Scott Drysdale.

"Sal would give me the knockdown sign from the dugout," Drysdale once said. "One time he gave me the sign with Henry Aaron up, and I knocked him down. Before the next pitch he gave me the sign again, so I knocked Henry down again. When I asked him why later, Sal said, 'You do it the second time to let him know you meant it the first time.' "

Thus encouraged, Drysdale took it a step further, hitting 154 batters in 3,432 innings en route to the Hall of Fame. By contrast, in his own belated 1,722 innings in the major leagues, Maglie would hit only forty-four batters, showing that it was the perception that counted.

Maglie's time with Drysdale was short. The Dodgers were fixing to move to Los Angeles, and Bavasi was in charge of lightening the load. He sold Maglie to the Yankees for $27,500 and a minor league pitcher—"plus dinner," Bavasi insisted.

"Ten minutes after the deal was announced," Bavasi recalled, "Carl called me and said, 'You dumb Dago.' And hung up."

Maglie finished up his career with the Cardinals, with a lifetime record of 119 victories and 62 losses, a superb percentage of .657. If not for the war and the Mexican League, he might have had Hall of Fame numbers. Or maybe without Dolf Luque, nobody would have heard of Sal the Barber.

Wearing down, Carl Furillo moved west with the Dodgers, lasting long enough to hit a seeing-eye single that drove in the winning run as the Dodgers beat the Braves in a playoff en route to the 1959 World Championship. Early the next year, his thirty-eight-year-old body was fading fast, and Bavasi tried to ship him to Spokane, ostensibly to coach. But Furillo, using a clause in his contract that said he could not be released while injured, eventually sued for his full salary that season.

"That was a dumbest Dago thing you ever did," Bavasi is quoted as saying. Furillo had already been paid $12,000 on his 1960 contract, and he wound up gaining the other $21,000 from his suit, but he had enraged Bavasi. To this day, Furillo's family thinks he was blackballed, but Bavasi denies it. At the very least, Furillo had challenged the power structure, and no law said anybody had to give him a job.

The son of the Depression did what he could. He helped run a delicatessen in the Flushing section of Queens, a mile or two from where a new expansion team called the Mets wound up playing in a ballpark that could have belonged to the Dodgers if the O'Malley clan had been serious about staying.

As close as he was, Furillo rarely went to the ballpark, but in 1971, another grizzled Brooklyn man, sports writer Dick Young, ran into Furillo and Maglie together at an old-timers game at Shea. Young still referred to Furillo in print as "The Daig," and he wrote that Maglie's eyes were "even more sinister than before, if that is possible."

By this time, it was safe to discuss the old fights.

"I always thought it was Jim Hearn who stepped on your hand," Maglie said to Furillo about the melee in 1953.

"I thought it was Whitey Lockman," Pee Wee Reese said.

"Naw, it was Durocher all right," Furillo said. "He did it. He took my finger and bent it back like this."

"How could he?" asked Johnny Podres. "You had both hands wrapped around his throat. He was turning blue."

At another old-timers game, the two old foes arranged for Maglie to sail a pitch over Furillo's head, for old-times' sake.

"Instead of throwing over my head, Sal throws the first pitch down the middle," Furillo said. "So I make a motion to him, like to ask why he didn't throw over my head the way he was supposed to. And you know what Maglie hollers back? He says, 'Not with a man on first!' How about that? In an old-timers game? The Barber's got to put out, even then."

In 1976, the old players were invited to Yankee Stadium to note the twenty-fifth anniversary of the Thomson home run.

"I told the story about how I was trying to set up Thomson for a curve by coming up and in," Branca said. "When I sat down at the table, Maglie turned to me and said, 'Hey, Dago, if you wanted to throw him a curve, why didn't you throw a damn curve?'"

The Dodgers pulled Furillo back into the fold, inviting him to tutor young players in their camp in Vero Beach and including him in fantasy camps. (He had a thing about appearing old and awkward, and would not wear spikes or play in any games.) However, he loved being around the Dodgers.

Life was not easy for the old combatants. Furillo went from the delicatessen to installing elevator doors on two skyscrapers going up at the tip of Manhattan, buildings that would be known as the World Trade Center.

That was where Roger Kahn met him around 1970. Furillo fit in with the other construction guys, with one major difference: Many of them had once paid their way into Ebbets Field to watch him play the wall.

In Kahn's wonderful book, the chapter on Furillo is entitled "The Hard Hat Who Sued Baseball." To this day, Carl Jr. does not like the chapter, or the title.

Eventually, Furillo went back to Pennsylvania, where he served for a while as a deputy sheriff. He learned he had leukemia, but he kept working and died in his sleep on January 21, 1989.

"I've seen other relatives slipping away, and I realize God did my dad a favor," said Butch Furillo.

Fern Furillo, still living in their old house, watches baseball, particularly on that insidious superstation out of Atlanta. Like many other older people with a clicker, she roots for the Atlanta Braves.

Sal Maglie's life was not easy after baseball, either. He and his first wife, the former Katherine Pileggi, adopted two sons—Salvatore, who died as a young adult, and Joseph, who would have a long career in the Air Force. After Katherine died, Maglie married Doris Ellman, also from the Niagara Falls area. He worked as a pitching coach for the Red Sox, and for the expansion Seattle Pilots in 1969. Eventually, he represented a whiskey company in his region, and was a deputy commissioner for the New York State Athletic Commission. He had a stroke and for several years he was under intensive care in a nursing wing of a hospital. He died on December 28, 1992.

His second wife never saw him as Sal the Barber, but a gentle man who enjoyed meeting old friends at reunions.

"The only time I met Mrs. Furillo was at an old-timers game somewhere," Doris Maglie said recently. "They gave the players rocking chairs. The wives all loved that. I loved hearing them talk about the old days. Sal said they used to be enemies, but they got to be good friends."

ERNIE LOMBARDI'S BUM RAP

Lawrence Baldassaro

For years, Ernie Lombardi remained silent as players he considered less worthy were elected to the Hall of Fame while he was left out. Then, in 1974, seventeen years after he had played his last game in the majors, he voiced his resentment to Ed Leavitt, a sportswriter for the *Oakland Tribune* who had accidentally discovered the former catcher working at a local gas station. "If they elected me, I wouldn't show up for the ceremony," he said. "They've waited too long and they've ignored me too long. That sounds terrible. But every year I see my chances getting smaller and smaller. Sure, who wouldn't be bitter?"

Lombardi would eventually be elected to the baseball shrine—in 1986 by the Veterans Committee—but by then it was too late to know if he would have shown up for the ceremony; he had been dead for almost nine years.

There's some pretty solid evidence that Lombardi had a right to be bitter about his repeated rejection. His statistics and the judgment of his peers clearly identify him as one of the best hitters of his era. No less an authority than Ted Williams considered him to be one of the best ever. A seven-time All-Star and the only catcher to win two batting titles, he hit over .300 ten times during his seventeen years in the big leagues and compiled a lifetime average of .306. In 1938, the year he caught both of

Johnny Vander Meer's consecutive no-hitters and won his first batting title, he became the first Italian American to win an MVP Award.

Yet, for all that, Lombardi was remembered less for his prodigious hitting than for his ungainly physique, lead feet, comic nickname, and a single lapse in a World Series game. In the pantheon of baseball heroes, Lombardi plays the role of a comic figure, a Falstaff among so many Prince Hals. Even in his own time, he was often depicted as a caricature of a major league ballplayer, more ridiculed than revered. Increasingly despondent after his retirement, he once attempted suicide, and his life ended in isolation and bitterness.

A Hall of Fame Career

That Ernie Lombardi ever made it to the major leagues, much less the Hall of Fame, was in itself a triumph against great odds. At the time he made his debut in 1931, only twenty-six players of Italian descent had ever played big league baseball, and five of those had been rookies in 1930. Slim as they were, his chances were improved somewhat because he grew up in the San Francisco Bay area, a hotbed of amateur baseball that produced most of the important early Italian American major-leaguers, including Ping Bodie, Tony Lazzeri, Frank Crosetti, and the DiMaggio brothers. Unlike the crowded eastern cities where the majority of Italian Americans lived, the Bay Area, whose rich baseball tradition predated the Civil War, had numerous playgrounds where boys could hone their skills.

Ernesto Natali Lombardi was born in Oakland on April 6, 1908. A standout on the local sandlots, he quit school as a teenager to work in the grocery store run by his father, Dominic, an immigrant from Piedmont. But he continued to play amateur and semi-pro ball, and when the Oakland Oaks offered him a contract in 1926 to play in the Pacific Coast League, he gladly moved out from behind the grocery counter. In 1927, the Oaks sent the eighteen-year-old catcher to their farm team in Ogden, Utah, for seasoning, and then recalled him when he was hitting .398 after fifty games. Over the next three years he hit .377, .366, and .370.

It was while playing for Oakland that Lombardi adopted the unorthodox batting grip that would become his trademark. When a blister on the little finger of his right hand made it painful to swing the bat, he wrapped that finger over the index finger of his left hand in the manner of an interlocking golf grip. The grip not only alleviated the pain but also improved his hitting so much that Lombardi never went back to the traditional way of holding the bat.

At the end of the 1930 season, the Brooklyn Dodgers purchased his contract for $50,000 and two players. On the occasion of his signing, the *Sporting News* reported that Lombardi "would appeal greatly to the Italian vote, which makes up a comparatively large portion of the summertime customers at Ebbets Field." But Lombardi spent only one season in Brooklyn; after hitting .297 in seventy-three games as a backup to Al Lopez, he was traded to the Cincinnati Reds.

Lombardi immediately became the Reds' starting catcher in 1932, hitting .303 in 118 games. In his ten years in Cincinnati he played in an average of 120 games a year and hit over .300 seven times. Between 1935 and '37 he hit .343, .333, and .334, and was selected to the All-Star team each year from 1936 to 1940.

His best all-around year came in 1938 when he helped lift the Reds from last place to fourth. That year Lombardi became only the second catcher (after Bubbles Hargrave in 1926) to win a batting title, when he hit .342. He also hit nineteen homers and had career-highs in RBIs (ninety-five) and slugging average (.524) while striking out only fourteen times in 489 times at bat. It was also the year he caught Johnny Vander Meer's back-to-back no-hitters. Following the season, the Baseball Writers' Association of America named him the National League's Most Valuable Player.

In his 1948 history of the Cincinnati Reds, Lee Allen wrote: "[I]n the summer of 1938, when the ominous clouds of war were growing ever darker, the people of Cincinnati, one slice of the isolationist Midwest of America, were cheering the names of Johnny Vander Meer and Ernie Lombardi, the sons, respectively, of a Dutch stonecutter and an Italian grocer, living testimony as to the value of the melting-pot tradition and the glory of a game."

In 1939, Lombardi's average dropped to .287 but he hit a career-high twenty homers to help lead Cincinnati to the pennant. The Reds were swept in four straight by the Yankees, but the following year, when Lombardi's average bounced back to .318, they won a second straight pennant. This time the Reds took the Series by defeating the Tigers in seven games, but a late-season ankle injury limited Lombardi to four plate appearances, in which he collected a double and a walk.

After hitting only .264 in 1941, Lombardi was traded to the Boston Braves. Whether rejuvenated by the change of scenery or motivated by revenge, he came back to hit .330 and win his second batting crown (though by current standards his 309 times at bat would be too few to qualify for the title). He remains the only catcher ever to twice lead the league in hitting.

A salary cap imposed during World War II forced the Braves to trade Lombardi to the Giants in 1943. He spent his last five seasons in New York, his career doubtless prolonged by the depletion of major league talent due to the war. (Lombardi was exempt from military service as the sole supporter of his father and sister.) For three years he was their regular catcher, hitting .305, .255 (the lowest average of his career), and .307. In his final two seasons he played in a backup role, appearing in a total of 136 games, but continued to hit well, averaging .290 and .282.

Like many others before him, Lombardi returned to his roots to play in the Pacific Coast League when his major league career ended. In 1948, he finished his professional career where it began, with the Oakland Oaks. Affectionately known as the "Nine Old Men," the Oaks featured several other Italian American major league veterans, including Dario Lodigiani, Les Scarsella, and Cookie Lavagetto. The youngest player was another Italian American, twenty-year-old Oakland native Billy Martin, who was two years away from his major league debut. Their manager, Casey Stengel, was four years younger than the forty-year-old Lombardi, who played in 102 games and hit .264 with eleven home runs.

That year, the Oaks won the Pacific Coast League pennant for the first time since 1927, Lombardi's first full year as a professional.

Among his contemporaries, there were varying opinions on Lombardi's defensive skills. The 6'3", 230-pound catcher was routinely described in the press as "lumbering" and "cumbersome," but the general consensus was that he was a solid receiver who handled pitchers well and possessed one of the strongest and most accurate throwing arms in the majors. Reds pitcher Kirby Higbe, a teammate for three years, considered Lombardi the greatest catcher of his time. While that was not a widely shared opinion, Lombardi was both dependable and durable; in only his first and last two years in the majors did he play in fewer than 104 games.

The big catcher's major weakness, of course, was his lack of mobility, which meant that he was not particularly adept at fielding bunts or pop flies, or at preventing passed balls, a category in which he led the league several times.

In addition to his strong arm, Lombardi had a huge pair of hands—one photo shows him holding seven baseballs in his right hand. Several sources report that when a pitcher would throw a ball wide to Lombardi's right, he would simply reach out and snare it barehanded. Bill Werber, a teammate with the Reds, wrote in his memoirs: "Pitching to him was like throwing to a warehouse behind the plate. Our staff liked throwing to him. He knew the opposition's strengths and weaknesses and called a great game. He was a shrewd operator. Lombardi could throw better than anybody—anybody."

Johnny Vander Meer had high praise for the man who caught both his no-hitters. "I never knew a greater one and I saw the best of 'em," he said. "Cochrane, Dickey, Hartnett. None of 'em could throw like Lom, and his hitting speaks for itself."

Whatever his abilities as a catcher, it was with his bat, not his glove, that Ernie Lombardi made his mark in the major leagues. In ten of his seventeen big league seasons he hit over .300, five times hitting .330 or above, including his two league-leading years. His lifetime average of .306

Ernie Lombardi holds seven baseballs among the fingers of one hand.
(National Baseball Hall of Fame Library, Cooperstown, New York)

is third highest among the twelve catchers in the Hall of Fame, trailing only Mickey Cochrane (.320) and Bill Dickey (.313).

In spite of his size, Lombardi was not the prototypical power hitter. He never hit more than twenty homers in a season and his seventeen-year total of 190 averages out to one home run every thirty-one times at bat. He was, however, an outstanding contact hitter; in 5,855 career at-bats, he struck out only 262 times, an average of one strikeout every twenty-two times at bat. "He was one of the toughest hitters in the history of baseball to strike out," said Vander Meer.

What Ernie Lombardi did better than just about anyone was hit blistering line drives that terrified opposing pitchers and infielders. Giants' pitcher Carl Hubbell once said, "I thought he might hurt me, even kill me, with one of those liners. They were screamers." In fact, in 1937, one of Lombardi's line drives did break three fingers on the right hand of Cubs pitcher Larry French.

Lombardi's lifetime average of .306 is all the more remarkable given his legendary slowness on the base paths. There were few if any "leg hits" in his career. In baseball lingo, a "piano man" is someone who runs as if he were carrying a piano on his back; by that standard, Lombardi, considered the slowest runner of his time, lugged a large pipe organ. Kirby Higbe used a different image: "I could run faster with a mule on my back than Ernie." *New York Times* columnist Arthur Daley wrote that the big catcher "ran on a treadmill and couldn't outrace a snail even with a head start."

It was common for infielders to play on the outfield grass when Lombardi came to the plate, knowing they had plenty of time to throw him out, both because he was slow and because he hit the ball so hard. Lombardi once told Dodgers shortstop Pee Wee Reese, "It was five years before I learned you weren't an outfielder."

As unlikely as it seems, Dick Bartell, a teammate with the New York Giants, claimed that Lombardi was thrown out at first after hitting the ball off the short right field fence in Philadelphia's Baker Bowl. But in his autobiography, *Rowdy Richard,* Bartell also defended Lombardi as a smart base runner, saying that "he never made any bad moves on the bases, even though it might take three singles to get him home."

One of the standard lines about Lombardi's lack of speed was that he would turn doubles into singles. All the more remarkable, then, that on May 8, 1935, he equaled the major league record by hitting four doubles in four consecutive innings, each off a different pitcher.

Lombardi was still hitting those screaming line drives at the age of forty, when he returned to the Oakland Oaks in 1948. Teammate Dario Lodigiani recalled Lombardi's ability to hit even at his advanced age. "Ernie Lombardi was the oldest on the club," he told this writer. "Come the seventh, eighth, ninth inning, if it was a close game and we had a chance to win, Casey would send Ernie up and it seems he'd always come through. Even then he was a great hitter. They'd play him back on the outfield grass because he was so slow, but he would hit those wicked line drives."

Praise and Ridicule

Lombardi's greatness as a hitter was widely acknowledged by his peers and the press. Harry Craft, a teammate for six years, called him "the best right-handed hitter I ever saw. And he was an exceptional player in every department except running. If he hadn't been so slow, he would have had an even better batting average." Kirby Higbe simply called him "the greatest hitter I ever saw, including everybody."

Lee Allen, the late historian of the Hall of Fame, recalled the scene as Ted Williams toured the baseball shrine on the morning of his own induction. As he looked at an exhibit listing the game's lifetime batting leaders, Williams said to former teammate Bobby Doerr, "Do you know who was one of the greatest batters of all time? Ernie Lombardi! If he had had normal speed, he would have made batting marks that would still be on the books."

Arthur Daley wrote: "When you look back on him and his seventeen years in the majors, you almost come to the conclusion that he was the greatest hitter of all time. Every hit he made was an honest one. . . . When

Lom would grasp a bat with that interlocking grip of his, his bat looked like a matchstick. And the ball would ricochet off it like a shell leaving a howitzer."

At the same time he was being praised for his hitting, Lombardi was also subject to frequent ridicule because of his appearance. Carrying 230 pounds on his 6'3" body and wearing the baggy uniform of his era, he gave the impression of being lumpy rather than burly. Even in his prime, Lombardi looked more like a rumpled manager than a batting champion. And atop his ungainly body sat a doughy face dominated by a large, bulbous nose. Never camera-friendly, he simply did not look like an athlete.

Disparaging comments on his appearance began to appear in print as soon as he was signed by the Brooklyn Dodgers. Tommy Holmes wrote in the January 29, 1931 issue of the *Sporting News* that "Ernie is a big lumbering kid with huge feet and a notable nose. His feet have been compared to those of [Primo] Carnera and his nose to that of [former major league infielder] Rollie Zeider."

The thirties was a decade marked by colorful nicknames, many of which appear insensitive by today's standards. There was Stinky Davis, Fat Freddie Fitzsimmons, Ducky Wucky Medwick, and Twinkletoes Selkirk. But one of the more disparaging nicknames based on appearance was hung on Lombardi, whose conspicuous nose earned him the handle of "Schnozz." Inevitably, his most prominent feature was compared to that of another Italian American, entertainer Jimmy Durante, who shared Lombardi's nickname. Lee Allen, in his history of the Reds, wrote that Lombardi "brought to baseball a nose so lavish in its geography that the more famous schnozzola of Jimmy Durante's seems picayunish by comparison."

Other, less offensive, nicknames were used by teammates and those afraid to call him "Schnozz" to his face, including Lom, Lumbago, and Bocce, a name he acquired as a child because of his skill at the Italian bowling game. But it was his best-known nickname that most clearly identified him as an object of ridicule. Lombardi was a gentle man who took the ribbing in good humor, but the time would come when his outlook changed.

The "Snooze" Play

From Fred Merkle in 1908 to Bill Buckner in 1986, "goats" have been a staple of baseball lore. A source of nostalgic anecdotes for fans, the label can leave an indelible stain on an otherwise stellar career. Tony Lazzeri, the first Italian American star and a key member of the Yankees' Murderers Row lineup, had a Hall of Fame career. But he is often remembered for his bases-loaded strikeout against Grover Cleveland Alexander in the seventh game of the 1926 World Series. Thirteen years later, it would be Ernie Lombardi's turn.

In 1939, the Reds won their first pennant since 1919, the year of their tainted Series win over the Chicago Black Sox. This time their opponents were the Yankees, who were seeking their fourth consecutive Series title. There is a photo of the Reds celebrating in the locker room after clinching the pennant. Partially obscured by a teammate on whose shoulder his hand is resting, Lombardi is seen looking straight into the camera, a big grin on his face. In a few days that smile would be wiped away by a single play that was to haunt him for the rest of his life.

At the time of the Series, incidentally, Lombardi may have been the most popular Reds player, but he apparently was not the best-known Italian ballplayer, at least among younger Cincinnati fans. Tom Knight, writing in the January 13, 1982 edition of the *Brooklyn Spectator,* told the story of a visit by Leo Perra, the Italian consul in Cincinnati, to a school where most of the children were of Italian descent. Perra gave a talk to one of the classes extolling the many contributions Italians had made to the U.S. At one point he said, "I'm sure you all know the name of one Italian whose efforts have been most important to America." Presumably he expected to hear the children name Christopher Columbus, but instead they yelled in unison, "Joe DiMaggio." When Perra shook his head, one boy raised his hand. "Who was it?" the Consul asked hopefully, and the boy proudly replied, "Ernie Lombardi."

The Yanks, led by DiMaggio, Bill Dickey, and Charlie Keller, won the first three games of the Series as the Reds scored a total of four runs. It was in the fourth and final game, on October 8, before a crowd of 32,794, that Lombardi was involved in the play that would forever tarnish his reputation. Ironically, his moment of infamy involved two other prominent Italian American players and an Italian American umpire.

The Reds held a 4–2 lead going into the ninth, but the Yankees came back to tie the game. In the top of the tenth inning, Joe DiMaggio came to the plate with Frank Crosetti on third and Charlie Keller on first. DiMaggio hit a single to right, scoring Crosetti with the go-ahead run. When Ival Goodman, the Reds' right fielder, bobbled the ball, Keller rounded third and headed for home. The throw came in, but as Lombardi applied the tag, Keller bowled him over, leaving the catcher momentarily stunned. (Some accounts have Keller hitting Lombardi in the head with his knee; others claim it was a blow to the groin.) DiMaggio, seeing Lombardi lying on the ground and the ball a few feet away, kept running, slid across home plate, and was signaled safe by umpire Babe Pinelli.

Grantland Rice, then the dean of American sportswriters, set the tone for future accounts of the play. "You won't believe what I am telling you—and I don't blame you," he wrote. "But it happened this way—the greatest World Series anticlimax I've ever seen in 35 years of close inspection. . . . Senor Lombardi fell squarely on his broad back. The ball bounded out of his hands and lay at rest two feet from either hand. At this point, DiMaggio was just rounding third. Joe kept on traveling over the intervening 90 feet as Lombardi still lay at rest, a stricken being. . . . He had no idea the roving DiMaggio was on his way to the plate."

The problem is, it didn't happen "this way." Rice's description of the play was as unfair as it was clever. Film of the play, as well as still photographs, clearly reveal that Lombardi did not "lay at rest." The film shows Lombardi getting knocked down by Keller, then lying face down on the ground (not on his back, as Rice reported) as the ball rolls a few feet away. As a Yankee player waves DiMaggio home, Lombardi regains his senses and picks up the ball. He then makes a lunging tag, which DiMaggio gracefully eludes with a perfect hook slide away from Lombardi's outstretched glove.

There was at least one other contemporary writer who surpassed even Rice in his fanciful account of the play. On October 10, two days after the game, John Kieran of the *New York Times* wrote a column that was condescendingly dismissive of the Reds' futile effort against the Yanks. But his most acerbic barbs were directed at "Ernesto Cyrano de Bergerac Lombardi, huge and cumbersome." According to Kieran's account, Keller did not even touch the Reds' catcher, but instead "slid past lumbering Lombardi without being touched." If that were true, what Kieran describes next would be truly remarkable. Apparently for no reason whatsoever, "Signor Ernesto collapsed heavily on the ground, spreading out in all directions like a flow of lava from a lazy volcano. . . . He was not dead, he was not sleeping; he was just brooding." In fairness to Kieran, he (unlike Rice) does acknowledge that "Lombardi, aroused by the horrified shouts of the spectators, came out of his brooding trance just in time to grab the ball and miss tagging DiMaggio."

But, regardless of its inaccuracy, it was Rice's typically colorful version of the play that stuck and apparently became the source of virtually all future accounts. Lee Allen, who was generally sympathetic to Lombardi in his history of the Reds, echoed Rice's portrayal of the play. Lombardi, wrote Allen, "lay prostrate on the ground as DiMaggio completed the circuit of the bases. . . . That play has gone down in history as the act of the dying swan, and the sportswriters, who always seem to feel each World Series must have a hero and a goat, have long remembered Ernie Lombardi as the man who swooned at home plate, while Yankees scampered all over him."

Other astute baseball historians have perpetuated the image of a lifeless Lombardi sprawled helpless on the dirt. Donald Honig, in his 1992 history of the Reds, wrote that DiMaggio "scored without a play being made on him." And Bill James, in his *New Historical Baseball Abstract,* wrote: "While [Lombardi] lay on his back a few feet from home plate, the ball on the ground beside him, DiMaggio raced around the bases. . . . Ernie's Snooze, Lombardi's Sit-down Strike, the Schnozz's Swan Dive. The play grew to have as many names as the player."

Allen, Honig, and James all acknowledge that Lombardi didn't deserve to be labeled as the goat of the Series, but they all reiterate Rice's imprecise depiction of the play that has ever since been known as Ernie's Snooze, and which Lombardi was never able to live down. Not even the Cincinnati Reds' official website is immune from the infection of inaccuracy that has endured for over half a century. Its description of the play concludes: " 'Lom' was knocked unconscious and lay prone at the plate while Joe DiMaggio scored the go-ahead run."

Lombardi himself had little to say about the play. Only years later was he quoted as saying, "It was an awful hot day in Cincinnati, and I was feeling dizzy. When Keller came in, he spun me around at the plate and I couldn't get up."

Apart from the blatant inaccuracy, which survives to this day, the question remains: Why has this play assumed mythic proportions in the annals of baseball history? Since his was the final run in a 7–4 victory, DiMaggio's tally was meaningless: the play had no effect on the outcome of the game or the Series. Was it because there was so little else of dramatic interest in the Series that this one episode became its signature play? (The Yankees swept the Series and the Reds scored a total of eight runs in the four games.) Would the play have received so much attention if the player sliding across home plate had been anyone other than Joe DiMaggio, who won his first MVP Award that year? Would the same play have received so much attention had it been made by a catcher whose physical appearance had not already made him an object of ridicule? Had the same thing happened, say, to Mickey Cochrane, would the play be remembered today as "Mickey's Snooze"? Not likely.

Unfair as it may be, the play was to become Lombardi's legacy, and he's been stuck with the bum rap ever since. He was a victim of his own reputation. Had it not been for his well-established image as a clumsy backstop—not to mention the ridicule heaped on him for his appearance—it is unlikely that the "snooze" play would have gained the prominence it did, thereby cementing Lombardi's reputation as a comic character.

A Tarnished Legacy

By all accounts, Lombardi was a gentle giant during his playing days, a friendly, quiet guy who was well liked by teammates and adored by Cincinnati fans. Dick Bartell wrote that everybody liked Lombardi, who "loaned money to players all over the league and never pressured them to pay it back." According to Lee Allen, by the time Lombardi won his first batting title in '38, "he had become the most popular player in the history of the [Cincinnati] club, even more of a hero than Edd Roush had been." And, against all odds, he was even something of a matinee idol. "The ladies shrieked with joy at every move the big catcher made," wrote Allen. There was "a Sinatra-like adulation of Lom that affected women of all ages."

But in the years following his retirement, Lombardi became embittered and depressed. Perhaps the indignities he had quietly endured throughout his career, together with the stigma of the "snooze," had done more damage than he knew or was willing to admit. Whatever the reasons, Lombardi's mental state deteriorated to the point where, on the night of April 8, 1953 he succumbed to his inner demons. On the advice of doctors, he had agreed to check into a sanitarium for treatment of depression. On the way there, he and his wife, Berice, stopped at the home of friends in Castro Valley, California. At some point in the evening, Lombardi said he was not feeling well, excused himself, and went into a bedroom. When his wife later went to check on him, she found him lying on the bed, his throat slit with a razor. Then, when police and medical personnel arrived, Lombardi resisted their efforts to assist him, reportedly saying, "Let me alone. I want to die." He soon recovered, however, and was transferred to the sanitarium.

The suicide attempt was an eerie replay of a tragic incident thirteen years earlier involving Willard Hershberger, Lombardi's backup as the

Reds' catcher. Apparently despondent over his role in the team's three-game losing streak, on August 3, 1940, Hershberger, age twenty-nine, committed suicide by slashing his throat in his room in Boston's Copley Plaza Hotel while the team was on a road trip.

In subsequent years, Lombardi grew even more despondent and reclusive. Nothing did more to fuel his bitterness than his failure to be elected to the Hall of Fame, first by the Baseball Writers' Association and then by the Veterans Committee. As the years passed he became more and more convinced that he was being snubbed merely because of his lack of speed. In the 1974 interview cited earlier, he said, "All anybody wants to remember about me was that I couldn't run. They still make jokes." Then, noting that Yogi Berra—"one of the great catchers of modern times"—was elected to the Hall of Fame with a lifetime average twenty points lower than his own, he concluded, "I'm not putting him down, but he wasn't that much faster than I was."

According to his obituary in the *Sporting News,* Lombardi's resentment at being snubbed was justified: "His credentials are far superior to many elected or named to the Cooperstown shrine." Former teammates expressed surprise over the years at Lombardi's failure to be elected. Pitcher Bucky Walters: "Lombardi belongs in the Hall of Fame. He did everything but run good. And he was a hell of a guy on the club. Everybody loved him." And Johnny Vander Meer: "How he's not in the Hall of Fame, I don't know. If you took a survey of every big league pitcher, they'd tell you Lombardi was the last guy they ever wanted to face in a clutch situation."

While no public explanations were ever offered, it was widely speculated that Lombardi's chances were hurt both by the perception that he was a one-dimensional player and by the memory of his "snooze" play in the '39 Series, not to mention his long-standing image as a comic figure. There was also speculation that Lombardi's prospects were further hindered by National League President Warren Giles, who served on the Veterans Committee from 1953 until 1978, the year after Lombardi died. There was bad blood between the two dating back to the years when

Giles—the Reds' general manager from 1937 to 1951—routinely clashed with Lombardi over salary negotiations. During a radio interview following the 1938 season, the Reds' catcher, reportedly under the influence, accused Giles of being cheap. Lombardi was convinced Giles never forgave him.

For some years following his retirement, Lombardi operated a liquor store in San Leandro, California. Then, from 1957 to 1963, he worked as an attendant in the San Francisco Giants press box, reportedly quitting after being insulted by a young sportswriter. For several years he disappeared from public view until being discovered in 1974 by Ed Leavitt in that Oakland gas station. After spending his final years as a virtual recluse, he died on September 26, 1977.

Sadly, Ernie Lombardi's legacy was undermined by a combination of genetics and bad press. Throughout his career he was plagued by a tragicomic flaw—the two Achilles heels that made him the slowest runner in baseball. And few major league players with significant careers have looked less suited to the role. With his baggy, disheveled uniform and homely face, he looked more like Al Schacht, the "Clown Prince of Baseball," than like Mickey Cochrane or Gabby Hartnett, the other Hall of Fame catchers of his era.

The fans loved him, but writers and the baseball establishment were less generous. His flaws were routinely noted by the press, which treated him more as a pathetic than a heroic figure. And the "snooze" play provided the perfect opportunity to perpetuate his image as a comic character, an image that, over time, diminished the memory of the screaming line drives, two batting titles, an MVP award, and his stature as one of the most feared hitters in the game.

But there may yet be hope for a Lombardi revival. At least in Cincinnati, where he was loved by the fans, Lombardi's greatness has not been forgotten. When the Great American Ballpark, the new home of the Cincinnati Reds, opened in 2003, Ernie Lombardi was one of four heroes of the Crosley Field era to be honored with statues (along with Joe Nuxhall, Ted Kluszewski, and Frank Robinson). Nuxhall, the longtime

Reds pitcher and now radio broadcaster, recalled Lombardi's reputation with the fans in an interview with this writer. "If you talk to the older generation that went to Cincinnati games," he said, "you'd find they bring up Ernie's name now because he was so popular with the fans." Then he added, "It's going to be very nice to be remembered with that type person."

Lombardi would no doubt have appreciated this symbol of the recognition and respect that had been denied him for so long, just as he would have appreciated his belated entry into the Hall of Fame, in spite of his longstanding resentment. Would he have maintained his vow to boycott his own induction ceremony? Not according to Johnny Vander Meer, who was a vocal advocate of his teammate's selection. "He'd have been there," he said on the day of Lombardi's posthumous induction in 1986. "The thing you have to know about Lom is that baseball was his life."

BOYS OF THE GOLDEN WEST

Joseph J. Vecchione

I n 1958 the Brooklyn Dodgers broke every heart in the borough that called itself the fourth largest city in the nation—and in terms of population that claim was probably true—by moving to the actual third largest, Los Angeles. Referring to Walter O'Malley, the Dodgers' owner at the time, Tim Cohane, a sportswriter, commented: "The City of Angels offered him more than the key to the city—it gave him the keys to the kingdom. New York balked at twelve acres and Los Angeles enthusiastically proffered three hundred acres. This is the biggest haul since the Brinks robbery."

That same year the New York Giants broke this writer's heart by heading west to San Francisco.

The migration, which left New York without a National League team for four years, would be the beginning of major league baseball's manifest destiny of having franchises all across the North American continent. In 1961 the Dodgers and Giants were joined by the Los Angeles—later California, now Anaheim—Angels. The Athletics or A's got to Oakland from Philadelphia via Kansas City in 1968. In 1969 the Seattle Pilots moved to Milwaukee and became the Brewers. The San Diego Padres became an expansion major league team in 1969, the Seattle Mariners in 1977, and the Arizona Diamondbacks in 1998. In 2003,

Young Oakland lefthander Barry Zito makes Yogi's All-Time All-Star roster. (National Baseball Hall of Fame Library, Cooperstown, New York)

Portland was making a run at acquiring the financially struggling Montreal Expos franchise and a major league berth.

In some ways the arrival of major league baseball on the West Coast was long overdue. Even by 1958 many major league players came from western states, particularly California. The Golden State has produced more major-leaguers than any other state in the union: according to baseball-reference.com, 1,697 out of the 14,023, or twelve percent, of all major-leaguers by 2002. (Second is Pennsylvania with 1,298, then New York, 1,073, and Ohio with 928.)

In fact, of the twenty-five players competing for selection to Yogi Berra's All-Time All–Italian American All-Star Team, eleven were born out west. The DiMaggio brothers, Billy Martin, Ernie Lombardi, Dolf Camilli, Jason Giambi, Tony Lazzeri, Frank Crosetti, and Dave Righetti were born in California. Barry Zito comes from Las Vegas and played for Southern Cal, and Ron Santo hails from Seattle. The only two positions not represented are shortstop and manager. But Jim Fregosi, who was

Jim Fregosi
(Private Archive)

born in San Francisco and had his best years with the Angels wouldn't be a bad backup for the Scooter. Arguably he, and perhaps Rich Aurilia, should have been candidates anyway. Joe Torre was born in Brooklyn, but Billy Martin could double up as second baseman and manager.

As for Martin the ballplayer, Casey Stengel, who managed Martin as a Yankee, described him in inimitable Stengelese. In the following commentary, Stengel referred to the seventh inning of the seventh game of the 1952 World Series at Ebbets Field. The Yankees were ahead 4–2 and the Dodgers had the bases loaded with two outs. Martin made a diving catch near the mound that saved the Series for the Yankees.

"What about Martin, what if he didn't catch Robinson's popup in the World Series, who was gonna catch it, 'cause the wind was blowing, but he went and got it for the out, and three runs were coming around the bases, so he's not such a bad fellow like they make him out if he can do that for you."

As for Martin the manager, Don Baylor once said, "Playing for Yogi

Dave "Rags" Righetti,
All-Star starter and reliever
(National Baseball Hall
of Fame Library,
Cooperstown, New York)

is like playing for your father; playing for Billy is like playing for your father-in-law."

The Italian American players who went west with the Dodgers were Carl Furillo, Gino Cimoli (also born in San Francisco), and Joe Pignatano, plus a few cups of coffee. Johnny Antonelli went with the Giants. The first regularly scheduled major league game played west of the Rockies was the season opener on April 15, 1958 between the Dodgers and the Giants before more than 23,000 people in Seals Stadium in San Francisco. The Giants and Reuben Gomez shut out the Dodgers 8–0.

But big-time baseball certainly was not new on the West Coast. The Pacific Coast League, organized in 1903, had a long and colorful history of its own by 1958, and it continues today. In 1925 Tony Lazzeri, playing for the Salt Lake City Bees, hit sixty home runs in one season a full two years before Babe Ruth did. Joe DiMaggio began his professional career at seventeen with the San Francisco Seals in 1932. In his first full season with the club, he hit successfully in sixty-one straight games, eight years

Jason Giambi,
another Oakland youngster and
All-Time All-Star, now with the
New York Yankees
(National Baseball Hall of Fame
Library, Cooperstown, New York)

before completing "The Streak" for New York. The following year the Yankees gave the Seals five players and $25,000 for DiMaggio.

In 1951 Larry MacPhail, the great innovator, although no longer in baseball, proposed the addition of two leagues to the majors, one of them being the Pacific Coast League, an idea that had wide circulation prior to 1957. The San Diego Padres and Los Angeles Angels already existed under those names in the Pacific Coast League before expansion.

Since 1958 there have been a number of good players of Italian extraction who either got their start or made their mark with West Coast teams. Mike Piazza, who was drafted by the Dodgers in the sixty-second round as a favor to Tommy Lasorda, an old friend of Piazza's family, was Rookie of the Year in 1993 and caught for them until he was traded in 1998. Jason Giambi spent his first seven years in the major leagues with the Oakland A's, and Barry Zito still pitches for them. All three have been selected for the All-Time All–Italian American All-Star Team. But there are some others who would probably qualify.

Mike Scioscia spent his whole career behind the plate for the

Dodgers and was known for his ability to block home plate on defense and to hit home runs at crucial times on offense. Al Campanis said Scioscia was the best plate-blocking catcher he had ever seen.

In 1985, in a game against the Cardinals, Scioscia, 6′2″, 220 pounds, was knocked unconscious by Jack Clark, 6′3″, 205 pounds, while defending home plate but never let go of the ball. "It literally sounded like he was dying," Brian Harper, who was playing for St. Louis then, told the *New York Times.* "There was blood coming out of his nose. It was real ugly."

"I was knocked out by Clark so I can't say I remember that one." Scioscia added, "It's one of the hardest I've ever been hit."

During the 1988 postseason he hit two key home runs, one off Dwight Gooden in the National League Championship Series against the Mets, which tied the score of the fourth game, which the Dodgers went on to win in the twelfth. The other was a two-run homer against the Athletics, also in the twelfth, that tied that World Series game, which the Dodgers won with Kirk Gibson's fabled home run later in the inning. Mike Scioscia was the manager of the 2002 World Champion Anaheim Angels.

Jim Fregosi was one of the twenty-eight players selected by the Los Angeles Angels to be part of that newly formed expansion organization. The power-hitting shortstop played there for eleven years, was a member of the American League All-Star team six times, and was awarded a Gold Glove in 1967. He is one of the few players to hit for the cycle twice.

In December 1971 Fregosi was sent to the Mets in exchange for four players, one of them Nolan Ryan. That trade was the beginning of Ryan's ascent as a pitcher and Fregosi's descent as a player. Due to injuries and being switched to third base, in the eight seasons he spent with the Mets, Texas Rangers, and Pittsburgh Pirates, he never quite came up to his performance with the Angels. One day in 1977, as he was approaching the end of his playing career, someone referred to a play Fregosi had just made as a "routine ground ball."

"I just want you to know one thing," Fregosi declared. "When you get to be my age, there are no routine ground balls."

Fregosi retired in 1978 with a career .265 average, 706 RBIs, 1,726 hits, and 151 home runs. That same year he was named manager of the Angels, who still had Ryan on their pitching staff. The following year they won the division title for the first time. In 1980 Ryan became a free agent and went to the Houston Astros, and the Angels finished in sixth place. Fregosi was let go the following year and did not get another chance to manage until 1986, when he took over the Chicago White Sox from Tony La Russa. After two-plus uneventful seasons, he was released again and waited until 1991 before taking the helm of the Philadelphia Phillies.

The Phillies won ninety-seven games in 1993 and took the National League pennant but lost the World Series to the Toronto Blue Jays in six games. Fregosi managed the Phillies for three more years, but they never were able to regain their winning ways and he was released again.

In 1999 he was named manager of the Blue Jays. After his first home opener in Toronto's SkyDome, he compared that state-of-the-art stadium to some of the other ballparks he had worked in as a manager. "This is a beautiful place—quite a bit better than the dungeons of Veterans Stadium in Philadelphia," he said, and then added, "I also managed in [old] Comiskey Park, where the rats were bigger than some of my players."

The Blue Jays finished the 2000 season in third place and let him go. He once remarked that the best a manager can hope for is that "when you're fired you'll leave the team in better shape than when you were hired."

Sal Bando was the outspoken cocaptain of Charlie Finley's contentious Oakland A's. After losing a game in 1974, Bando publicly complained that his manager, Alvin Dark, "couldn't manage a meat market." And that was a year in which they won the World Series.

A slugging third baseman, Bando was with the A's for eleven seasons, beginning in Kansas City in 1966. But he is best remembered, as are all his teammates, for what he did during the glory years in Oakland—from 1971 to '75, when the A's won five straight division titles, and three straight World Series from 1972 to 1974.

In 1973, his best year, Bando batted .287, hit twenty-nine home runs, had ninety-eight RBIs, and led the league in doubles with thirty-two. In the second game of the playoffs that year he hit two home runs and was robbed of a third on a spectacular catch by Al Bumbry. His fielding percentage at third base was well above .900 for his entire career. He was elected an All-Star four times but always had to wait his turn to play, behind Brooks Robinson.

Ken Caminiti, another native Californian, played third base in Houston for most of his career but had four outstanding years, 1995–98, with the San Diego Padres after a blockbuster eleven-player trade with the Astros. In 1995 he became the first player to homer from both sides of the plate three times in a season.

He was voted the National League Most Valuable Player of 1996, the only one the Padres ever had, and helped them win two division titles and their second pennant, in 1998. A switch-hitter, he batted .326, hit forty home runs, and had 178 hits during his MVP season. His fielding percentage was .954 that year and he won his second of three Gold Gloves, the other two coming in '95 and '97. Clete Boyer (not a bad third baseman himself) once autographed a photo for Caminiti: "You're better than Graig Nettles, Brooks, and myself. You're the best third baseman I've ever seen."

The fascinating thing about Caminiti was that throughout his career, which lasted fifteen years, he played while trying to overcome an addiction to alcohol and painkillers, plus any number of physical injuries to his abdomen, thigh, shoulder, elbow, back, groin, and hamstrings.

John Montefusco, a right-hander with a good fastball, made a sensational debut with the Giants in September 1974 by pitching nine innings of relief in a 9–5 victory over the Dodgers and hitting a home run in his first major league at-bat. He finished his first full year with the Giants with a 15–9 record, 2.88 ERA, and 215 strikeouts. He was voted the National League Rookie of the Year. The following season he pitched a no-hitter against the Atlanta Braves, and was elected to the National League All-Star team. He finished that season with a 16–14 record and a 2.84 ERA.

But injuries slowed the Count of Montefusco and he never had another season like the first two. His high opinion of himself and his pitching ability earned him the nickname "The Mouth That Roared." In 1975 he boasted that he would shut out the Dodgers and he did, 1–0. That same year he predicted an identical fate for the Reds, and added that he would strike out Johnny Bench four times. The Reds scored seven runs in one-and-a-third innings off the Count, three of them coming off a Bench homer.

After a clubhouse altercation with Giants manager Dave Bristol, he was sent to the Braves for one year and then pitched with varying degrees of success over the next six years for the Padres and the Yankees.

While these players were making their contributions on the field, there were other sons of Italy working the dugouts as coaches and managers. Fregosi and Scioscia managed the Angels. Joe Altobelli ran the Giants in the late seventies. Billy Martin and Tony La Russa managed the A's in the eighties and nineties. And there were two others who had a hand in shaping West Coast ballclubs; one a great player and the other an outstanding manager: Joe DiMaggio and Tommy Lasorda.

The only other major league uniform Joe DiMaggio ever wore was that of the Oakland A's. In 1968, when Charles O. Finley moved the Kansas City A's to Oakland, he made DiMaggio executive vice president, public relations man, and coach.

The association of baseball's most respected entity with the game's most flamboyant was perceived as, and might have been, yet another Finley stunt to gain attention and fans. Joltin' Joe was a Bay Area boy after all, and Finley, who owned the Athletics for twenty years from 1960 to 1980, was known for his tricks. He was the man who pushed for the designated hitter and night games during the World Series—blessings or, as some see them, curses, that are still with us today. On the other hand, he wanted to color the ball orange and, when the team was in Kansas City, had a mechanical rabbit pop up next to home plate with a fresh supply of balls for the umpire, while sheep grazed outside the outfield fence. He also introduced the green-and-gold uniform with white shoes.

But DiMaggio put numerous restrictions on what he would and wouldn't do for the contentious owner, and they stuck. For instance he would not be required to work the baselines or make personal appearances if he didn't want to, and he insisted that his official duties be confined to the ballpark, thereby keeping his free time his own. However, he did have to wear that uniform, a far cry from pinstripes, and it didn't go unnoticed by the fans.

As vice-president one of the first things DiMaggio did was have the infield moved in order to make home plate visible to all the fans. Just prior to opening day in 1968, while walking around the Oakland-Alameda County Coliseum, DiMaggio noticed that certain seats in the upper decks did not have a view of home plate, so he had the team move the infield farther away from the stands. The move created the largest foul territory in the majors, which was a dream for pitchers and a nightmare for batters—but a full view for all the paying customers.

The Clipper helped a number of young players on the team who would go on to dominate the game in the first half of the seventies. Recognizing Reggie Jackson's hitting ability, DiMaggio spent an hour every day during batting practice teaching him how to make contact with the ball despite his feeling that hitting couldn't be taught. In an interview with Ira Berkow at the time he said, "You can't teach someone how to hit. He has to see a lot of pitching. You can teach an outfielder how to chase a fly ball, which base to throw to. You can teach a pitcher how to work a hitter. But you can't teach a hitter how to hit. If you could, I'd still be playing. It's the reflexes that count. You can show him little things like improving the stance though."

Joltin' Joe must have shown Mr. October a lot of little things. He is also credited with having corrected Sal Bando's batting stance, a tip that raised the third baseman's average from .147 in 1967 to .287 in 1973.

And it was DiMaggio who taught Joe Rudi how to turn his back to home plate when chasing long fly balls. That lesson resulted in one of the great catches in World Series history. In the second game of the 1972 series, with the A's ahead of the Cincinnati Reds 2–0 in the last inning,

Cincinnati had a man on base and Carl Menke hit a long fly ball to left field. Rudi turned his back to the plate and made a leaping, backhanded catch, keeping the tying run off base and gaining a 2–1 win for the A's, who eventually took the series.

Wanting more free time, DiMaggio quietly left the A's in 1969 and, except for helping out the Yankees during spring training and Old Timer's Day appearances, he never donned a uniform again. The A's went on to win the Western Division title from 1971 to 1975, plus the pennant and World Series from 1972 to 1974. Reggie Jackson was the most valuable player of the 1973 World Series.

But probably the best-known Italian name in western baseball has to be that of Tommy Lasorda, who managed the Dodgers for twenty years—one of those larger than life characters who attracted as much attention to himself as to his organization. In the clubhouse and the dugout he would shout language that Roger Kahn said "tends to electric blue." He also pitched batting practice every day and didn't like anyone hitting his curve ball. He maintained that the practice was good for his health. "You ever see a batting practice pitcher drop dead?" Lasorda once asked. "Men drop dead shoveling snow, but not pitching batting practice. That's why I pitch batting practice."

A master of self-promotion, he fed the sports press the things they crave the most: usable quotes and a colorful lifestyle with a heavy emphasis on his ethnicity. As a consequence, one reads that he so loved Italian food he had tortellini for breakfast and devoured linguine with clam sauce for dinner. He had a full wall of autographed Frank Sinatra photos in his office. One sports columnist actually wrote that if the Dodgers beat the A's in the 1988 World Series (which they did), Lasorda's ring should be "bigger than a plate of linguine."

None of the above indicates that he wasn't a good baseball man or manager. When he took over the Dodgers in 1976, seventeen players on the roster had played for him in the minor leagues. His teams went on to win two World Series, four National League pennants, and eight West Division titles. Under his watch the Dodgers won 1,599 games and pro-

Hall of Famer Tom Lasorda as a young lefthanded pitcher
(National Baseball Hall of Fame Library, Cooperstown, New York)

duced one Most Valuable Player, Kirk Gibson in 1988, and two Cy Young Award pitchers: Fernando Valenzuela in 1981 and Orel Hershiser in 1988. His teams also fielded nine Rookies of the Year: Rick Sutcliffe, 1979; Steve Howe, 1980; Fernando Valenzuela, 1981; Steve Sax, 1982; Eric Karros, 1992; Mike Piazza, 1993; Raul Mondesi, 1994; Hideo Nomo, 1995; and Todd Hollandsworth, 1996.

Lasorda's knowledge of the game seemed to be as sharp as his eye for talent. During a game in 1995, with the Dodgers and Pirates tied 10–10 in the eleventh inning, Lasorda cited an obscure rule even the umpires didn't seem to remember. With a man on third, Matt Webster swung at a pitch in the dirt that the Pirates' rookie catcher, Angelo Incarnacion, fielded with his mask. Lasorda immediately cited the rule that awards a runner two bases if a catcher uses his mask to touch a thrown ball. The umpires agreed and the winning run scored.

Thomas Charles Lasorda was born on September 22, 1927 in Norristown, Pennsylvania. He was a left-handed pitcher who had a major minor-league career and a really minor one in the majors.

He caught the eye of the Dodgers organization on June 1, 1948 when he struck out twenty-five batters (a since broken professional record) for the Schenectady Blue Jays of the class-C Canadian-American League in a game that lasted fifteen innings. He also drove in the winning run with a single. He went on to strike out fifteen and thirteen batters in his next two starts.

He was signed by the Dodgers and sent to their International League farm team in Montreal. He played there a total of nine years, compiling a 98–49 record, and helped them win the league championship five times.

Lasorda was called up to the Dodgers in 1954 and pitched in eight games during the two years he was with them, a total of thirteen innings. His most famous inning was his first start on May 5, 1955 against the St. Louis Cardinals at Ebbets Field. He walked the first batter, Wally Moon, and then proceeded to tie a major league record by throwing three wild pitches in the same inning. He threw the first to Bill Virdon, the next batter, and then two to Stan Musial batting third. He then had an injury added to the insult when he was spiked by Moon while covering home plate for Roy Campanella, who was chasing Lasorda's second wild pitch to Musial. Moon's score was the only run in that fateful inning, however, because Lasorda eventually struck out first Musial, then Rip Repulski, and forced the last batter into a groundout. But that was enough for Walter Alston, the Dodgers' manager; Lasorda went to the showers. He pitched a total of four innings for the Dodgers that season and amassed a 13.50 ERA before being sent down to make room for Sandy Koufax—another benchmark in Lasorda's career.

The Dodgers went on to win the World Series that season, and Lasorda went on to the Kansas City Athletics. Pitching for the A's in 1956, he appeared in eighteen games and was 0–4, which turned out to be his major league record. Lasorda once commented on his major league pitching career by saying, "Statistics are misleading. When Drysdale or Gibson pitched, for example, the other team never scored any runs, but when I pitch, they always scored runs."

Lasorda returned to Montreal in 1957 and completed his playing career in 1960. He became a Dodgers scout in 1961 and was a minor league manager in their organization from 1965 to 1972. His minor league teams won five pennants, finished second twice and third once. He moved up to the Dodgers as a coach until September 29, 1976, when he replaced Alston as manager.

His twenty-year stint as manager of the same team is the fourth longest, behind Alston, who ran the Dodgers for the twenty-three years before him, John McGraw's thirty-one with the New York Giants, and Connie Mack, who owned as well as managed the Philadelphia Athletics for fifty years.

Perhaps among his teams' finest hours were in the postseason of 1988, the year he won his one thousandth game. The Dodgers finished first in the West with a 94–67 record. They had to face the Mets in the

National League Championship Series. New York had beaten the Dodgers ten out of the eleven times they met during the regular season, and was bringing a 100–60 record to the series.

This was the Mets of Gary Carter, Lenny Dykstra, Keith Hernandez, Darryl Strawberry, and Mookie Wilson in the field, and Dwight Gooden, David Cone, and Ron Darling on the mound. The Dodgers had Kirk Gibson, Mike Marshall, Steve Sax, and Mike Scioscia, along with such starting pitchers as Tim Belcher, Tim Leary, and, especially, Orel Hershiser. Not a bad matchup, but if one listened to Lasorda it made David and Goliath look like even money.

Lasorda played the underdog role to the hilt, particularly after losing the first game at home. He told anyone who would listen how good the Mets were, how the Dodgers shouldn't even be there, and made sure his team heard every negative thing the Mets or anyone else said or wrote about them. It worked. The Dodgers got angry and took the series four out of seven, even after losing the opener at home and having their ace reliever, Jay Howell, suspended for three games when pine tar was discovered on his glove in game three.

Hershiser, who had broken the regular season consecutive-scoreless-innings record by pitching fifty-nine of them, one more than former Dodger Don Drysdale, shut out the Mets 6–0 in the last game. He was named the series' Most Valuable Player. But it had cost the Dodgers also. Kirk Gibson, their top home run hitter, hurt his knee during the series, making it unlikely that he could play in the World Series.

The hard-fought victory gave the Dodgers the opportunity to meet the Oakland A's in the second World Series to be played between two West Coast teams. (The first was in 1974, also between the A's and the Dodgers. The A's won). Oakland came into that series having won 104 regular season games, in addition to taking four straight from the Boston Red Sox in the American League Championship Series. Which meant they had had five days to rest while the Dodgers struggled to beat the Mets.

The Athletics featured Jose Canseco and Mark McGwire, the Bash

Brothers, who had hit forty-two and thirty-two home runs respectively, and had 124 and 99 RBIs apiece in the regular season. Then there was Dave Henderson, who hit .304 with 24 homers and 94 RBIs. The pitching staff had Dave Stewart, 21–12, Bob Welch, 17–9, Storm Davis, 17–9, and Curt Young, 11–8. Their chief reliever was Dennis Eckersley, who had 45 saves and a 2.35 ERA.

Lasorda, however, made the most of being up against one of the most formidable teams of all time. To hear him tell it, if he was the underdog against the Mets he was a mangy cur before the A's. In a piece that appeared in the *New York Times* on October 15, the first day of the series, he told Joseph Durso, "We shouldn't even be on the same field with the Athletics. The whole team scares me. We're a team nobody thought could win our division. A team nobody thought could beat the mighty Mets in the playoff. A team nobody thinks can beat the mighty Athletics in the World Series.

"Las Vegas told me we have no chance against a team that won 104 games and four more in the American League playoff. I don't even know if the 1927 Yankees won 108 games. [Editor's note: They were 110–44.] Now my poor little old team's got to play them in the World Series."

The story was headlined LASORDA SERVES PASTA WITH BALONEY because the night before the Series he had hosted a linguine dinner for the team and their families to celebrate the win over the Mets. You missed the pasta but got a good helping of the baloney.

If you're wondering why Lasorda felt the need to wring every last drop out of his hands, Steve Sax, their second baseman, summed it up in the same *Times* story. "Underdogs again? It's great. All the pressure is on them. As we showed against the Mets, our guys can play inspired. We're kind of a group of misfits taken from other clubs, guys who don't know what it means to lose. People keep expecting the Dodgers to buckle, but we didn't."

And inspired they were. The Dodgers took the World Series in five games. In the first game, Kirk Gibson came off the bench injured to pinch hit a game-ending, two-run homer with two out in the bottom of the ninth off Eckersley. Then Hershiser took over. In the second game he held the A's to three hits and got three himself in the Dodgers' 6–0 victory. Oakland did manage to win the third game when Mark McGwire hit a homer off Jay Howell in the bottom of the ninth. But that was it for the A's. Tim Belcher, aided by some Oakland errors, won the fourth game 4–3, and Hershiser held the A's to four hits in the fifth game with a 5–2 win and was named the series MVP.

That was to be the last World Series for Lasorda's teams. The Dodgers would win two more West Division titles: in 1994, the strike-shortened season, and 1995 when they lost the Championship Series to the Cincinnati Reds.

In June of 1996 Lasorda suffered a minor heart attack and decided to retire from managing. The Dodgers made him a vice president and gave him an office overlooking left field. He is most likely the last of the longtime managers. There were 185 managerial changes in the major leagues during his tenure, and even the Dodgers had changed managers four times by 2003.

But Lasorda didn't go quietly into the sunset. In 2000 he managed the United States baseball team in the Olympics held in Sydney, Australia. Under his guidance the U.S. won its first gold medal since its native game became an official Olympic sport in 1992, thereby adding red and white to Lasorda's Dodger blue.

After assuring the veterans committee that he would never manage again, Lasorda was elected to the Hall of Fame in 1997, and his number 2 was retired by the Dodgers that same year. Fitting tributes for the man whose blood runs Dodger blue and wants to join that big Dodger in the sky when his time comes. But one can't be too sure. Lasorda told the following story during his induction speech at Cooperstown:

> You've gotta win. And if you don't win, like many, you'll fall
> by the wayside. To tell you how bad I want to win: A few years ago,
> we were playing in Cincinnati. I got up Sunday morning and

went to church. Who came in and sat right next to me was the manager of the Cincinnati Reds, Johnny McNamara.

Now, I knew why he was in church, and he knew why I was there. At the conclusion of the mass, we walked out the center aisle together and I'm thinking, "Man, I've got to beat this guy today."

As we approached the front door, he said to me very quietly, "Wait for me outside, Tommy, I'll be right out."

I said, "OK, Johnny." But then I thought, "Where's he going? The mass is over."

I watched him and he went over to that side of the church, knelt down, and he lit a candle. Instead of me going out the door, I went over to that side of the church, and I went in front of the altar and waited. When he left, I went down and I blew that candle out! I knew one thing, he was not lighting that candle for a dead relative.

Throughout the game I kept hollering, "Hey, Mac, it ain't gonna work, pal. I blew it out!" We clobbered them that day, thirteen to two.

Last year Johnny Mac went to Rome and he sent me a card. And all that it said was, "Try blowing this candle out!"

Perhaps it is belaboring the obvious, but in many ways no one can hold a candle to Tommy Lasorda.

SAL MAGLIE IN PARADISE

Anthony Valerio

Every ball I throw has a purpose.
—Sal Maglie

Brooklyn, New York, 1950

By the ninth grade, I was already wearing eyeglasses, which is why I kept a close eye on the bespectacled Dom DiMaggio, who played in seven All-Star games, six with his great elder brother, Joe, and two, in 1950 and '51, with Sal Maglie. Bright and early my mother sent me out to the street. Geraniums flourished in our cement flower boxes that lasted generations. It was spring again.

The street was the first stage in earning fan allegiance. Fan allegiance was not a divine right or entirely hereditary. First I had to leave my sweat and blood on the street, then I could say: "The Brooklyn Dodgers played for Brooklyn's streets."

My father, nicknamed Lefty, and my uncle, nicknamed Slim, remembered their sandlot and semi-pro ball-playing days. The way their parents told stories about life years back in Italy, Lefty and Slim and their friends told stories about their youth in sport, especially baseball, in America. Baseball was a major tradition. Baseball's oral history connected the generations. Lefty was a slow-running long-ball hitter for the Red Devils; Slim, a scrappy, Eddie Stanky–type infielder for the Concords. The teams had clubhouses and held dances and went on outings. Lefty married Slim's sister. Slim and Zack, ace hurler for the Concords, remained friends for life. Zack and Romeo, who had played for the Brooklyn Juniors and was a guardian angel of our streets, continued their tradition in practical ways. Romeo coached the Falcons and taught us baseball's fundamentals. Sometimes we practiced on the New Utrecht high school field, a home run away from the West End El. The great baritone Robert Merrill, who sings the National Anthem in ballparks, had attended New Utrecht, Lefty told me. Zack was recreation director at Brooklyn State Hospital, and organized baseball games for the sacred.

Whoever owned the house or paid the rent, that's the TV channel you watched. In our house, the channel was set to the Brooklyn Dodgers games. The living room, with club chairs and hassocks and sofas, was a new kind of theater. Other teams came and went, but time unraveled on the Brooklyn Dodgers. Lefty and Slim had attended St. John's University. Rooting for the Brooklyn Dodgers was tantamount to rooting for St. John Himself.

In time the Brooklyn Dodgers players established themselves in their own right in my vision and in my heart.

One step remained before I could call myself a Brooklyn Dodgers fan.

◆　　◆　　◆

I took the West End line toward New York and got off at DeKalb Avenue. Up one flight of stairs, across and down, then I took another train one stop back toward Brooklyn. I bought my own ticket with monies earned from my seasonal business of car simonizing. Walking along the inclined ramp through the massive shadow cast by the stands above, I glanced up at the maze of supporting steel girders. You could hear the buzz from back in there. Suddenly a celestial light bathed me. Spread out before my wide-open eyes was a level, raked, dirt infield. Clean white bases. Perfect chalk foul lines. An outfield so green, the field, like a womb, was embraced by stands packed with fans. I was in Ebbets Field. I was in Paradise.

◆　◆　◆

If you placed a radio on top of the train tracks where the West End line crossed Bay Ridge Parkway, all of Bianca Gatusso's eight children and their families could have heard Red Barber's call of a Brooklyn Dodgers ballgame.

Though future Hall of Fame broadcaster Walter "Red" Barber was a Floridian and a Protestant, and spoke English with an accent, we forgave him and clasped him to our hearts, for Red Barber believed, and, as he said, broadcast the Brooklyn Dodgers games "with a Brooklyn heart."

Bianca Gattuso's family lived within walking distance of the revered matriarch, in the spirit of Italy's ancient Communes. Between doubleheaders, I ducked into my grandmother's house for milk and cookies.

She sat on her couch in the cool basement, knitting.

"Testa di cazzo," she muttered.

She was referring to her husband, Don Franco. Whatever the man had done to her had earned him this imprecation of the most scathing male organ sort.

Bianca Gattuso rocked back and forth, knitting.

"Testa di cazzo. . . ."

Don Franco had been a budding baritone and was a tailor now. Working with his straight tailor's pins in his lips, he hummed along to the great baritone arias that played in the background, including Figaro's tour de force, "Largo al Factotum," from Gioachino Rossini's *The Barber of Seville.*

Don Franco took his afternoon coffee out on the cool, airy front porch that looked out to the street. I had to pass him on my way into the kitchen. His abdomen and stomach were one large mound, held tightly in place by a thick black belt. He was as bald as a nine ball, and rivulets of capillaries coursed the base and sides of his mushroom nose. As a rule, we exchanged hello and goodbye. This particular afternoon, Don Franco turned toward me and opened wide his small beady eyes.

"MAHL-YEE!" He scowled at me.

I stopped, and my eyes and mouth opened wide in horror. Immediately, I knew that he was saying "Maglie" in southern Italian dialect, and that, somehow, Sal Maglie was hurting the Brooklyn Dodgers. But Don Franco was not a fan of any sort. His own son, Slim, had had to steal out of the house with his bat and glove because he was supposed to be studying to become a doctor, which he became anyway. Don Franco's blurting of Sal Maglie's name in my face while I was engaged in real life, hustling in from another hard day on the street, my glasses running with sweat, launched me topsy-turvy through time and space.

Mexico, 1946

Maglie pitched in 110-degree heat. After one month, twenty players were batting over .400 against him. In Puebla's high altitude and thinner air, his curveballs were hanging. He rode in the Puebla team's bouncing bus. Mexico's paved road network was just getting under way. Dante Alighieri wrote all but one and a half cantos of *The Divine Comedy* in exile from his hometown of Florence. Dante's pilgrim, himself, with his guide, Virgil, must journey through Hell and Purgatory in order to reach Paradise.

The ubiquitous Dolf Luque, Puebla's manager (who had known the great Mathewson) and Maglie's guide and mentor, worked with him on his fastball. He could show the curveball, but the fastball was his out pitch. Maglie began snapping the sharp curveball, instead of over the inside corner, over the outside corner, so that if the ball hung, batters couldn't get their power behind it. Also, Maglie noticed that the Mexican hitters didn't like sidearm pitching. He developed that delivery. Maglie won twenty games in the 1946 season, and he won twenty games in the 1947 season. Mexico's dream of a major leagues ended after two seasons, gate receipts and salaries plummeting. Maglie pitched another season of winter ball in Cuba. Then he joined the Max Lanier All-Stars in a barnstorming bus tour of the United States. Lanier pitched one day, Maglie the other. They played the outfield. The All-Stars won fifty-one out of fifty-one games. Once again, Commissioner Happy Chandler acted to preserve the major leagues' sanctity, eliminating ballparks that the All-Stars could play in, and teams against which they could play. Maglie pitched in freezing temperatures and biting winds and snow in Quebec's Provincial League. He returned to Niagara Falls and bought into a gas station–auto repair shop, and worked in the grease pit under cars and trucks.

An obscure Italian American ballplayer, Danny Gardella, sued the major leagues, challenging its reserve clause. The U.S. Court of Appeals reversed a lower court's decision, ruling in Gardella's favor. Max Lanier and Sal Maglie joined the suit. Fearing an adverse decision on the major leagues' reserve clause and free agency, which would wait two decades for Curt Flood, in 1949, Chandler reinstated the banned players.

An older player reported to the 1950 New York Giants' spring training camp in Phoenix, Arizona. "I had the funny feeling that they weren't counting on me. They were taking a look just because they owned me," Sal Maglie said at the end of the 1950 season.

Risen Star, 1950

Sal Maglie's name had infused into Brooklyn's air. Sal Maglie had become the source of great pride in an enemy Brooklyn Italian household, without a television set and with a *testa di cazzo*.

It could have been any one of Sal Maglie's outings during the month of August and the first weeks of September 1950. They all led to a game against the Pittsburgh Pirates on September 13.

The sky was overcast and a drizzle was falling at game time, but a capacity crowd filled the Polo Grounds, as if the sun was out. Sal Maglie was pitching for two records: consecutive shutouts and consecutive scoreless innings.

In an incredible streak of ten straight wins, Maglie's last four had been shutouts. One more and he'd tie the National League record, established by Doc White in 1904. During his tear, Maglie had pitched thirty-nine consecutive scoreless innings. That day, he was within reach of Carl Hubbell's 1933 National League record of forty-six-and-a-third consecutive scoreless innings.

The Pirates did not score in the first inning. In the top half of the second inning, Maglie backed up third base and caught rookie Gus Bell at the plate. A sigh of relief went up from the eleven-thousand-plus fans. Maglie took the mound in the seventh inning, leading 3–0. The drizzle turned to a downpour.

His spectacular run had begun in late July against the St. Louis Cardinals in Sportsman's Park. The Giants were coming off nine straight losses and were one game out of last place. It was then that Leo Durocher gave Sal Maglie the ball.

Maglie kept a book on hitters and conditions in the different stadiums. When he sat in the dugout talking to players and reporters, he kept one eye on the hitters. Sal Maglie's book on Stan "The Man" Musial: "Throw and pray."

Maglie threw Musial a curveball that Musial pulled for a home run over the right field wall, tying the score 4–4. It stayed that way into extra innings. Maglie was going all the way. The Giants went ahead on Eddie "The Brat" Stanky's infield hit. In the bottom half of the eleventh inning, catcher Joe Garagiola, who would go on to become a fine, popular broadcaster, bounced out for the second out. Eddie Kazak pinch hit for the pitcher. Coach Freddie Fitzsimmons came out to the mound. The fastball was suggested.

"I don't care if he eats curveballs for breakfast," Maglie told Fitzsimmons and Wes Westrum. "He's going to hit my best pitch."

After Maglie threw two curveballs for strikes, Westrum called for a third curveball. Maglie shook it off and threw a high inside fastball that sent Kazak down to the dirt. Again Westrum called for the curveball. Maglie threw another high inside fastball, brushing Kazak back. Finally, Wes Westrum got his way, and Kazak swung and missed and the ballgame was over.

Maglie's win halted the Giants' skid and gave his team a tremendous lift. They won their next six games. Maglie's single drove in the winning run against the Cincinnati Reds for the Giants' seventh straight win.

Future Hall-of-Famers Ralph Kiner and Stan Musial told Leo Durocher that Sal Maglie had the sharpest curveball and the best control in baseball. Durocher, who had begun the season with only two starters, Larry Jansen and Jim Hearn, installed Maglie in the starting rotation.

The Maglies moved from their small Manhattan hotel to an apartment on the Upper West Side.

"MAHL-YEE!"

◆　◆　◆

Sal Maglie's wife said, "He lets his beard grow before a game so he'll look fierce. I used to wonder what people were talking about when they said he scowled ferociously at batters. Then I stayed home one day and watched him on TV. I didn't know who he was."

But in the clubhouse before a Maglie start, Leo "The Lip" Durocher decided that he knew who Sal Maglie was. Durocher looked over at Maglie and said, "He looks like the guy at the third chair at the barbershop."

Sportswriter Jim McCully overheard and conflated, and in his columns for the New York *Daily News* began referring to Sal Maglie as "The Barber."

Maglie's high inside fastball came so close to the batter's face that it acted as a straight razor, "shaving" it. Sal Maglie's sharp-breaking curveball just nicked the corners of the plate for strikes, "shaving" it.

Leo Frank wrote that "The Barber" was a "derisive nickname, akin to 'Curly' for a bald-headed man. In baseball parlance," Frank continued, "a barber is a guy who talks the ear off a brass monkey. Maglie is a lone wolf who does not engage in card games or go to the movies on the road."

Sal Maglie was a barber in need of a shave. Even a close shave could not conceal Sal Maglie's tawny complexion. An older man, Sal Maglie's face was unlike the normal-age ballplayers' faces, clean-shaven, of soft, downy skin.

Our neighborhood barber, Tito, had three chairs in his shop. In chair number one, closest to the street, Tito gave the children their haircuts. A full-time barber worked at chair number two, mostly on the non-regular customers. Chair number three was kept empty, except before big holidays like Ascension Thursday, Thanksgiving, and Christmas, when Tito hired a part-time barber. The only other person who hung around the barbershop all day was Sam the Bookie, but Sam sat at his desk near the window, under the radio, taking down the scores and looking out for police cars. Sam wore his fedora back on his head and tossed me a smile from his toothless mouth. Tito was not without his mystery. He was a barber of a few broken English words, and was serious with the children, and wore eyeglasses and had piercing eyes, and, when Sam was in jail, men came in and slipped scraps of paper into Tito's hand. Another barber of that time held mysterious allure: Perry Como. Had Perry Como been so handsome and calm and sung so beautifully when he was a real barber? The barber was as popular an Italian American stereotype as the crooner and the gangster. Tito sharpened his straight razor on a leather strop hanging from the side of the chair. Towels steamed in a globe-shaped, metal-plated steamer with a small window that looked like a giant tabernacle. After sculpting the sideburns, Tito laid a steaming towel over your face, except for the nose. Suddenly everything went dark and moist and warm, like the womb, and we were as vulnerable as Mr. Albert Anastasia must have been, lying in the same position in *his* barber's chair.

After Maglie's fourth straight win against the Pittsburgh Pirates, the New York Giants climbed into fourth place. Then Maglie faced the Philadelphia Phillies, who were battling the Brooklyn Dodgers for the pennant. The Giants-Phillies feud began.

One of Maglie's high inside fastballs knocked the strong, hefty catcher, Andy Seminick, down to the dirt. In the meantime, Eddie Stanky was waving his arms from second base, distracting Seminick, but such behavior was expected from Stanky. The next day, after Maglie had shut out the Phillies for his fifth straight win, Andy Seminick bowled over Hank Thomson at third base, knocking him unconscious. Two innings later, Seminick slid into second base with his spikes high. Stanky pounced on him, and the benches cleared.

Eddie Stanky once said, "I would spike my mother if it meant scoring a run." What kind of a good Christian person would say such a thing? In the stultifying heat of August 11, Sal Maglie beat the Brooklyn Dodgers again, coasting to a 16–7 victory. Gil Hodges' home run in the eighth inning marked the last run any team would score against Maglie for the next month.

Maglie shut out the Cardinals, then the Pirates. The Giants climbed into fourth place. During the second game of the Labor Day double-header, the Phillies' pitcher Russ Meyers hit Maglie on the arm with a pitch. In turn, Monte Irvin knocked Andy Seminick, who was blocking home plate, head over heels, injuring Seminick's ankle. Sal Maglie responded by shutting out the Phils for his third straight shutout and ninth straight win. With his fourth consecutive shutout against the Brooklyn Dodgers, which was becoming routine, Maglie tied Grover Cleveland Alexander. At the same time, Maglie had pitched thirty-nine consecutive scoreless innings.

◆　　◆　　◆

Maglie stood in the downpour on the mound in the Polo Grounds. Gus Bell was the first Pirates batter in the top half of the seventh inning. Maglie was four outs away from tying Carl Hubbell's record.

Maglie got ahead in the count 2–0. Then he threw a low inside fastball, a pitch that he had gotten Bell out on all year, and Bell lofted a soft fly ball to right field. It hugged the foul line—and then nestled in the eighteen-inch screen in fair territory, 287.8 feet away from home plate, for a home run.

Later on, Gus Bell said that he was just trying to foul off the pitch.

Sal Maglie said, "The pitch was so far inside that it might've nicked him on the leg if he hadn't hit it."

Eddie Stanky came in from second base and dried off a new ball.

"Get this fuckin' game over with and let's get out of the rain," Stanky said.

Maglie got the next two batters, then the home-plate umpire called the game on account of the rain.

◆　◆　◆

After the Philadelphia Phillies lost to the New York Yankees in the World Series, a few of the Phillies players said that playing with a hobbled Andy Seminick had hurt their chances, and that Sal Maglie's near beaning of Seminick back on August 11 had begun a string of retaliations, culminating in Monte Irvin's crushing, injurious slide. Though Sal Maglie was known for his pinpoint control, the players pointed out, he had hit ten batters, second only to the Cincinnati Reds' Ewell Blackwell.

Sal Maglie was concentrating on his 1951 contract.

"I'm asking for twenty-thousand dollars. I think I had a good season," Maglie told reporters after the season ended.

After Maglie had snapped the Giants' nine-game losing streak, the team went on to win forty-nine of its next ninety-one games and finish the season in third place, five games out of first place. Maglie was unbeaten against the pennant-winning Philadelphia Phillies and the second-place Brooklyn Dodgers. His 18–4 record was the best winning percentage in the National League.

Horace Stoneham offered Maglie a contract. "I pitch for money," Sal Maglie said. "I've got maybe four more years left"—he would have eight—"to make up for the time I lost in Mexico." Then he smiled a bitter smile. "Of course, I'm getting from the Giants what I got in Cuba and Mexico five years ago, when nobody heard of me."

"MAHL-YEE!"

◆　◆　◆

During a recent talk at the University of Palermo, I mentioned that Palermo was my paternal grandfather's old hometown. In the four decades since Don Franco's passing, I discovered, he had progressed from a family member to an ancestor, and his characterization had changed. Allegiances, human foibles, even the love or lack of it between grandfather and grandson, had grown trite, fallen away. I thought about Don Franco's work. He did his tailoring on the dinette table and allowed me to sit beside him and watch. Now and then he pressed the straight pins in his lips, like a fish out of water attempting to breathe. A customer came, and Don Franco measured and fit the cloth of the customer's choosing, smoothing the shoulders and neck, pulling and cuffing the sleeves and pants. The double-edged chalk he used free-hand made sharp, precise lines, mapping out the cuts. He pinned, using the straight pins in his lips. Then, after the customer left, he cut the cloth with his large tailor's shears. Above the dinette table was a pitched skylight fortified with crosshatched chicken wire. The sun shined in, and you could also hear the rain. More of the outside filtered in through the windows all around that looked out to the backyard garden. Biting her tongue, all flushed and beautiful, Elena, Don Franco and Bianca's youngest, worked in her garden of pink and red roses. It was spring again.

The Little Miracle of Coogan's Bluff

Coogan's Bluff was the land site on 155th Street in the Bronx on which the Polo Grounds stood. The "Little Miracle" referred to the New York Giants' impossible but true comeback from thirteen-and-a-half games behind the Brooklyn Dodgers on August 11. Winning thirty-seven of the next forty-two games, ending the season in a dead heat with the Brooklyn Dodgers, the Giants won the sudden-death playoff game on Bobby Thomson's "Shot Heard Round the World."

The Giants performed a "little" miracle as opposed to a "major" one because, otherwise, winning a pennant would have been tantamount to multiplying fish and changing bread into wine. Baseball was just a game.

◆　　◆　　◆

The New York Giants began the 1951 season in horrendous fashion, losing eleven of their first twelve games, plunging them into the National League cellar, and Sal Maglie lost his first two starts. The Giants were picked for the second division. The Brooklyn Dodgers had gotten off to a flying start. I turned and looked at Tommy Ceravalo, the sole New York Giants fan in the family. Tommy owned the house, and we sat on his couch in his living room. He was smiling.

The Giants had begun the 1950 season in about the same way, and remember the enormous amount of ground the team had made up. The pennant was not exactly preordained in the Giants' favor, but the race was a toss-up.

Tommy was odd in other ways, too. He was very good friends with Tito the Barber and looked like he got a haircut every day. Tommy's thick, straight, black hair was always neat and shiny and parted perfectly, slightly left of center. He watched the Giants games in a white shirt, the sleeves rolled up, baring his tattooed forearms, and wearing the pants of his black silk suits.

Lefty, Slim, and Zack, and their wives, left Brooklyn for Saratoga Springs: walks in the country, the waters, then, in August, the Yearling Sales and the races. Lefty owned a few thoroughbreds. I was staying with his elder sister, Lucia, and Uncle Tommy.

Aunt Lucia wore eyeglasses, too, and had been named after Santa Lucia, who, in Domenico Beccafumi's visionary painting, which I saw the other day in Sienna, is depicted wearing a white dress, a crown of lights, and, in her hands, holds a small dish in which sit her eyes. In order not to see the calumnies inflicted upon her person—dragged by bulls, raked over hot coals—for vowing her virginity and distributing her family's wealth, Lucia had torn out her eyes. Years back, Don Pietro, Lucia's father, a wiry sheet-metal worker from Naples, told Tommy that the same thing was going to happen to his eyes if he did not find gainful employment. Which Tommy did. Lucia was a real angel, and Tommy loved her.

It was through Tommy Ceravalo that I first saw Sal Maglie pitch.

◆ ◆ ◆

Sal Maglie mesmerized me. I could not take my eyes from him. It was not so much the "special effects:" the scowl down at the batters, the stubble of a beard, the so-called five o'clock shadow. The Italian American performer Liberace played a gold piano, day and night his candelabra sat on his piano, and he wore jackets studded with colorful sequins. It was Sal Maglie's motion to home plate that I can still see. His stillness, his concentration while getting the sign—suddenly his body broke into long, low, swift, fierce, determined motion down toward home plate.

St. Sebastian is depicted with an arrow in his side. Every pitch that Sal Maglie threw to a Brooklyn Dodgers batter was an arrow into my heart.

◆ ◆ ◆

Jackie Robinson was my favorite player. Nobody broke from a base on a steal like Jackie Robinson: the instant acceleration, his legs churning close to the ground, his arms propelling his body forward and side to side; finally, the slide wide of the base, his winglike arms spread along the dirt, toe on the base. I longed to be pigeon-toed like Jackie Robinson. The night had come down into this one player's face and arms.

◆ ◆ ◆

"I was hated in Brooklyn," Sal Maglie said. "At Ebbets Field they booed me, yelled at me, and I loved it. The first time Campanella would come to bat I'd put the ball about two feet over his head. They'd get so damn angry that they'd try to kill me with home runs and they'd break their necks swinging at bad balls. They didn't get anything. I had their number."

Jackie Robinson sought to retaliate against Sal Maglie.

In the April 30 game at Ebbets Field, Sal Maglie took an 8–3 lead into the third inning. Jackie Robinson came up to bat for the second time. Normally Sal Maglie brushed batters back on a 2–2 count. But Jackie Robinson had hit a home run in the first inning. With the count 0–0, Maglie threw two consecutive high inside fastballs that sent Jackie Robinson jumping back. Robinson bunted the next pitch up the first base line. Maglie came over to field it, but the ball rolled foul. Jackie Robinson, however, kept running full speed and rammed Sal Maglie, knocking him back. Then Maglie went after Robinson. Of all people, Eddie Stanky ran in from second base to restrain his pitcher. The home plate umpire, Babe Pinelli, mask in hand, walked up the line to calm Robinson down, then the two of them returned to home plate.

Wes Westrum said to Robinson, "Sal wasn't trying to hit you. He was just trying to brush you back."

Jackie Robinson, an educated man, said, "That's too fine a distinction for me." Then he lined Maglie's next pitch for a single to center field.

After the game, which the Giants won, a reporter said to Sal Maglie, "Robinson believes you are trying to hit him."

The batting helmet had not as yet come into use, and, on April 16, 1920, Cleveland Indians shortstop Ray Chapman had died after being hit in the head by a side-armed fastball thrown by Carl Mays of the New York Yankees.

Sal Maglie reacted as if he had been criminalized again.

"That's almost like accusing a guy of attempted murder," Maglie said. "If I was really aiming at the guy, I wouldn't have missed." Then Sal Maglie dispelled any mystery surrounding his success. "Look, I pitch like this: throw 'em high inside and low outside. I got to figure that the guy is trying to beat my brains out. So I pitch him tight, he can't get set. Then when I come back with the breaking stuff on the outside, he really has to reach for it. That's the only way to pitch and win."

Tommy Ceravalo was smiling. That was baseball.

Sal Maglie was also accused of throwing spitballs. It was not humanly possible for a curveball like his to break so sharply. Maglie's illegal saliva was making his balls curve. Opposing managers sought to distract Maglie by asking the home plate umpire to examine the ball; so much so that, once, Maglie threw the ball back over the umpire's head, into the stands.

Steve O'Neill came back into Maglie's life in a supportive way. O'Neill, who had drafted Maglie for the Buffalo Bisons of the International League, went on to manage the Philadelphia Phillies. After being tossed from a game at the Polo Grounds, O'Neill watched the rest of it from the center field clubhouse. After his team lost to the Giants and Maglie, the Phillies batters, and coach Eddie Mayo, insisted that Maglie was throwing spitballs.

"Boys," O'Neill told them, "I've got to let you in on a secret. What you thought were spitballs were extra-special curveballs."

Sal Maglie was accused of throwing the illegal "cut" ball. Either Maglie himself or one of his infielders was nicking the horsehide with something sharp, and that's what was making his balls curve so.

Jackie Robinson spoke up in Sal Maglie's behalf: "You can't take anything away from Sal. I'm not going to accuse him of anything."

◆   ◆   ◆

Once again, as he had the previous season, Sal Maglie's win, this time against the Brooklyn Dodgers on April 30, reversed his team's fortunes. Maglie and Larry Jansen became a phenomenal one-two punch, mirror images, of one another's wins. Maglie won his third game; Jansen won his third game. Jansen won his twelfth game, Maglie won his twelfth game. At the same time, Leo Durocher made some interesting changes. He brought Whitey Lockman in from the outfield to first base, returned Monte Irvin to the outfield, and installed Bobby Thomson at third base. A good-natured kid from the Minneapolis farm team was brought up, Willie Mays, "The Say Hey Kid."

Maglie pointed to his three-hit shutout of the Philadelphia Phillies on May 22 as his best-pitched game of the season. The win pulled his team up to the .500 mark, and it was the first of his three wins against the previous year's pennant winners.

In his June 26 outing against the Brooklyn Dodgers, a three-hit shutout in Ebbets Field, Maglie threw a fastball behind Andy Pafko's neck. Pafko had hit three home runs against Maglie in one game the previous year, playing for the Chicago Cubs.

Sal Maglie was the winning pitcher in the All-Star game.

Larry Jansen and Sal Maglie won their thirteenth then their fourteenth then their fifteenth games. The Brooklyn Dodgers were still ahead by fifteen games.

On August 11, the New York Giants pulled within thirteen-and-a-half games of the Brooklyn Dodgers. The rest is the stuff of the Little Miracle of Coogan's Bluff.

Uncle Tommy did not bother to witness it. About the same thing had happened in mid-August of the previous season. Gil Hodges had hit a home run during a Dodgers rout, then Sal Maglie didn't give up another run for a month, and the Giants won seventy percent of their remaining games.

The night before the sudden-death playoff game, Sal Maglie and his family and a few friends from Niagara Falls went out to dinner. The elevator operator at the Henry Hudson Hotel told a reporter, "We got twenty Giants, the Galway Curling team, the Meath football team, and the American League umpires staying here. Sal is the nicest guy of all."

I watched the sudden-death playoff game alone, from Uncle Tommy's couch. He was in New York, working. Every day at lunch he called Lucia from work.

Don Newcombe (20–9 on the year, 5–2 against the Giants) and Sal Maglie (26–6 on the year, 5–1 against the Dodgers) began the game.

◆ ◆ ◆

My father told me at least two memorable things: Ted Williams had better-than-perfect 20/15 vision, and Leo Durocher was a high-stakes poker player and was married to a beautiful actress, Lorraine Day. Then I spent the next fifty years attempting to reconcile Leo Durocher's gleeful slap of

Bobby Thomson's backside as he jumped for joy to home plate with the pennant-winning run, with Leo Durocher's high style of living and his marriage to a most beautiful woman.

When Ralph Branca walked off the mound with his head bowed, I loved him.

I got up and shut off the television. I looked toward the kitchen. Aunt Lucia, (wearing eyeglasses with opaque frames and a long, white cotton dress) was standing at a small table on which sat her telephone. I glanced down at the ground. I had aged. I felt and saw a silent, vast, inner world. Grave disappointment, loss was possible there, and born was the love of the game of baseball for the game.

That night, Bobby Thomson appeared on the Perry Como show.

◆   ◆   ◆

My father picked me up. As we began to walk home, he looked up, and my eyes followed his gaze. The sky was filled with stars. You know how the human eye is really seeing the light of stars that shone a long, long time ago. Lefty said, "I like to think that those stars are shining now."

Extra Inning

Next-door neighbor Teddy the Oil Man came out of his unlocked screen door, looked out at our corner, and smiled.

"This is God's Country," he said.

Our neighbors down on the street looked about the same, their skin the color of Italian bread, the crust, and Teddy's oil had kept us warm through the winter months, and his odd, thin, beautiful wife with reddish hair and a lilting voice had come up behind the door to smile and wave Teddy on his way to work. Brooklyn was God's country for one other reason—Sal Maglie had come to the Brooklyn Dodgers.

The angels sing hosannas in Heaven all the time.

In 1955 the Cleveland Indians picked Maglie up on waivers from the New York Giants. The year before, the Giants had traded its miracu-

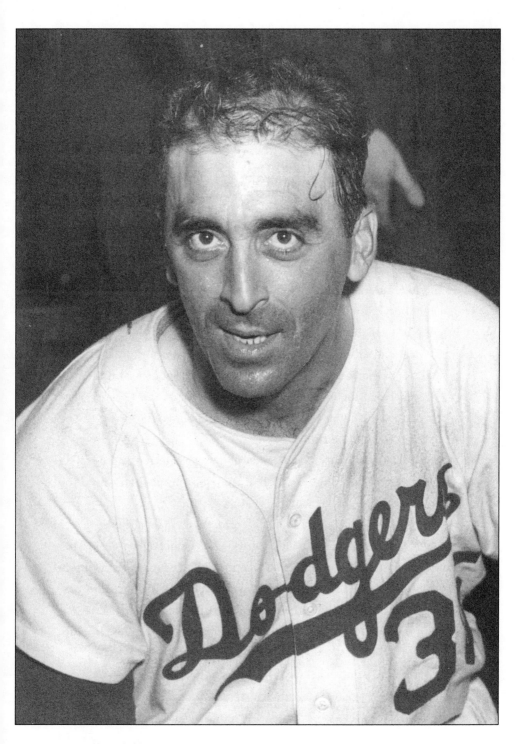

Sal Maglie's trade to the Brooklyn Dodgers turned Brooklyn's hatred to love.
(National Baseball Hall of Fame Library, Cooperstown, New York)

lous hero, Bobby Thomson, to the Milwaukee Braves for a young, talented left-handed Italian American pitcher, Johnny Antonelli. That was baseball. In 1956 the Dodgers purchased Maglie from the Indians for a pittance. He was thirty-nine years old, had won ninety-five games and lost forty-four, and felt he could still pitch.

When he started out in baseball, Maglie had three goals: win 20 games, pitch a no-hitter, and win a World Series game. He accomplished the first by winning 23 games in 1951 with the Giants. On the way to winning thirteen more games in the Dodgers' 1956 pennant-winning season, Maglie pitched a no-hitter in September against the Phillies, thus achieving his second goal. He finished the season with a record of 13–5. His 7.26 hits allowed per nine innings was best in the majors. He was second in the voting for National League Most Valuable Player and second in the voting for the Cy Young Award. The Baseball Writers' Association voted Maglie the Comeback Player of the Year.

Maglie was the last player to wear all three New York franchise jerseys, those of the New York Giants, the Brooklyn Dodgers, and the New York Yankees. In the end, he unified all New York baseball fans. A few other players, including Tony Lazzeri, who had played for the three New York teams were in the Hall of Fame.

Bill Madden writes: "Sal Maglie will never be elected to the Hall of Fame. Unless, that is, there's a Hall of Fame just for pitchers whom you wanted to have the ball in a game you had to win."

For the first game of the 1956 World Series against the New York Yankees, Dodgers manager Walter Alston, with whom I once rode in a bus down Flatbush Avenue, gave Sal Maglie the ball. He beat Whitey Ford in a 6–3 game. President Dwight D. Eisenhower phoned Maglie to congratulate him. According to Maglie himself, the fifth game of that Series was "one of the greatest games of my life." He allowed two runs and five hits, and the only well-hit ball was Mickey Mantle's home run to right field. But Maglie lost the game. That day, Don Larsen was perfect. That was baseball.

Sal Maglie's days ended in his hometown of Niagara Falls, New York, surrounded by family and friends. He was one of the great curveball pitchers and clutch performers in baseball history. Just to mention another little miracle, a bit of magic: Salvatore, son of Maria and Giuiseppe, pitched 1,723 innings and hit only forty-four batters.

When he had first walked into the Brooklyn Dodgers clubhouse in Paradise as a team member, a few other players were there. Maglie had beaten the Dodgers on twenty-three occasions, and had wrecked my childhood.

Dodger captain Harold "Pee Wee" Reese said, "Leo Durocher going to the Giants from Brooklyn in 1948 was about the most unbelievable thing that happened in my career. But Sal coming over to us in 1956 was hard to believe. He spent a lifetime brushing us back."

Carl Furillo was in the clubhouse. The nature of the Reading Rifle and the Barber's exchange, and their civil war, appears in George Vecsey's essay in this volume.

CONTRIBUTORS

LAWRENCE BALDASSARO *is a native of Chicopee, Massachusetts, home of the A.G. Spalding plant that manufactured major league baseballs until 1973. A professor of Italian and director of the University Honors Program at the University of Wisconsin–Milwaukee, he is coeditor of* The American Game: Baseball and Ethnicity *(2002), and editor of* The Ted Williams Reader *(1991) and* Ted Williams: Reflections on a Splendid Life *(2003).*

IRA BERKOW *has written sports and features for* The New York Times *for more than twenty years. He has been a finalist for the Pulitzer Prize for Distinguished Commentary and in 2000 shared the Pulitzer Prize for National Reporting. Among his books are* The Minority Quarterback; To the Hoop; Pitchers Do Get Lonely; Red: A Biography of Red Smith; *and* Maxwell Street: Survival in a Bazaar.

LARRY FREUNDLICH *has had a long career as an editor and book publisher. He is the founder of the New York publishing and media consulting firm Freundlich Communications. He is the author of the international bestseller* Blue Dog *with Cajun artist George Rodrigue, and* A Life Well Spent: A Biography of the Restaurateur Jerome Brody. *He is the coauthor with Pia Mellody of* The Intimacy Factor.

A. BARTLETT GIAMATTI *had been Sterling Professor of Italian and Renaissance studies at Yale, president of Yale, president of the National League, and at his death in 1989, commissioner of baseball. Among his several books is* Take Time for Paradise.

DONALD HONIG *is one of baseball's most renowned historians and has written a number of nonfiction bestsellers on the game, including* The Image of Their Greatness *with Lawrence Ritter and the classic* Baseball When the Grass Was Real.

ROBERT LEUCI *was a narcotics detective in New York City for more than twenty years. He was the subject of the book and movie* Prince of the City. *He is the author of several books, including* Fence Jumpers, Double Edge, *and* The Snitch.

WILFRID SHEED *is a critic, novelist, and sportswriter whose books* Baseball and Lesser Sports *and* My Life as a Fan *were nominated for the National Book Award, as were his novels* Office Politics, People Will Always Be Kind, *and* Max Jamison. *He was the recipient of the Book Critics Circle award for his* Essays in Criticism.

ANTHONY VALERIO *is the author of five books, including* Bart: A Life of A. Bartlett Giamatti. *His most recent book is* Anita Garibaldi: A Biography.

JOSEPH J. VECCHIONE *retired from* The New York Times *as a senior editor in 2001 having worked there for forty-one years. In 1978 he became the first editor of "SportsMonday," then a separate weekly section. He was made sports editor in 1980 and was in charge of the entire sports staff until 1990. Vecchione compiled and edited* The New York Times Book of Sports Legends, *a collection of profiles of some of the greatest athletes of the twentieth century, and coauthored, with David W. Dunlap,* Glory in Gotham: Manhattan's Houses of Worship.

GEORGE VECSEY *is a sports columnist with* The New York Times *and author of over a dozen books, including* Coal Miner's Daughter *and* Martina. *Although profoundly sad that he has no Italian ancestry, he has tried to compensate by reading Italian papers regularly, following Italian soccer, and visiting Italy whenever possible. He was a Brooklyn Dodgers fan as a child and has never gotten over their departure. He lives in Port Washington, Long Island, with his wife, Marianne, an artist. They have three children, who are all involved in journalism.*

EDITOR'S NOTE

We can only hope that we have identified all the major leaguers with at least one Italian or Italian American parent. We invite our readers to alert us to any errors and omissions to our roster by writing to the editor, Larry Freundlich, care of Ballantine Books or by e-mail directly to Freundlich at *lsf246@rcn.com*. We will make the appropriate corrections in subsequent editions of *Reaching for the Stars*. Acknowledgment is made to the National Italian American Sports Museum in Chicago, Illinois, for making available its list of all Italian American major leaguers through 2001. This list represents a considerable work of research, but it is still a work in progress, and, inevitably, some errors and omissions exist, which we intend to correct in future printings of *Reaching for the Stars*. Two omissions that have been discovered too late for inclusion in this printing are the names of Cookie Lavagetto and Jerry Casale, to whose fans we apologize. Lavagetto is a Brooklyn Dodger folk hero, celebrated in the pages of this book, and Jerry Casale, who spent the majority of his five-year career as a pitcher with Boston of the American League, compiled a lifetime win-lost record of 17–24. He is active today as the proprietor of the celebrated Pino's Italian restaurant in New York City.

Italian Americans and the Hall of Fame

	Elected
Yogi Berra	1972
Roy Campanella	1969
Ernie Lombardi	1986
Tony Lazzeri	1991
Phil Rizzuto	1994
Joe DiMaggio	1955
Tommy Lasorda	1997

Broadcasters (Ford Frick Award)

Harry Caray	1989
Joe Garagiola	1991

Writers (J. G. Taylor Spink Award)

Bob Addie	1981
Joseph Durso	1995

Retired Numbers

Jim Fregosi	11	Anaheim Angels
Yogi Berra	8	New York Yankees
Joe DiMaggio	5	New York Yankees
Billy Martin	1	New York Yankees
Phil Rizzuto	10	New York Yankees
Roy Campanella	39	Los Angeles Dodgers
Tom Lasorda	2	Los Angeles Dodgers

Italian American
Records of Achievement

NATIONAL LEAGUE

Rookie of the Year

John Montefusco	1975
Steve Sax	1982
Mike Piazza	1993

MVP

Phil Cavarretta	1945
Roy Campanella	1951
Roy Campanella	1953
Roy Campanella	1955
Joe Torre	1971
Ken Caminiti	1996

Manager of the Year

Tom Lasorda	1983
Tom Lasorda	1988

Home Run Leader

Dolph Camilli	34	1941

AMERICAN LEAGUE

Rookie of the Year

John Castino	1979
Dave Righetti	1981

MVP

Joe DiMaggio	1939
Joe DiMaggio	1941
Joe DiMaggio	1947
Phil Rizzuto	1950
Yogi Berra	1951
Yogi Berra	1954
Yogi Berra	1955
Jason Giambi	2000

Manager of the Year

Sam Mele	1965
Billy Martin	1981
Tony LaRussa	1983
Tony LaRussa	1988
Tony LaRussa	1992
Joe Torre	1996
Joe Torre	1998
Joe Torre	2000

Cy Young Award

Frank Viola	1988

Home Run Leader

Joe DiMaggio	46	1937
Joe DiMaggio	39	1948
Rocky Colavito	42	1959
Tony Conigliaro	32	1965

NATIONAL LEAGUE

Winningest Pitcher

1950	Sal Maglie, New York	18–4	.818
1954	Johnny Antonelli, New York	21–7	.750
1960	Ernie Brogli, St. Louis	21–9	.700

Batting Average Leaders

1938	Ernie Lombardi, Cincinnati	.342
1942	Ernie Lombardi, Boston	.339
1945	Phil Cavarretta, Chicago	.355
1953	Carl Furillo, Brooklyn	.344
1971	Joe Torre, St. Louis	.363

Runs Batted in Leaders

1941	Dolph Camilli, Brooklyn	120
1953	Roy Campanella, Brooklyn	142
1971	Joe Torre, St. Louis	137

Stolen Bases

1935	Augie Galan, Chicago	22

All-Time Saves

Dave Righetti	252
John Franco	420+ still pitching

AMERICAN LEAGUE

Winningest Pitcher

1950	Vic Raschi, New York	21–8	.724
1988	Frank Viola, Minnesota	24–7	.774

Hitting Streaks

1941	Joe DiMaggio, New York	Gm 56
1949	Dom DiMaggio, Boston	Gm 34

Four Home Runs in One Game

Rocky Colavito, Cleveland 6/10/59	Inn 9

Runs Batted in Leader

1941	Joe DiMaggio, New York	125
1948	Joe DiMaggio, New York	155
1965	Rocky Colavito, Cleveland	108

Stolen Bases

1938	Frank Crosetti, New York	27
1950	Dom DiMaggio, Boston	15

Italian American Players Season by Season

PLAYER STATISTICS KEY

g = games

ab = at bats

r = runs

h = hits

2b = doubles

3b = triples

hr = home runs

rbi = runs batted in

bb = bases on balls

so = strike outs

avg = batting average

slug = slugs (total bases divided by at bats)

sb = stolen bases

FIRST	LAST	YEAR	TEAM	LEAGUE	G	AB	R	H	2B	3B	HR	RBI	BB	SO	AVG	SLUG	SB
ED	ABBATICCHIO	1897	Philadelphia Phillies	NL	3	10	0	3	0	0	0	0	1		.300	.300	0
ED	ABBATICCHIO	1898	Philadelphia Phillies	NL	25	92	9	21	4	0	0	14	7		.228	.272	4
ED	ABBATICCHIO	1903	Boston Beaneaters	NL	136	489	61	111	18	5	1	46	52		.227	.290	23
ED	ABBATICCHIO	1904	Boston Beaneaters	NL	154	579	76	148	18	10	3	54	40		.256	.337	24
ED	ABBATICCHIO	1905	Boston Beaneaters	NL	153	610	70	170	25	12	3	41	35		.279	.374	30
ED	ABBATICCHIO	1907	Pittsburgh Pirates	NL	147	496	63	130	14	7	2	82	65		.262	.331	35
ED	ABBATICCHIO	1908	Pittsburgh Pirates	NL	146	500	43	125	16	7	1	61	58		.250	.316	22
ED	ABBATICCHIO	1909	Pittsburgh Pirates	NL	36	87	13	20	0	0	0	16	19		.230	.264	2
ED	ABBATICCHIO	1910	Boston Beaneaters	NL	52	178	20	44	4	2	1	10	12	16	.247	.292	2
ED	ABBATICCHIO	1910	Pittsburgh Pirates	NL	3	3	0	0	0	0	0	0	0	0	.000		0
JIM	ADDUCI	1983	St. Louis Cardinals	NL	10	20	0	1	0	0	0	0	1	6	.050	.050	0
JIM	ADDUCI	1986	Milwaukee Brewers	AL	3	11	2	1	1	1	0	0	0	2	.091		0
JIM	ADDUCI	1988	Milwaukee Brewers	AL	44	94	8	25	6	1	1	15	1	15	.266	.383	0
JIM	ADDUCI	1989	Philadelphia Phillies	NL	13	19	4	7	1	0	0	2	0	4	.368	.421	0
BOB	ALLIETTA	1975	California Angels	AL	21	45	4	8	3	0	1	2	0	6	.178	.267	0
JOE	ALTOBELLI	1955	Cleveland Indians	AL	42	75	8	15	3	0	2	5	5	14	.200	.320	0
JOE	ALTOBELLI	1957	Cleveland Indians	AL	83	87	9	18	3	0	0	9	5	14	.207	.287	3
JOE	ALTOBELLI	1961	Minnesota Twins	AL	41	95	10	21	2	1	3	14	13	14	.221	.358	0
JOEY	AMALFITANO	1954	New York Giants	NL	9	5	2	0	0	1	0	0	0	4	.000		0
JOEY	AMALFITANO	1955	New York Giants	NL	36	22	8	5	1	1	0	2	2	2	.227	.364	2
JOEY	AMALFITANO	1960	San Francisco Giants	NL	106	328	47	91	15	3	1	27	26	31	.277	.351	2
JOEY	AMALFITANO	1961	San Francisco Giants	NL	109	384	64	98	11	4	2	23	44	59	.255	.320	7
JOEY	AMALFITANO	1962	Houston Colt .45s	NL	117	380	44	90	12	5	1	27	45	43	.237	.303	4
JOEY	AMALFITANO	1963	San Francisco Giants	NL	54	137	11	24	3	3	0	7	12	18	.175	.219	2
JOEY	AMALFITANO	1964	Chicago Cubs	NL	100	324	51	78	19	6	4	27	40	42	.241	.373	2
JOEY	AMALFITANO	1965	Chicago Cubs	NL	67	96	13	26	4	0	0	8	12	14	.271	.312	2
JOEY	AMALFITANO	1966	Chicago Cubs	NL	41	38	8	6	2	0	0	3	4	10	.158	.211	0
JOEY	AMALFITANO	1967	Chicago Cubs	NL	4	1	0	0	0	0	0	0	0		.000		0
JOHN	ANTONELLI	1944	St. Louis Cardinals	NL	8	21	0	4	1	0	0	1	0	4	.190	.238	0
JOHN	ANTONELLI	1945	Philadelphia Phillies	NL	125	504	50	129	27	2	1	28	24	24	.256	.323	1
JOHN	ANTONELLI	1945	St. Louis Cardinals	NL	2	3	0	0	0	0	0	0	0	1	.000		0
BILL	ANTONELLO	1953	Brooklyn Dodgers	NL	40	43	9	7	1	1	0	4	2	11	.163	.302	0
KEN	ASPROMONTE	1957	Boston Red Sox	AL	24	78	9	21	5	0	0	4	17	10	.269	.333	0
KEN	ASPROMONTE	1958	Boston Red Sox	AL	6	16	0	2	0	0	0	0	3		.125	.125	0
KEN	ASPROMONTE	1958	Washington Senators	AL	92	253	15	57	9	1	5	27	25	28	.225	.328	1

FIRST	LAST	YEAR	TEAM	LEAGUE	G	AB	R	H	2B	3B	HR	RBI	BB	SO	AVG	SLUG	SB
KEN	ASPROMONTE	1959	Washington Senators	AL	70	225	31	55	12	0	2	14	26	39	.244	.324	2
KEN	ASPROMONTE	1960	Cleveland Indians	AL	117	459	65	133	20	1	10	48	53	32	.290	.403	4
KEN	ASPROMONTE	1960	Washington Senators	AL	4	3	0	0	0	0	0	0	0	1	.000		0
KEN	ASPROMONTE	1961	Cleveland Indians	AL	22	70	5	16	6	1	0	5	6	3	.229	.343	0
KEN	ASPROMONTE	1961	Los Angeles Angels	AL	66	238	29	53	10	0	2	14	33	21	.223	.290	0
KEN	ASPROMONTE	1962	Cleveland Indians	AL	20	28	4	4	2	0	0	1	6	5	.143	.214	0
KEN	ASPROMONTE	1962	Milwaukee Braves	NL	34	79	11	23	2	0	0	7	6	5	.291	.316	0
KEN	ASPROMONTE	1963	Chicago Cubs	NL	20	34	2	5	3	0	0	4	4	4	.147	.235	0
BOB	ASPROMONTE	1956	Brooklyn Dodgers	NL	1	1	0	0	0	0	0	0	0	1	.000		0
BOB	ASPROMONTE	1960	Los Angeles Dodgers	NL	21	55	1	10	1	0	1	6	0	6	.182	.255	1
BOB	ASPROMONTE	1961	Los Angeles Dodgers	NL	47	58	7	14	3	0	0	2	4	12	.241	.293	1
BOB	ASPROMONTE	1962	Houston Colt .45s	NL	149	534	59	142	18	4	11	59	46	54	.266	.376	4
BOB	ASPROMONTE	1963	Houston Colt .45s	NL	136	468	42	100	9	5	8	49	40	57	.214	.306	3
BOB	ASPROMONTE	1964	Houston Colt .45s	NL	157	553	51	155	20	3	12	69	35	54	.280	.392	6
BOB	ASPROMONTE	1965	Houston Colt .45s	NL	152	578	53	152	15	2	5	52	38	54	.263	.322	2
BOB	ASPROMONTE	1966	Houston Astros	NL	152	560	55	141	16	3	8	52	35	63	.252	.334	2
BOB	ASPROMONTE	1967	Houston Astros	NL	137	486	51	143	24	3	6	58	45	44	.294	.401	2
BOB	ASPROMONTE	1968	Houston Astros	NL	124	409	25	92	9	5	1	46	35	57	.225	.264	1
BOB	ASPROMONTE	1969	Atlanta Braves	NL	82	198	16	50	8	2	3	24	13	19	.253	.348	0
BOB	ASPROMONTE	1970	Atlanta Braves	NL	62	127	5	27	3	0	3	7	13	13	.213	.236	0
BOB	ASPROMONTE	1971	New York Mets	NL	104	342	21	77	9	1	5	33	29	25	.225	.301	1
RICH	AURILIA	1995	San Francisco Giants	NL	9	19	4	9	3	0	2	4	1	2	.474	.947	1
RICH	AURILIA	1996	San Francisco Giants	NL	105	318	27	76	7	1	3	26	25	52	.239	.296	4
RICH	AURILIA	1997	San Francisco Giants	NL	46	102	16	28	8	0	1	19	8	15	.275	.500	1
RICH	AURILIA	1998	San Francisco Giants	NL	122	413	54	110	27	2	9	49	31	62	.266	.407	2
RICH	AURILIA	1999	San Francisco Giants	NL	152	558	68	157	23	1	22	80	43	71	.281	.444	3
RICH	AURILIA	2000	San Francisco Giants	NL	141	509	67	138	24	2	20	79	54	90	.271	.444	1
RICH	AURILIA	2001	San Francisco Giants	NL	156	636	114	206	37	5	37	97	47	83	.324	.572	1
STEVE	BALBONI	1981	New York Yankees	AL	4	7	2	2	1	0	0	2	1		.286		0
STEVE	BALBONI	1982	New York Yankees	AL	33	107	8	20	2	1	2	4	6	34	.187	.280	0
STEVE	BALBONI	1983	New York Yankees	AL	32	86	8	20	2	0	5	17	8	23	.233	.450	0
STEVE	BALBONI	1984	Kansas City Royals	AL	126	438	58	107	23	2	28	77	45	139	.244	.498	1
STEVE	BALBONI	1985	Kansas City Royals	AL	160	600	74	146	28	2	36	88	52	166	.243	.477	1
STEVE	BALBONI	1986	Kansas City Royals	AL	138	512	54	117	25	1	29	88	43	146	.229	.451	0
STEVE	BALBONI	1987	Kansas City Royals	AL	121	386	44	80	11	1	24	60	34	97	.207	.427	0

FIRST	LAST	YEAR	TEAM	LEAGUE	G	AB	R	H	2B	3B	HR	RBI	BB	SO	AVG	SLUG	SB
STEVE	BALBONI	1988	Kansas City Royals	AL	21	63	2	9	2	1	2	5	1	20	.143	.270	0
STEVE	BALBONI	1988	Seattle Mariners	AL	97	350	44	88	15	1	21	61	23	67	.251	.480	0
STEVE	BALBONI	1989	New York Yankees	AL	110	300	33	71	12	2	17	59	25	67	.237	.460	0
STEVE	BALBONI	1990	New York Yankees	AL	116	266	24	51	6	0	17	34	35	91	.192	.406	0
STEVE	BALBONI	1993	Texas Rangers	AL	2	5	0	3	0	0	0	0	0	2	.600	.600	0
MIKE	BALENTI	1911	Cincinnati Reds	NL	8	8	2	2	0	0	0	0	0	1	.250	.250	0
MIKE	BALENTI	1913	St. Louis Browns	AL	70	211	17	38	2	4	0	11	6	32	.180	.227	3
CHRIS	BANDO	1981	Cleveland Indians	AL	21	47	3	10	3	0	0	6	2	2	.213	.277	3
CHRIS	BANDO	1982	Cleveland Indians	AL	66	184	13	39	6	1	3	16	24	30	.212	.304	0
CHRIS	BANDO	1983	Cleveland Indians	AL	48	121	15	31	3	0	4	15	15	19	.256	.380	0
CHRIS	BANDO	1984	Cleveland Indians	AL	75	220	38	64	11	0	12	41	33	35	.291	.505	1
CHRIS	BANDO	1985	Cleveland Indians	AL	73	173	11	24	4	1	0	13	22	21	.139	.173	0
CHRIS	BANDO	1986	Cleveland Indians	AL	92	254	28	68	9	0	2	26	22	49	.268	.327	0
CHRIS	BANDO	1987	Cleveland Indians	AL	89	211	20	46	9	0	5	16	12	28	.218	.332	0
CHRIS	BANDO	1988	Cleveland Indians	AL	32	72	6	9	1	0	0	8	8	12	.125	.181	0
CHRIS	BANDO	1988	Detroit Tigers	AL	1	0	0	0	0	0	0	0	0	0			0
CHRIS	BANDO	1989	Oakland Athletics	AL	1	2	0	1	0	0	0	1	0	1	.500	.500	0
SAL	BANDO	1966	Kansas City Athletics	AL	11	24	3	7	1	0	0	1	2	3	.292	.417	0
SAL	BANDO	1967	Kansas City Athletics	AL	47	130	11	25	4	2	0	6	16	24	.192	.246	1
SAL	BANDO	1968	Oakland Athletics	AL	162	605	67	152	25	5	9	67	51	78	.251	.354	13
SAL	BANDO	1969	Oakland Athletics	AL	162	609	106	171	25	3	31	113	111	82	.281	.484	1
SAL	BANDO	1970	Oakland Athletics	AL	155	502	93	132	20	2	20	75	118	88	.263	.430	6
SAL	BANDO	1971	Oakland Athletics	AL	153	538	75	146	23	1	24	94	86	55	.271	.452	3
SAL	BANDO	1972	Oakland Athletics	AL	152	535	64	126	20	3	15	77	78	55	.236	.368	3
SAL	BANDO	1973	Oakland Athletics	AL	162	592	97	170	32	3	29	98	82	84	.287	.498	4
SAL	BANDO	1974	Oakland Athletics	AL	146	498	84	121	21	2	22	103	86	79	.243	.426	2
SAL	BANDO	1975	Oakland Athletics	AL	160	562	64	129	24	1	15	78	87	80	.230	.356	7
SAL	BANDO	1976	Oakland Athletics	AL	158	550	75	132	18	2	27	84	76	74	.240	.427	20
SAL	BANDO	1977	Milwaukee Brewers	AL	159	580	65	145	27	3	17	82	75	89	.250	.395	4
SAL	BANDO	1978	Milwaukee Brewers	AL	152	540	85	154	20	6	17	78	72	52	.285	.439	3
SAL	BANDO	1979	Milwaukee Brewers	AL	130	476	57	117	14	3	9	43	57	42	.246	.345	2
SAL	BANDO	1980	Milwaukee Brewers	AL	78	254	28	50	12	1	5	31	29	35	.197	.311	5
SAL	BANDO	1981	Milwaukee Brewers	AL	32	65	10	13	4	0	2	9	6	6	.200	.354	1
DICK	BARONE	1960	Pittsburgh Pirates	NL	3	6	0	0	0	0	0	0	0	3	.000	.000	0
TONY	BARTIROME	1952	Pittsburgh Pirates	NL	124	355	32	78	10	3	0	16	26	37	.220	.265	3

FIRST	LAST	YEAR	TEAM	LEAGUE	G	AB	R	H	2B	3B	HR	RBI	BB	SO	AVG	SLUG	SB
MARK	BELANGER	1965	Baltimore Orioles	AL	11	3	1	1	0	0	0	0	0	0	.333	.333	0
MARK	BELANGER	1966	Baltimore Orioles	AL	8	19	2	3	1	0	0	0	0	3	.158	.211	0
MARK	BELANGER	1967	Baltimore Orioles	AL	69	184	19	32	5	0	1	10	12	46	.174	.217	6
MARK	BELANGER	1968	Baltimore Orioles	AL	145	472	40	98	13	4	2	21	40	114	.208	.248	10
MARK	BELANGER	1969	Baltimore Orioles	AL	150	530	76	152	17	5	2	50	53	54	.287	.345	14
MARK	BELANGER	1970	Baltimore Orioles	AL	145	459	53	100	6	5	1	36	52	65	.218	.259	13
MARK	BELANGER	1971	Baltimore Orioles	AL	150	500	67	133	19	4	0	35	73	48	.266	.320	10
MARK	BELANGER	1972	Baltimore Orioles	AL	113	285	36	53	9	1	2	16	18	53	.186	.246	6
MARK	BELANGER	1973	Baltimore Orioles	AL	154	470	60	106	15	4	5	27	49	54	.226	.262	13
MARK	BELANGER	1974	Baltimore Orioles	AL	155	493	54	111	14	4	5	36	51	69	.225	.300	17
MARK	BELANGER	1975	Baltimore Orioles	AL	152	442	44	100	11	1	3	27	36	53	.226	.276	16
MARK	BELANGER	1976	Baltimore Orioles	AL	153	522	66	141	22	2	1	40	51	64	.270	.326	27
MARK	BELANGER	1977	Baltimore Orioles	AL	144	402	39	83	13	4	2	30	43	68	.206	.274	15
MARK	BELANGER	1978	Baltimore Orioles	AL	135	348	39	74	13	5	0	16	40	55	.213	.250	6
MARK	BELANGER	1979	Baltimore Orioles	AL	101	198	28	33	6	2	0	9	29	33	.167	.217	5
MARK	BELANGER	1980	Baltimore Orioles	AL	113	268	37	61	7	3	0	22	12	25	.228	.276	6
MARK	BELANGER	1981	Baltimore Orioles	AL	64	139	9	23	3	2	1	10	12	25	.165	.237	2
MARK	BELANGER	1982	Los Angeles Dodgers	NL	54	50	6	12	1	0	0	4	5	10	.240	.260	1
WAYNE	BELARDI	1950	Brooklyn Dodgers	NL	10	10	0	0	0	0	0	0	0	4	.000		1
WAYNE	BELARDI	1951	Brooklyn Dodgers	NL	3	3	1	1	0	1	0	0	0	2	.333	.333	0
WAYNE	BELARDI	1953	Brooklyn Dodgers	NL	69	163	19	39	3	2	11	34	16	40	.239	.485	0
WAYNE	BELARDI	1954	Brooklyn Dodgers	NL	11	9	0	2	0	0	0	1	2	3	.222	.222	0
WAYNE	BELARDI	1954	Detroit Tigers	AL	88	250	27	58	7	0	11	24	33	34	.232	.400	1
WAYNE	BELARDI	1955	Detroit Tigers	AL	3	3	0	0	0	0	0	0	0	1	.000		0
WAYNE	BELARDI	1956	Detroit Tigers	AL	79	154	24	43	3	1	6	15	15	13	.279	.429	0
ZEKE	BELLA	1957	New York Yankees	AL	5	10	0	1	0	0	0	0	1	2	.100	.100	0
ZEKE	BELLA	1959	Kansas City Athletics	AL	47	82	10	17	2	0	1	9	9	14	.207	.293	0
JOHNNY	BERARDINO	1939	St. Louis Browns	AL	126	468	42	120	24	5	5	58	37	36	.256	.361	6
JOHNNY	BERARDINO	1940	St. Louis Browns	AL	142	523	71	135	31	4	16	85	32	46	.258	.424	6
JOHNNY	BERARDINO	1941	St. Louis Browns	AL	128	469	48	127	30	4	5	89	41	27	.271	.384	3
JOHNNY	BERARDINO	1942	St. Louis Browns	AL	29	74	11	21	6	0	1	10	4	2	.284	.405	3
JOHNNY	BERARDINO	1946	St. Louis Browns	AL	144	582	70	154	29	5	5	68	34	58	.265	.357	2
JOHNNY	BERARDINO	1947	St. Louis Browns	AL	90	306	29	80	22	1	5	20	44	26	.261	.350	6
JOHNNY	BERARDINO	1948	Cleveland Indians	AL	66	147	19	28	5	2	2	10	27	16	.190	.279	0
JOHNNY	BERARDINO	1949	Cleveland Indians	AL	50	116	11	23	6	1	0	13	14	14	.198	.267	0

FIRST	LAST	YEAR	TEAM	LEAGUE	G	AB	R	H	2B	3B	HR	RBI	BB	SO	AVG	SLUG	SB
JOHNNY	BERARDINO	1950	Cleveland Indians	AL	4	5	1	2	0	0	0	3	1	0	.400	.400	0
JOHNNY	BERARDINO	1950	Pittsburgh Pirates	NL	40	131	12	27	3	1	1	12	19	11	.206	.267	0
JOHNNY	BERARDINO	1951	St. Louis Browns	AL	39	119	13	27	7	1	0	13	17	18	.227	.303	1
JOHNNY	BERARDINO	1952	Cleveland Indians	AL	35	32	5	3	0	0	0	2	10	8	.094	.094	0
JOHNNY	BERARDINO	1952	Pittsburgh Pirates	NL	19	56	2	8	4	0	0	4	4	6	.143	.214	0
AUGIE	BERGAMO	1944	St. Louis Cardinals	NL	80	192	35	55	6	3	2	19	35	23	.286	.380	0
AUGIE	BERGAMO	1945	St. Louis Cardinals	NL	94	304	51	96	17	2	3	44	43	21	.316	.414	0
DALE	BERRA	1977	Pittsburgh Pirates	NL	17	40	0	7	1	0	0	3	3	11	.175	.200	0
DALE	BERRA	1978	Pittsburgh Pirates	NL	56	135	16	28	2	0	6	14	13	20	.207	.356	3
DALE	BERRA	1979	Pittsburgh Pirates	NL	44	123	11	26	5	0	3	15	11	17	.211	.325	0
DALE	BERRA	1980	Pittsburgh Pirates	NL	93	245	21	54	8	2	6	31	16	52	.220	.343	2
DALE	BERRA	1981	Pittsburgh Pirates	NL	81	232	21	56	12	0	6	27	17	34	.241	.319	11
DALE	BERRA	1982	Pittsburgh Pirates	NL	156	529	64	139	25	5	10	61	33	83	.263	.386	6
DALE	BERRA	1983	Pittsburgh Pirates	NL	161	537	51	135	25	0	10	52	61	84	.251	.358	8
DALE	BERRA	1984	Pittsburgh Pirates	NL	136	450	31	100	16	0	9	52	34	78	.222	.318	1
DALE	BERRA	1985	New York Yankees	AL	48	109	8	25	5	1	1	8	7	20	.229	.321	1
DALE	BERRA	1986	New York Yankees	AL	42	108	10	25	7	0	2	13	9	14	.231	.352	0
DALE	BERRA	1987	Houston Astros	NL	19	45	3	8	3	0	0	4	8	12	.178	.244	0
YOGI	BERRA	1946	New York Yankees	AL	7	22	3	8	1	0	2	4	1	1	.364	.682	0
YOGI	BERRA	1947	New York Yankees	AL	83	293	41	82	15	3	11	54	13	12	.280	.464	0
YOGI	BERRA	1948	New York Yankees	AL	125	469	70	143	24	10	14	98	25	24	.305	.488	3
YOGI	BERRA	1949	New York Yankees	AL	116	415	59	115	20	2	20	91	22	25	.277	.480	2
YOGI	BERRA	1950	New York Yankees	AL	151	597	116	192	30	6	28	124	55	12	.322	.533	4
YOGI	BERRA	1951	New York Yankees	AL	141	547	92	161	19	4	27	88	44	20	.294	.492	5
YOGI	BERRA	1952	New York Yankees	AL	142	534	97	146	17	1	30	98	66	24	.273	.478	2
YOGI	BERRA	1953	New York Yankees	AL	137	503	80	149	23	5	27	108	50	32	.296	.523	0
YOGI	BERRA	1954	New York Yankees	AL	151	584	88	179	28	6	22	125	56	29	.307	.488	0
YOGI	BERRA	1955	New York Yankees	AL	147	541	84	147	20	3	27	108	60	20	.272	.470	1
YOGI	BERRA	1956	New York Yankees	AL	140	521	93	155	29	2	30	105	65	29	.298	.534	3
YOGI	BERRA	1957	New York Yankees	AL	134	482	74	121	14	2	24	82	57	24	.251	.438	1
YOGI	BERRA	1958	New York Yankees	AL	122	433	60	115	17	3	22	90	35	35	.266	.471	3
YOGI	BERRA	1959	New York Yankees	AL	131	472	64	134	25	1	19	69	43	38	.284	.462	1
YOGI	BERRA	1960	New York Yankees	AL	120	359	46	99	14	1	15	62	38	23	.276	.446	2
YOGI	BERRA	1961	New York Yankees	AL	119	395	62	107	11	0	22	61	35	28	.271	.466	2
YOGI	BERRA	1962	New York Yankees	AL	86	232	25	52	8	0	10	35	24	18	.224	.388	0

FIRST	LAST	YEAR	TEAM	LEAGUE	G	AB	R	H	2B	3B	HR	RBI	BB	SO	AVG	SLUG	SB
YOGI	BERRA	1963	New York Yankees	AL	64	147	20	43	6	0	8	28	15	17	.293	.497	1
YOGI	BERRA	1965	NewYorkMets	NL	4	9	1	2	0	0	0	0	0	3	.222	.222	0
BUDDY	BIANCALANA	1982	Kansas City Royals	AL	3	2	0	1	0	1	0	0	1	0	.500	.500	0
BUDDY	BIANCALANA	1983	Kansas City Royals	AL	6	15	2	3	0	0	0	0	0	7	.200	.200	1
BUDDY	BIANCALANA	1984	Kansas City Royals	AL	66	134	18	26	6	1	2	9	6	44	.194	.299	1
BUDDY	BIANCALANA	1985	Kansas City Royals	AL	81	138	21	26	5	1	1	6	17	34	.188	.261	1
BUDDY	BIANCALANA	1986	Kansas City Royals	AL	100	190	24	46	4	4	2	8	15	50	.242	.337	5
BUDDY	BIANCALANA	1987	Houston Astros	NL	18	24	1	1	0	0	0	0	1	12	.042	.042	0
BUDDY	BIANCALANA	1987	Kansas City Royals	AL	37	47	4	10	1	0	0	7	1	10	.213	.298	0
TOMMY	BIANCO	1975	Milwaukee Brewers	AL	18	34	6	6	1	0	0	1	3	7	.176	.206	0
HANK	BIASATTI	1949	Philadelphia Athletics	AL	21	24	6	2	0	0	0	0	8	5	.083	.083	6
CRAIG	BIGGIO	1988	Houston Astros	NL	50	123	14	26	6	1	3	5	7	29	.211	.350	6
CRAIG	BIGGIO	1989	Houston Astros	NL	134	443	64	114	21	2	13	60	49	64	.257	.402	21
CRAIG	BIGGIO	1990	Houston Astros	NL	150	555	53	153	24	2	4	42	53	79	.276	.348	25
CRAIG	BIGGIO	1991	Houston Astros	NL	149	546	79	161	23	4	4	46	53	71	.295	.374	19
CRAIG	BIGGIO	1992	Houston Astros	NL	162	613	96	170	32	3	6	39	94	95	.277	.369	38
CRAIG	BIGGIO	1993	Houston Astros	NL	155	610	98	175	41	5	21	64	77	93	.287	.474	15
CRAIG	BIGGIO	1994	Houston Astros	NL	114	437	88	139	44	5	6	56	62	58	.318	.483	39
CRAIG	BIGGIO	1995	Houston Astros	NL	141	553	123	167	30	4	22	77	80	85	.302	.483	33
CRAIG	BIGGIO	1996	Houston Astros	NL	162	605	113	174	24	4	15	75	75	72	.288	.415	25
CRAIG	BIGGIO	1997	Houston Astros	NL	162	619	146	191	37	8	22	81	84	107	.309	.501	47
CRAIG	BIGGIO	1998	Houston Astros	NL	160	646	123	210	51	2	20	88	64	113	.325	.503	50
CRAIG	BIGGIO	1999	Houston Astros	NL	160	639	123	188	56	0	16	73	88	107	.294	.457	28
CRAIG	BIGGIO	2000	Houston Astros	NL	101	377	67	101	13	3	8	35	61	73	.268	.393	12
CRAIG	BIGGIO	2001	Houston Astros	NL	155	617	118	180	35	3	20	70	66	100	.292	.455	7
DANN	BILARDELLO	1983	Cincinnati Reds	NL	109	298	27	71	18	0	9	38	15	49	.238	.389	2
DANN	BILARDELLO	1984	Cincinnati Reds	NL	68	182	16	38	7	0	2	10	19	34	.209	.280	0
DANN	BILARDELLO	1985	Cincinnati Reds	NL	42	102	6	17	0	0	1	9	4	15	.167	.196	0
DANN	BILARDELLO	1986	Montreal Expos	NL	79	191	12	37	5	0	4	17	14	32	.194	.283	1
DANN	BILARDELLO	1989	Pittsburgh Pirates	NL	33	80	11	18	6	0	2	8	2	18	.225	.375	0
DANN	BILARDELLO	1990	Pittsburgh Pirates	NL	19	37	1	2	0	0	0	3	4	10	.054	.054	1
DANN	BILARDELLO	1991	SanDiego Padres	NL	15	26	4	7	2	1	0	5	3	4	.269	.423	0
DANN	BILARDELLO	1992	SanDiego Padres	NL	17	33	2	4	0	0	1	1	4	8	.121	.152	0
JOHN	BOCCABELLA	1963	Chicago Cubs	NL	24	74	7	14	4	1	1	5	6	21	.189	.311	0
JOHN	BOCCABELLA	1964	Chicago Cubs	NL	9	23	4	9	2	1	0	6	0	3	.391	.565	0

FIRST	LAST	YEAR	TEAM	LEAGUE	G	AB	R	H	2B	3B	HR	RBI	BB	SO	AVG	SLUG	SB
JOHN	BOCCABELLA	1965	Chicago Cubs	NL	6	12	2	4	0	0	2	4	1	2	.333	.833	0
JOHN	BOCCABELLA	1966	Chicago Cubs	NL	75	206	22	47	9	0	6	25	14	39	.228	.359	0
JOHN	BOCCABELLA	1967	Chicago Cubs	NL	25	35	0	6	1	1	0	8	3	7	.171	.257	0
JOHN	BOCCABELLA	1968	Chicago Cubs	NL	7	14	0	1	0	0	0	1	2	5	.071	.071	0
JOHN	BOCCABELLA	1969	Montreal Expos	NL	40	86	4	9	2	0	1	6	6	30	.105	.163	1
JOHN	BOCCABELLA	1970	Montreal Expos	NL	61	145	18	39	3	1	5	17	11	24	.269	.407	0
JOHN	BOCCABELLA	1971	Montreal Expos	NL	74	177	15	39	11	0	3	15	14	26	.220	.333	0
JOHN	BOCCABELLA	1972	Montreal Expos	NL	83	207	14	47	8	1	3	10	9	29	.227	.290	1
JOHN	BOCCABELLA	1973	Montreal Expos	NL	118	403	25	94	13	0	7	46	26	57	.233	.318	1
JOHN	BOCCABELLA	1974	San Francisco Giants	NL	29	80	6	11	3	0	0	5	4	6	.138	.175	0
SAL	BUTERA	1980	Minnesota Twins	AL	34	85	4	23	7	0	0	2	3	6	.271	.282	0
SAL	BUTERA	1981	Minnesota Twins	AL	62	167	13	40	7	1	0	18	22	14	.240	.293	0
SAL	BUTERA	1982	Minnesota Twins	AL	54	126	9	32	2	0	0	8	17	12	.254	.270	0
SAL	BUTERA	1983	Detroit Tigers	AL	4	5	0	1	0	0	0	0	0	0	.200	.200	0
SAL	BUTERA	1984	Montreal Expos	NL	3	3	0	0	0	0	0	0	1	0	.000	.000	0
SAL	BUTERA	1985	Montreal Expos	NL	67	120	11	24	1	0	3	12	13	12	.200	.283	0
SAL	BUTERA	1986	Cincinnati Reds	NL	56	113	14	27	6	1	2	16	21	10	.239	.363	0
SAL	BUTERA	1987	Cincinnati Reds	NL	5	11	1	2	0	0	0	2	1	6	.182	.455	0
SAL	BUTERA	1987	Minnesota Twins	AL	51	111	7	19	5	0	1	12	7	16	.171	.243	0
SAL	BUTERA	1988	Toronto Blue Jays	AL	23	60	3	14	2	1	1	6	7	9	.233	.350	0
PING	BODIE	1911	Chicago White Sox	AL	145	551	75	159	27	13	4	97	49		.289	.407	14
PING	BODIE	1912	Chicago White Sox	AL	138	472	58	139	24	7	5	72	43		.294	.407	12
PING	BODIE	1913	Chicago WhiteSox	AL	127	406	39	107	14	8	3	48	35	57	.264	.397	5
PING	BODIE	1914	Chicago White Sox	AL	107	327	21	75	9	5	3	29	21	35	.229	.315	12
PING	BODIE	1917	PhiladelphiaAthletics	AL	148	557	51	162	28	11	7	74	53	40	.291	.418	13
PING	BODIE	1918	New York Yankees	AL	91	324	36	83	12	6	3	46	27	24	.256	.358	6
PING	BODIE	1919	New York Yankees	AL	134	475	45	132	27	8	6	59	36	46	.278	.406	15
PING	BODIE	1920	New York Yankees	AL	129	471	63	139	26	12	7	79	40	30	.295	.446	6
PING	BODIE	1921	New York Yankees	AL	31	87	5	15	2	2	0	12	8	8	.172	.241	0
NINO	BONGIOVANNI	1938	Cincinnati Reds	NL	2	7	0	2	1	0	0	0	0	0	.286	.429	0
NINO	BONGIOVANNI	1939	Cincinnati Reds	NL	66	159	17	41	6	0	0	16	9	8	.258	.296	0
ZEKE	BONURA	1934	Chicago White Sox	AL	127	510	86	154	35	4	27	110	64	31	.302	.545	4
ZEKE	BONURA	1935	Chicago White Sox	AL	138	550	107	162	34	4	21	92	57	28	.295	.485	0
ZEKE	BONURA	1936	Chicago White Sox	AL	148	587	120	194	39	7	12	138	94	29	.330	.482	4
ZEKE	BONURA	1937	Chicago White Sox	AL	116	447	79	154	41	2	19	100	49	24	.345	.573	5

FIRST	LAST	YEAR	TEAM	LEAGUE	G	AB	R	H	2B	3B	HR	RBI	BB	SO	AVG	SLUG	SB
ZEKE	BONURA	1938	Washington Senators	AL	137	540	72	156	27	3	22	114	44	29	.289	.472	2
ZEKE	BONURA	1939	New York Giants	NL	123	455	75	146	26	6	11	85	46	22	.321	.477	1
ZEKE	BONURA	1940	Chicago Cubs	NL	49	182	20	48	14	0	4	20	10	4	.264	.407	1
ZEKE	BONURA	1940	Washington Senators	AL	79	311	41	85	16	3	3	45	40	13	.273	.373	2
RICK	BOSETTI	1976	Philadelphia Phillies	NL	13	18	6	5	1	0	0	0	1	13	.278	.333	3
RICK	BOSETTI	1977	St. Louis Cardinals	NL	41	69	12	16	0	0	0	3	6	11	.232	.232	3
RICK	BOSETTI	1978	Toronto Blue Jays	AL	136	568	61	147	25	5	5	42	30	65	.259	.347	4
RICK	BOSETTI	1979	Toronto Blue Jays	AL	162	619	59	161	35	2	8	65	22	70	.260	.362	6
RICK	BOSETTI	1980	Toronto Blue Jays	AL	53	188	24	40	7	1	4	18	15	29	.213	.324	13
RICK	BOSETTI	1981	Oakland Athletics	AL	9	19	4	2	0	0	0	1	3	3	.105	.105	4
RICK	BOSETTI	1981	Toronto Blue Jays	AL	25	47	5	11	2	0	0	4	2	6	.234	.277	0
RICK	BOSETTI	1982	Oakland Athletics	AL	6	15	1	3	0	0	0	0	0	3	.200	.200	0
JOHN	BOTTARINI	1937	Chicago Cubs	NL	26	40	3	11	3	0	1	7	5	10	.275	.425	0
LARRY	BOWA	1970	Philadelphia Phillies	NL	145	547	50	137	17	6	0	34	21	48	.250	.303	24
LARRY	BOWA	1971	Philadelphia Phillies	NL	159	650	74	162	18	5	0	25	36	61	.249	.292	28
LARRY	BOWA	1972	Philadelphia Phillies	NL	152	579	67	145	11	13	1	31	32	51	.250	.320	17
LARRY	BOWA	1973	Philadelphia Phillies	NL	122	446	42	94	11	3	0	23	24	31	.211	.249	10
LARRY	BOWA	1974	Philadelphia Phillies	NL	162	669	97	184	19	10	1	36	23	31	.275	.338	39
LARRY	BOWA	1975	Philadelphia Phillies	NL	136	583	79	178	18	9	2	38	24	52	.305	.377	24
LARRY	BOWA	1976	Philadelphia Phillies	NL	156	624	71	155	15	9	0	49	32	31	.248	.301	30
LARRY	BOWA	1977	Philadelphia Phillies	NL	154	624	93	175	19	3	4	41	24	32	.280	.340	32
LARRY	BOWA	1978	Philadelphia Phillies	NL	156	654	78	192	31	5	3	43	24	40	.294	.370	27
LARRY	BOWA	1979	Philadelphia Phillies	NL	147	539	74	130	17	11	0	31	61	32	.241	.314	20
LARRY	BOWA	1980	Philadelphia Phillies	NL	147	540	57	144	16	4	2	39	24	28	.267	.322	21
LARRY	BOWA	1981	Philadelphia Phillies	NL	103	360	34	102	14	3	0	31	26	17	.283	.339	16
LARRY	BOWA	1982	Chicago Cubs	NL	142	499	50	123	15	7	0	29	39	38	.246	.305	8
LARRY	BOWA	1983	Chicago Cubs	NL	147	499	73	133	20	5	2	43	35	30	.267	.339	7
LARRY	BOWA	1984	Chicago Cubs	NL	133	391	33	87	14	4	0	17	28	24	.223	.269	10
LARRY	BOWA	1985	Chicago Cubs	NL	72	195	13	48	6	4	0	13	11	20	.246	.318	5
LARRY	BOWA	1985	New York Mets	NL	14	19	2	2	1	0	0	2	2	2	.105	.158	0
AL	BRANCATO	1939	Philadelphia Athletics	AL	21	68	12	14	5	2	1	8	8	4	.206	.324	1
AL	BRANCATO	1940	Philadelphia Athletics	AL	107	298	42	57	11	2	0	23	28	36	.191	.252	3
AL	BRANCATO	1941	Philadelphia Athletics	AL	144	530	60	124	20	9	2	49	59	49	.234	.317	1
AL	BRANCATO	1945	Philadelphia Athletics	AL	10	34	3	4	1	0	0	0	1	3	.118	.147	0
FRED	BRATSCHI	1921	Chicago White Sox	AL	16	28	0	8	1	0	0	3	0	2	.286	.321	0

FIRST	LAST	YEAR	TEAM	LEAGUE	G	AB	R	H	2B	3B	HR	RBI	BB	SO	AVG	SLUG	SB
FRED	BRATSCHI	1926	Boston Red Sox	AL	72	167	12	46	10	1	0	19	14	15	.275	.347	0
FRED	BRATSCHI	1927	Boston Red Sox	AL	1	1	0	0	0	0	0	0	0	0	.000		0
RICO	BROGNA	1992	Detroit Tigers	AL	9	26	3	5	1	0	0	3	3	5	.192	.346	0
RICO	BROGNA	1994	New York Mets	NL	39	131	16	46	11	2	7	20	6	29	.351	.626	1
RICO	BROGNA	1995	New York Mets	NL	134	495	72	143	27	2	22	76	39	111	.289	.485	1
RICO	BROGNA	1996	New York Mets	NL	55	188	18	48	10	1	7	30	19	50	.255	.431	0
RICO	BROGNA	1997	Philadelphia Phillies	NL	148	543	68	137	36	1	20	81	33	116	.252	.433	12
RICO	BROGNA	1998	Philadelphia Phillies	NL	153	565	77	150	36	3	20	104	49	125	.265	.446	7
RICO	BROGNA	1999	Philadelphia Phillies	NL	157	619	90	172	29	4	24	102	54	132	.278	.454	8
RICO	BROGNA	2000	Boston Red Sox	AL	43	56	8	11	3	0	1	8	3	13	.196	.304	1
RICO	BROGNA	2000	Philadelphia Phillies	NL	38	129	12	32	14	0	3	13	7	28	.248	.380	3
RICO	BROGNA	2001	Atlanta Braves	NL	72	206	15	51	9	0	3	21	14	46	.248	.355	0
JOE	BROVIA	1955	Cincinnati Reds	NL	21	18	0	2	0	0	0	4	1	6	.111	.111	0
PUTSY	CABALLERO	1944	Philadelphia Phillies	NL	4	4	0	0	0	0	0	0	0		.000		0
PUTSY	CABALLERO	1945	Philadelphia Phillies	NL	9	7	1	0	0	0	0	0	1	0	.000		0
PUTSY	CABALLERO	1947	Philadelphia Phillies	NL	2	7	2	1	0	0	0	0	1	0	.143	.143	0
PUTSY	CABALLERO	1948	Philadelphia Phillies	NL	113	351	33	86	12	1	0	19	24	18	.245	.285	7
PUTSY	CABALLERO	1949	Philadelphia Phillies	NL	29	68	8	19	3	0	0	3	2	3	.279	.324	0
PUTSY	CABALLERO	1950	Philadelphia Phillies	NL	46	24	12	4	0	0	0	0	0	7	.167	.167	1
PUTSY	CABALLERO	1951	Philadelphia Phillies	NL	84	161	15	30	3	2	1	11	12	7	.186	.248	1
PUTSY	CABALLERO	1952	Philadelphia Phillies	NL	35	42	10	10	3	0	0	6	2	3	.238	.310	1
SAM	CALDERONE	1950	New York Giants	NL	34	67	9	20	1	0	0	12	2	5	.299	.358	0
SAM	CALDERONE	1953	New York Giants	NL	35	45	4	10	2	0	0	8	2	4	.222	.267	0
SAM	CALDERONE	1954	Milwaukee Braves	NL	22	29	3	11	2	0	0	5	4	4	.379	.448	0
HANK	CAMELLI	1943	Pittsburgh Pirates	NL	1	3	1	0	0	0	0	0	1	0	.000		0
HANK	CAMELLI	1944	Pittsburgh Pirates	NL	63	125	14	37	5	1	1	10	18	12	.296	.376	0
HANK	CAMELLI	1945	Pittsburgh Pirates	NL	1	2	0	0	0	0	0	0	0	0	.000		0
HANK	CAMELLI	1946	Pittsburgh Pirates	NL	42	96	8	20	2	2	0	5	8	9	.208	.271	0
HANK	CAMELLI	1947	Boston Braves	NL	52	150	10	29	8	1	1	11	18	18	.193	.280	0
DOLPH	CAMILLI	1933	Chicago Cubs	NL	16	58	8	13	2	0	2	7	4	11	.224	.397	3
DOLPH	CAMILLI	1934	Chicago Cubs	NL	32	120	17	33	8	0	4	19	5	25	.275	.442	1
DOLPH	CAMILLI	1934	Philadelphia Phillies	NL	102	378	52	100	20	3	12	68	48	69	.265	.429	3
DOLPH	CAMILLI	1935	Philadelphia Phillies	NL	156	602	88	157	23	5	25	83	65	113	.261	.440	9
DOLPH	CAMILLI	1936	Philadelphia Phillies	NL	151	530	106	167	29	13	28	102	116	84	.315	.577	5
DOLPH	CAMILLI	1937	Philadelphia Phillies	NL	131	475	101	161	23	7	27	80	90	82	.339	.587	6

FIRST	LAST	YEAR	TEAM	LEAGUE	G	AB	R	H	2B	3B	HR	RBI	BB	SO	AVG	SLUG	SB
DOLPH	CAMILLI	1938	Brooklyn Dodgers	NL	146	509	106	128	25	11	24	100	119	101	.251	.485	6
DOLPH	CAMILLI	1939	Brooklyn Dodgers	NL	157	565	105	164	30	12	26	104	110	107	.290	.524	1
DOLPH	CAMILLI	1940	Brooklyn Dodgers	NL	142	512	92	147	29	13	23	96	89	83	.287	.529	9
DOLPH	CAMILLI	1941	Brooklyn Dodgers	NL	149	529	92	151	29	6	34	120	104	115	.285	.556	3
DOLPH	CAMILLI	1942	Brooklyn Dodgers	NL	150	524	89	132	23	7	26	109	97	85	.252	.471	10
DOLPH	CAMILLI	1943	Brooklyn Dodgers	NL	95	353	56	87	15	6	6	43	65	48	.246	.374	2
DOLPH	CAMILLI	1945	Boston Red Sox	AL	63	198	24	42	5	2	2	19	35	38	.212	.288	2
DOUG	CAMILLI	1960	LosAngeles Dodgers	NL	6	24	4	8	2	0	1	3	1	4	.333	.542	0
DOUG	CAMILLI	1961	Los Angeles Dodgers	NL	13	30	3	4	0	0	3	4	9	9	.133	.433	0
DOUG	CAMILLI	1962	Los Angeles Dodgers	NL	45	88	16	25	5	2	4	22	12	21	.284	.523	0
DOUG	CAMILLI	1963	Los Angeles Dodgers	NL	49	117	9	19	1	1	3	10	11	22	.162	.265	0
DOUG	CAMILLI	1964	Los Angeles Dodgers	NL	50	123	1	22	3	0	0	10	8	19	.179	.203	0
LOU	CAMILLI	1969	Cleveland Indians	AL	13	14	0	0	0	0	0	0	0	3	.000		0
LOU	CAMILLI	1970	Cleveland Indians	AL	16	15	0	0	0	0	0	0	2	2	.000	.000	0
LOU	CAMILLI	1971	Cleveland Indians	AL	39	81	5	16	2	0	0	0	8	10	.198	.222	0
LOU	CAMILLI	1972	Cleveland Indians	AL	39	41	2	6	2	0	0	3	3	8	.146	.195	0
KEN	CAMINITI	1987	Houston Astros	NL	63	203	10	50	7	1	3	23	12	44	.246	.335	0
KEN	CAMINITI	1988	Houston Astros	NL	30	83	5	15	2	3	1	7	5	18	.181	.241	0
KEN	CAMINITI	1989	Houston Astros	NL	161	585	71	149	31	3	10	72	51	93	.255	.369	4
KEN	CAMINITI	1990	Houston Astros	NL	153	541	52	131	20	2	4	51	48	97	.242	.309	9
KEN	CAMINITI	1991	Houston Astros	NL	152	574	65	145	30	3	13	80	46	85	.253	.383	4
KEN	CAMINITI	1992	Houston Astros	NL	135	506	68	149	31	0	13	62	44	68	.294	.441	10
KEN	CAMINITI	1993	Houston Astros	NL	143	543	75	142	31	2	13	75	49	88	.262	.390	8
KEN	CAMINITI	1994	Houston Astros	NL	143	406	63	115	28	0	18	75	43	71	.283	.495	4
KEN	CAMINITI	1995	San Diego Padres	NL	143	526	74	159	33	2	26	94	69	94	.302	.513	12
KEN	CAMINITI	1996	San Diego Padres	NL	146	546	109	178	37	0	40	130	78	99	.326	.621	11
KEN	CAMINITI	1997	San Diego Padres	NL	137	486	92	141	28	0	26	90	80	108	.290	.508	11
KEN	CAMINITI	1998	Houston Astros	NL	131	452	87	114	29	1	29	82	71	58	.252	.509	6
KEN	CAMINITI	1999	Houston Astros	NL	78	273	45	78	11	0	13	56	46	37	.286	.476	6
KEN	CAMINITI	2000	Houston Astros	NL	59	208	42	63	13	0	15	45	42	44	.303	.582	3
KEN	CAMINITI	2001	Atlanta Braves	NL	64	171	12	38	9	0	6	16	21	41	.222	.380	0
KEN	CAMINITI	2001	Texas Rangers	AL	54	185	24	43	8	0	9	25	22	45	.232	.432	3
ROY	CAMPANELLA	1948	Brooklyn Dodgers	NL	83	279	32	72	11	3	9	45	36	45	.258	.416	3
ROY	CAMPANELLA	1949	Brooklyn Dodgers	NL	130	436	65	125	22	2	22	82	67	36	.287	.498	3
ROY	CAMPANELLA	1950	Brooklyn Dodgers	NL	126	437	70	123	19	3	31	89	55	51	.281	.551	1

FIRST	LAST	YEAR	TEAM	LEAGUE	G	AB	R	H	2B	3B	HR	RBI	BB	SO	AVG	SLUG	SB
ROY	CAMPANELLA	1951	Brooklyn Dodgers	NL	143	505	90	164	33	1	33	108	53	51	.325	.590	1
ROY	CAMPANELLA	1952	Brooklyn Dodgers	NL	128	468	73	126	18	1	22	97	57	59	.269	.453	8
ROY	CAMPANELLA	1953	Brooklyn Dodgers	NL	144	519	103	162	26	3	41	142	67	58	.312	.611	4
ROY	CAMPANELLA	1954	Brooklyn Dodgers	NL	111	397	43	82	14	3	19	51	42	49	.207	.401	1
ROY	CAMPANELLA	1955	Brooklyn Dodgers	NL	123	446	81	142	20	1	32	107	56	41	.318	.583	2
ROY	CAMPANELLA	1956	Brooklyn Dodgers	NL	124	388	39	85	6	1	20	73	66	61	.219	.394	1
ROY	CAMPANELLA	1957	Brooklyn Dodgers	NL	103	330	31	80	9	0	13	62	34	50	.242	.388	1
AL	CAMPANIS	1943	Brooklyn Dodgers	NL	7	20	3	2	0	0	0	0	4	5	.100	.100	0
GEORGE	CANALE	1989	Milwaukee Brewers	AL	13	26	5	5	1	0	1	3	2	5	.192	.346	0
GEORGE	CANALE	1990	Milwaukee Brewers	AL	10	13	4	1	0	0	0	0	2	6	.077	.077	0
GEORGE	CANALE	1991	Milwaukee Brewers	AL	21	34	6	6	2	0	3	10	8	6	.176	.500	0
JOHN	CANGELOSI	1985	Chicago White Sox	AL	5	2	2	0	0	0	0	0	0	1	.000		0
JOHN	CANGELOSI	1986	Chicago White Sox	AL	137	438	65	103	16	3	2	32	71	61	.235	.299	50
JOHN	CANGELOSI	1987	Pittsburgh Pirates	NL	104	182	44	50	8	3	4	18	46	33	.275	.418	21
JOHN	CANGELOSI	1988	Pittsburgh Pirates	NL	75	118	18	30	4	1	0	8	17	16	.254	.305	9
JOHN	CANGELOSI	1989	Pittsburgh Pirates	NL	112	160	18	35	4	2	0	9	35	20	.219	.269	11
JOHN	CANGELOSI	1990	Pittsburgh Pirates	NL	58	76	13	15	2	0	0	1	11	12	.197	.224	7
JOHN	CANGELOSI	1992	Texas Rangers	AL	73	85	12	16	2	0	0	6	18	16	.188	.247	6
JOHN	CANGELOSI	1994	New York Mets	NL	62	111	14	28	4	0	0	4	19	20	.252	.288	5
JOHN	CANGELOSI	1995	Houston Astros	NL	90	201	46	64	5	2	2	18	48	42	.318	.393	21
JOHN	CANGELOSI	1996	Houston Astros	NL	108	262	49	69	11	4	1	16	44	41	.263	.347	17
JOHN	CANGELOSI	1997	Florida Marlins	NL	103	192	28	47	8	0	1	12	19	33	.245	.302	5
JOHN	CANGELOSI	1998	Florida Marlins	NL	104	171	19	43	8	0	0	10	30	23	.251	.316	2
JOHN	CANGELOSI	1999	Colorado Rockies	NL	7	6	4	1	0	0	0	0	0	4	.167	.167	0
JAY	CANIZARO	1996	San Francisco Giants	NL	43	120	11	24	4	1	2	8	9	38	.200	.300	0
JAY	CANIZARO	1999	San Francisco Giants	NL	12	18	5	8	2	0	0	2	1	2	.444	.722	1
JAY	CANIZARO	2000	Minnesota Twins	AL	102	346	43	93	21	1	7	40	24	57	.269	.396	4
CHRIS	CANNIZZARO	1960	St. Louis Cardinals	NL	6	9	0	2	0	0	0	0	1	3	.222	.222	0
CHRIS	CANNIZZARO	1961	St. Louis Cardinals	NL	6	2	0	1	0	0	0	0	0		.500	.500	1
CHRIS	CANNIZZARO	1962	New York Mets	NL	59	133	9	32	2	1	0	9	19	26	.241	.271	0
CHRIS	CANNIZZARO	1963	New York Mets	NL	16	33	4	8	1	0	0	4	1	8	.242	.273	1
CHRIS	CANNIZZARO	1964	New York Mets	NL	60	164	11	51	10	0	2	20	14	28	.311	.372	0
CHRIS	CANNIZZARO	1965	New York Mets	NL	114	251	17	46	8	2	0	7	28	60	.183	.231	0
CHRIS	CANNIZZARO	1968	Pittsburgh Pirates	NL	25	58	5	14	2	2	1	7	9	13	.241	.397	0
CHRIS	CANNIZZARO	1969	SanDiego Padres	NL	134	418	23	92	14	3	4	33	42	81	.220	.297	0

FIRST	LAST	YEAR	TEAM	LEAGUE	G	AB	R	H	2B	3B	HR	RBI	BB	SO	AVG	SLUG	SB
CHRIS	CANNIZZARO	1970	SanDiego Padres	NL	111	341	27	95	13	3	5	42	48	49	.279	.378	2
CHRIS	CANNIZZARO	1971	Chicago Cubs	NL	71	197	18	42	8	1	5	23	28	24	.213	.340	0
CHRIS	CANNIZZARO	1971	SanDiego Padres	NL	21	63	2	12	1	0	1	8	11	10	.190	.254	0
CHRIS	CANNIZZARO	1972	Los Angeles Dodgers	NL	73	200	14	48	6	0	2	18	31	38	.240	.300	0
CHRIS	CANNIZZARO	1973	Los Angeles Dodgers	NL	17	21	0	4	0	0	0	3	3	3	.190	.190	0
CHRIS	CANNIZZARO	1974	San Diego Padres	NL	26	60	2	11	1	0	0	4	6	11	.183	.200	2
NICK	CAPRA	1982	Texas Rangers	AL	13	15	2	4	0	0	1	1	3	4	.267	.467	2
NICK	CAPRA	1983	Texas Rangers	AL	8	2	2	0	0	0	0	0	0	0	.000		0
NICK	CAPRA	1985	Texas Rangers	AL	8	8	1	1	0	0	0	0	2	0	.125	.125	1
NICK	CAPRA	1988	Kansas City Royals	AL	14	29	3	4	1	0	0	0	2	3	.138	.172	0
NICK	CAPRA	1991	Texas Rangers	AL	2	0	1	0	0	0	0	0	1	0			0
PAT	CAPRI	1944	Boston Braves	NL	7	1	1	0	0	0	0	0	0	1	.000		0
MIKE	CARUSO	1998	Chicago White Sox	AL	133	523	81	160	17	6	5	55	14	38	.306	.390	22
MIKE	CARUSO	1999	Chicago White Sox	AL	136	529	60	132	11	4	2	35	20	36	.250	.297	12
JACK	CASSINI	1949	Pittsburgh Pirates	NL	8	0	3	0	0	0	0	0	0	0			0
JIM	CASTIGLIA	1942	Philadelphia Athletics	AL	16	18	6	7	0	0	0	2	1	3	.389	.389	0
PETE	CASTIGLIONE	1947	Pittsburgh Pirates	NL	13	50	6	14	0	0	0	1	0	5	.280	.280	1
PETE	CASTIGLIONE	1948	Pittsburgh Pirates	NL	4	2	0	0	0	0	0	0	0	0	.000		2
PETE	CASTIGLIONE	1949	Pittsburgh Pirates	NL	118	448	57	120	20	2	6	43	20	43	.268	.362	2
PETE	CASTIGLIONE	1950	Pittsburgh Pirates	NL	94	263	29	67	10	3	3	22	23	23	.255	.350	1
PETE	CASTIGLIONE	1951	Pittsburgh Pirates	NL	132	482	62	126	19	7	7	42	34	28	.261	.361	2
PETE	CASTIGLIONE	1952	Pittsburgh Pirates	NL	67	214	27	57	9	1	4	18	17	8	.266	.374	3
PETE	CASTIGLIONE	1953	Pittsburgh Pirates	NL	45	159	14	33	2	1	4	21	5	14	.208	.308	1
PETE	CASTIGLIONE	1953	St. Louis Cardinals	NL	67	52	9	9	2	0	0	3	2	5	.173	.212	0
PETE	CASTIGLIONE	1954	St. Louis Cardinals	NL	5	0	1	0	0	0	0	0	0	0			0
JOHN	CASTINO	1979	Minnesota Twins	AL	148	393	49	112	13	8	5	52	27	72	.285	.397	5
JOHN	CASTINO	1980	Minnesota Twins	AL	150	546	67	165	17	7	13	64	29	67	.302	.430	7
JOHN	CASTINO	1981	Minnesota Twins	AL	101	381	41	102	13	9	6	36	18	52	.268	.396	4
JOHN	CASTINO	1982	Minnesota Twins	AL	117	410	48	99	12	6	6	37	36	51	.241	.344	2
JOHN	CASTINO	1983	Minnesota Twins	AL	142	563	83	156	30	4	11	57	62	54	.277	.403	4
JOHN	CASTINO	1984	Minnesota Twins	AL	8	27	5	12	1	0	0	3	5	11	.444	.481	0
VINCE	CASTINO	1943	Chicago White Sox	AL	33	101	14	23	1	0	2	16	12	11	.228	.297	0
VINCE	CASTINO	1944	Chicago White Sox	AL	29	78	8	18	5	0	0	3	10	13	.231	.295	0
VINCE	CASTINO	1945	Chicago White Sox	AL	26	36	2	8	1	0	0	4	3	7	.222	.250	0
FRANK	CATALANOTTO	1997	Detroit Tigers	AL	13	26	2	8	2	0	0	3	3	7	.308	.385	0

FIRST	LAST	YEAR	TEAM	LEAGUE	G	AB	R	H	2B	3B	HR	RBI	BB	SO	AVG	SLUG	SB
FRANK	CATALANOTTO	1998	Detroit Tigers	AL	89	213	23	60	13	2	6	25	12	39	.282	.446	3
FRANK	CATALANOTTO	1999	Detroit Tigers	AL	100	286	41	79	19	0	11	35	15	49	.276	.458	3
FRANK	CATALANOTTO	2000	Texas Rangers	AL	103	282	55	82	13	2	10	42	33	36	.291	.457	6
FRANK	CATALANOTTO	2001	Texas Rangers	AL	133	463	77	153	31	5	11	54	39	55	.330	.490	15
PHIL	CAVARRETTA	1934	Chicago Cubs	NL	7	21	5	8	0	1	1	6	2	3	.381	.619	1
PHIL	CAVARRETTA	1935	Chicago Cubs	NL	146	589	85	162	28	12	8	82	39	61	.275	.404	4
PHIL	CAVARRETTA	1936	Chicago Cubs	NL	124	458	55	125	18	5	9	56	17	36	.273	.376	8
PHIL	CAVARRETTA	1937	Chicago Cubs	NL	106	329	43	94	18	7	5	56	32	35	.286	.429	7
PHIL	CAVARRETTA	1938	Chicago Cubs	NL	92	268	29	64	11	4	1	28	14	27	.239	.321	4
PHIL	CAVARRETTA	1939	Chicago Cubs	NL	22	55	4	15	3	1	0	0	4	3	.273	.364	2
PHIL	CAVARRETTA	1940	Chicago Cubs	NL	65	193	34	54	11	4	2	22	31	18	.280	.409	3
PHIL	CAVARRETTA	1941	Chicago Cubs	NL	107	346	46	99	18	4	6	40	53	28	.286	.413	2
PHIL	CAVARRETTA	1942	Chicago Cubs	NL	136	482	59	130	28	4	3	54	71	42	.270	.363	3
PHIL	CAVARRETTA	1943	Chicago Cubs	NL	143	530	93	154	27	9	8	73	75	42	.291	.421	4
PHIL	CAVARRETTA	1944	Chicago Cubs	NL	152	614	106	197	35	15	5	82	67	42	.321	.451	5
PHIL	CAVARRETTA	1945	Chicago Cubs	NL	132	498	94	177	34	10	6	97	81	34	.355	.500	5
PHIL	CAVARRETTA	1946	Chicago Cubs	NL	139	510	89	150	28	10	8	78	88	54	.294	.435	2
PHIL	CAVARRETTA	1947	Chicago Cubs	NL	127	459	56	144	22	5	2	63	58	35	.314	.397	4
PHIL	CAVARRETTA	1948	Chicago Cubs	NL	111	334	41	93	16	5	3	40	35	29	.278	.383	4
PHIL	CAVARRETTA	1949	Chicago Cubs	NL	105	360	46	106	22	4	8	49	45	31	.294	.444	2
PHIL	CAVARRETTA	1950	Chicago Cubs	NL	82	256	49	70	11	1	10	31	40	31	.273	.441	1
PHIL	CAVARRETTA	1951	Chicago Cubs	NL	89	206	24	64	7	1	6	28	27	28	.311	.442	0
PHIL	CAVARRETTA	1952	Chicago Cubs	NL	41	63	7	15	1	1	0	8	9	3	.238	.333	0
PHIL	CAVARRETTA	1953	Chicago Cubs	NL	27	21	3	6	3	0	0	3	6	3	.286	.429	0
PHIL	CAVARRETTA	1954	Chicago White Sox	AL	71	158	21	50	6	2	3	24	26	12	.316	.411	4
PHIL	CAVARRETTA	1955	Chicago White Sox	AL	6	4	1	0	0	0	0	0	0	1	.000		0
RICK	CERONE	1975	Cleveland Indians	AL	7	12	1	3	1	0	0	0	0	0	.250	.333	0
RICK	CERONE	1976	Cleveland Indians	AL	7	16	1	2	0	0	0	0	1	2	.125	.125	0
RICK	CERONE	1977	Toronto Blue Jays	AL	31	100	7	20	4	0	3	10	6	12	.200	.270	0
RICK	CERONE	1978	Toronto Blue Jays	AL	88	282	25	63	8	2	3	20	23	32	.223	.298	0
RICK	CERONE	1979	Toronto Blue Jays	AL	136	469	47	112	27	4	7	61	37	40	.239	.358	1
RICK	CERONE	1980	New York Yankees	AL	147	519	70	144	30	4	14	85	32	56	.277	.432	1
RICK	CERONE	1981	New York Yankees	AL	71	234	23	57	13	2	2	21	12	24	.244	.342	0
RICK	CERONE	1982	New York Yankees	AL	89	300	29	68	10	0	5	28	19	27	.227	.310	0
RICK	CERONE	1983	New York Yankees	AL	80	246	18	54	7	0	2	22	15	29	.220	.272	0

FIRST	LAST	YEAR	TEAM	LEAGUE	G	AB	R	H	2B	3B	HR	RBI	BB	SO	AVG	SLUG	SB
RICK	CERONE	1984	New York Yankees	AL	38	120	8	25	3	0	2	13	9	15	.208	.283	1
RICK	CERONE	1985	Atlanta Braves	NL	96	282	15	61	9	0	3	25	29	25	.216	.280	0
RICK	CERONE	1986	Milwaukee Brewers	AL	68	216	22	56	14	0	4	18	15	28	.259	.380	1
RICK	CERONE	1987	New York Yankees	AL	113	284	28	69	12	1	4	23	30	46	.243	.335	0
RICK	CERONE	1988	Boston Red Sox	AL	84	264	31	71	13	1	3	27	20	32	.269	.360	0
RICK	CERONE	1989	Boston Red Sox	AL	102	296	28	72	16	0	4	48	34	40	.243	.345	0
RICK	CERONE	1990	New York Yankees	AL	49	139	12	42	6	0	2	11	5	13	.302	.388	0
RICK	CERONE	1991	New York Mets	NL	90	227	18	62	13	0	2	16	30	24	.273	.357	1
RICK	CERONE	1992	Montreal Expos	NL	33	63	10	17	4	0	1	7	3	5	.270	.381	0
DINO	CHIOZZA	1935	Philadelphia Phillies	NL	2	0	1	0	0	0	0	0	0	0			0
LOU	CHIOZZA	1934	Philadelphia Phillies	NL	134	484	66	147	28	5	0	44	34	35	.304	.382	9
LOU	CHIOZZA	1935	Philadelphia Phillies	NL	124	472	71	134	26	6	3	47	33	44	.284	.383	5
LOU	CHIOZZA	1936	Philadelphia Phillies	NL	144	572	83	170	32	6	1	48	37	39	.297	.379	17
LOU	CHIOZZA	1937	New York Giants	NL	117	439	49	102	11	2	4	29	20	30	.232	.294	6
LOU	CHIOZZA	1938	New York Giants	NL	57	179	15	42	7	2	3	17	12	7	.235	.346	5
LOU	CHIOZZA	1939	New York Giants	NL	40	142	19	38	3	1	3	12	9	10	.268	.366	3
HARRY	CHITI	1950	Chicago Cubs	NL	3	6	0	2	0	0	0	0	0	7	.333	.333	0
HARRY	CHITI	1951	Chicago Cubs	NL	9	31	1	11	2	0	0	5	2	2	.355	.419	0
HARRY	CHITI	1952	Chicago Cubs	NL	32	113	14	31	5	0	5	13	5	8	.274	.451	0
HARRY	CHITI	1955	Chicago Cubs	NL	113	338	24	78	6	1	11	41	25	68	.231	.352	0
HARRY	CHITI	1956	Chicago Cubs	NL	72	203	17	43	6	4	9	18	19	35	.212	.340	0
HARRY	CHITI	1958	Kansas City Athletics	AL	103	295	32	79	11	3	4	44	18	48	.268	.417	3
HARRY	CHITI	1959	Kansas City Athletics	AL	55	162	20	44	11	0	5	25	17	26	.272	.444	0
HARRY	CHITI	1960	Detroit Tigers	AL	37	104	9	17	0	0	2	5	10	12	.163	.221	0
HARRY	CHITI	1960	Kansas City Athletics	AL	58	190	16	42	7	0	5	28	17	33	.221	.337	1
HARRY	CHITI	1961	Detroit Tigers	AL	5	12	0	1	0	0	0	0	1	2	.083	.083	0
HARRY	CHITI	1962	New York Mets	NL	15	41	2	8	1	0	0	2	1	8	.195	.220	0
ARCHI	CIANFROCCO	1992	Montreal Expos	NL	86	232	25	56	5	2	6	30	11	66	.241	.358	3
ARCHI	CIANFROCCO	1993	Montreal Expos	NL	12	17	3	4	1	0	1	1	0	5	.235	.471	0
ARCHI	CIANFROCCO	1993	San Diego Padres	NL	84	279	27	68	10	2	11	47	17	64	.244	.412	2
ARCHI	CIANFROCCO	1994	San Diego Padres	NL	59	146	9	32	8	0	4	13	3	39	.219	.356	2
ARCHI	CIANFROCCO	1995	San Diego Padres	NL	51	118	22	31	7	0	5	31	11	28	.263	.449	0
ARCHI	CIANFROCCO	1996	San Diego Padres	NL	79	192	21	54	13	3	2	32	8	56	.281	.411	1
ARCHI	CIANFROCCO	1997	San Diego Padres	NL	89	220	25	54	12	0	4	26	25	80	.245	.355	7
ARCHI	CIANFROCCO	1998	San Diego Padres	NL	40	72	4	9	3	0	1	5	5	22	.125	.208	1

FIRST	LAST	YEAR	TEAM	LEAGUE	G	AB	R	H	2B	3B	HR	RBI	BB	SO	AVG	SLUG	SB
LARRY	CIAFFONE	1951	St. Louis Cardinals	NL	5	5	0	0	0	0	0	0	1	2	.000	.000	0
JOE	CICERO	1929	Boston Red Sox	AL	10	32	6	10	2	2	0	4	1	5	.312	.500	0
JOE	CICERO	1930	Boston Red Sox	AL	18	30	5	5	1	2	0	4	1	5	.167	.333	0
GINO	CICERO	1945	Philadelphia Athletics	AL	12	19	3	3	0	0	0	0		6	.158	.158	0
GINO	CIMOLI	1956	Brooklyn Dodgers	NL	73	36		4	1	0	0	4		8	.111	.139	1
GINO	CIMOLI	1957	Brooklyn Dodgers	NL	142	532	88	156	22	5	10	57	39	86	.293	.410	3
GINO	CIMOLI	1958	Los Angeles Dodgers	NL	109	325	35	80	6	3	9	27	18	49	.246	.366	3
GINO	CIMOLI	1959	St. Louis Cardinals	NL	143	519	61	145	40	7	8	72	37	83	.279	.430	7
GINO	CIMOLI	1960	Pittsburgh Pirates	NL	101	307	36	82	14	4	0	28	32	43	.267	.339	1
GINO	CIMOLI	1961	Milwaukee Braves	NL	57	117	12	23	5	1	3	4	11	15	.197	.316	1
GINO	CIMOLI	1961	Pittsburgh Pirates	NL	21	67	4	20	3	0	0	6	2	13	.299	.373	1
GINO	CIMOLI	1962	Kansas City Athletics	AL	152	550	67	151	20	15	10	71	40	89	.275	.420	2
GINO	CIMOLI	1963	Kansas City Athletics	AL	145	529	56	139	19	11	4	48	39	72	.263	.363	3
GINO	CIMOLI	1964	Baltimore Orioles	AL	38	58	6	8	3	2	0	3	2	13	.138	.259	0
GINO	CIMOLI	1964	Kansas City Athletics	AL	4	9	1	0	0	0	0	0	0	2	.000	.000	0
GINO	CIMOLI	1965	California Angels	AL													0
FRANK	CIPRIANI	1961	Kansas City Athletics	AL	13	36	2	9	0	0	0	2	2	4	.250	.250	0
JEFF	CIRILLO	1994	Milwaukee Brewers	AL	39	126	17	30	9	0	3	12	11	16	.238	.381	0
JEFF	CIRILLO	1995	Milwaukee Brewers	AL	125	328	57	91	19	4	9	39	47	42	.277	.442	7
JEFF	CIRILLO	1996	Milwaukee Brewers	AL	158	566	101	184	46	5	15	83	58	69	.325	.504	4
JEFF	CIRILLO	1997	Milwaukee Brewers	AL	154	580	74	167	46	2	10	82	60	74	.288	.426	4
JEFF	CIRILLO	1998	Milwaukee Brewers	NL	156	604	97	194	31	1	14	68	79	88	.321	.445	10
JEFF	CIRILLO	1999	Milwaukee Brewers	NL	157	607	98	198	35	1	15	88	75	83	.326	.461	7
JEFF	CIRILLO	2000	Colorado Rockies	NL	138	598	111	195	53	4	11	115	67	72	.326	.477	3
JEFF	CIRILLO	2001	Colorado Rockies	NL	157	528	72	165	26	2	17	83	43	63	.312	.473	12
JACK	CLARK	1975	San Francisco Giants	NL	8	17	3	4	0	0	0	2	1	2	.235	.235	1
JACK	CLARK	1976	San Francisco Giants	NL	26	102	14	23	6	2	2	10	8	18	.225	.382	6
JACK	CLARK	1977	San Francisco Giants	NL	136	413	64	104	17	4	13	51	49	73	.252	.407	12
JACK	CLARK	1978	San Francisco Giants	NL	156	592	90	181	46	8	25	98	50	72	.306	.537	15
JACK	CLARK	1979	San Francisco Giants	NL	143	527	84	144	25	2	26	86	63	95	.273	.476	11
JACK	CLARK	1980	San Francisco Giants	NL	127	437	77	124	20	8	22	82	74	52	.284	.517	2
JACK	CLARK	1981	San Francisco Giants	NL	99	385	60	103	19	2	17	53	45	45	.268	.460	1
JACK	CLARK	1982	San Francisco Giants	NL	157	563	90	154	30	3	27	103	90	91	.274	.481	6
JACK	CLARK	1983	San Francisco Giants	NL	135	492	82	132	25	0	20	66	74	79	.268	.441	5
JACK	CLARK	1984	San Francisco Giants	NL	57	203	33	65	9	1	11	44	43	29	.320	.537	1

FIRST	LAST	YEAR	TEAM	LEAGUE	G	AB	R	H	2B	3B	HR	RBI	BB	SO	AVG	SLUG	SB
JACK	CLARK	1985	St. Louis Cardinals	NL	126	442	71	124	26	3	22	87	83	88	.281	.502	1
JACK	CLARK	1986	St. Louis Cardinals	NL	65	232	34	55	12	2	9	23	45	61	.237	.422	1
JACK	CLARK	1987	St. Louis Cardinals	NL	131	419	93	120	23	1	35	106	136	139	.286	.597	1
JACK	CLARK	1988	New York Yankees	AL	150	496	81	120	14	0	27	93	113	141	.242	.433	3
JACK	CLARK	1989	San Diego Padres	NL	142	455	76	110	19	1	26	94	132	145	.242	.459	6
JACK	CLARK	1990	San Diego Padres	NL	115	334	59	89	12	1	25	62	104	91	.266	.533	4
JACK	CLARK	1991	Boston Red Sox	AL	140	481	75	120	18	0	28	87	96	133	.249	.466	0
JACK	CLARK	1992	Boston Red Sox	AL	81	257	32	54	11	0	5	33	56	87	.210	.311	1
ROCKY	COLAVITO	1955	Cleveland Indians	AL	5	9	3	4	2	0	0	0	0	2	.444	.667	0
ROCKY	COLAVITO	1956	Cleveland Indians	AL	101	322	55	89	11	0	21	65	49	46	.276	.531	0
ROCKY	COLAVITO	1957	Cleveland Indians	AL	134	461	66	116	26	0	25	84	71	80	.252	.471	0
ROCKY	COLAVITO	1958	Cleveland Indians	AL	143	489	80	148	26	3	41	113	84	89	.303	.620	0
ROCKY	COLAVITO	1959	Cleveland Indians	AL	154	588	90	151	24	0	42	111	71	86	.257	.512	3
ROCKY	COLAVITO	1960	Detroit Tigers	AL	145	555	67	138	18	1	35	87	53	80	.249	.474	3
ROCKY	COLAVITO	1961	Detroit Tigers	AL	163	583	129	169	30	2	45	140	113	75	.290	.580	1
ROCKY	COLAVITO	1962	Detroit Tigers	AL	161	601	90	164	30	2	37	112	96	68	.273	.514	2
ROCKY	COLAVITO	1963	Detroit Tigers	AL	160	597	91	162	29	2	22	91	84	78	.271	.437	0
ROCKY	COLAVITO	1964	Kansas City Athletics	AL	160	588	89	161	31	2	34	102	83	56	.274	.507	3
ROCKY	COLAVITO	1965	Cleveland Indians	AL	162	592	92	170	25	2	26	108	93	63	.287	.468	1
ROCKY	COLAVITO	1966	Cleveland Indians	AL	151	533	68	127	13	0	30	72	76	81	.238	.432	2
ROCKY	COLAVITO	1967	Chicago White Sox	AL	60	190	20	42	4	1	3	29	25	10	.221	.300	1
ROCKY	COLAVITO	1967	Cleveland Indians	AL	63	191	10	46	9	0	5	21	24	31	.241	.366	2
ROCKY	COLAVITO	1968	Los Angeles Dodgers	NL	40	113	8	23	3	0	3	11	15	18	.204	.310	0
ROCKY	COLAVITO	1968	New York Yankees	AL	39	91	13	20	1	0	5	13	14	17	.220	.451	0
MICHAEL	COLANGELO	1999	Anaheim Angels	AL	1	2	0	1	0	0	0	0	8	0	.500	.500	0
MICHAEL	COLANGELO	2001	San Diego Padres	NL	50	91	10	22	3	1	2	8	8	30	.242	.407	0
CHRIS	COLETTA	1972	California Angels	AL	14	30	5	9	1	0	0	7	1	4	.300	.433	0
BOB	COLUCCIO	1973	Milwaukee Brewers	AL	124	438	65	98	21	8	15	58	54	92	.224	.411	13
BOB	COLUCCIO	1974	Milwaukee Brewers	AL	138	394	42	88	13	4	6	31	43	61	.223	.322	15
BOB	COLUCCIO	1975	Chicago White Sox	AL	61	161	22	33	4	2	4	13	13	34	.205	.329	4
BOB	COLUCCIO	1975	Milwaukee Brewers	AL	22	62	8	12	0	1	1	5	11	11	.194	.274	1
BOB	COLUCCIO	1977	Chicago White Sox	AL	20	37	4	10	0	0	0	7	6	2	.270	.270	0
BOB	COLUCCIO	1978	St. Louis Cardinals	NL	5	3	0	0	0	0	0	0	1	2	.000	.000	0
TONY	CONIGLIARO	1964	Boston RedSox	AL	111	404	69	117	21	2	24	52	35	78	.290	.530	2
TONY	CONIGLIARO	1965	Boston RedSox	AL	138	521	82	140	21	5	32	82	51	116	.269	.512	4

FIRST	LAST	YEAR	TEAM	LEAGUE	G	AB	R	H	2B	3B	HR	RBI	BB	SO	AVG	SLUG	SB
TONY	CONIGLIARO	1966	Boston RedSox	AL	150	558	77	148	26	7	28	93	52	112	.265	.487	0
TONY	CONIGLIARO	1967	Boston RedSox	AL	95	349	59	100	11	5	20	67	27	58	.287	.519	4
TONY	CONIGLIARO	1969	Boston RedSox	AL	141	506	57	129	21	3	20	82	48	111	.255	.427	2
TONY	CONIGLIARO	1970	Boston RedSox	AL	146	560	89	149	20	1	36	116	43	93	.266	.498	4
TONY	CONIGLIARO	1971	California Angels	AL	74	266	23	59	18	0	4	15	23	52	.222	.335	3
TONY	CONIGLIARO	1975	Boston Red Sox	AL	21	57	8	7	1	0	2	9	8	9	.123	.246	1
BILLY	CONIGLIARO	1969	Boston Red Sox	AL	32	80	14	23	6	0	4	7	9	23	.287	.562	1
BILLY	CONIGLIARO	1970	Boston Red Sox	AL	114	398	59	108	16	3	18	58	35	73	.271	.462	3
BILLY	CONIGLIARO	1971	Boston Red Sox	AL	101	351	42	92	26	1	11	33	25	68	.262	.436	3
BILLY	CONIGLIARO	1972	Milwaukee Brewers	AL	52	191	22	44	6	2	7	16	8	54	.230	.393	1
BILLY	CONIGLIARO	1973	Oakland Athletics	AL	48	110	5	22	2	2	0	14	9	26	.200	.255	1
BILLY	CONSOLO	1953	Boston Red Sox	AL	47	65	9	14	2	1	1	6	2	23	.215	.323	2
BILLY	CONSOLO	1954	Boston Red Sox	AL	91	242	23	55	7	1	1	11	33	69	.227	.277	0
BILLY	CONSOLO	1955	Boston Red Sox	AL	8	18	4	4	0	0	0	0	5	4	.222	.222	0
BILLY	CONSOLO	1956	Boston Red Sox	AL	48	11	13	2	0	0	0	1	3	5	.182	.182	0
BILLY	CONSOLO	1957	Boston Red Sox	AL	68	196	26	53	6	1	4	19	23	48	.270	.372	1
BILLY	CONSOLO	1958	Boston Red Sox	AL	46	72	13	9	2	1	0	5	6	14	.125	.181	0
BILLY	CONSOLO	1959	Boston Red Sox	AL	10	14	3	3	1	0	0	0	2	5	.214	.286	0
BILLY	CONSOLO	1959	Washington Senators	AL	79	202	25	43	5	3	0	10	36	54	.213	.267	1
BILLY	CONSOLO	1960	Washington Senators	AL	100	174	23	36	4	2	3	15	25	29	.207	.305	1
BILLY	CONSOLO	1961	Minnesota Twins	AL	11	5	1	0	0	0	0	0	0	1	.000		0
BILLY	CONSOLO	1962	Kansas City Athletics	AL	54	154	11	37	4	2	0	16	23	33	.240	.292	1
BILLY	CONSOLO	1962	Los Angeles Angels	AL	28	20	4	2	0	0	0	0	3	11	.100	.100	2
BILLY	CONSOLO	1962	Philadelphia Phillies	NL	13	5	3	2	0	0	0	0	0	1	.400	.400	0
DAN	COSTELLO	1913	New York Yankees	AL	2	2	1	1	0	0	0	0	0	0	.500	.500	0
DAN	COSTELLO	1914	Pittsburgh Pirates	NL	21	64	7	19	1	0	0	5	8	16	.297	.312	2
DAN	COSTELLO	1915	Pittsburgh Pirates	NL	71	125	16	27	4	1	0	11	7	23	.216	.264	7
DAN	COSTELLO	1916	Pittsburgh Pirates	NL	60	159	11	38	1	3	0	8	6	23	.239	.283	3
TIM	COSTO	1992	Cincinnati Reds	NL	12	36	3	8	2	0	0	2	5	6	.222	.278	0
TIM	COSTO	1993	Cincinnati Reds	NL	31	98	13	22	5	0	3	12	4	17	.224	.367	0
CREEPY	CRESPI	1938	St. Louis Cardinals	NL	7	19	2	5	2	0	0	1	2	7	.263	.368	0
CREEPY	CRESPI	1939	St. Louis Cardinals	NL	15	29	3	5	1	0	0	6	3	6	.172	.207	0
CREEPY	CRESPI	1940	St. Louis Cardinals	NL	3	11	2	3	1	0	0	0	1	2	.273	.364	1
CREEPY	CRESPI	1941	St. Louis Cardinals	NL	146	560	85	156	24	2	4	46	57	58	.279	.350	3
CREEPY	CRESPI	1942	St. Louis Cardinals	NL	93	292	33	71	4	2	0	35	27	29	.243	.271	4

FIRST	LAST	YEAR	TEAM	LEAGUE	G	AB	R	H	2B	3B	HR	RBI	BB	SO	AVG	SLUG	SB
DAVE	CRISCIONE	1977	Baltimore Orioles	AL	7	9	1	3	0	0	1	1	0	1	.333	.667	0
TONY	CRISCOLA	1942	St. Louis Browns	AL	91	158	17	47	9	2	1	13	8	13	.297	.399	2
TONY	CRISCOLA	1943	St. Louis Browns	AL	29	52	4	8	0	2	0	1	8	12	.154	.154	0
TONY	CRISCOLA	1944	Cincinnati Reds	NL	64	157	14	36	3	2	0	14	14	7	.229	.274	3
FRANKIE	CROSETTI	1932	New York Yankees	AL	116	398	47	96	20	9	5	57	51	51	.241	.374	4
FRANKIE	CROSETTI	1933	New York Yankees	AL	136	451	71	114	20	5	9	60	55	40	.253	.379	5
FRANKIE	CROSETTI	1934	New York Yankees	AL	138	554	85	147	22	10	11	67	61	58	.265	.401	5
FRANKIE	CROSETTI	1935	New York Yankees	AL	87	305	49	78	17	6	8	50	41	27	.256	.430	3
FRANKIE	CROSETTI	1936	New York Yankees	AL	151	632	137	182	35	7	15	78	90	83	.288	.437	18
FRANKIE	CROSETTI	1937	New York Yankees	AL	149	611	127	143	29	5	11	49	86	105	.234	.352	13
FRANKIE	CROSETTI	1938	New York Yankees	AL	157	631	113	166	35	3	9	55	106	97	.263	.371	27
FRANKIE	CROSETTI	1939	New York Yankees	AL	152	656	109	153	25	5	10	56	65	81	.233	.332	11
FRANKIE	CROSETTI	1940	New York Yankees	AL	145	546	84	106	23	4	4	31	72	77	.194	.273	14
FRANKIE	CROSETTI	1941	New York Yankees	AL	50	148	13	33	2	2	1	22	18	14	.223	.284	0
FRANKIE	CROSETTI	1942	New York Yankees	AL	74	285	50	69	5	5	4	23	31	31	.242	.337	1
FRANKIE	CROSETTI	1943	New York Yankees	AL	95	348	36	81	8	1	2	20	36	47	.233	.279	4
FRANKIE	CROSETTI	1944	New York Yankees	AL	55	197	20	47	4	2	5	30	11	21	.239	.355	3
FRANKIE	CROSETTI	1945	New York Yankees	AL	130	441	57	105	12	0	4	48	59	65	.238	.293	7
FRANKIE	CROSETTI	1946	New York Yankees	AL	28	59	4	17	3	0	0	3	8	2	.288	.339	0
FRANKIE	CROSETTI	1947	New York Yankees	AL	3	1	0	0	0	0	0	0	0	0	.000		0
FRANKIE	CROSETTI	1948	New York Yankees	AL	17	14	4	4	0	0	0	0	2	0	.286	.429	0
TONY	CUCCINELLO	1930	Cincinnati Reds	NL	125	443	64	138	22	5	10	78	47	44	.312	.451	5
TONY	CUCCINELLO	1931	Cincinnati Reds	NL	154	575	67	181	39	11	2	93	54	28	.315	.431	1
TONY	CUCCINELLO	1932	Brooklyn Dodgers	NL	154	597	76	168	32	6	12	77	46	47	.281	.415	5
TONY	CUCCINELLO	1933	Brooklyn Dodgers	NL	134	485	58	122	31	4	9	65	44	40	.252	.388	4
TONY	CUCCINELLO	1934	Brooklyn Dodgers	NL	140	528	59	138	32	3	14	94	49	45	.261	.409	0
TONY	CUCCINELLO	1935	Brooklyn Dodgers	NL	102	360	49	105	20	3	8	53	40	35	.292	.431	3
TONY	CUCCINELLO	1936	Boston Braves	NL	150	565	68	174	26	3	7	86	58	49	.308	.402	1
TONY	CUCCINELLO	1937	Boston Braves	NL	152	575	77	156	36	4	11	80	61	40	.271	.405	2
TONY	CUCCINELLO	1938	Boston Braves	NL	147	555	62	147	25	2	9	76	52	32	.265	.366	4
TONY	CUCCINELLO	1939	Boston Braves	NL	81	310	42	95	17	1	2	40	26	26	.306	.387	5
TONY	CUCCINELLO	1940	Boston Braves	NL	34	126	14	34	9	0	0	19	8	9	.270	.341	1
TONY	CUCCINELLO	1940	New York Giants	NL	88	307	26	64	9	2	5	36	16	42	.208	.300	1
TONY	CUCCINELLO	1942	Boston Braves	NL	40	104	8	21	3	0	1	8	9	11	.202	.260	1
TONY	CUCCINELLO	1943	Boston Braves	NL	13	19	0	0	0	0	0	2	3	1	.000		0

FIRST	LAST	YEAR	TEAM	LEAGUE	G	AB	R	H	2B	3B	HR	RBI	BB	SO	AVG	SLUG	SB
TONY	CUCCINELLO	1943	Chicago WhiteSox	AL	34	103	5	28	5	0	2	11	13	13	.272	.379	3
TONY	CUCCINELLO	1944	Chicago WhiteSox	AL	38	130	5	34	3	3	0	17	8	16	.262	.285	0
TONY	CUCCINELLO	1945	Chicago WhiteSox	AL	118	402	50	124	25	3	2	49	45	19	.308	.400	6
AL	CUCCINELLO	1935	New York Giants	NL	54	165	27	41	7	1	4	20	1	20	.248	.376	0
MARK	DALESANDRO	1994	California Angels	AL	19	25	5	5	1	0	0	2	2	4	.200	.360	0
MARK	DALESANDRO	1995	California Angels	AL	11	10	1	1	0	0	0	0	1	2	.100	.100	0
MARK	DALESANDRO	1998	Toronto BlueJays	AL	32	67	8	20	5	0	2	14	0	6	.299	.463	1
MARK	DALESANDRO	1999	Toronto Blue Jays	AL	16	27	3	5	0	0	0	1	0	2	.185	.185	0
MARK	DALESANDRO	2001	Chicago White Sox	AL	1	0	0	0	0	0	0	0	0	0			0
DOM	DALLESSANDRO	1937	Boston Red Sox	AL	68	147	18	34	7	0	0	11	27	16	.231	.293	2
DOM	DALLESSANDRO	1940	Chicago Cubs	NL	107	287	33	77	19	6	1	36	34	13	.268	.387	4
DOM	DALLESSANDRO	1941	Chicago Cubs	NL	140	486	73	132	36	2	6	85	68	37	.272	.391	3
DOM	DALLESSANDRO	1942	Chicago Cubs	NL	96	264	30	69	12	4	4	43	36	18	.261	.383	4
DOM	DALLESSANDRO	1943	Chicago Cubs	NL	87	176	13	39	8	3	0	31	40	14	.222	.318	1
DOM	DALLESSANDRO	1944	Chicago Cubs	NL	117	381	53	116	19	4	8	74	61	29	.304	.438	1
DOM	DALLESSANDRO	1946	Chicago Cubs	NL	65	89	4	20	2	1	0	9	23	12	.225	.326	1
DOM	DALLESSANDRO	1947	Chicago Cubs	NL	66	115	18	33	7	1	1	14	21	11	.287	.391	0
FATS	DANTONIO	1944	Brooklyn Dodgers	NL	3	7	0	1	0	0	0	0	0	1	.143	.143	0
FATS	DANTONIO	1945	Brooklyn Dodgers	NL	47	128	12	32	6	1	0	12	11	6	.250	.312	3
DOUG	DASCENZO	1988	Chicago Cubs	NL	26	75	9	16	3	0	0	4	9	4	.213	.253	6
DOUG	DASCENZO	1989	Chicago Cubs	NL	47	139	20	23	1	0	0	12	13	13	.165	.194	6
DOUG	DASCENZO	1990	Chicago Cubs	NL	113	241	27	61	9	5	1	26	21	18	.253	.344	15
DOUG	DASCENZO	1991	Chicago Cubs	NL	118	239	40	61	11	0	1	18	24	26	.255	.314	14
DOUG	DASCENZO	1992	Chicago Cubs	NL	139	376	37	96	13	4	0	20	27	32	.255	.311	6
DOUG	DASCENZO	1993	Texas Rangers	AL	76	146	20	29	5	2	2	20	8	22	.199	.288	2
DOUG	DASCENZO	1996	San Diego Padres	NL	21	9	3	2	0	0	0	0	1	2	.111	.111	0
DOUG	DeCINCES	1973	Baltimore Orioles	AL	10	18	2	2	0	0	0	3	1	5	.111	.111	0
DOUG	DeCINCES	1974	Baltimore Orioles	AL	1	1	0	0	0	0	0	0	0	0	.000		0
DOUG	DeCINCES	1975	Baltimore Orioles	AL	61	167	20	42	6	3	4	23	13	32	.251	.395	0
DOUG	DeCINCES	1976	Baltimore Orioles	AL	129	440	36	103	17	2	11	42	29	68	.234	.357	8
DOUG	DeCINCES	1977	Baltimore Orioles	AL	150	522	63	135	28	3	19	69	64	86	.259	.433	8
DOUG	DeCINCES	1978	Baltimore Orioles	AL	142	511	72	146	37	1	28	80	46	81	.286	.526	7
DOUG	DeCINCES	1979	Baltimore Orioles	AL	120	422	67	97	27	1	16	61	54	68	.230	.412	5
DOUG	DeCINCES	1980	Baltimore Orioles	AL	145	489	64	122	23	2	16	64	49	83	.249	.403	11
DOUG	DeCINCES	1981	Baltimore Orioles	AL	100	346	49	91	23	2	13	55	41	32	.263	.454	0

FIRST	LAST	YEAR	TEAM	LEAGUE	G	AB	R	H	2B	3B	HR	RBI	BB	SO	AVG	SLUG	SB
DOUG	DeCINCES	1982	California Angels	AL	153	575	94	173	42	5	30	97	66	80	.301	.548	7
DOUG	DeCINCES	1983	California Angels	AL	95	370	49	104	19	3	18	65	32	56	.281	.495	2
DOUG	DeCINCES	1984	California Angels	AL	146	547	77	147	23	3	20	82	53	79	.269	.431	4
DOUG	DeCINCES	1985	California Angels	AL	120	427	50	104	22	1	20	78	47	71	.244	.440	1
DOUG	DeCINCES	1986	California Angels	AL	140	512	69	131	20	3	26	96	52	74	.256	.459	2
DOUG	DeCINCES	1987	California Angels	AL	133	453	65	106	23	3	16	63	70	87	.234	.391	3
DOUG	DeCINCES	1987	St. Louis Cardinals	NL	4	9		2	2	0	0	1	0	2	.222		0
BOBBY	DelGRECO	1952	Pittsburgh Pirates	NL	99	341	34	74	14	2	1	20	38	70	.217	.279	6
BOBBY	DelGRECO	1956	Pittsburgh Pirates	NL	14	20	4	4	0	0	2	3	3	3	.200	.500	0
BOBBY	DelGRECO	1956	St. Louis Cardinals	NL	102	270	29	58	16	2	5	18	32	50	.215	.344	1
BOBBY	DelGRECO	1957	Chicago Cubs	NL	20	40	2	8	2	0	0	3	10	17	.200	.250	1
BOBBY	DelGRECO	1957	New York Yankees	AL	8	7	3	3	0	0	0	0	2	2	.429	.429	1
BOBBY	DelGRECO	1958	New York Yankees	AL	12	5	1	1	0	0	0	0	1		.200	.200	0
BOBBY	DelGRECO	1960	Philadelphia Phillies	NL	100	300	48	71	16	4	10	26	54	64	.237	.417	1
BOBBY	DelGRECO	1961	Kansas City Athletics	AL	74	239	34	55	14	1	5	21	30	31	.230	.360	0
BOBBY	DelGRECO	1961	Philadelphia Phillies	NL	41	112	14	29	5	0	1	11	12	17	.259	.357	4
BOBBY	DelGRECO	1962	Kansas City Athletics	AL	132	338	61	86	21	1	9	38	49	62	.254	.402	0
BOBBY	DelGRECO	1963	Kansas City Athletics	AL	121	306	40	65	7	1	8	29	40	52	.212	.320	0
BOBBY	DelGRECO	1965	Philadelphia Phillies	NL	8	4	1	0	0	0	0	0	0	3	.000		0
DAVE	DELLUCCI	1997	Baltimore Orioles	AL	17	27	3	6	1	0	0	3	4	7	.222	.370	0
DAVE	DELLUCCI	1998	Arizona Diamondbacks	NL	124	416	43	108	19	12	5	51	33	103	.260	.399	3
DAVE	DELLUCCI	1999	Arizona Diamondbacks	NL	63	109	27	43	7	1	5	15	11	24	.394	.505	2
DAVE	DELLUCCI	2000	Arizona Diamondbacks	NL	34	50	2	15	3	0	0	2	4	9	.300	.360	0
DAVE	DELLUCCI	2001	Arizona Diamondbacks	NL	115	217	28	60	10	2	10	40	22	52	.276	.479	2
JOE	DeMAESTRI	1951	Chicago White Sox	AL	56	74	8	15	0	2	1	3	5	11	.203	.297	0
JOE	DeMAESTRI	1952	St. Louis Browns	AL	81	186	13	42	9	2	1	18	8	25	.226	.301	0
JOE	DeMAESTRI	1953	Philadelphia Athletics	AL	111	420	53	107	17	3	6	35	24	39	.255	.352	1
JOE	DeMAESTRI	1954	Philadelphia Athletics	AL	146	539	49	124	16	3	8	40	20	63	.230	.315	3
JOE	DeMAESTRI	1955	Kansas City Athletics	AL	123	457	42	114	14	1	6	37	20	47	.249	.324	3
JOE	DeMAESTRI	1956	Kansas City Athletics	AL	133	434	41	101	16	1	6	39	25	73	.233	.316	6
JOE	DeMAESTRI	1957	Kansas City Athletics	AL	135	461	44	113	14	6	9	33	22	82	.245	.360	1
JOE	DeMAESTRI	1958	Kansas City Athletics	AL	139	442	32	97	11	6	6	38	16	84	.219	.290	3
JOE	DeMAESTRI	1959	Kansas City Athletics	AL	118	352	31	86	16	5	6	34	28	65	.244	.369	1
JOE	DeMAESTRI	1960	New York Yankees	AL	49	35	8	8	1	0	0	2	0	9	.229	.257	0
JOE	DeMAESTRI	1961	New York Yankees	AL	50	41	1	6	0	0	0	2	0	13	.146	.146	0

FIRST	LAST	YEAR	LEAGUE	TEAM	G	AB	R	H	2B	3B	HR	RBI	BB	SO	AVG	SLUG	SB
AL	DEMAREE	1912	NL	New York Giants	2	5	0	0	0	0	0	0	0	1	.000		0
AL	DEMAREE	1913	NL	New York Giants	31	66	5	7	0	1	0	1	3	22	.106	.136	0
AL	DEMAREE	1914	NL	New York Giants	38	68	5	9	0	0	0	0	4	12	.132	.132	0
AL	DEMAREE	1915	NL	Philadelphia Phillies	32	68	6	12	1	0	0	4	4	32	.176	.191	0
AL	DEMAREE	1916	NL	Philadelphia Phillies	39	101	6	11	2	0	0	5	6	36	.109	.129	2
AL	DEMAREE	1917	NL	Chicago Cubs	24	41	0	5	0	0	0	1	4	17	.122	.122	0
AL	DEMAREE	1917	NL	New York Giants	15	18	2	2	0	0	0	2	1	6	.111	.111	2
AL	DEMAREE	1918	NL	New York Giants	26	47	5	6	0	0	0	2	1	11	.128	.128	1
AL	DEMAREE	1919	NL	Boston Braves	25	42	1	2	0	0	0	1	1	11	.048	.048	1
SAM	DENTE	1947	AL	Boston Red Sox	46	168	14	39	4	2	0	11	19	15	.232	.280	0
SAM	DENTE	1948	AL	St. Louis Browns	98	267	26	72	11	2	1	22	22	12	.270	.326	1
SAM	DENTE	1949	AL	Washington Senators	153	590	48	161	24	4	1	53	31	24	.273	.332	4
SAM	DENTE	1950	AL	Washington Senators	155	603	56	144	20	5	2	59	39	19	.239	.299	1
SAM	DENTE	1951	AL	Washington Senators	88	273	21	65	8	1	0	29	25	10	.238	.275	3
SAM	DENTE	1952	AL	Chicago White Sox	62	145	12	32	0	0	0	11	5	8	.221	.234	3
SAM	DENTE	1953	AL	Chicago White Sox	2	0	0	0	0	0	0	0	0	0			0
SAM	DENTE	1954	AL	Cleveland Indians	68	169	18	45	7	1	1	19	14	4	.266	.337	0
SAM	DENTE	1955	AL	Cleveland Indians	73	105	10	27	4	1	0	10	12	8	.257	.295	0
MARK	DEROSA	1998	NL	Atlanta Braves	5	3	2	1	0	0	0	0	0	1	.333	.333	0
MARK	DEROSA	1999	NL	Atlanta Braves	7	8	1	0	0	0	0	0	0	2	.000		0
MARK	DEROSA	2000	NL	Atlanta Braves	22	13	9	4	1	0	0	3	2	2	.308	.385	0
MARK	DEROSA	2001	NL	Atlanta Braves	66	164	27	47	8	0	3	20	12	19	.287	.390	2
BUTTERCUP	DICKERSON	1878	NL	Cincinnati Red Stockings	29	123	17	38	5	1	2	9	0	7	.309	.366	
BUTTERCUP	DICKERSON	1879	NL	Cincinnati Red Stockings	81	350	73	102	18	14	2	57	3	27	.291	.440	
BUTTERCUP	DICKERSON	1880	NL	Troy Trojans	30	119	15	23	2	2	0	10	2	3	.193	.244	
BUTTERCUP	DICKERSON	1880	NL	Worcester Brown Stockings	31	133	22	39	8	6	0	20	1	2	.293	.444	
BUTTERCUP	DICKERSON	1881	NL	Worcester Brown Stockings	80	367	48	116	18	6	1	31	8	8	.316	.406	
BUTTERCUP	DICKERSON	1883	AA	Pittsburgh Alleghenys	85	354	62	88	15	1	0		18		.249	.297	
BUTTERCUP	DICKERSON	1884	AA	Baltimore Orioles	13	56	9	12	2	2	1		4		.214	.286	
BUTTERCUP	DICKERSON	1884	AA	Louisville Colonels	8	28	6	4	0	2	0		3		.143	.393	
BUTTERCUP	DICKERSON	1884	UA	St. Louis Maroons	46	211	49	77	15	1	0		8		.365	.445	
BUTTERCUP	DICKERSON	1885	NL	Buffalo Bisons	5	21	1	1	1	0	0	0	1	4	.048	.048	
JAY	DIFANI	1948	AL	Washington Senators	2	2	0	1	0	0	0	0	0	2	.000		0
JAY	DIFANI	1949	AL	Washington Senators	2	1	0	1	1	0	0	0	0	0	1.000		0
MIKE	DIFELICE	1996	NL	St. Louis Cardinals	4	7	0	2	1	0	0	2	0	1	.286	.429	0

FIRST	LAST	YEAR	TEAM	LEAGUE	G	AB	R	H	2B	3B	HR	RBI	BB	SO	AVG	SLUG	SB
MIKE	DIFELICE	1997	St. Louis Cardinals	NL	93	260	16	62	10	1	4	30	19	61	.258	.331	1
MIKE	DIFELICE	1998	Tampa Bay Devil Rays	AL	84	248	17	57	12	3	3	23	15	56	.230	.339	0
MIKE	DIFELICE	1999	Tampa Bay Devil Rays	AL	51	179	21	55	11	0	6	27	8	23	.307	.469	0
MIKE	DIFELICE	2000	Tampa Bay Devil Rays	AL	60	204	23	49	13	1	6	19	12	40	.240	.402	0
MIKE	DIFELICE	2001	Arizona Diamondbacks	NL	12	21	1	1	0	0	0	1	0	10	.048	.048	0
MIKE	DIFELICE	2001	Tampa Bay Devil Rays	AL	48	149	13	31	5	1	2	9	8	39	.208	.295	1
DOM	DIMAGGIO	1940	Boston Red Sox	AL	108	418	81	126	32	6	8	46	41	46	.301	.464	7
DOM	DIMAGGIO	1941	Boston Red Sox	AL	144	584	117	165	37	6	8	58	90	57	.283	.408	13
DOM	DIMAGGIO	1942	Boston Red Sox	AL	151	622	110	178	36	8	14	48	70	52	.286	.437	16
DOM	DIMAGGIO	1946	Boston Red Sox	AL	142	554	85	169	24	7	7	73	66	58	.316	.427	10
DOM	DIMAGGIO	1947	Boston Red Sox	AL	136	513	75	145	21	5	8	71	74	62	.283	.390	10
DOM	DIMAGGIO	1948	Boston Red Sox	AL	155	648	127	185	40	4	9	87	101	58	.285	.401	10
DOM	DIMAGGIO	1949	Boston Red Sox	AL	145	605	126	186	34	5	8	60	96	55	.307	.420	9
DOM	DIMAGGIO	1950	Boston Red Sox	AL	141	588	131	193	30	11	7	70	82	68	.328	.452	15
DOM	DIMAGGIO	1951	Boston Red Sox	AL	146	639	113	189	34	4	12	72	73	53	.296	.418	4
DOM	DIMAGGIO	1952	Boston Red Sox	AL	128	486	81	143	20	1	6	33	57	61	.294	.377	6
DOM	DIMAGGIO	1953	Boston Red Sox	AL	3	3	0	1	0	0	0	0	0	0	.333	.333	0
JOE	DIMAGGIO	1936	New York Yankees	AL	138	637	132	206	44	15	29	125	24	39	.323	.576	4
JOE	DIMAGGIO	1937	New York Yankees	AL	151	621	151	215	35	15	46	167	64	37	.346	.673	3
JOE	DIMAGGIO	1938	New York Yankees	AL	145	599	129	194	32	13	32	140	59	21	.324	.581	6
JOE	DIMAGGIO	1939	New York Yankees	AL	120	462	108	176	32	6	30	126	52	20	.381	.671	3
JOE	DIMAGGIO	1940	New York Yankees	AL	132	508	93	179	28	9	31	133	61	30	.352	.626	1
JOE	DIMAGGIO	1941	New York Yankees	AL	139	541	122	193	43	11	30	125	76	13	.357	.643	4
JOE	DIMAGGIO	1942	New York Yankees	AL	154	610	123	186	29	13	21	114	68	36	.305	.498	4
JOE	DIMAGGIO	1946	New York Yankees	AL	132	503	81	146	20	8	25	95	59	24	.290	.511	1
JOE	DIMAGGIO	1947	New York Yankees	AL	141	534	97	168	31	10	20	97	64	32	.315	.522	3
JOE	DIMAGGIO	1948	New York Yankees	AL	153	594	110	190	26	11	39	155	67	30	.320	.598	1
JOE	DIMAGGIO	1949	New York Yankees	AL	76	272	58	94	14	6	14	67	55	18	.346	.596	0
JOE	DIMAGGIO	1950	New York Yankees	AL	139	525	114	158	33	10	32	122	80	33	.301	.585	0
JOE	DIMAGGIO	1951	New York Yankees	AL	116	415	72	109	22	4	12	71	61	36	.263	.422	0
VINCE	DIMAGGIO	1937	Boston Braves	NL	132	493	56	126	18	3	13	69	39	111	.256	.387	8
VINCE	DIMAGGIO	1938	Boston Braves	NL	150	540	71	123	28	3	14	61	65	134	.228	.369	11
VINCE	DIMAGGIO	1939	Cincinnati Reds	NL	8	14	1	1	1	0	0	2	2	10	.071	.143	0
VINCE	DIMAGGIO	1940	Cincinnati Reds	NL	2	4	2	1	0	0	0	0	1	0	.250	.250	0
VINCE	DIMAGGIO	1940	Pittsburgh Pirates	NL	110	356	59	103	26	0	19	54	37	83	.289	.522	11

FIRST	LAST	YEAR	LEAGUE	TEAM	G	AB	R	H	2B	3B	HR	RBI	BB	SO	AVG	SLUG	SB
VINCE	DIMAGGIO	1941	NL	Pittsburgh Pirates	151	528	73	141	27	5	21	100	68	100	.267	.456	10
VINCE	DIMAGGIO	1942	NL	Pittsburgh Pirates	143	496	57	118	22	3	15	75	52	87	.238	.385	10
VINCE	DIMAGGIO	1943	NL	Pittsburgh Pirates	157	580	64	144	41	2	15	88	70	126	.248	.403	11
VINCE	DIMAGGIO	1944	NL	Pittsburgh Pirates	109	342	41	82	20	4	9	50	33	83	.240	.401	6
VINCE	DIMAGGIO	1945	NL	Philadelphia Phillies	127	452	64	116	25	3	19	84	43	91	.257	.451	12
VINCE	DIMAGGIO	1946	NL	New York Giants	15	25	2	0			0	0	2	5	.000		0
VINCE	DIMAGGIO	1946	NL	Philadelphia Phillies	6	19	1	4	1	0	0	1	0	7	.211	.263	0
BOB	DiPIETRO	1951	AL	Boston Red Sox	4	11	0	1	0	0	0	0	1	1	.091	.091	0
GARY	DiSARCINA	1989	AL	California Angels	2	0	0							0			0
GARY	DiSARCINA	1990	AL	California Angels	18	57	8	8	1	1	0	0	0	10	.140	.193	1
GARY	DiSARCINA	1991	AL	California Angels	18	57	5	12	2	0	0	3	3	4	.211	.246	0
GARY	DiSARCINA	1992	AL	California Angels	157	518	48	128	19	1	3	42	20	50	.247	.301	9
GARY	DiSARCINA	1993	AL	California Angels	126	416	44	99	20	2	3	45	15	38	.238	.312	5
GARY	DiSARCINA	1994	AL	California Angels	112	389	53	101	14	2	3	33	18	28	.260	.329	3
GARY	DiSARCINA	1995	AL	California Angels	99	362	61	111	28	6	5	41	20	25	.307	.459	7
GARY	DiSARCINA	1996	AL	California Angels	150	536	62	137	26	4	5	48	21	36	.256	.347	7
GARY	DiSARCINA	1997	AL	Anaheim Angels	154	549	52	135	28	2	4	47	17	29	.246	.326	2
GARY	DiSARCINA	1998	AL	Anaheim Angels	157	551	73	158	39	3	3	56	21	51	.287	.385	7
GARY	DiSARCINA	1999	AL	Anaheim Angels	81	271	32	62	7	1	1	29	15	32	.229	.273	2
GARY	DiSARCINA	2000	AL	Anaheim Angels	12	38	6	15	2	2	1	11	5	13	.395	.526	0
BENNY	DiSTEFANO	1984	NL	Pittsburgh Pirates	45	78	10	13	1	0	3	9	5	5	.167	.346	0
BENNY	DiSTEFANO	1986	NL	Pittsburgh Pirates	31	39	3	7	1	1	1	5	1	4	.179	.282	0
BENNY	DiSTEFANO	1988	NL	Pittsburgh Pirates	16	29	6	10	3	0	1	6	3	4	.345	.621	0
BENNY	DiSTEFANO	1989	NL	Pittsburgh Pirates	96	154	12	38	8	2	2	15	17	30	.247	.358	1
BENNY	DiSTEFANO	1992	NL	Houston Astros	52	60	4	14	0	0	0	7	5	14	.233	.300	0
SAMMY	ESPOSITO	1952	AL	Chicago White Sox	1	4	0	1	0	0	0	0	0	2	.250	.250	0
SAMMY	ESPOSITO	1955	AL	Chicago White Sox	3	4	3	1	0	0	0	0	1	0	.250	.250	0
SAMMY	ESPOSITO	1956	AL	Chicago White Sox	81	184	30	42	8	2	3	25	41	19	.228	.342	1
SAMMY	ESPOSITO	1957	AL	Chicago White Sox	94	176	26	36	3	0	2	15	38	27	.205	.256	5
SAMMY	ESPOSITO	1958	AL	Chicago White Sox	98	81	16	20	3	0	1	3	12	16	.247	.284	1
SAMMY	ESPOSITO	1959	AL	Chicago White Sox	69	66	12	11	1	0	1	5	11	20	.167	.227	0
SAMMY	ESPOSITO	1960	AL	Chicago White Sox	57	77	14	14	5	0	1	11	10	21	.182	.286	0
SAMMY	ESPOSITO	1961	AL	Chicago White Sox	63	94	12	16	5	0	1	8	12	13	.170	.255	0
SAMMY	ESPOSITO	1962	AL	Chicago White Sox	75	81	14	19	1	0	0	4	17	0	.235	.247	0
SAMMY	ESPOSITO	1963	AL	Chicago White Sox	1	0	0	0	0	0	0	0	0	0			0

REACHING FOR THE STARS

FIRST	LAST	YEAR	TEAM	LEAGUE	G	AB	R	H	2B	3B	HR	RBI	BB	SO	AVG	SLUG	SB
SAMMY	ESPOSITO	1963	Kansas City Athletics	AL	18	25	3	5	1	0	0	2	3	3	.200	.240	0
CARMEN	FANZONE	1970	Boston Red Sox	AL	10	15	0	3	1	0	0	3	2	2	.200	.267	0
CARMEN	FANZONE	1971	ChicagoCubs	NL	12	43	5	8	2	0	2	5	2	7	.186	.372	0
CARMEN	FANZONE	1972	Chicago Cubs	NL	86	222	26	50	11	0	8	42	35	45	.225	.383	2
CARMEN	FANZONE	1973	Chicago Cubs	NL	64	150	22	41	7	0	6	22	20	38	.273	.440	1
CARMEN	FANZONE	1974	Chicago Cubs	NL	65	158	13	30	6	0	4	22	15	27	.190	.304	0
SAL	FASANO	1996	Kansas City Royals	AL	51	143	20	29	2	0	6	19	14	25	.203	.343	1
SAL	FASANO	1997	Kansas City Royals	AL	13	38	4	8	2	0	2	1	1	12	.211	.342	0
SAL	FASANO	1998	Kansas City Royals	AL	74	216	21	49	10	0	8	31	10	56	.227	.384	1
SAL	FASANO	1999	Kansas City Royals	AL	23	60	11	14	2	0	5	16	7	17	.233	.517	0
SAL	FASANO	2000	Oakland Athletics	AL	52	126	21	27	6	0	7	19	14	47	.214	.429	0
SAL	FASANO	2001	Colorado Rockies	NL	25	63	10	16	5	0	3	9	4	19	.254	.476	0
SAL	FASANO	2001	Kansas City Royals	AL	3	1	0	0	0	0	0	0	0	0	.000	.000	0
SAL	FASANO	2001	Oakland Athletics	AL	11	21	2	1	0	0	0	1	1	12	.048	.048	0
ERNIE	FAZIO	1962	Houston Colt. 45s	NL	12	12	3	1	0	0	0	0	2	5	.083	.083	0
ERNIE	FAZIO	1963	Houston Colt. 45s	NL	102	228	31	42	10	3	2	5	27	70	.184	.281	4
ERNIE	FAZIO	1966	Kansas City Athletics	AL	27	34	0	7	0	0	0	2	4	10	.206	.265	1
JOE	FERGUSON	1970	Los Angeles Dodgers	NL	5	4	0	1	0	0	0	1	1	2	.250	.250	0
JOE	FERGUSON	1971	Los Angeles Dodgers	NL	36	102	13	22	3	0	2	7	12	15	.216	.304	1
JOE	FERGUSON	1972	Los Angeles Dodgers	NL	8	24	2	7	3	0	1	5	2	4	.292	.542	0
JOE	FERGUSON	1973	Los Angeles Dodgers	NL	136	487	84	128	26	1	25	88	87	81	.263	.470	1
JOE	FERGUSON	1974	Los Angeles Dodgers	NL	111	349	54	88	14	1	16	57	75	73	.252	.456	2
JOE	FERGUSON	1975	Los Angeles Dodgers	NL	66	202	15	42	2	1	5	23	35	47	.208	.302	2
JOE	FERGUSON	1976	Los Angeles Dodgers	NL	54	185	24	41	7	0	6	18	25	41	.222	.357	2
JOE	FERGUSON	1976	St. Louis Cardinals	NL	71	189	22	38	8	4	4	21	32	40	.201	.349	4
JOE	FERGUSON	1977	Houston Astros	NL	132	421	59	108	21	3	16	61	85	79	.257	.435	6
JOE	FERGUSON	1978	Houston Astros	NL	51	150	20	31	5	0	7	22	37	30	.207	.380	0
JOE	FERGUSON	1978	Los Angeles Dodgers	NL	67	198	20	47	11	0	7	28	34	41	.237	.399	1
JOE	FERGUSON	1979	Los Angeles Dodgers	NL	122	363	54	95	14	0	20	69	70	68	.262	.466	1
JOE	FERGUSON	1980	Los Angeles Dodgers	NL	77	172	20	41	3	2	9	29	38	46	.238	.456	2
JOE	FERGUSON	1981	California Angels	AL	12	30	5	7	1	0	0	5	9	8	.233	.367	0
JOE	FERGUSON	1981	Los Angeles Dodgers	NL	17	14	2	2	1	0	0	1	9	5	.143	.214	0
JOE	FERGUSON	1982	California Angels	AL	36	84	10	19	2	0	3	8	12	19	.226	.357	2
JOE	FERGUSON	1983	California Angels	AL	12	27	3	2	0	0	0	2	5	8	.074	.074	0
AL	FERRARA	1963	Los Angeles Dodgers	NL	21	44	2	7	0	0	1	1	6	9	.159	.227	0

FIRST	LAST	YEAR	TEAM	LEAGUE	G	AB	R	H	2B	3B	HR	RBI	BB	SO	AVG	SLUG	SB
AL	FERRARA	1965	Los Angeles Dodgers	NL	41	81	5	17	2	1	1	10	9	20	.210	.296	0
AL	FERRARA	1966	Los Angeles Dodgers	NL	63	115	15	31	4	0	5	23	9	35	.270	.435	0
AL	FERRARA	1967	Los Angeles Dodgers	NL	122	347	41	96	16	0	16	50	33	73	.277	.467	0
AL	FERRARA	1968	Los Angeles Dodgers	NL	2	7	0	1	0	1	0	0	0	2	.143	.143	0
AL	FERRARA	1969	San Diego Padres	NL	138	366	39	95	22	1	14	56	45	69	.260	.440	0
AL	FERRARA	1970	San Diego Padres	NL	138	372	44	103	15	0	13	51	46	63	.277	.444	0
AL	FERRARA	1971	Cincinnati Reds	NL	32	33	2	6	0	0	0	5	3	10	.182	.273	0
AL	FERRARA	1971	San Diego Padres	NL	17	17	0	2	1	0	0	2	5	5	.118	.176	0
MIKE	FERRARO	1966	New York Yankees	AL	10	28	4	5	0	0	0	1	3	3	.179	.179	0
MIKE	FERRARO	1968	New York Yankees	AL	23	87	5	14	0	1	0	1	2	17	.161	.184	0
MIKE	FERRARO	1969	Seattle Pilots	AL	5	4	0	0	0	0	0	0	1	1	.000		0
MIKE	FERRARO	1972	Milwaukee Brewers	AL	124	381	19	97	18	1	2	29	17	41	.255	.323	0
NEIL	FIALA	1981	Cincinnati Reds	NL	2	2	1	1	0	0	0	0	0	1	.500	.500	0
NEIL	FIALA	1981	St. Louis Cardinals	NL	3	3	0	0	0	0	0	0	0	1	.000		0
MIKE	FIGGA	1997	New York Yankees	AL	2	4	1	1	0	0	0	0	0	3	.250	.250	0
MIKE	FIGGA	1998	New York Yankees	AL	1	4	1	1	0	0	0	1	0	3	.250	.250	0
MIKE	FIGGA	1999	Baltimore Orioles	AL	41	86	12	19	4	0	1	5	2	27	.221	.302	0
MIKE	FIGGA	1999	New York Yankees	AL	2	0	0	0	0	0	0	0	0	0			0
MIKE	FIORE	1968	Baltimore Orioles	AL	6	17	2	0	0	0	0	0	4	4	.059	.059	0
MIKE	FIORE	1969	Kansas City Royals	AL	107	339	53	93	14	1	12	35	84	63	.274	.428	4
MIKE	FIORE	1970	Boston Red Sox	AL	41	50	5	7	0	0	0	4	8	4	.140	.140	0
MIKE	FIORE	1970	Kansas City Royals	AL	25	72	6	13	2	0	1	4	13	24	.181	.208	1
MIKE	FIORE	1971	Boston Red Sox	AL	51	62	9	11	2	0	0	6	12	14	.177	.258	0
MIKE	FIORE	1972	San Diego Padres	NL	7	6	0	0	0	0	0	0	1	3	.000		0
MIKE	FIORE	1972	St. Louis Cardinals	NL	17	10	0	1	0	0	0	1	2	3	.100	.100	0
DAN	FIROVA	1981	Seattle Mariners	AL	13	2	0	0	0	0	0	0	0	1	.000		0
DAN	FIROVA	1982	Seattle Mariners	AL	3	5	0	0	0	0	0	0	0	0	.000		0
DAN	FIROVA	1988	Cleveland Indians	AL	1	0	0	0	0	0	0	0	0	0			0
KEVIN	FLORA	1991	California Angels	AL	3	8	1	1	0	0	0	0	1	5	.125	.125	0
KEVIN	FLORA	1995	California Angels	AL	2	3	0	0	0	0	0	0	0	1	.000		0
KEVIN	FLORA	1995	Philadelphia Phillies	NL	24	75	12	16	3	0	2	7	4	22	.213	.333	1
TIM	FOLI	1970	New York Mets	NL	5	11	0	4	0	0	0	1	0	2	.364	.364	1
TIM	FOLI	1971	New York Mets	NL	97	288	32	65	12	2	0	24	18	50	.226	.281	5
TIM	FOLI	1972	Montreal Expos	NL	149	540	45	130	12	2	2	35	25	43	.241	.281	11
TIM	FOLI	1973	Montreal Expos	NL	126	458	37	110	11	0	2	36	28	40	.240	.277	6

FIRST	LAST	YEAR	TEAM	LEAGUE	G	AB	R	H	2B	3B	HR	RBI	BB	SO	AVG	SLUG	SB
TIM	FOLI	1974	Montreal Expos	NL	121	441	41	112	10	3	0	39	28	27	.254	.290	8
TIM	FOLI	1975	Montreal Expos	NL	152	572	64	136	25	2	1	29	36	49	.238	.294	13
TIM	FOLI	1976	Montreal Expos	NL	149	546	41	144	36	1	6	54	16	33	.264	.366	6
TIM	FOLI	1977	Montreal Expos	NL	13	57	2	10	5	1	0	3	0	4	.175	.298	0
TIM	FOLI	1977	San Francisco Giants	NL	104	368	30	84	17	3	4	27	11	16	.228	.323	2
TIM	FOLI	1978	New York Mets	NL	113	413	37	106	21	1	1	27	14	30	.257	.320	2
TIM	FOLI	1979	New York Mets	NL	3	7	0	0	0	0	0	0	0	0	.000		0
TIM	FOLI	1979	Pittsburgh Pirates	NL	133	525	70	153	23	0	1	65	28	14	.291	.345	6
TIM	FOLI	1980	Pittsburgh Pirates	NL	127	495	61	131	22	0	3	38	19	23	.265	.327	11
TIM	FOLI	1981	Pittsburgh Pirates	NL	86	316	32	78	12	2	0	20	17	10	.247	.297	7
TIM	FOLI	1982	California Angels	AL	150	480	46	121	14	2	3	56	14	22	.252	.308	2
TIM	FOLI	1983	California Angels	AL	88	330	29	83	10	0	0	29	5	18	.252	.300	2
TIM	FOLI	1984	New York Yankees	AL	61	163	8	41	11	0	0	16	2	16	.252	.319	0
TIM	FOLI	1985	Pittsburgh Pirates	NL	19	57	1	7	0	0	0	2	4	2	.189	.189	0
MATT	FRANCO	1995	Chicago Cubs	NL	16	17	3	5	1	0	0	1	0	4	.294	.353	0
MATT	FRANCO	1996	New York Mets	NL	14	31	3	6	1	0	0	2	1	5	.194	.323	0
MATT	FRANCO	1997	New York Mets	NL	112	163	21	45	5	0	5	21	13	23	.276	.399	1
MATT	FRANCO	1998	New York Mets	NL	103	161	20	44	7	2	1	13	23	26	.273	.360	0
MATT	FRANCO	1999	New York Mets	NL	122	132	18	31	5	0	4	21	28	21	.235	.364	0
MATT	FRANCO	2000	New York Mets	NL	101	134	9	32	4	0	2	14	21	22	.239	.333	0
TITO	FRANCONA	1956	Baltimore Orioles	AL	139	445	62	115	16	4	9	57	51	60	.258	.373	11
TITO	FRANCONA	1957	Baltimore Orioles	AL	97	279	35	65	8	3	7	38	29	48	.233	.358	7
TITO	FRANCONA	1958	Chicago White Sox	AL	41	128	10	33	3	2	1	10	14	24	.258	.336	2
TITO	FRANCONA	1958	Detroit Tigers	AL	45	69	11	17	5	0	0	10	15	16	.246	.319	0
TITO	FRANCONA	1959	Cleveland Indians	AL	122	399	68	145	17	2	20	79	35	42	.363	.566	2
TITO	FRANCONA	1960	Cleveland Indians	AL	147	544	84	159	36	3	17	79	67	67	.292	.460	4
TITO	FRANCONA	1961	Cleveland Indians	AL	155	592	87	178	30	8	16	85	56	52	.301	.459	2
TITO	FRANCONA	1962	Cleveland Indians	AL	158	621	82	169	28	5	14	70	47	74	.272	.401	3
TITO	FRANCONA	1963	Cleveland Indians	AL	142	500	57	114	29	0	10	41	47	77	.228	.346	9
TITO	FRANCONA	1964	Cleveland Indians	AL	111	270	35	67	13	2	8	24	44	46	.248	.400	1
TITO	FRANCONA	1965	St. Louis Cardinals	NL	81	174	15	45	6	1	5	19	17	30	.259	.402	0
TITO	FRANCONA	1966	St. Louis Cardinals	NL	83	156	14	33	4	1	4	17	20	27	.212	.327	0
TITO	FRANCONA	1967	Atlanta Braves	NL	82	254	28	63	5	0	6	25	7	34	.248	.346	1
TITO	FRANCONA	1967	Philadelphia Phillies	NL	27	73	7	15	1	0	0	3	7	10	.205	.219	0
TITO	FRANCONA	1968	Atlanta Braves	NL	122	346	32	99	13	1	2	47	51	45	.286	.347	3

FIRST	LAST	YEAR	LEAGUE	TEAM	G	AB	R	H	2B	3B	HR	RBI	BB	SO	AVG	SLUG	SB
TITO	FRANCONA	1969	NL	Atlanta Braves	51	88	5	26	1	0	2	22	13	10	.295	.375	0
TITO	FRANCONA	1969	AL	Oakland Athletics	32	85	12	29	6	1	3	20	12	15	.341	.541	0
TITO	FRANCONA	1970	AL	Milwaukee Brewers	52	65	4	15	3	0	0	4	6	15	.231	.277	1
TITO	FRANCONA	1970	AL	Oakland Athletics	32	33	2	8	0	1	1	6	6	6	.242	.333	1
TERRY	FRANCONA	1981	NL	Montreal Expos	34	95	11	26	3	0	1	8	5	6	.274	.326	1
TERRY	FRANCONA	1982	NL	Montreal Expos	46	131	14	42	3	1	0	9	8	11	.321	.344	2
TERRY	FRANCONA	1983	NL	Montreal Expos	120	230	21	59	11	1	3	22	6	20	.257	.352	2
TERRY	FRANCONA	1984	NL	Montreal Expos	58	214	18	74	19	2	1	18	5	12	.346	.467	0
TERRY	FRANCONA	1985	NL	Montreal Expos	107	281	19	75	15	1	2	31	12	12	.267	.349	5
TERRY	FRANCONA	1986	NL	Chicago Cubs	86	124	13	31	3	0	2	8	6	8	.250	.323	0
TERRY	FRANCONA	1987	NL	Cincinnati Reds	102	207	16	47	5	0	3	12	10	12	.227	.295	2
TERRY	FRANCONA	1988	AL	Cleveland Indians	62	212	24	66	8	0	1	12	5	18	.311	.363	2
TERRY	FRANCONA	1989	AL	Milwaukee Brewers	90	233	26	54	10	1	3	23	8	20	.232	.322	2
TERRY	FRANCONA	1990	AL	Milwaukee Brewers	3	4	1	0	0	0	0	0	0	0	.000		0
HERMAN	FRANKS	1939	NL	St.Louis Cardinals	17	17	1	1	0	0	0	3	3	3	.059	.059	0
HERMAN	FRANKS	1940	NL	Brooklyn Dodgers	65	131	11	24	4	0	1	14	20	16	.183	.237	2
HERMAN	FRANKS	1941	NL	Brooklyn Dodgers	57	139	10	28	7	0	1	11	14	13	.201	.273	0
HERMAN	FRANKS	1947	AL	Philadelphia Athletics	8	15	2	3	0	1	0	1	4	4	.200	.333	0
HERMAN	FRANKS	1948	AL	Philadelphia Athletics	40	98	10	22	7	1	0	14	16	11	.224	.347	0
HERMAN	FRANKS	1949	NL	New York Giants	1	3	2	2	0	0	0	0	0	0	.667	.667	0
JIM	FREGOSI	1961	AL	Los Angeles Angels	11	27	7	6	0	0	0	3	1	4	.222	.222	0
JIM	FREGOSI	1962	AL	Los Angeles Angels	58	175	15	51	3	4	3	23	18	27	.291	.406	2
JIM	FREGOSI	1963	AL	Los Angeles Angels	154	592	83	170	29	12	9	50	36	104	.287	.422	2
JIM	FREGOSI	1964	AL	Los Angeles Angels	147	505	86	140	22	9	18	72	72	87	.277	.463	8
JIM	FREGOSI	1965	AL	California Angels	161	602	66	167	19	7	15	64	54	107	.277	.407	13
JIM	FREGOSI	1966	AL	California Angels	162	611	78	154	32	7	13	67	67	89	.252	.391	17
JIM	FREGOSI	1967	AL	California Angels	151	590	75	171	23	6	9	56	49	77	.290	.395	9
JIM	FREGOSI	1968	AL	California Angels	159	614	77	150	21	13	9	49	60	101	.244	.365	9
JIM	FREGOSI	1969	AL	California Angels	161	580	78	151	22	6	12	47	93	86	.260	.381	9
JIM	FREGOSI	1970	AL	California Angels	158	601	95	167	33	5	22	82	69	92	.278	.459	0
JIM	FREGOSI	1971	AL	California Angels	107	347	31	81	15	4	5	33	39	61	.233	.326	2
JIM	FREGOSI	1972	NL	New York Mets	101	340	37	79	15	1	5	32	38	71	.232	.344	0
JIM	FREGOSI	1973	NL	New York Mets	45	124	7	29	4	2	0	11	20	25	.234	.282	1
JIM	FREGOSI	1973	AL	Texas Rangers	45	157	25	42	6	2	6	16	12	31	.268	.446	0
JIM	FREGOSI	1974	AL	Texas Rangers	78	230	31	60	5	0	12	34	22	41	.261	.439	0

FIRST	LAST	YEAR	TEAM	LEAGUE	G	AB	R	H	2B	3B	HR	RBI	BB	SO	AVG	SLUG	SB
JIM	FREGOSI	1975	Texas Rangers	AL	77	191	25	50	5	0	7	33	20	39	.262	.398	0
JIM	FREGOSI	1976	Texas Rangers	AL	58	133	17	31	7	0	2	12	23	33	.233	.331	2
JIM	FREGOSI	1977	Pittsburgh Pirates	NL	36	56	10	16	1	1	3	16	13	10	.286	.500	2
JIM	FREGOSI	1977	Texas Rangers	AL	13	28	4	7	1	0	0	5	3	4	.250	.393	0
JIM	FREGOSI	1978	Pittsburgh Pirates	NL	20	20	3	4	1	0	0	1	6	8	.200	.250	0
CARL	FURILLO	1946	Brooklyn Dodgers	NL	117	335	29	95	18	6	3	35	21	20	.284	.400	6
CARL	FURILLO	1947	Brooklyn Dodgers	NL	124	437	61	129	24	7	8	88	31	24	.295	.437	7
CARL	FURILLO	1948	Brooklyn Dodgers	NL	108	364	55	108	20	4	4	44	34	32	.297	.407	6
CARL	FURILLO	1949	Brooklyn Dodgers	NL	142	549	95	177	27	10	18	106	43	29	.322	.506	4
CARL	FURILLO	1950	Brooklyn Dodgers	NL	155	620	99	189	30	6	18	106	37	40	.305	.460	8
CARL	FURILLO	1951	Brooklyn Dodgers	NL	158	667	93	197	32	4	16	91	41	33	.295	.427	8
CARL	FURILLO	1952	Brooklyn Dodgers	NL	134	425	52	105	18	1	8	59	31	33	.247	.351	1
CARL	FURILLO	1953	Brooklyn Dodgers	NL	132	479	82	165	38	6	21	92	34	32	.344	.580	1
CARL	FURILLO	1954	Brooklyn Dodgers	NL	150	547	56	161	23	1	19	96	49	35	.294	.444	2
CARL	FURILLO	1955	Brooklyn Dodgers	NL	140	523	83	164	24	3	26	95	43	43	.314	.520	4
CARL	FURILLO	1956	Brooklyn Dodgers	NL	149	523	66	151	30	0	21	83	57	41	.289	.467	1
CARL	FURILLO	1957	Brooklyn Dodgers	NL	119	395	61	121	17	4	12	66	29	33	.306	.461	0
CARL	FURILLO	1958	Los Angeles Dodgers	NL	122	411	54	119	19	3	18	83	35	28	.290	.482	0
CARL	FURILLO	1959	Los Angeles Dodgers	NL	50	93	8	27	4	0	0	13	7	11	.290	.333	0
CARL	FURILLO	1960	Los Angeles Dodgers	NL	8	10	1	2	0	0	0	1	0	2	.200	.400	0
GARY	GAETTI	1981	Minnesota Twins	AL	9	26	4	5	0	0	2	3	0	6	.192	.423	0
GARY	GAETTI	1982	Minnesota Twins	AL	145	508	59	117	25	4	25	84	37	107	.230	.443	0
GARY	GAETTI	1983	Minnesota Twins	AL	157	584	81	143	30	4	21	78	54	121	.245	.414	7
GARY	GAETTI	1984	Minnesota Twins	AL	162	588	55	154	29	3	5	65	44	81	.262	.350	11
GARY	GAETTI	1985	Minnesota Twins	AL	160	560	71	138	31	0	20	63	37	89	.246	.409	13
GARY	GAETTI	1986	Minnesota Twins	AL	157	596	91	171	34	1	34	108	52	108	.287	.518	14
GARY	GAETTI	1987	Minnesota Twins	AL	154	584	95	150	36	2	31	109	37	92	.257	.485	10
GARY	GAETTI	1988	Minnesota Twins	AL	133	468	66	141	29	2	28	88	36	85	.301	.551	7
GARY	GAETTI	1989	Minnesota Twins	AL	130	498	63	125	11	4	19	75	25	87	.251	.404	6
GARY	GAETTI	1990	Minnesota Twins	AL	154	577	61	132	27	5	16	85	36	101	.229	.376	6
GARY	GAETTI	1991	California Angels	AL	152	586	58	144	22	1	18	66	33	104	.246	.379	5
GARY	GAETTI	1992	California Angels	AL	130	456	41	103	13	2	12	48	21	79	.226	.342	3
GARY	GAETTI	1993	California Angels	AL	20	50	3	9	2	0	0	4	5	12	.180	.220	1
GARY	GAETTI	1993	Kansas City Royals	AL	82	281	37	72	18	1	14	46	16	75	.256	.477	0
GARY	GAETTI	1994	Kansas City Royals	AL	90	327	53	94	15	3	12	57	19	63	.287	.462	0

FIRST	LAST	YEAR	TEAM	LEAGUE	G	AB	R	H	2B	3B	HR	RBI	BB	SO	AVG	SLUG	SB
GARY	GAETTI	1995	Kansas City Royals	AL	137	514	76	134	27	0	35	96	47	91	.261	.518	3
GARY	GAETTI	1996	St. Louis Cardinals	NL	141	522	71	143	27	4	23	80	35	97	.274	.473	2
GARY	GAETTI	1997	St. Louis Cardinals	NL	148	502	63	126	24	1	17	69	36	88	.251	.404	7
GARY	GAETTI	1998	Chicago Cubs	NL	37	128	21	41	11	0	8	27	12	23	.320	.594	0
GARY	GAETTI	1998	St. Louis Cardinals	NL	91	306	39	81	23	1	11	43	31	39	.265	.454	1
GARY	GAETTI	1999	Chicago Cubs	NL	113	280	22	57	9	0	9	46	21	51	.204	.339	1
GARY	GAETTI	2000	Boston Red Sox	AL	5	10	0	0	0	0	0	1	0	3	.000		0
PHIL	GAGLIANO	1963	St. Louis Cardinals	NL	10	5	1	2	0	0	0	1	1	1	.400	.400	0
PHIL	GAGLIANO	1964	St. Louis Cardinals	NL	40	58	5	15	4	0	1	9	3	10	.259	.379	0
PHIL	GAGLIANO	1965	St. Louis Cardinals	NL	122	363	46	87	14	2	8	53	40	45	.240	.355	2
PHIL	GAGLIANO	1966	St. Louis Cardinals	NL	90	213	23	54	8	2	2	15	24	29	.254	.338	2
PHIL	GAGLIANO	1967	St. Louis Cardinals	NL	73	217	20	48	7	0	2	21	19	26	.221	.281	0
PHIL	GAGLIANO	1968	St. Louis Cardinals	NL	53	105	13	24	4	2	1	13	7	12	.229	.305	0
PHIL	GAGLIANO	1969	St. Louis Cardinals	NL	62	128	7	29	2	2	0	10	14	12	.227	.266	0
PHIL	GAGLIANO	1970	Chicago Cubs	NL	26	40	5	6	0	0	1	5	5	5	.150	.150	0
PHIL	GAGLIANO	1970	St. Louis Cardinals	NL	18	32	0	6	0	0	0	2	1	3	.188	.188	0
PHIL	GAGLIANO	1971	Boston Red Sox	AL	47	68	11	22	5	0	0	13	11	5	.324	.397	0
PHIL	GAGLIANO	1972	Boston Red Sox	AL	52	82	9	21	4	1	0	10	10	13	.256	.329	1
PHIL	GAGLIANO	1973	Cincinnati Reds	NL	63	69	8	20	2	0	0	7	13	16	.290	.319	0
PHIL	GAGLIANO	1974	Cincinnati Reds	NL	46	31	2	2	0	0	0	0	15	7	.065	.065	0
RALPH	GAGLIANO	1965	Cleveland Indians	AL	1	0	0	0	0	0	0	0	0	0			0
MIKE	GALLEGO	1985	Oakland Athletics	AL	76	77	13	16	5	1	1	9	12	14	.208	.338	1
MIKE	GALLEGO	1986	Oakland Athletics	AL	20	37	2	10	2	0	0	4	1	6	.270	.324	0
MIKE	GALLEGO	1987	Oakland Athletics	AL	72	124	18	31	6	0	2	14	12	21	.250	.347	0
MIKE	GALLEGO	1988	Oakland Athletics	AL	129	277	38	58	8	0	2	20	34	53	.209	.260	2
MIKE	GALLEGO	1989	Oakland Athletics	AL	133	357	45	90	14	2	3	30	35	43	.252	.328	7
MIKE	GALLEGO	1990	Oakland Athletics	AL	140	389	36	80	13	2	3	34	35	50	.206	.272	5
MIKE	GALLEGO	1991	Oakland Athletics	AL	159	482	67	119	15	4	12	49	67	84	.247	.369	6
MIKE	GALLEGO	1992	New York Yankees	AL	53	173	24	44	7	1	3	14	20	22	.254	.358	0
MIKE	GALLEGO	1993	New York Yankees	AL	119	403	63	114	20	1	10	54	50	65	.283	.412	3
MIKE	GALLEGO	1994	New York Yankees	AL	89	306	39	73	17	0	6	41	38	46	.239	.359	0
MIKE	GALLEGO	1995	Oakland Athletics	AL	43	120	11	28	2	0	0	8	9	24	.233	.233	0
MIKE	GALLEGO	1996	St. Louis Cardinals	NL	51	143	12	30	2	0	0	4	12	31	.210	.224	0
MIKE	GALLEGO	1997	St. Louis Cardinals	NL	27	43	6	7	2	0	0	1	1	6	.163	.209	0
JOE	GARAGIOLA	1946	St. Louis Cardinals	NL	74	211	21	50	4	1	3	22	23	25	.237	.308	0

FIRST	LAST	YEAR	TEAM	LEAGUE	G	AB	R	H	2B	3B	HR	RBI	BB	SO	AVG	SLUG	SB
JOE	GARAGIOLA	1947	St. Louis Cardinals	NL	77	183	20	47	10	2	5	25	40	14	.257	.415	0
JOE	GARAGIOLA	1948	St. Louis Cardinals	NL	24	56	9	6	1	0	2	7	12	9	.107	.232	0
JOE	GARAGIOLA	1949	St. Louis Cardinals	NL	81	241	25	63	14	0	3	26	31	19	.261	.357	0
JOE	GARAGIOLA	1950	Pittsburgh Pirates	NL	34	88	8	28	6	1	2	20	10	20	.318	.477	0
JOE	GARAGIOLA	1951	St. Louis Cardinals	NL	72	212	24	54	8	2	9	35	32	20	.255	.439	4
JOE	GARAGIOLA	1951	Pittsburgh Pirates	NL	27	72	9	14	3	2	2	9	9	7	.194	.375	0
JOE	GARAGIOLA	1952	St. Louis Cardinals	NL	118	344	35	94	15	4	8	54	50	24	.273	.410	0
JOE	GARAGIOLA	1953	Chicago Cubs	NL	74	228	21	62	9	4	1	21	21	23	.272	.360	0
JOE	GARAGIOLA	1953	Pittsburgh Pirates	NL	27	73	9	17	5	0	2	14	10	11	.233	.384	1
JOE	GARAGIOLA	1954	Chicago Cubs	NL	63	153	16	43	5	0	5	21	28	12	.281	.412	0
JOE	GARAGIOLA	1954	New York Giants	NL	5	11	1	3	2	0	0	1	1	2	.273	.455	0
DANNY	GARDELLA	1944	New York Giants	NL	47	112	20	28	2	2	6	14	11	13	.250	.464	2
DANNY	GARDELLA	1945	New York Giants	NL	121	430	54	117	10	1	18	71	46	55	.272	.426	2
DANNY	GARDELLA	1950	St. Louis Cardinals	NL	1	1	0	0	0	0	0	0	1	0	.000		0
AL	GARDELLA	1945	New York Giants	NL	16	26	2	2	0	0	0	1	4	3	.077	.077	0
ART	GARIBALDI	1936	St. Louis Cardinals	NL	71	232	30	64	12	0	1	20	16	30	.276	.341	3
MIKE	GAZELLA	1923	New York Yankees	AL	8	13	2	1	0	0	0	1	2	3	.077	.077	0
MIKE	GAZELLA	1926	New York Yankees	AL	66	168	21	39	6	0	0	20	25	24	.232	.268	2
MIKE	GAZELLA	1927	New York Yankees	AL	54	115	17	32	8	4	0	9	23	16	.278	.417	4
MIKE	GAZELLA	1928	New York Yankees	AL	32	56	11	13	0	0	0	2	6	7	.232	.232	2
GEORGE	GENOVESE	1950	Washington Senators	AL	3	1	1	0	0	0	0	0	1	0	.000		0
JIM	GENTILE	1957	Brooklyn Dodgers	NL	4	6	1	1	0	0	0	1	1	1	.167	.167	0
JIM	GENTILE	1958	Los Angeles Dodgers	NL	12	30	0	4	1	0	0	4	4	6	.133	.167	0
JIM	GENTILE	1960	Baltimore Orioles	AL	138	384	67	112	17	0	21	98	68	72	.292	.500	0
JIM	GENTILE	1961	Baltimore Orioles	AL	148	486	96	147	25	2	46	141	96	106	.302	.646	1
JIM	GENTILE	1962	Baltimore Orioles	AL	152	545	80	137	21	1	33	87	77	100	.251	.475	1
JIM	GENTILE	1963	Baltimore Orioles	AL	145	496	65	123	16	1	24	72	76	101	.248	.429	1
JIM	GENTILE	1964	Kansas City Athletics	AL	136	439	71	110	10	0	28	71	84	122	.251	.465	0
JIM	GENTILE	1965	Houston Colt .45s	NL	81	227	22	55	11	1	7	31	34	72	.242	.392	0
JIM	GENTILE	1965	Kansas City Athletics	AL	38	118	14	29	5	0	10	22	9	26	.246	.542	0
JIM	GENTILE	1966	Cleveland Indians	AL	33	47	2	6	1	0	2	4	5	18	.128	.277	0
JIM	GENTILE	1966	Houston Astros	NL	49	144	16	35	6	0	7	18	21	39	.243	.444	0
SAM	GENTILE	1943	Boston Braves	NL	8	4	1	1	1	0	0	0	0	0	.250	.500	0
JASON	GIAMBI	1995	Oakland Athletics	AL	54	176	27	45	7	0	6	25	28	31	.256	.398	2
JASON	GIAMBI	1996	Oakland Athletics	AL	140	536	84	156	40	1	20	79	51	95	.291	.481	0

FIRST	LAST	YEAR	TEAM	LEAGUE	G	AB	R	H	2B	3B	HR	RBI	BB	SO	AVG	SLUG	SB
JASON	GIAMBI	1997	Oakland Athletics	AL	142	519	66	152	41	2	20	81	55	89	.293	.495	0
JASON	GIAMBI	1998	Oakland Athletics	AL	153	562	92	166	28	0	27	110	81	102	.295	.489	2
JASON	GIAMBI	1999	Oakland Athletics	AL	158	575	115	181	36	1	33	123	105	106	.315	.553	1
JASON	GIAMBI	2000	Oakland Athletics	AL	152	510	108	170	29	1	43	137	137	96	.333	.647	2
JASON	GIAMBI	2001	Oakland Athletics	AL	154	520	109	178	47	2	38	120	129	83	.342	.660	2
JEREMY	GIAMBI	1998	Kansas City Royals	AL	18	58	6	13	4	0	2	8	11	9	.224	.397	0
JEREMY	GIAMBI	1999	Kansas City Royals	AL	90	288	34	82	13	1	3	34	40	67	.285	.368	0
JEREMY	GIAMBI	2000	Oakland Athletics	AL	104	260	42	66	10	2	10	50	32	61	.254	.423	0
JEREMY	GIAMBI	2001	Oakland Athletics	AL	124	371	64	105	26	0	12	57	63	83	.283	.450	0
RAY	GIANNELLI	1991	Toronto Blue Jays	AL	9	24	2	4	1	0	0	0	5	9	.167	.208	1
RAY	GIANNELLI	1995	St. Louis Cardinals	NL	9	11	0	1	1	0	0	0	3	4	.091	.091	0
JOE	GIANNINI	1911	Boston Red Sox	AL	1	2	0	1	0	0	0	0	0		.500	.500	0
AL	GIONFRIDDO	1944	Pittsburgh Pirates	NL	4	6	0	1	0	0	0	0	1	1	.167	.167	0
AL	GIONFRIDDO	1945	Pittsburgh Pirates	NL	122	409	74	116	18	9	2	42	60	22	.284	.386	12
AL	GIONFRIDDO	1946	Pittsburgh Pirates	NL	64	102	11	26	2	2	0	10	14	5	.255	.314	2
AL	GIONFRIDDO	1947	Brooklyn Dodgers	NL	37	62	10	11	2	1	0	6	16	11	.177	.242	0
AL	GIONFRIDDO	1947	Pittsburgh Pirates	NL	3	1	0	0	0	0	0	0	0	0	.000		0
TOMMY	GIORDANO	1953	Philadelphia Athletics	AL	11	40	2	7	2	0	2	5	5	6	.175	.375	0
ED	GIOVANOLA	1995	Atlanta Braves	NL	13	14	2	1	0	0	0	0	3	5	.071	.071	1
ED	GIOVANOLA	1996	Atlanta Braves	NL	43	82	10	19	2	0	0	7	8	13	.232	.256	0
ED	GIOVANOLA	1997	Atlanta Braves	NL	14	8	0	2	0	0	0	0	2	1	.250	.250	1
ED	GIOVANOLA	1998	San Diego Padres	NL	92	139	19	32	3	3	1	9	22	22	.230	.317	2
ED	GIOVANOLA	1999	San Diego Padres	NL	56	58	10	11	2	0	0	3	9	8	.190	.224	2
JOE	GIRARDI	1989	Chicago Cubs	NL	59	157	15	39	10	0	1	14	11	26	.248	.331	2
JOE	GIRARDI	1990	Chicago Cubs	NL	133	419	36	113	24	2	1	38	17	50	.270	.344	8
JOE	GIRARDI	1991	Chicago Cubs	NL	21	47	3	9	2	2	0	6	6	6	.191	.234	0
JOE	GIRARDI	1992	Chicago Cubs	NL	91	270	19	73	14	0	1	12	19	38	.270	.333	0
JOE	GIRARDI	1993	Colorado Rockies	NL	86	310	35	90	14	5	3	31	24	41	.290	.397	6
JOE	GIRARDI	1994	Colorado Rockies	NL	93	330	47	91	9	4	4	34	21	48	.276	.364	3
JOE	GIRARDI	1995	Colorado Rockies	NL	125	462	63	121	17	2	8	55	29	76	.262	.359	3
JOE	GIRARDI	1996	New York Yankees	AL	124	422	55	124	22	3	2	45	30	55	.294	.374	13
JOE	GIRARDI	1997	New York Yankees	AL	112	398	38	105	23	1	1	50	26	53	.264	.334	2
JOE	GIRARDI	1998	New York Yankees	AL	78	254	31	70	11	4	3	31	14	38	.276	.386	3
JOE	GIRARDI	1999	New York Yankees	AL	65	209	23	50	16	1	2	27	10	26	.239	.354	3
JOE	GIRARDI	2000	Chicago Cubs	NL	106	363	47	101	15	1	6	40	32	61	.278	.375	1

FIRST	LAST	YEAR	TEAM	LEAGUE	G	AB	R	H	2B	3B	HR	RBI	BB	SO	AVG	SLUG	SB
JOE	GIRARDI	2001	Chicago Cubs	NL	78	229	22	58	10	1	3	25	21	50	.253	.345	0
TONY	GIULIANI	1936	St. Louis Browns	AL	71	198	17	43	3	0	0	13	11	13	.217	.232	0
TONY	GIULIANI	1937	St. Louis Browns	AL	19	53	6	16	1	0	0	3	3	3	.302	.321	0
TONY	GIULIANI	1938	Washington Senators	AL	46	115	10	25	4	2	0	15	8	3	.217	.252	1
TONY	GIULIANI	1939	Washington Senators	AL	54	172	20	43	6	0	0	18	4	7	.250	.308	0
TONY	GIULIANI	1940	Brooklyn Dodgers	NL	1	1	0	0	0	0	0	0	0	1	.000		0
TONY	GIULIANI	1941	Brooklyn Dodgers	NL	3	2	0	0	0	0	0	0	0	0	.000		0
TONY	GIULIANI	1943	Washington Senators	AL	49	133	5	30	4	1	0	20	12	14	.226	.271	0
TOMMY	GLAVIANO	1949	St. Louis Cardinals	NL	87	258	32	69	16	2	6	36	41	35	.267	.407	6
TOMMY	GLAVIANO	1950	St. Louis Cardinals	NL	115	410	92	117	29	2	11	44	90	74	.285	.446	6
TOMMY	GLAVIANO	1951	St. Louis Cardinals	NL	54	104	20	19	4	0	1	4	26	18	.183	.250	3
TOMMY	GLAVIANO	1952	St. Louis Cardinals	NL	80	162	30	39	5	1	3	19	27	26	.241	.340	0
TOMMY	GLAVIANO	1953	Philadelphia Phillies	NL	53	74	17	15	1	2	0	5	24	20	.203	.392	2
TONY	GRAFFANINO	1996	Atlanta Braves	NL	22	46	7	8	1	1	3	2	4	13	.174	.239	0
TONY	GRAFFANINO	1997	Atlanta Braves	NL	104	186	33	48	9	1	8	20	26	46	.258	.446	6
TONY	GRAFFANINO	1998	Atlanta Braves	NL	105	289	32	61	14	1	5	22	24	68	.211	.318	1
TONY	GRAFFANINO	1999	Tampa Bay Devil Rays	AL	39	130	20	41	9	4	2	19	9	22	.315	.492	3
TONY	GRAFFANINO	2000	Chicago White Sox	AL	57	148	25	40	5	1	2	16	21	25	.270	.358	7
TONY	GRAFFANINO	2000	Tampa Bay Devil Rays	AL	13	20	8	6	1	0	0	1	1	2	.300	.350	0
TONY	GRAFFANINO	2001	Chicago White Sox	AL	74	145	23	44	9	0	2	15	16	29	.303	.407	4
MICKEY	GRASSO	1946	New York Giants	NL	7	22	1	3	0	0	0	1	0	3	.136	.136	0
MICKEY	GRASSO	1950	Washington Senators	AL	75	195	25	56	4	1	1	22	25	31	.287	.333	1
MICKEY	GRASSO	1951	Washington Senators	AL	52	175	16	36	3	0	0	14	14	17	.206	.240	0
MICKEY	GRASSO	1952	Washington Senators	AL	115	361	22	78	9	0	0	27	29	36	.216	.241	1
MICKEY	GRASSO	1953	Washington Senators	AL	61	196	13	41	7	0	2	22	9	20	.209	.276	0
MICKEY	GRASSO	1954	Cleveland Indians	AL	4	6	1	2	0	0	0	1	1	1	.333	.833	0
MICKEY	GRASSO	1955	New York Giants	NL	8	2	0	0	0	0	0	0	3	0	.000		0
BEN	GUINTINI	1946	Pittsburgh Pirates	NL	2	3	0	0	0	0	0	0	0	0	.000		0
BEN	GUINTINI	1950	Philadelphia Athletics	AL	3	4	0	0	0	0	0	0	0	1	.000		0
LOU	GUISTO	1916	Cleveland Indians	AL	6	19	2	3	0	0	0	2	4	3	.158	.158	1
LOU	GUISTO	1917	Cleveland Indians	AL	73	200	9	37	4	2	0	29	25	18	.185	.225	3
LOU	GUISTO	1921	Cleveland Indians	AL	2	2	0	1	0	0	0		0	7	.500	.500	0
LOU	GUISTO	1922	Cleveland Indians	AL	35	84	7	21	10	1	0	9	2	7	.250	.393	0
LOU	GUISTO	1923	Cleveland Indians	AL	40	144	17	26	5	0	0	18	15	15	.181	.215	1
FRANKIE	GUSTINE	1939	Pittsburgh Pirates	NL	22	70	5	13	3	0	0	3	9	4	.186	.229	0

FIRST	LAST	YEAR	TEAM	LEAGUE	G	AB	R	H	2B	3B	HR	RBI	BB	SO	AVG	SLUG	SB
FRANKIE	GUSTINE	1940	Pittsburgh Pirates	NL	133	524	59	147	32	7	1	55	35	39	.281	.374	7
FRANKIE	GUSTINE	1941	Pittsburgh Pirates	NL	121	463	46	125	24	7	1	46	28	38	.270	.359	5
FRANKIE	GUSTINE	1942	Pittsburgh Pirates	NL	115	388	34	89	11	4	2	35	29	27	.229	.294	5
FRANKIE	GUSTINE	1943	Pittsburgh Pirates	NL	112	414	40	120	21	3	0	43	32	36	.290	.355	12
FRANKIE	GUSTINE	1944	Pittsburgh Pirates	NL	127	405	42	93	18	5	2	42	33	41	.230	.304	8
FRANKIE	GUSTINE	1945	Pittsburgh Pirates	NL	128	478	67	134	27	5	2	66	37	33	.280	.370	8
FRANKIE	GUSTINE	1946	Pittsburgh Pirates	NL	131	495	60	128	23	6	8	52	40	52	.259	.378	2
FRANKIE	GUSTINE	1947	Pittsburgh Pirates	NL	156	616	102	183	30	6	9	67	63	65	.297	.409	5
FRANKIE	GUSTINE	1948	Pittsburgh Pirates	NL	131	449	68	120	19	2	9	42	42	62	.267	.379	5
FRANKIE	GUSTINE	1949	Chicago Cubs	NL	76	261	29	59	13	4	4	27	18	22	.226	.352	3
FRANKIE	GUSTINE	1950	St. Louis Browns	AL	9	19	1	3	1	0	0	2	3	8	.158	.211	3
PETE	INCAVIGLIA	1986	Texas Rangers	AL	153	540	82	135	21	2	30	88	55	185	.250	.463	3
PETE	INCAVIGLIA	1987	Texas Rangers	AL	139	509	85	138	26	4	27	80	48	168	.271	.497	9
PETE	INCAVIGLIA	1988	Texas Rangers	AL	116	418	59	104	19	3	22	54	39	153	.249	.467	6
PETE	INCAVIGLIA	1989	Texas Rangers	AL	133	453	48	107	27	4	21	81	32	136	.236	.453	5
PETE	INCAVIGLIA	1990	Texas Rangers	AL	153	529	59	123	27	0	24	85	45	146	.233	.420	3
PETE	INCAVIGLIA	1991	Detroit Tigers	AL	97	337	38	72	12	1	11	38	36	92	.214	.353	1
PETE	INCAVIGLIA	1992	Houston Astros	NL	113	349	31	93	22	1	11	44	25	99	.266	.430	2
PETE	INCAVIGLIA	1993	Philadelphia Phillies	NL	116	368	60	101	16	3	24	89	21	82	.274	.530	1
PETE	INCAVIGLIA	1994	Philadelphia Phillies	NL	80	244	28	56	10	1	13	32	16	71	.230	.439	1
PETE	INCAVIGLIA	1996	Baltimore Orioles	AL	12	33	4	10	2	0	2	8	0	7	.303	.545	0
PETE	INCAVIGLIA	1996	Philadelphia Phillies	NL	99	269	33	63	7	2	16	42	30	82	.234	.454	2
PETE	INCAVIGLIA	1997	Baltimore Orioles	AL	48	138	18	34	4	0	5	12	11	43	.246	.384	0
PETE	INCAVIGLIA	1997	New York Yankees	AL	5	16	1	4	0	0	0	0	0	3	.250	.250	0
PETE	INCAVIGLIA	1998	Detroit Tigers	AL	7	14	0	1	0	0	0	0	1	6	.071	.071	0
PETE	INCAVIGLIA	1998	Houston Astros	NL	13	16	0	2	1	0	0	2	1	4	.125	.188	0
PAUL	KONERKO	1997	Los Angeles Dodgers	NL	6	7	0	1	0	0	0	0	1	2	.143	.143	0
PAUL	KONERKO	1998	Cincinnati Reds	NL	26	73	7	16	3	0	3	13	6	10	.219	.384	0
PAUL	KONERKO	1998	Los Angeles Dodgers	NL	49	144	14	31	1	0	4	16	10	30	.215	.306	0
PAUL	KONERKO	1999	Chicago White Sox	AL	142	513	71	151	31	4	24	81	45	68	.294	.511	1
PAUL	KONERKO	2000	Chicago White Sox	AL	143	524	84	156	31	1	21	97	47	72	.298	.481	1
PAUL	KONERKO	2001	Chicago White Sox	AL	156	582	92	164	35	0	32	99	54	89	.282	.507	1
JOE	LAFATA	1947	New York Giants	NL	62	95	13	21	1	0	0	18	15	18	.221	.295	1
JOE	LAFATA	1948	New York Giants	NL	1	1	0	0	0	0	0	0	0	0	.000		1
JOE	LAFATA	1949	New York Giants	NL	64	140	18	33	2	2	3	16	9	23	.236	.343	1

FIRST	LAST	YEAR	TEAM	LEAGUE	G	AB	R	H	2B	3B	HR	RBI	BB	SO	AVG	SLUG	SB
MIKE	LAGA	1982	Detroit Tigers	AL	27	88	6	23	9	0	3	11	4	23	.261	.466	1
MIKE	LAGA	1983	Detroit Tigers	AL	12	21	2	4	0	0	0	2	1	9	.190	.190	0
MIKE	LAGA	1984	Detroit Tigers	AL	9	11	1	6	0	0	2	1	0	2	.545	.545	0
MIKE	LAGA	1985	Detroit Tigers	AL	9	36	3	6	1	0	2	6	0	13	.167	.361	0
MIKE	LAGA	1986	Detroit Tigers	AL	15	45	6	9	1	0	3	8	5	13	.200	.422	0
MIKE	LAGA	1986	St. Louis Cardinals	NL	18	46	7	10	4	0	3	8	2	18	.217	.500	0
MIKE	LAGA	1987	St. Louis Cardinals	NL	17	29	4	4	0	0	1	4	2	7	.138	.276	0
MIKE	LAGA	1988	St. Louis Cardinals	NL	41	100	5	13	1	0	1	4	2	21	.130	.160	0
MIKE	LAGA	1989	San Francisco Giants	NL	17	20	4	4	1	0	2	7	1	6	.200	.400	0
MIKE	LAGA	1990	San Francisco Giants	NL	23	27	4	5	0	0	0	4	1	7	.185	.444	0
RAY	LAMANNO	1941	Cincinnati Reds	NL	1	0	0	0	0	0	0	0	0	0			0
RAY	LAMANNO	1942	Cincinnati Reds	NL	111	371	40	98	12	2	12	43	31	54	.264	.404	0
RAY	LAMANNO	1946	Cincinnati Reds	NL	85	239	18	58	12	2	1	30	11	26	.243	.305	0
RAY	LAMANNO	1947	Cincinnati Reds	NL	118	413	33	106	21	3	5	50	28	39	.257	.358	2
RAY	LAMANNO	1948	Cincinnati Reds	NL	127	385	31	93	12	3	0	27	48	32	.242	.273	0
RICK	LANCELLOTTI	1982	San Diego Padres	NL	17	39	2	7	2	0	0	4	2	8	.179	.231	0
RICK	LANCELLOTTI	1986	San Francisco Giants	NL	15	18	2	4	0	0	2	6	0	7	.222	.556	0
RICK	LANCELLOTTI	1990	Boston Red Sox	AL	4	8	0	0	0	0	0	1	0	3	.000	.000	1
FRANK	LaPORTE	1905	New York Highlanders	AL	11	40	4	16	4	0	0	12	1		.400	.500	0
FRANK	LaPORTE	1906	New York Highlanders	AL	123	454	60	120	23	9	2	54	22		.264	.368	10
FRANK	LaPORTE	1907	New York Highlanders	AL	130	470	56	127	20	11	0	48	27		.270	.360	10
FRANK	LaPORTE	1908	Boston Pilgrims	AL	62	156	14	37	1	3	0	15	12		.237	.282	3
FRANK	LaPORTE	1908	New York Highlanders	AL	39	145	7	38	3	4	1	15	8		.262	.359	3
FRANK	LaPORTE	1909	New York Highlanders	AL	89	309	35	92	19	3	3	31	18		.298	.379	5
FRANK	LaPORTE	1910	New York Highlanders	AL	124	432	43	114	14	6	2	67	33		.264	.338	16
FRANK	LaPORTE	1911	St. Louis Browns	AL	136	507	71	159	37	12	2	82	34		.314	.446	4
FRANK	LaPORTE	1912	St. Louis Browns	AL	80	266	32	83	11	4	1	38	20		.312	.395	7
FRANK	LaPORTE	1912	Washington Senators	AL	40	136	13	42	9	0	0	17	12	16	.309	.390	3
FRANK	LaPORTE	1913	Washington Senators	AL	79	242	25	61	5	4	0	18	17	36	.252	.306	10
FRANK	LaPORTE	1914	Indianapolis Hoosiers	FL	133	505	86	157	27	12	4	107	36	33	.311	.456	15
FRANK	LaPORTE	1915	Newark Peppers	FL	148	550	55	139	28	10	2	56	48		.253	.351	14
TONY	LaRUSSA	1963	Kansas City Athletics	AL	34	44	4	11	1	0	0	1	7	12	.250	.318	0
TONY	LaRUSSA	1968	Oakland Athletics	AL	5	3	0	1	0	0	0	0	0	0	.333	.333	0
TONY	LaRUSSA	1969	Oakland Athletics	AL	8	8	0	0	0	0	0	0	0	1	.000		0
TONY	LaRUSSA	1970	Oakland Athletics	AL	52	106	6	21	4	1	0	6	15	19	.198	.255	0

FIRST	LAST	YEAR	TEAM	LEAGUE	G	AB	R	H	2B	3B	HR	RBI	BB	SO	AVG	SLUG	SB
TONY	LaRUSSA	1971	Atlanta Braves	NL	9	7	1	2	0	0	0	0	1	1	.286	.286	0
TONY	LaRUSSA	1971	Oakland Athletics	AL	23	8	3	0	0	0	0	0	0	4	.000		0
TONY	LaRUSSA	1973	Chicago Cubs	NL	1	0	1	0	0	0	0	0	0	0			0
TOM	LASORDA	1954	Brooklyn Dodgers	NL	4	1	0	0	0	0	0	0	0	0			0
TOM	LASORDA	1955	Brooklyn Dodgers	NL	4	0	0	0	0	0	0	0	0	0	.000		0
TOM	LASORDA	1956	Kansas City Athletics	AL	19	13	0	1	0	0	0	0	0	4	.077	.077	0
TONY	LAZZERI	1926	New York Yankees	AL	155	589	79	162	28	14	18	114	54	96	.275	.462	16
TONY	LAZZERI	1927	New York Yankees	AL	153	570	92	176	29	8	18	102	69	82	.309	.482	22
TONY	LAZZERI	1928	New York Yankees	AL	116	404	62	134	30	11	10	82	43	50	.332	.535	15
TONY	LAZZERI	1929	New York Yankees	AL	147	545	101	193	37	11	18	106	68	45	.354	.561	9
TONY	LAZZERI	1930	New York Yankees	AL	143	571	109	173	34	15	9	121	60	62	.303	.462	4
TONY	LAZZERI	1931	New York Yankees	AL	135	484	67	129	27	7	8	83	79	80	.267	.401	18
TONY	LAZZERI	1932	New York Yankees	AL	142	510	79	153	28	16	15	113	82	64	.300	.506	11
TONY	LAZZERI	1933	New York Yankees	AL	139	523	94	154	22	12	18	104	73	62	.294	.486	15
TONY	LAZZERI	1934	New York Yankees	AL	123	438	59	117	24	6	14	67	71	64	.267	.445	11
TONY	LAZZERI	1935	New York Yankees	AL	130	477	72	130	18	6	13	83	63	75	.273	.417	11
TONY	LAZZERI	1936	New York Yankees	AL	150	557	82	154	29	6	14	109	97	65	.287	.441	8
TONY	LAZZERI	1937	New York Yankees	AL	126	446	56	109	21	3	14	70	71	76	.244	.399	7
TONY	LAZZERI	1938	Chicago Cubs	NL	54	120	21	32	5	0	5	23	22	30	.267	.433	0
TONY	LAZZERI	1939	Brooklyn Dodgers	NL	14	39	6	11	2	0	3	6	10	7	.282	.564	1
TONY	LAZZERI	1939	New York Giants	NL	13	44	7	13	1	0	1	8	7	6	.295	.364	0
JIM	LENTINE	1978	St. Louis Cardinals	NL	8	11	1	2	0	0	0	—	0	6	.182	.182	1
JIM	LENTINE	1979	St. Louis Cardinals	NL	11	23	2	9	1	0	0	1	3	6	.391	.435	0
JIM	LENTINE	1980	Detroit Tigers	AL	67	161	19	42	8	1	1	17	28	30	.261	.342	2
JIM	LENTINE	1980	St. Louis Cardinals	NL	9	10	1	1	0	0	0	—	0	2	.100	.100	0
DARIO	LODIGIANI	1938	Philadelphia Athletics	AL	93	325	36	91	15	1	6	44	34	25	.280	.388	3
DARIO	LODIGIANI	1939	Philadelphia Athletics	AL	121	393	46	102	22	4	6	44	42	18	.260	.382	2
DARIO	LODIGIANI	1940	Philadelphia Athletics	AL	1	0	0	0	0	0	0	—	0	0	.000		0
DARIO	LODIGIANI	1941	Chicago White Sox	AL	87	322	39	77	19	2	4	40	31	19	.239	.348	0
DARIO	LODIGIANI	1942	Chicago White Sox	AL	59	168	9	47	7	0	0	15	18	10	.280	.321	3
DARIO	LODIGIANI	1946	Chicago White Sox	AL	44	155	12	38	8	0	0	13	16	14	.245	.297	4
PAUL	LODUCA	1998	Los Angeles Dodgers	NL	6	14	2	4	1	0	0	—	0	7	.286	.357	0
PAUL	LODUCA	1999	Los Angeles Dodgers	NL	36	95	11	22	1	0	3	11	10	9	.232	.337	1
PAUL	LODUCA	2000	Los Angeles Dodgers	NL	34	65	6	16	2	0	2	8	6	8	.246	.369	0
PAUL	LODUCA	2001	Los Angeles Dodgers	NL	125	460	71	147	28	0	25	90	39	30	.320	.543	2

FIRST	LAST	YEAR	TEAM	LEAGUE	G	AB	R	H	2B	3B	HR	RBI	BB	SO	AVG	SLUG	SB
ERNIE	LOMBARDI	1931	Brooklyn Dodgers	NL	73	182	20	54	7	1	4	23	12	12	.297	.412	1
ERNIE	LOMBARDI	1932	Cincinnati Reds	NL	118	413	43	125	22	9	11	68	41	19	.303	.479	0
ERNIE	LOMBARDI	1933	Cincinnati Reds	NL	107	350	30	99	21	1	4	47	16	17	.283	.383	2
ERNIE	LOMBARDI	1934	Cincinnati Reds	NL	132	417	42	127	19	4	9	62	16	22	.305	.434	0
ERNIE	LOMBARDI	1935	Cincinnati Reds	NL	120	332	36	114	23	3	12	64	16	6	.343	.539	0
ERNIE	LOMBARDI	1936	Cincinnati Reds	NL	121	387	42	129	23	2	12	68	19	16	.333	.496	1
ERNIE	LOMBARDI	1937	Cincinnati Reds	NL	120	368	41	123	22	1	9	59	14	17	.334	.473	1
ERNIE	LOMBARDI	1938	Cincinnati Reds	NL	129	489	60	167	30	1	19	95	40	14	.342	.524	0
ERNIE	LOMBARDI	1939	Cincinnati Reds	NL	130	450	43	129	26	2	20	85	35	19	.287	.487	0
ERNIE	LOMBARDI	1940	Cincinnati Reds	NL	109	376	50	120	22	0	14	74	31	14	.319	.489	1
ERNIE	LOMBARDI	1941	Cincinnati Reds	NL	117	398	33	105	12	1	10	60	36	14	.264	.374	0
ERNIE	LOMBARDI	1942	Boston Braves	NL	105	309	32	102	14	0	11	46	37	12	.330	.482	1
ERNIE	LOMBARDI	1943	New York Giants	NL	104	295	19	90	7	0	10	51	16	11	.305	.451	1
ERNIE	LOMBARDI	1944	New York Giants	NL	117	373	37	95	13	0	10	58	33	25	.255	.370	0
ERNIE	LOMBARDI	1945	New York Giants	NL	115	368	46	113	7	1	19	70	43	11	.307	.486	0
ERNIE	LOMBARDI	1946	New York Giants	NL	88	238	19	69	4	1	12	39	18	24	.290	.466	0
ERNIE	LOMBARDI	1947	New York Giants	NL	48	110	8	31	5	0	4	21	7	9	.282	.436	0
PHIL	LOMBARDI	1986	New York Yankees	AL	20	36	6	10	3	0	2	6	4	7	.278	.528	0
PHIL	LOMBARDI	1987	New York Yankees	AL	5	8	0	1	0	0	0	0	0	2	.125	.125	0
PHIL	LOMBARDI	1989	New York Mets	NL	18	48	4	11	1	0	1	3	5	8	.229	.312	0
STEVE	LOMBARDOZZI	1985	Minnesota Twins	AL	28	54	10	20	4	1	0	6	6	6	.370	.481	3
STEVE	LOMBARDOZZI	1986	Minnesota Twins	AL	156	453	53	103	20	5	8	33	52	76	.227	.347	3
STEVE	LOMBARDOZZI	1987	Minnesota Twins	AL	136	432	51	103	19	3	8	38	33	66	.238	.352	5
STEVE	LOMBARDOZZI	1988	Minnesota Twins	AL	103	287	34	60	15	2	3	27	35	48	.209	.307	2
STEVE	LOMBARDOZZI	1989	Houston Astros	NL	21	37	5	8	3	1	1	3	4	9	.216	.432	0
STEVE	LOMBARDOZZI	1990	Houston Astros	NL	2	1	0	0	0	0	0	0	1		.000		0
MARK	LORETTA	1995	Milwaukee Brewers	AL	19	50	13	13	3	0	1	3	4	7	.260	.380	1
MARK	LORETTA	1996	Milwaukee Brewers	AL	73	154	20	43	3	0	1	13	14	15	.279	.318	2
MARK	LORETTA	1997	Milwaukee Brewers	AL	132	418	56	120	17	5	5	47	47	60	.287	.388	5
MARK	LORETTA	1998	Milwaukee Brewers	NL	140	434	55	137	29	2	6	54	42	47	.316	.424	9
MARK	LORETTA	1999	Milwaukee Brewers	NL	153	587	93	170	34	1	5	67	52	59	.290	.390	4
MARK	LORETTA	2000	Milwaukee Brewers	NL	91	352	49	99	21	2	7	40	37	38	.281	.406	0
MARK	LORETTA	2001	Milwaukee Brewers	NL	102	384	40	111	14	2	2	29	28	46	.289	.352	1
JAY	LOVIGLIO	1980	Philadelphia Phillies	NL	16	5	5	0	0	0	0	0	1	1	.000		1
JAY	LOVIGLIO	1981	Chicago White Sox	AL	14	15	5	4	0	0	0	2	1	1	.267	.267	2

FIRST	LAST	YEAR	TEAM	LEAGUE	G	AB	R	H	2B	3B	HR	RBI	BB	SO	AVG	SLUG	SB
JAY	LOVIGLIO	1982	Chicago White Sox	AL	15	31	5	6	0	0	0	2	1	4	.194	.194	2
JAY	LOVIGLIO	1983	Chicago Cubs	NL	1	1	0	0	0	0	0	0	0	1	.000		0
JOE	LOVITTO	1972	Texas Rangers	AL	117	330	23	74	9	1	1	19	37	54	.224	.267	13
JOE	LOVITTO	1973	Texas Rangers	AL	26	44	3	6	1	0	0	0	5	7	.136	.159	1
JOE	LOVITTO	1974	Texas Rangers	AL	113	283	27	63	9	3	2	26	25	36	.223	.297	6
JOE	LOVITTO	1975	Texas Rangers	AL	50	106	17	22	3	0	1	8	13	16	.208	.264	2
TOREY	LOVULLO	1988	Detroit Tigers	AL	12	21	2	8	1	1	0	2	1	2	.381	.667	0
TOREY	LOVULLO	1989	Detroit Tigers	AL	29	87	8	10	2	0	1	4	14	20	.115	.172	0
TOREY	LOVULLO	1991	New York Yankees	AL	22	51	0	9	2	0	0	2	5	11	.176	.216	0
TOREY	LOVULLO	1993	California Angels	AL	116	367	42	92	20	0	6	30	36	49	.251	.354	7
TOREY	LOVULLO	1994	Seattle Mariners	AL	36	72	9	16	5	0	2	7	9	13	.222	.375	1
TOREY	LOVULLO	1996	Oakland Athletics	AL	65	82	15	18	4	0	3	9	11	17	.220	.378	0
TOREY	LOVULLO	1998	Cleveland Indians	AL	6	19	1	4	1	0	0	1	1	2	.211	.263	0
TOREY	LOVULLO	1999	Philadelphia Phillies	NL	17	38	3	8	0	0	2	5	3	11	.211	.368	0
JOHNNY	LUCADELLO	1938	St. Louis Browns	AL	7	20	1	3	1	0	0	0	1	0	.150	.200	0
JOHNNY	LUCADELLO	1939	St. Louis Browns	AL	9	30	0	7	2	0	0	4	2	4	.233	.300	1
JOHNNY	LUCADELLO	1940	St. Louis Browns	AL	17	63	15	20	4	2	2	10	6	4	.317	.540	5
JOHNNY	LUCADELLO	1941	St. Louis Browns	AL	107	351	58	98	22	4	4	31	48	23	.279	.382	5
JOHNNY	LUCADELLO	1946	St. Louis Browns	AL	87	210	21	52	7	1	1	15	36	20	.248	.305	0
JOHNNY	LUCADELLO	1947	New York Yankees	AL	12	12	0	1	0	0	0	0	1	5	.083	.083	0
LEW	MALONE	1915	Philadelphia Athletics	AL	76	201	17	41	4	4	1	17	21	40	.204	.279	7
LEW	MALONE	1916	Philadelphia Athletics	AL	5	4	1	0	0	0	0	0	1	2	.000		0
LEW	MALONE	1917	Brooklyn Dodgers	NL	1	0	0	0									
LEW	MALONE	1919	Brooklyn Dodgers	NL	51	162	9	33	7	3	0	11	6	18	.204	.284	1
FRANK	MALZONE	1955	Boston Red Sox	AL	6	20	2	7	1	1	0	1	1	3	.350	.400	0
FRANK	MALZONE	1956	Boston Red Sox	AL	27	103	15	17	3	1	2	11	9	8	.165	.272	1
FRANK	MALZONE	1957	Boston Red Sox	AL	153	634	82	185	31	5	15	103	31	41	.292	.427	2
FRANK	MALZONE	1958	Boston Red Sox	AL	155	627	76	185	30	2	15	87	33	53	.295	.421	1
FRANK	MALZONE	1959	Boston Red Sox	AL	154	604	90	169	34	2	19	92	42	58	.280	.437	6
FRANK	MALZONE	1960	Boston Red Sox	AL	152	595	60	161	30	2	14	79	36	42	.271	.398	2
FRANK	MALZONE	1961	Boston Red Sox	AL	151	590	74	157	21	4	14	87	44	49	.266	.386	1
FRANK	MALZONE	1962	Boston Red Sox	AL	156	619	74	175	20	3	21	95	35	43	.283	.426	0
FRANK	MALZONE	1963	Boston Red Sox	AL	151	580	66	169	25	2	15	71	31	45	.291	.419	0
FRANK	MALZONE	1964	Boston Red Sox	AL	148	537	62	142	19	0	13	56	57	43	.264	.372	0
FRANK	MALZONE	1965	Boston Red Sox	AL	106	364	40	87	20	0	3	34	28	38	.239	.319	1

FIRST	LAST	YEAR	TEAM	LEAGUE	G	AB	R	H	2B	3B	HR	RBI	BB	SO	AVG	SLUG	SB
FRANK	MALZONE	1966	California Angels	AL	82	155	6	32	5	0	2	12	10	11	.206	.277	0
GUS	MANCUSO	1928	St. Louis Cardinals	NL	11	38	2	7	0	1	0	3	0	5	.184	.237	0
GUS	MANCUSO	1930	St. Louis Cardinals	NL	76	227	39	83	17	2	7	59	18	16	.366	.551	1
GUS	MANCUSO	1931	St. Louis Cardinals	NL	67	187	13	49	16	1	1	23	18	13	.262	.374	2
GUS	MANCUSO	1932	St. Louis Cardinals	NL	103	310	25	88	23	1	5	43	30	15	.284	.413	0
GUS	MANCUSO	1933	New York Giants	NL	144	481	39	127	17	1	6	56	48	21	.264	.345	0
GUS	MANCUSO	1934	New York Giants	NL	122	383	32	94	14	0	7	46	27	19	.245	.337	0
GUS	MANCUSO	1935	New York Giants	NL	128	447	33	133	18	2	5	56	30	16	.298	.380	1
GUS	MANCUSO	1936	New York Giants	NL	139	519	55	156	21	3	9	63	39	28	.301	.405	0
GUS	MANCUSO	1937	New York Giants	NL	86	287	30	80	17	0	4	39	17	20	.279	.387	1
GUS	MANCUSO	1938	New York Giants	NL	52	158	19	55	8	0	2	15	17	13	.348	.437	0
GUS	MANCUSO	1939	Chicago Cubs	NL	80	251	17	58	10	0	2	17	24	19	.231	.295	0
GUS	MANCUSO	1940	Brooklyn Dodgers	NL	60	144	16	33	8	0	0	16	13	7	.229	.285	0
GUS	MANCUSO	1941	St. Louis Cardinals	NL	106	328	25	75	13	1	2	37	37	19	.229	.293	1
GUS	MANCUSO	1942	New York Giants	NL	39	109	4	21	1	0	0	8	14	7	.193	.220	0
GUS	MANCUSO	1942	St. Louis Cardinals	NL	5	13	0	1	0	0	0	1	0	0	.077	.077	0
GUS	MANCUSO	1943	New York Giants	NL	94	252	11	50	5	0	2	20	28	16	.198	.242	0
GUS	MANCUSO	1944	New York Giants	NL	78	195	15	49	4	1	1	25	30	20	.251	.297	2
GUS	MANCUSO	1945	Philadelphia Phillies	NL	70	176	11	35	5	0	0	16	28	10	.199	.227	1
FRANK	MANCUSO	1944	St. Louis Browns	AL	88	244	19	50	11	0	1	24	20	32	.205	.262	1
FRANK	MANCUSO	1945	St. Louis Browns	AL	119	365	39	98	13	3	1	38	46	44	.268	.329	0
FRANK	MANCUSO	1946	St. Louis Browns	AL	87	262	22	63	8	3	3	23	30	31	.240	.328	1
FRANK	MANCUSO	1947	Washington Senators	AL	43	131	5	30	5	1	0	13	5	11	.229	.282	0
DON	MANNO	1940	Boston Braves	NL	3	7	1	2	0	0	0	4	0	2	.286	.714	0
DON	MANNO	1941	Boston Braves	NL	22	30	2	5	0	0	0	4	3	7	.167	.200	0
JEFF	MANTO	1990	Cleveland Indians	AL	30	76	12	17	5	1	2	14	21	18	.224	.395	0
JEFF	MANTO	1991	Cleveland Indians	AL	47	128	15	27	7	0	2	13	14	22	.211	.312	2
JEFF	MANTO	1993	Philadelphia Phillies	NL	8	18	0	1	0	0	0	0	0	5	.056	.056	0
JEFF	MANTO	1995	Baltimore Orioles	AL	89	254	31	65	9	0	17	38	24	69	.256	.492	0
JEFF	MANTO	1996	Boston Red Sox	AL	22	48	8	10	3	0	2	6	8	12	.208	.438	0
JEFF	MANTO	1996	Seattle Mariners	AL	21	54	7	10	3	1	1	4	9	12	.185	.296	0
JEFF	MANTO	1997	Cleveland Indians	AL	16	30	3	8	3	0	2	7	1	10	.267	.567	0
JEFF	MANTO	1998	Cleveland Indians	AL	15	37	8	8	1	0	2	6	2	10	.216	.405	0
JEFF	MANTO	1998	Detroit Tigers	AL	16	30	6	8	2	0	1	3	3	11	.267	.433	0
JEFF	MANTO	1999	Cleveland Indians	AL	12	25	5	5	0	0	1	2	11	11	.200	.320	0

FIRST	LAST	YEAR	TEAM	LEAGUE	G	AB	R	H	2B	3B	HR	RBI	BB	SO	AVG	SLUG	SB
JEFF	MANTO	1999	New York Yankees	AL	6	8	0	1	0	0	0	0	2	4	.125	.125	0
JEFF	MANTO	2000	Colorado Rockies	NL	7	5	2	4	2	0	1	4	2	0	.800	1.800	0
BILLY	MARTIN	1950	New York Yankees	AL	34	36	10	9	1	0	1	8	3	3	.250	.361	0
BILLY	MARTIN	1951	New York Yankees	AL	51	58	10	15	1	2	0	2	4	9	.259	.345	0
BILLY	MARTIN	1952	New York Yankees	AL	109	363	32	97	13	3	3	33	22	31	.267	.344	3
BILLY	MARTIN	1953	New York Yankees	AL	149	587	72	151	24	6	15	75	43	56	.257	.395	6
BILLY	MARTIN	1955	New York Yankees	AL	20	70	8	21	2	0	1	9	7	9	.300	.371	1
BILLY	MARTIN	1956	New York Yankees	AL	121	458	76	121	24	5	9	49	30	56	.264	.397	7
BILLY	MARTIN	1957	Kansas City Athletics	AL	73	265	33	68	9	2	9	27	12	20	.257	.415	7
BILLY	MARTIN	1957	New York Yankees	AL	43	145	12	35	5	2	1	12	12	14	.241	.324	2
BILLY	MARTIN	1958	Detroit Tigers	AL	131	498	56	127	19	1	7	42	16	62	.255	.339	5
BILLY	MARTIN	1959	Cleveland Indians	AL	73	242	37	63	7	0	9	24	8	18	.260	.401	0
BILLY	MARTIN	1960	Cincinnati Reds	NL	103	317	34	78	17	1	3	16	27	34	.246	.334	0
BILLY	MARTIN	1961	Milwaukee Braves	NL	6	6	1	0	0	0	0	0	0	1	.000	.000	0
BILLY	MARTIN	1961	Minnesota Twins	AL	108	374	44	92	15	5	6	36	13	42	.246	.361	3
JOHN	MARZANO	1987	Boston Red Sox	AL	52	168	20	41	11	0	5	24	7	41	.244	.399	0
JOHN	MARZANO	1988	Boston Red Sox	AL	10	29	3	4	1	0	0	1	1	3	.138	.172	0
JOHN	MARZANO	1989	Boston Red Sox	AL	7	18	5	8	3	0	1	3	0	3	.444	.778	0
JOHN	MARZANO	1990	Boston Red Sox	AL	32	83	8	20	4	0	0	6	5	10	.241	.289	0
JOHN	MARZANO	1991	Boston Red Sox	AL	49	114	10	30	8	0	0	9	1	16	.263	.333	0
JOHN	MARZANO	1992	Boston Red Sox	AL	19	50	4	4	2	1	0	1	2	12	.080	.160	0
JOHN	MARZANO	1995	Texas Rangers	AL	2	6	2	2	0	0	0	0	0	0	.333	.333	0
JOHN	MARZANO	1996	Seattle Mariners	AL	41	106	8	26	6	0	0	6	7	15	.245	.302	0
JOHN	MARZANO	1997	Seattle Mariners	AL	39	87	7	25	3	0	1	10	7	15	.287	.356	0
JOHN	MARZANO	1998	Seattle Mariners	AL	50	133	13	31	7	1	4	12	9	24	.233	.391	0
PHIL	MASI	1939	Boston Braves	NL	46	114	14	29	7	2	1	14	9	15	.254	.377	0
PHIL	MASI	1940	Boston Braves	NL	63	138	11	27	4	0	0	14	14	14	.196	.261	0
PHIL	MASI	1941	Boston Braves	NL	87	180	17	40	8	2	3	18	16	13	.222	.339	4
PHIL	MASI	1942	Boston Braves	NL	57	87	14	19	3	1	0	9	12	4	.218	.276	2
PHIL	MASI	1943	Boston Braves	NL	80	238	27	65	9	1	2	28	27	20	.273	.345	7
PHIL	MASI	1944	Boston Braves	NL	89	251	33	69	13	5	3	23	31	20	.275	.402	4
PHIL	MASI	1945	Boston Braves	NL	114	371	55	101	25	4	7	46	42	32	.272	.418	9
PHIL	MASI	1946	Boston Braves	NL	133	397	52	106	17	5	3	62	55	41	.267	.358	5
PHIL	MASI	1947	Boston Braves	NL	126	411	54	125	22	4	9	50	47	27	.304	.443	7
PHIL	MASI	1948	Boston Braves	NL	113	376	43	95	19	0	5	44	35	26	.253	.343	2

FIRST	LAST	YEAR	TEAM	LEAGUE	G	AB	R	H	2B	3B	HR	RBI	BB	SO	AVG	SLUG	SB
PHIL	MASI	1949	Boston Braves	NL	37	105	13	22	2	2	0	6	14	10	.210	.229	1
PHIL	MASI	1949	Pittsburgh Pirates	NL	48	135	16	37	6	1	2	13	17	16	.274	.378	1
PHIL	MASI	1950	Chicago White Sox	AL	122	377	38	105	17	2	7	55	49	36	.279	.390	2
PHIL	MASI	1951	Chicago White Sox	AL	84	225	24	61	11	2	4	28	32	27	.271	.391	1
PHIL	MASI	1952	Chicago White Sox	AL	30	63	9	16	1	0	0	7	10	10	.254	.302	0
GORDON	MASSA	1957	Chicago Cubs	NL	6	15	2	7	1	0	0	3	4	3	.467	.533	0
GORDON	MASSA	1958	Chicago Cubs	NL	2	2	0	0	0	0	0	0	0	2	.000		0
CARMEN	MAURO	1948	Chicago Cubs	NL	3	5	2	1	0	0	1	1	2	0	.200	.200	0
CARMEN	MAURO	1950	Chicago Cubs	NL	62	185	19	42	4	3	0	10	13	31	.227	.297	3
CARMEN	MAURO	1951	Chicago Cubs	NL	13	29	3	5	1	0	0	3	2	6	.172	.207	0
CARMEN	MAURO	1953	Brooklyn Dodgers	NL	8	9	1	0	0	0	0	0	0	4	.000		3
CARMEN	MAURO	1953	Philadelphia Athletics	AL	64	165	14	44	4	4	0	17	19	21	.267	.339	3
CARMEN	MAURO	1955	Washington Senators	AL	17	23	1	4	0	1	0	2	1	3	.174	.261	0
MEL	MAZZERA	1935	St. Louis Browns	AL	12	30	4	7	2	0	0	2	4	9	.233	.400	0
MEL	MAZZERA	1937	St. Louis Browns	AL	7	7	1	2	2	0	0	0	0	2	.286		0
MEL	MAZZERA	1938	St. Louis Browns	AL	86	204	33	57	8	2	6	29	12	25	.279	.426	1
MEL	MAZZERA	1939	St. Louis Browns	AL	33	110	21	33	5	2	3	22	10	20	.300	.464	0
MEL	MAZZERA	1940	Philadelphia Phillies	NL	69	156	16	37	5	4	0	13	19	15	.237	.321	1
LEE	MAZZILLI	1976	New York Mets	NL	24	77	9	15	1	0	2	7	14	10	.195	.299	5
LEE	MAZZILLI	1977	New York Mets	NL	159	537	66	134	24	3	6	46	72	72	.250	.339	22
LEE	MAZZILLI	1978	New York Mets	NL	148	542	78	148	28	5	16	61	69	82	.273	.432	20
LEE	MAZZILLI	1979	New York Mets	NL	158	597	78	181	34	4	15	79	93	74	.303	.449	34
LEE	MAZZILLI	1980	New York Mets	NL	152	578	82	162	31	4	16	76	82	92	.280	.431	41
LEE	MAZZILLI	1981	New York Mets	NL	95	324	36	74	14	5	6	34	46	53	.228	.358	17
LEE	MAZZILLI	1982	New York Yankees	AL	37	128	20	34	2	0	6	17	15	15	.266	.422	7
LEE	MAZZILLI	1982	Texas Rangers	AL	58	195	23	47	8	0	4	17	28	26	.241	.344	2
LEE	MAZZILLI	1983	Pittsburgh Pirates	NL	109	246	37	59	9	0	5	24	49	43	.240	.337	11
LEE	MAZZILLI	1984	Pittsburgh Pirates	NL	111	266	37	63	11	0	4	21	40	42	.237	.331	15
LEE	MAZZILLI	1985	Pittsburgh Pirates	NL	92	117	20	33	8	1	1	9	29	17	.282	.376	8
LEE	MAZZILLI	1986	New York Mets	NL	39	58	10	16	3	0	2	7	12	11	.276	.431	4
LEE	MAZZILLI	1986	Pittsburgh Pirates	NL	61	93	18	21	2	1	1	8	26	25	.226	.301	1
LEE	MAZZILLI	1987	New York Mets	NL	88	124	26	38	8	0	3	24	21	14	.306	.460	3
LEE	MAZZILLI	1988	New York Mets	NL	68	116	9	17	2	1	0	12	12	16	.147	.164	5
LEE	MAZZILLI	1989	New York Mets	NL	48	60	10	11	2	0	2	7	17	19	.183	.317	4
LEE	MAZZILLI	1989	Toronto Blue Jays	AL	28	66	12	15	3	0	4	11	17	16	.227	.455	2

FIRST	LAST	YEAR	TEAM	LEAGUE	G	AB	R	H	2B	3B	HR	RBI	BB	SO	AVG	SLUG	SB
DUTCH	MELE	1937	Cincinnati Reds	NL	6	14	1	2	1	0	0	1	1	1	.143	.214	0
SAM	MELE	1947	Boston Red Sox	AL	123	453	71	137	14	8	12	73	37	35	.302	.448	0
SAM	MELE	1948	Boston Red Sox	AL	66	180	25	42	12	1	2	25	13	21	.233	.344	1
SAM	MELE	1949	Boston Red Sox	AL	18	46	7	9	1	1	0	7	7	14	.196	.261	2
SAM	MELE	1949	Washington Senators	AL	78	264	21	64	12	6	3	25	17	34	.242	.337	2
SAM	MELE	1950	Washington Senators	AL	126	435	57	119	21	7	12	86	51	40	.274	.432	2
SAM	MELE	1951	Washington Senators	AL	143	558	58	153	36	2	5	94	32	31	.274	.391	2
SAM	MELE	1952	Chicago White Sox	AL	123	423	46	105	18	7	14	59	48	40	.248	.400	1
SAM	MELE	1952	Washington Senators	AL	9	28	2	12	3	2	0	10	1	2	.429	.750	0
SAM	MELE	1953	Chicago White Sox	AL	140	481	64	132	26	8	12	82	58	47	.274	.437	3
SAM	MELE	1954	Baltimore Orioles	AL	72	230	17	55	9	4	5	32	18	26	.239	.378	0
SAM	MELE	1954	Boston Red Sox	AL	42	132	22	42	6	0	7	23	12	12	.318	.523	1
SAM	MELE	1955	Boston Red Sox	AL	14	31	4	4	2	0	0	1	0	7	.129	.194	0
SAM	MELE	1955	Cincinnati Reds	NL	35	62	17	13	1	0	2	7	5	13	.210	.323	0
SAM	MELE	1956	Cleveland Indians	AL	57	114	17	29	7	0	4	20	12	20	.254	.421	6
SKI	MELILLO	1926	St. Louis Browns	AL	99	385	54	98	18	5	1	30	32	31	.255	.335	3
SKI	MELILLO	1927	St. Louis Browns	AL	107	356	45	80	18	2	0	26	25	28	.225	.287	2
SKI	MELILLO	1928	St. Louis Browns	AL	51	132	9	25	2	0	0	9	9	11	.189	.205	2
SKI	MELILLO	1929	St. Louis Browns	AL	141	494	57	146	17	10	5	67	29	30	.296	.401	11
SKI	MELILLO	1930	St. Louis Browns	AL	149	574	62	147	30	10	5	59	23	44	.256	.369	15
SKI	MELILLO	1931	St. Louis Browns	AL	151	617	88	189	34	11	2	75	37	29	.306	.407	7
SKI	MELILLO	1932	St. Louis Browns	AL	154	612	71	148	19	11	3	66	36	42	.242	.324	6
SKI	MELILLO	1933	St. Louis Browns	AL	132	496	50	145	23	6	2	79	29	18	.292	.381	12
SKI	MELILLO	1934	St. Louis Browns	AL	144	552	54	133	19	3	1	55	28	27	.241	.297	4
SKI	MELILLO	1935	Boston Red Sox	AL	106	400	45	104	13	2	0	39	38	22	.260	.310	3
SKI	MELILLO	1935	St. Louis Browns	AL	19	62	8	13	3	0	0	5	8	4	.210	.258	0
SKI	MELILLO	1935	Boston Red Sox	AL	98	327	39	74	12	4	0	32	28	16	.226	.287	0
SKI	MELILLO	1936	Boston Red Sox	AL	26	56	8	14	2	0	0	6	5	4	.250	.286	0
JOE	MELLANA	1927	Philadelphia Athletics	AL	4	7	1	2	0	0	0	2	0	1	.286	.286	0
RUDY	MEOLI	1971	California Angels	AL	7	3	0	0	0	0	0	0	0	1	.000	.000	0
RUDY	MEOLI	1973	California Angels	AL	120	305	36	68	12	1	2	23	31	38	.223	.289	2
RUDY	MEOLI	1974	California Angels	AL	36	90	9	22	2	0	0	3	8	10	.244	.267	2
RUDY	MEOLI	1975	California Angels	AL	70	126	12	27	2	1	0	6	15	20	.214	.246	3
RUDY	MEOLI	1978	Chicago Cubs	NL	47	29	10	3	0	0	0	2	6	4	.103	.172	1
RUDY	MEOLI	1979	Philadelphia Phillies	NL	30	73	2	13	4	1	0	6	9	15	.178	.260	2

FIRST	LAST	YEAR	TEAM	LEAGUE	G	AB	R	H	2B	3B	HR	RBI	BB	SO	AVG	SLUG	SB
FRANK	MENECHINO	1999	Oakland Athletics	AL	9	9	0	2	0	0	0	0	0	4	.222	.222	0
FRANK	MENECHINO	2000	Oakland Athletics	AL	66	145	31	37	9	1	6	26	20	45	.255	.455	1
FRANK	MENECHINO	2001	Oakland Athletics	AL	139	471	82	114	22	2	12	60	79	97	.242	.374	1
LOU	MERLONI	1998	Boston Red Sox	AL	39	96	10	27	6	0	1	15	7	20	.281	.375	0
LOU	MERLONI	1999	Boston Red Sox	AL	43	126	18	32	7	2	1	13	8	16	.254	.333	1
LOU	MERLONI	2000	Boston Red Sox	AL	40	128	10	41	11	0	3	18	4	22	.320	.438	1
LOU	MERLONI	2001	Boston Red Sox	AL	52	146	21	39	10	2	3	13	6	31	.267	.397	2
LENNIE	MERULLO	1941	Chicago Cubs	NL	7	17	3	6	1	0	0	1	2	0	.353	.412	2
LENNIE	MERULLO	1942	Chicago Cubs	NL	143	515	53	132	23	3	2	37	35	45	.256	.324	14
LENNIE	MERULLO	1943	Chicago Cubs	NL	129	453	37	115	18	3	1	25	26	42	.254	.313	7
LENNIE	MERULLO	1944	Chicago Cubs	NL	66	193	20	41	8	1	1	16	16	18	.212	.280	3
LENNIE	MERULLO	1945	Chicago Cubs	NL	121	394	40	94	18	0	2	37	31	30	.239	.299	7
LENNIE	MERULLO	1946	Chicago Cubs	NL	65	126	14	19	8	0	0	7	11	13	.151	.214	2
LENNIE	MERULLO	1947	Chicago Cubs	NL	108	373	24	90	16	1	0	29	15	26	.241	.290	4
MATT	MERULLO	1989	Chicago White Sox	AL	31	81	5	18	1	0	0	8	6	14	.222	.272	0
MATT	MERULLO	1991	Chicago White Sox	AL	80	140	8	32	1	0	5	21	9	18	.229	.343	0
MATT	MERULLO	1992	Chicago White Sox	AL	24	50	3	9	0	1	0	3	1	8	.180	.240	0
MATT	MERULLO	1993	Chicago White Sox	AL	8	20	1	1	0	0	0	0	0	1	.050	.050	0
MATT	MERULLO	1994	Cleveland Indians	AL	4	10	1	1	0	0	0	0	2	1	.100	.100	0
MATT	MERULLO	1995	Minnesota Twins	AL	76	195	19	55	14	0	0	27	14	27	.282	.379	0
MICKEY	MICELOTTA	1954	Philadelphia Phillies	NL	13	3	2	0	0	0	0	0	1	0	.000		0
MICKEY	MICELOTTA	1955	Philadelphia Phillies	NL	4	4	0	0	0	0	0	0	0	0	.000		0
DOUG	MIRABELLI	1996	San Francisco Giants	NL	9	18	2	4	1	0	0	1	3	4	.222	.278	0
DOUG	MIRABELLI	1997	San Francisco Giants	NL	6	7	0	1	0	0	0	0	0	3	.143	.143	0
DOUG	MIRABELLI	1998	San Francisco Giants	NL	10	17	2	4	2	0	1	4	2	6	.235	.529	0
DOUG	MIRABELLI	1999	San Francisco Giants	NL	33	87	10	22	6	0	1	10	9	25	.253	.356	0
DOUG	MIRABELLI	2000	San Francisco Giants	NL	82	230	23	53	10	2	6	28	36	57	.230	.370	1
DOUG	MIRABELLI	2001	Boston Red Sox	AL	54	141	16	38	8	0	9	26	17	36	.270	.518	0
DOUG	MIRABELLI	2001	Texas Rangers	AL	23	49	4	5	2	1	2	3	10	21	.102	.265	0
BOB	MOLINARO	1975	Detroit Tigers	AL	6	19	2	5	0	0	0	1	1	0	.263	.368	0
BOB	MOLINARO	1977	Chicago White Sox	AL	1	2	0	1	0	0	0	0	0	1	.500	.500	1
BOB	MOLINARO	1977	Detroit Tigers	AL	4	4	0	1	1	0	0	0	0	2	.250	.250	0
BOB	MOLINARO	1978	Chicago White Sox	AL	105	286	39	75	5	5	6	27	19	12	.262	.378	22
BOB	MOLINARO	1979	Baltimore Orioles	AL	8	6	0	0	0	0	0	0	1	3	.000		1
BOB	MOLINARO	1980	Chicago White Sox	AL	119	344	48	100	16	4	5	36	26	29	.291	.404	18

FIRST	LAST	YEAR	TEAM	LEAGUE	G	AB	R	H	2B	3B	HR	RBI	BB	SO	AVG	SLUG	SB
BOB	MOLINARO	1981	Chicago White Sox	AL	47	42	7	11	1	1	1	9	8	1	.262	.405	1
BOB	MOLINARO	1982	Chicago Cubs	NL	65	66	6	13	1	0	1	12	6	5	.197	.258	1
BOB	MOLINARO	1982	Philadelphia Phillies	NL	19	14	0	4	0	0	0	2	3	1	.286	.286	1
BOB	MOLINARO	1983	Detroit Tigers	AL	8	2	3	0	0	0	0	0	0	2	.000		1
BLAS	MOLINARO	1983	Philadelphia Phillies	NL	19	18	0	2	1	0	1	3	0	2	.111	.111	0
BLAS	MONACO	1937	Cleveland Indians	AL	5	7	0	2	0	1	0	3	0	1	.286	.571	0
ROSS	MONACO	1946	Cleveland Indians	AL	12	6	2	0	0	0	0	0	1	2	.000		0
ROSS	MOSCHITTO	1965	New York Yankees	AL	96	27	12	5	0	0	0	3	0	12	.185	.296	0
CHAD	MOSCHITTO	1967	New York Yankees	AL	14	9	0	1	0	0	0	0	0	1	.111	.111	2
CHAD	MOTTOLA	1996	Cincinnati Reds	NL	35	79	10	17	3	0	3	6	6	16	.215	.367	2
CHAD	MOTTOLA	2000	Toronto Blue Jays	AL	3	9	1	2	0	0	0	2	0	4	.222	.222	0
STEVE	MOTTOLA	2001	Florida Marlins	NL	5	7	0	0	0	0	0	0	2	2	.000		0
STEVE	NICOSIA	1978	Pittsburgh Pirates	NL	3	5	0	0	0	0	0	1	0	1	.000		0
STEVE	NICOSIA	1979	Pittsburgh Pirates	NL	70	191	22	55	16	0	4	13	23	17	.288	.435	3
STEVE	NICOSIA	1980	Pittsburgh Pirates	NL	60	176	16	38	8	0	1	22	19	16	.216	.278	3
STEVE	NICOSIA	1981	Pittsburgh Pirates	NL	54	169	21	39	10	1	2	18	13	10	.231	.337	0
STEVE	NICOSIA	1982	Pittsburgh Pirates	NL	39	100	6	28	3	0	2	7	11	13	.280	.340	0
STEVE	NICOSIA	1983	Pittsburgh Pirates	NL	21	46	4	6	2	0	1	1	3	7	.130	.239	0
STEVE	NICOSIA	1983	San Francisco Giants	NL	15	33	4	11	0	0	0	6	3	2	.333	.333	0
STEVE	NICOSIA	1984	San Francisco Giants	NL	48	132	9	40	11	2	2	19	8	14	.303	.462	1
STEVE	NICOSIA	1985	Montreal Expos	NL	42	71	4	12	2	0	0	1	7	11	.169	.197	0
ERNIE	NICOSIA	1985	Toronto Blue Jays	AL	6	15	0	4	0	0	0	0	0	0	.267	.267	0
ERNIE	ORSATTI	1927	St. Louis Cardinals	NL	27	92	15	29	7	3	0	12	11	12	.315	.457	2
ERNIE	ORSATTI	1928	St. Louis Cardinals	NL	27	69	10	21	6	0	1	15	10	11	.304	.522	0
ERNIE	ORSATTI	1929	St. Louis Cardinals	NL	113	346	64	115	21	7	3	39	33	43	.332	.460	7
ERNIE	ORSATTI	1930	St. Louis Cardinals	NL	48	131	24	42	8	4	0	19	12	18	.321	.466	1
ERNIE	ORSATTI	1931	St. Louis Cardinals	NL	70	158	27	46	16	6	1	44	14	16	.291	.468	1
ERNIE	ORSATTI	1932	St. Louis Cardinals	NL	101	375	44	126	27	6	2	38	18	29	.336	.456	5
ERNIE	ORSATTI	1933	St. Louis Cardinals	NL	120	456	55	130	21	6	0	31	33	33	.298	.374	14
ERNIE	ORSATTI	1934	St. Louis Cardinals	NL	105	337	39	101	14	4	0	24	27	31	.300	.365	6
JOHN	ORSATTI	1935	St. Louis Cardinals	NL	90	221	28	53	9	3	4	12	18	25	.240	.321	10
JOHN	ORSINO	1961	San Francisco Giants	NL	25	83	5	23	3	2	0	4	3	13	.277	.506	0
JOHN	ORSINO	1962	San Francisco Giants	NL	18	48	4	13	2	0	0	4	5	11	.271	.312	0
JOHN	ORSINO	1963	Baltimore Orioles	AL	116	379	53	103	18	1	19	56	38	53	.272	.475	2
JOHN	ORSINO	1964	Baltimore Orioles	AL	81	248	21	55	10	0	8	23	23	55	.222	.359	0

FIRST	LAST	YEAR	TEAM	LEAGUE	G	AB	R	H	2B	3B	HR	RBI	BB	SO	AVG	SLUG	SB
JOHN	ORSINO	1965	Baltimore Orioles	AL	77	232	30	54	10	2	9	28	23	51	.233	.409	1
FRANK	ORTENZIO	1973	Kansas City Royals	AL	9	25	1	7	2	0	1	6	2	6	.280	.480	0
JIM	PAGLIARONI	1955	Boston Red Sox	AL	1	0	0	0	0	0	0	1	0	0			0
JIM	PAGLIARONI	1960	Boston Red Sox	AL	28	62	7	19	5	2	2	9	13	11	.306	.548	0
JIM	PAGLIARONI	1961	Boston Red Sox	AL	120	376	50	91	17	0	16	58	55	74	.242	.415	1
JIM	PAGLIARONI	1962	Boston Red Sox	AL	90	260	39	67	14	0	11	37	36	55	.258	.438	2
JIM	PAGLIARONI	1963	Pittsburgh Pirates	NL	92	252	27	58	5	3	11	26	36	57	.230	.381	0
JIM	PAGLIARONI	1964	Pittsburgh Pirates	NL	97	302	33	89	12	3	10	36	41	56	.295	.454	1
JIM	PAGLIARONI	1965	Pittsburgh Pirates	NL	134	403	42	108	15	0	17	65	41	84	.268	.432	0
JIM	PAGLIARONI	1966	Pittsburgh Pirates	NL	123	374	37	88	20	0	11	49	50	71	.235	.377	0
JIM	PAGLIARONI	1967	Pittsburgh Pirates	NL	44	100	4	20	1	1	0	9	16	26	.200	.230	0
JIM	PAGLIARONI	1968	Oakland Athletics	AL	66	199	19	49	4	0	6	20	24	42	.246	.357	0
JIM	PAGLIARONI	1969	Oakland Athletics	AL	14	27	1	4	1	0	1	2	5	2	.148	.296	0
JIM	PAGLIARONI	1969	Seattle Pilots	AL	40	110	10	29	4	0	5	14	13	16	.264	.455	0
MIKE	PAGLIARULO	1984	New York Yankees	AL	67	201	24	48	15	3	7	34	15	46	.239	.448	0
MIKE	PAGLIARULO	1985	New York Yankees	AL	138	380	55	91	16	2	19	62	45	86	.239	.442	0
MIKE	PAGLIARULO	1986	New York Yankees	AL	149	504	71	120	24	3	28	71	54	120	.238	.464	4
MIKE	PAGLIARULO	1987	New York Yankees	AL	150	522	76	122	26	3	32	87	53	111	.234	.479	1
MIKE	PAGLIARULO	1988	New York Yankees	AL	125	444	46	96	20	1	15	67	37	104	.216	.367	1
MIKE	PAGLIARULO	1989	New York Yankees	AL	74	223	19	44	10	0	4	16	19	43	.197	.296	1
MIKE	PAGLIARULO	1989	San Diego Padres	NL	50	148	12	29	7	0	3	14	18	39	.196	.304	2
MIKE	PAGLIARULO	1990	San Diego Padres	NL	128	398	29	101	23	2	7	38	39	66	.254	.374	1
MIKE	PAGLIARULO	1991	Minnesota Twins	AL	121	365	38	102	20	0	6	36	21	55	.279	.384	1
MIKE	PAGLIARULO	1992	Minnesota Twins	AL	42	105	10	21	4	0	0	9	1	17	.200	.238	0
MIKE	PAGLIARULO	1993	Baltimore Orioles	AL	33	117	24	38	9	0	6	21	8	15	.325	.556	6
MIKE	PAGLIARULO	1993	Minnesota Twins	AL	83	253	31	74	16	4	3	23	18	34	.292	.423	0
MIKE	PAGLIARULO	1995	Texas Rangers	AL	86	241	27	56	16	0	2	27	15	49	.232	.349	0
TOM	PAGNOZZI	1987	St. Louis Cardinals	NL	27	48	8	9	1	0	2	9	4	13	.188	.333	0
TOM	PAGNOZZI	1988	St. Louis Cardinals	NL	81	195	17	55	9	0	0	15	11	32	.282	.328	0
TOM	PAGNOZZI	1989	St. Louis Cardinals	NL	52	80	3	12	2	0	0	3	6	19	.150	.175	0
TOM	PAGNOZZI	1990	St. Louis Cardinals	NL	69	220	20	61	15	0	2	23	14	37	.277	.373	1
TOM	PAGNOZZI	1991	St. Louis Cardinals	NL	140	459	38	121	24	5	2	57	36	63	.264	.351	9
TOM	PAGNOZZI	1992	St. Louis Cardinals	NL	139	485	33	121	26	3	7	44	28	64	.249	.359	2
TOM	PAGNOZZI	1993	St. Louis Cardinals	NL	92	330	31	85	15	1	7	41	19	30	.258	.373	1
TOM	PAGNOZZI	1994	St. Louis Cardinals	NL	70	243	21	66	12	1	7	40	21	39	.272	.416	0

FIRST	LAST	YEAR	TEAM	LEAGUE	G	AB	R	H	2B	3B	HR	RBI	BB	SO	AVG	SLUG	SB
TOM	PAGNOZZI	1995	St. Louis Cardinals	NL	62	219	17	47	14	1	2	15	11	31	.215	.315	0
TOM	PAGNOZZI	1996	St. Louis Cardinals	NL	119	407	48	110	23	0	13	55	24	78	.270	.423	4
TOM	PAGNOZZI	1997	St. Louis Cardinals	NL	25	50	4	11	3	0	1	8	1	7	.220	.340	0
TOM	PAGNOZZI	1998	St. Louis Cardinals	NL	51	160	7	35	9	0	1	10	14	37	.219	.294	0
JOE	PALMISANO	1931	Philadelphia Athletics	AL	19	44	5	10	2	0	0	4	6	5	.227	.273	0
TONY	PARISSE	1943	Philadelphia Athletics	AL	6	17	3	3	0	0	0	1	2	3	.176	.176	0
TONY	PARISSE	1944	Philadelphia Athletics	AL	4	4	0	0	0	0	0	0	0	1	.000		0
DAN	PASQUA	1985	New York Yankees	AL	60	148	17	31	3	1	9	25	16	38	.209	.426	0
DAN	PASQUA	1986	New York Yankees	AL	102	280	44	82	17	0	16	45	47	78	.293	.525	2
DAN	PASQUA	1987	New York Yankees	AL	113	318	42	74	7	1	17	42	40	99	.233	.421	0
DAN	PASQUA	1988	Chicago White Sox	AL	129	422	48	96	16	2	20	50	46	100	.227	.417	1
DAN	PASQUA	1989	Chicago White Sox	AL	73	246	26	61	9	1	11	47	25	58	.248	.427	1
DAN	PASQUA	1990	Chicago White Sox	AL	112	325	43	89	27	3	13	58	37	66	.274	.495	1
DAN	PASQUA	1991	Chicago White Sox	AL	134	417	71	108	22	5	18	66	62	86	.259	.465	0
DAN	PASQUA	1992	Chicago White Sox	AL	93	265	26	56	16	1	6	33	36	57	.211	.347	2
DAN	PASQUA	1993	Chicago White Sox	AL	78	176	22	36	10	0	5	20	26	51	.205	.358	0
DAN	PASQUA	1994	Chicago White Sox	AL	11	23	2	5	2	0	2	4	0	9	.217	.565	0
MIKE	PASQUELLA	1919	Philadelphia Phillies	NL	1	1	0	1	0	0	0	0	0	0	1.000	1.000	0
MIKE	PASQUELLA	1919	St. Louis Cardinals	NL	1	1	0	0	0	0	0	0	0	0	.000	.000	0
BILL	PECOTA	1986	Kansas City Royals	AL	12	29	3	6	2	0	0	2	3	3	.207	.276	0
BILL	PECOTA	1987	Kansas City Royals	AL	66	156	22	43	5	1	3	14	15	25	.276	.378	5
BILL	PECOTA	1988	Kansas City Royals	AL	90	178	25	37	3	3	1	15	18	34	.208	.275	7
BILL	PECOTA	1989	Kansas City Royals	AL	65	83	21	17	4	2	3	5	7	9	.205	.410	5
BILL	PECOTA	1990	Kansas City Royals	AL	87	240	43	58	15	2	5	20	33	39	.242	.383	8
BILL	PECOTA	1991	Kansas City Royals	AL	125	398	53	114	23	2	6	45	41	45	.286	.399	16
BILL	PECOTA	1992	New York Mets	NL	117	269	28	61	13	0	2	26	25	40	.227	.297	9
BILL	PECOTA	1993	Atlanta Braves	NL	72	62	17	20	2	1	0	5	2	5	.323	.387	1
BILL	PECOTA	1994	Atlanta Braves	NL	64	112	11	24	5	0	2	16	16	16	.214	.312	1
EDDIE	PELLAGRINI	1946	Boston Red Sox	AL	22	71	7	15	3	1	2	4	3	18	.211	.366	1
EDDIE	PELLAGRINI	1947	Boston Red Sox	AL	74	231	29	47	8	1	4	19	23	35	.203	.299	2
EDDIE	PELLAGRINI	1948	St. Louis Browns	AL	105	290	31	69	8	3	2	27	34	40	.238	.307	0
EDDIE	PELLAGRINI	1949	St. Louis Browns	AL	79	235	26	56	8	1	2	15	14	24	.238	.306	2
EDDIE	PELLAGRINI	1951	Philadelphia Phillies	NL	86	197	31	46	4	5	5	30	23	25	.234	.381	5
EDDIE	PELLAGRINI	1952	Cincinnati Reds	NL	46	100	15	17	2	0	0	3	8	18	.170	.220	1
EDDIE	PELLAGRINI	1953	Pittsburgh Pirates	NL	78	174	16	44	3	2	4	19	14	20	.253	.362	1

FIRST	LAST	YEAR	TEAM	LEAGUE	G	AB	R	H	2B	3B	HR	RBI	BB	SO	AVG	SLUG	SB
EDDIE	PELLAGRINI	1954	Pittsburgh Pirates	NL	73	125	12	27	6	0	0	16	9	21	.216	.264	0
JOE	PEPITONE	1962	New York Yankees	AL	63	138	14	33	3	2	7	17	3	21	.239	.442	1
JOE	PEPITONE	1963	New York Yankees	AL	157	580	79	157	16	3	27	89	23	63	.271	.448	3
JOE	PEPITONE	1964	New York Yankees	AL	160	613	71	154	12	3	28	100	24	63	.251	.418	2
JOE	PEPITONE	1965	New York Yankees	AL	143	531	51	131	18	4	18	62	43	59	.247	.394	4
JOE	PEPITONE	1966	New York Yankees	AL	152	585	85	149	21	3	31	83	29	58	.255	.463	4
JOE	PEPITONE	1967	New York Yankees	AL	133	501	45	126	18	3	13	64	34	62	.251	.377	1
JOE	PEPITONE	1968	New York Yankees	AL	108	380	41	93	9	3	15	56	37	45	.245	.403	8
JOE	PEPITONE	1969	New York Yankees	AL	135	513	49	124	16	2	27	70	30	42	.242	.442	8
JOE	PEPITONE	1970	Chicago Cubs	NL	56	213	38	57	9	2	12	44	15	15	.268	.498	0
JOE	PEPITONE	1970	Houston Astros	NL	75	279	44	70	9	5	14	35	18	28	.251	.470	5
JOE	PEPITONE	1971	Chicago Cubs	NL	115	427	50	131	19	4	16	61	24	41	.307	.482	1
JOE	PEPITONE	1972	Chicago Cubs	NL	66	214	23	56	5	0	8	21	13	22	.262	.397	1
JOE	PEPITONE	1973	Atlanta Braves	NL	3	11	0	4	0	0	0	1	1	1	.364	.364	0
JOE	PEPITONE	1973	Chicago Cubs	NL	31	112	16	30	3	0	3	18	8	6	.268	.375	3
JACK	PERCONTE	1980	Los Angeles Dodgers	NL	14	17	2	4	0	0	0	2	2	1	.235	.235	3
JACK	PERCONTE	1981	Los Angeles Dodgers	NL	8	9	2	2	0	1	0	1	2	2	.222	.444	1
JACK	PERCONTE	1982	Cleveland Indians	AL	93	219	27	52	4	4	0	15	22	25	.237	.292	9
JACK	PERCONTE	1983	Cleveland Indians	AL	14	26	1	7	1	0	0	0	5	2	.269	.308	3
JACK	PERCONTE	1984	Seattle Mariners	AL	155	612	93	180	24	4	0	31	57	47	.294	.346	29
JACK	PERCONTE	1985	Seattle Mariners	AL	125	485	60	128	17	7	2	23	50	36	.264	.340	31
JACK	PERCONTE	1986	Chicago White Sox	AL	24	73	6	16	1	0	0	4	11	10	.219	.233	2
SAM	PERLOZZO	1977	Minnesota Twins	AL	10	24	6	7	0	0	0	0	2	3	.292	.458	0
SAM	PERLOZZO	1979	San Diego Padres	NL	2	2	0	0	0	0	0	0	1	0	.000		0
GENO	PETRALLI	1982	Toronto Blue Jays	AL	16	44	3	16	2	0	0	1	4	6	.364	.409	0
GENO	PETRALLI	1983	Toronto Blue Jays	AL	6	4	0	0	0	0	0	0	1	1	.000		0
GENO	PETRALLI	1984	Toronto Blue Jays	AL	3	3	0	0	0	0	0	0	0	0	.000		0
GENO	PETRALLI	1985	Texas Rangers	AL	42	100	7	27	2	3	0	11	8	12	.270	.290	1
GENO	PETRALLI	1986	Texas Rangers	AL	69	137	17	35	9	2	2	18	5	14	.255	.409	3
GENO	PETRALLI	1987	Texas Rangers	AL	101	202	28	61	11	2	7	31	27	29	.302	.480	0
GENO	PETRALLI	1988	Texas Rangers	AL	129	351	35	99	14	2	7	36	41	52	.282	.393	0
GENO	PETRALLI	1989	Texas Rangers	AL	70	184	18	56	7	0	4	23	17	24	.304	.408	0
GENO	PETRALLI	1990	Texas Rangers	AL	133	325	28	83	13	1	0	21	50	49	.255	.302	0
GENO	PETRALLI	1991	Texas Rangers	AL	87	199	21	54	8	1	2	20	21	25	.271	.352	2
GENO	PETRALLI	1992	Texas Rangers	AL	94	192	11	38	12	0	1	18	20	34	.198	.276	0

FIRST	LAST	YEAR	TEAM	LEAGUE	G	AB	R	H	2B	3B	HR	RBI	BB	SO	AVG	SLUG	SB
GENO	PETRALLI	1993	Texas Rangers	AL	59	133	16	32	5	0	1	13	22	17	.241	.301	2
RICO	PETROCELLI	1963	Boston Red Sox	AL	1	4	0	1	1	0	0	1	0		.250		0
RICO	PETROCELLI	1965	Boston Red Sox	AL	103	323	38	75	15	2	13	33	36	71	.232	.412	1
RICO	PETROCELLI	1966	Boston Red Sox	AL	139	522	58	124	20	1	18	59	41	99	.238	.383	2
RICO	PETROCELLI	1967	Boston Red Sox	AL	142	491	53	127	24	2	17	66	49	93	.259	.420	2
RICO	PETROCELLI	1968	Boston Red Sox	AL	123	406	41	95	17	2	12	46	31	73	.234	.374	3
RICO	PETROCELLI	1969	Boston Red Sox	AL	154	535	92	159	32	2	40	97	98	68	.297	.589	1
RICO	PETROCELLI	1970	Boston Red Sox	AL	157	583	82	152	31	3	29	103	67	82	.261	.473	2
RICO	PETROCELLI	1971	Boston Red Sox	AL	158	553	82	139	24	4	28	89	91	108	.251	.461	2
RICO	PETROCELLI	1972	Boston Red Sox	AL	147	521	62	125	15	1	15	75	78	91	.240	.363	0
RICO	PETROCELLI	1973	Boston Red Sox	AL	100	356	44	87	13	1	13	45	47	64	.244	.396	1
RICO	PETROCELLI	1974	Boston Red Sox	AL	129	454	53	121	23	1	15	76	48	74	.267	.421	0
RICO	PETROCELLI	1975	Boston Red Sox	AL	115	402	31	96	15	0	7	59	41	66	.239	.333	0
RICO	PETROCELLI	1976	Boston RedSox	AL	85	240	17	51	7	1	3	24	34	36	.212	.287	0
JOE	PETTINI	1980	San Francisco Giants	NL	63	190	19	44	3	1	0	9	17	33	.232	.274	5
JOE	PETTINI	1981	San Francisco Giants	NL	35	29	3	2	1	0	0	2	4	5	.069	.103	1
JOE	PETTINI	1982	San Francisco Giants	NL	29	39	5	8	1	0	0	2	3	4	.205	.231	0
JOE	PETTINI	1983	San Francisco Giants	NL	61	86	11	16	0	0	0	7	9	11	.186	.209	4
MIKE	PIAZZA	1992	Los Angeles Dodgers	NL	21	69	5	16	3	0	1	7	4	12	.232	.319	0
MIKE	PIAZZA	1993	Los Angeles Dodgers	NL	149	547	81	174	24	2	35	112	46	86	.318	.561	3
MIKE	PIAZZA	1994	Los Angeles Dodgers	NL	107	405	64	129	18	0	24	92	33	65	.319	.541	1
MIKE	PIAZZA	1995	Los Angeles Dodgers	NL	112	434	82	150	17	0	32	93	39	80	.346	.606	1
MIKE	PIAZZA	1996	Los Angeles Dodgers	NL	148	547	87	184	16	0	36	105	81	93	.336	.563	0
MIKE	PIAZZA	1997	Los Angeles Dodgers	NL	152	556	104	201	32	1	40	124	69	77	.362	.638	5
MIKE	PIAZZA	1998	Florida Marlins	NL	5	18	1	5	0	0	0	5	0		.278	.389	0
MIKE	PIAZZA	1998	Los Angeles Dodgers	NL	37	149	20	42	5	0	9	30	11	27	.282	.497	1
MIKE	PIAZZA	1998	New York Mets	NL	109	394	67	137	33	0	23	76	47	53	.348	.607	1
MIKE	PIAZZA	1999	New York Mets	NL	141	534	100	162	25	0	40	124	51	70	.303	.575	2
MIKE	PIAZZA	2000	New York Mets	NL	136	482	90	156	26	0	38	113	58	69	.324	.614	4
MIKE	PIAZZA	2001	New York Mets	NL	141	503	81	151	29	0	36	94	67	87	.300	.573	0
JOE	PIGNATANO	1957	Brooklyn Dodgers	NL	8	14	0	3	1	0	0	1	0	5	.214	.286	0
JOE	PIGNATANO	1958	Los Angeles Dodgers	NL	63	142	18	31	4	1	9	17	16	26	.218	.437	4
JOE	PIGNATANO	1959	Los Angeles Dodgers	NL	52	139	17	33	4	0	1	11	21	15	.237	.302	1
JOE	PIGNATANO	1960	Los Angeles Dodgers	NL	58	90	11	21	4	0	2	9	15	17	.233	.344	1
JOE	PIGNATANO	1961	Kansas City Athletics	AL	92	243	31	59	10	3	4	22	36	42	.243	.358	2

FIRST	LAST	YEAR	TEAM	LEAGUE	G	AB	R	H	2B	3B	HR	RBI	BB	SO	AVG	SLUG	SB
JOE	PIGNATANO	1962	New York Mets	NL	27	56	2	13	2	0	0	2	2	11	.232	.268	0
JOE	PIGNATANO	1962	San Francisco Giants	NL	7	5	2	1	0	0	0	0	4	0	.200	.200	0
BABE	PINELLI	1918	Chicago White Sox	AL	24	78	7	18	1	1	0	7	7	8	.231	.308	3
BABE	PINELLI	1920	Detroit Tigers	AL	102	284	33	65	9	3	0	21	25	16	.229	.282	6
BABE	PINELLI	1922	Cincinnati Reds	NL	156	547	77	167	19	7	1	72	48	37	.305	.371	17
BABE	PINELLI	1923	Cincinnati Reds	NL	117	423	44	117	14	5	0	51	27	29	.277	.333	10
BABE	PINELLI	1924	Cincinnati Reds	NL	144	510	61	156	16	7	0	70	32	32	.306	.365	23
BABE	PINELLI	1925	Cincinnati Reds	NL	130	492	68	139	33	6	2	49	22	28	.283	.386	8
BABE	PINELLI	1926	Cincinnati Reds	NL	71	207	26	46	7	4	0	24	15	5	.222	.295	2
BABE	PINELLI	1927	Cincinnati Reds	NL	30	76	11	15	1	0	1	4	6	7	.197	.263	2
JIM	PISONI	1953	St. Louis Browns	AL	3	12	1	1	0	0	0	-	0	5	.083	.083	0
JIM	PISONI	1956	Kansas City Athletics	AL	10	30	4	8	0	0	2	5	2	8	.267	.467	0
JIM	PISONI	1957	Kansas City Athletics	AL	44	97	14	23	2	2	3	12	10	17	.237	.392	0
JIM	PISONI	1959	Milwaukee Braves	NL	9	24	4	4	1	0	0	0	2	6	.167	.208	0
JIM	PISONI	1959	New York Yankees	AL	17	17	2	3	0	1	0	-	1	9	.176	.294	0
JIM	PISONI	1960	New York Yankees	AL	20	9	1	1	0	0	0	1	1	2	.111	.111	0
CHRIS	PITTARO	1985	Detroit Tigers	AL	28	62	10	15	3	0	0	7	5	13	.242	.323	1
CHRIS	PITTARO	1986	Minnesota Twins	AL	11	21	0	2	0	0	0	0	0	8	.095	.095	0
CHRIS	PITTARO	1987	Minnesota Twins	AL	14	12	6	4	0	0	0	0	1	0	.333	.333	1
ROB	PICCIOLO	1977	Oakland Athletics	AL	148	419	35	84	12	3	2	22	9	55	.200	.258	1
ROB	PICCIOLO	1978	Oakland Athletics	AL	78	93	16	21	1	0	2	7	2	13	.226	.301	1
ROB	PICCIOLO	1979	Oakland Athletics	AL	115	348	37	88	16	2	2	27	3	45	.253	.328	2
ROB	PICCIOLO	1980	Oakland Athletics	AL	95	271	32	65	9	2	5	18	2	63	.240	.343	2
ROB	PICCIOLO	1981	Oakland Athletics	AL	82	179	23	48	5	3	4	13	5	22	.268	.397	0
ROB	PICCIOLO	1982	Milwaukee Brewers	AL	22	21	7	6	1	0	0	-	1	4	.286	.333	0
ROB	PICCIOLO	1982	Oakland Athletics	AL	18	49	3	11	1	0	0	3	1	10	.224	.245	1
ROB	PICCIOLO	1983	Milwaukee Brewers	AL	14	27	2	6	3	0	0	3	0	4	.222	.333	0
ROB	PICCIOLO	1984	California Angels	AL	87	119	18	24	6	0	1	9	0	21	.202	.277	0
ROB	PICCIOLO	1985	Oakland Athletics	AL	71	102	19	28	6	0	1	8	2	17	.275	.324	3
NICK	PICCIUTO	1945	Philadelphia Phillies	NL	36	89	7	12	6	0	0	6	6	17	.135	.202	0
JOHNNY	PRAMESA	1949	Cincinnati Reds	NL	17	25	2	6	1	0	1	2	3	5	.240	.400	0
JOHNNY	PRAMESA	1950	Cincinnati Reds	NL	74	228	14	70	10	2	5	30	19	15	.307	.425	0
JOHNNY	PRAMESA	1951	Cincinnati Reds	NL	72	227	12	52	5	2	6	22	5	17	.229	.348	0
JOHNNY	PRAMESA	1952	Chicago Cubs	NL	22	46	1	13	1	0	0	5	4	4	.283	.370	0
GEORGE	PUCCINELLI	1930	St. Louis Cardinals	NL	11	16	5	9	1	0	3	8	0	1	.562	1.188	0

FIRST	LAST	YEAR	TEAM	LEAGUE	G	AB	R	H	2B	3B	HR	RBI	BB	SO	AVG	SLUG	SB
GEORGE	PUCCINELLI	1932	St. Louis Cardinals	NL	31	108	17	30	8	0	3	11	12	13	.278	.435	1
GEORGE	PUCCINELLI	1934	St. Louis Browns	AL	10	26	4	6	1	0	2	5	1	8	.231	.500	0
GEORGE	PUCCINELLI	1936	Philadelphia Athletics	AL	135	457	83	127	30	3	11	78	65	70	.278	.429	2
FRANK	QUILICI	1965	Minnesota Twins	AL	56	149	16	31	5	1	0	7	15	33	.208	.255	1
FRANK	QUILICI	1967	Minnesota Twins	AL	23	19	2	2	1	0	0	1	3	4	.105	.158	0
FRANK	QUILICI	1968	Minnesota Twins	AL	97	229	22	56	11	4	1	22	21	45	.245	.341	0
FRANK	QUILICI	1969	Minnesota Twins	AL	118	144	19	25	3	1	2	12	12	22	.174	.250	2
BOB	QUILICI	1970	Minnesota Twins	AL	111	141	19	32	3	0	2	12	15	16	.227	.291	0
BOB	RAMAZZOTTI	1946	Brooklyn Dodgers	NL	62	120	10	25	4	0	0	7	9	13	.208	.242	0
BOB	RAMAZZOTTI	1948	Brooklyn Dodgers	NL	4	3	0	0	0	0	0	0		1	.000	.000	0
BOB	RAMAZZOTTI	1949	Brooklyn Dodgers	NL	5	13	1	2	0	0	0	3	0	3	.154	.385	0
BOB	RAMAZZOTTI	1949	Chicago Cubs	NL	65	190	14	34	3	1	0	6	5	33	.179	.205	9
BOB	RAMAZZOTTI	1950	Chicago Cubs	NL	61	145	19	38	3	3	1	6	4	16	.262	.345	3
BOB	RAMAZZOTTI	1951	Chicago Cubs	NL	73	158	13	39	5	2	1	15	10	23	.247	.323	0
BOB	RAMAZZOTTI	1952	Chicago Cubs	NL	50	183	26	52	5	3	1	12	14	14	.284	.361	3
BOB	RAMAZZOTTI	1953	Chicago Cubs	NL	26	39	3	6	2	0	0	4	3	4	.154	.205	0
BILL	RENNA	1953	New York Yankees	AL	61	121	19	38	6	3	2	13	13	31	.314	.463	0
BILL	RENNA	1954	Philadelphia Athletics	AL	123	422	52	98	15	4	13	53	41	60	.232	.379	1
BILL	RENNA	1955	Kansas City Athletics	AL	100	249	33	53	7	3	7	28	31	42	.213	.349	0
BILL	RENNA	1956	Kansas City Athletics	AL	33	48	12	13	5	2	2	5	3	10	.271	.458	1
BILL	RENNA	1958	Boston Red Sox	AL	39	56	5	15	5	0	4	18	6	14	.268	.571	0
BILL	RENNA	1959	Boston Red Sox	AL	14	22	2	2	0	0	0	2	5	9	.091	.091	0
TONY	RENSA	1930	Detroit Tigers	AL	20	37	6	10	2	1	1	3	6	7	.270	.459	1
TONY	RENSA	1930	Philadelphia Phillies	NL	54	172	31	49	11	2	3	31	10	18	.285	.424	0
TONY	RENSA	1931	Philadelphia Phillies	NL	19	29	2	3	1	0	0	3	6	2	.103	.138	0
TONY	RENSA	1933	New York Yankees	AL	8	29	4	9	2	1	0	3	1	3	.310	.448	0
TONY	RENSA	1937	Chicago White Sox	AL	26	57	10	17	5	0	0	5	8	6	.298	.421	3
TONY	RENSA	1938	Chicago White Sox	AL	59	165	15	41	5	0	3	19	25	16	.248	.333	1
TONY	RENSA	1939	Chicago White Sox	AL	14	25	3	5	0	0	0	2	1	2	.200	.200	0
DINO	RESTELLI	1949	Pittsburgh Pirates	NL	72	232	41	58	11	0	12	40	35	26	.250	.453	3
DINO	RESTELLI	1951	Pittsburgh Pirates	NL	21	38	1	7	1	0	1	3	2	4	.184	.289	0
HARRY	RICONDA	1923	Philadelphia Athletics	AL	55	175	23	46	11	4	0	12	12	18	.263	.371	4
HARRY	RICONDA	1924	Philadelphia Athletics	AL	83	281	34	71	16	3	1	21	27	43	.253	.342	3
HARRY	RICONDA	1926	Boston Braves	NL	4	12	1	2	0	0	0	0	2	2	.167	.167	0
HARRY	RICONDA	1928	Brooklyn Dodgers	NL	92	281	22	63	15	4	3	35	20	28	.224	.338	6

FIRST	LAST	YEAR	TEAM	LEAGUE	G	AB	R	H	2B	3B	HR	RBI	BB	SO	AVG	SLUG	SB
HARRY	RICONDA	1929	Pittsburgh Pirates	NL	8	15	3	7	2	0	0	2	0	0	.467	.600	0
HARRY	RICONDA	1930	Cincinnati Reds	NL	1	1	0	0	0	0	0	0	0	0	.000		0
JOHNNY	RIZZO	1938	Pittsburgh Pirates	NL	143	555	97	167	31	9	23	111	54	61	.301	.514	1
JOHNNY	RIZZO	1939	Pittsburgh Pirates	NL	94	330	49	86	23	3	6	55	42	27	.261	.403	0
JOHNNY	RIZZO	1940	Cincinnati Reds	NL	31	110	17	31	6	1	4	17	14	14	.282	.445	1
JOHNNY	RIZZO	1940	Philadelphia Phillies	NL	103	367	53	107	12	2	20	53	37	31	.292	.499	2
JOHNNY	RIZZO	1940	Pittsburgh Pirates	NL	9	28	1	5	1	0	0	2	5	5	.179	.214	0
JOHNNY	RIZZO	1941	Philadelphia Phillies	NL	99	235	20	51	9	2	4	24	24	34	.217	.323	1
JOHNNY	RIZZO	1942	Brooklyn Dodgers	NL	78	217	31	50	8	0	4	27	24	25	.230	.323	2
PHIL	RIZZUTO	1941	New York Yankees	AL	133	515	65	158	20	9	3	46	27	36	.307	.398	14
PHIL	RIZZUTO	1942	New York Yankees	AL	144	553	79	157	24	7	4	68	44	40	.284	.374	22
PHIL	RIZZUTO	1946	New York Yankees	AL	126	471	53	121	17	1	2	38	34	39	.257	.310	14
PHIL	RIZZUTO	1947	New York Yankees	AL	153	549	78	150	26	9	2	60	57	31	.273	.364	11
PHIL	RIZZUTO	1948	New York Yankees	AL	128	464	65	117	13	2	6	50	60	24	.252	.328	6
PHIL	RIZZUTO	1949	New York Yankees	AL	153	614	110	169	22	7	5	65	72	34	.275	.358	18
PHIL	RIZZUTO	1950	New York Yankees	AL	155	617	125	200	36	7	7	66	92	39	.324	.439	12
PHIL	RIZZUTO	1951	New York Yankees	AL	144	540	87	148	21	6	2	43	58	27	.274	.346	18
PHIL	RIZZUTO	1952	New York Yankees	AL	152	578	89	147	24	10	2	43	67	42	.254	.341	17
PHIL	RIZZUTO	1953	New York Yankees	AL	134	413	54	112	21	3	2	54	71	39	.271	.351	4
PHIL	RIZZUTO	1954	New York Yankees	AL	127	307	47	60	11	0	2	15	41	23	.195	.251	3
PHIL	RIZZUTO	1955	New York Yankees	AL	81	143	19	37	4	1	1	9	22	18	.259	.322	7
PHIL	RIZZUTO	1956	New York Yankees	AL	31	52	6	12	0	0	0	6	6	6	.231	.231	3
MICKEY	ROCCO	1943	Cleveland Indians	AL	108	405	43	97	14	4	5	46	51	40	.240	.331	1
MICKEY	ROCCO	1944	Cleveland Indians	AL	155	653	87	174	29	7	13	70	56	51	.266	.392	4
MICKEY	ROCCO	1945	Cleveland Indians	AL	143	565	81	149	28	6	10	56	52	40	.264	.388	0
MICKEY	ROCCO	1946	Cleveland Indians	AL	34	98	8	24	2	0	0	14	15	15	.245	.327	1
LOU	ROCHELLI	1944	Brooklyn Dodgers	NL	5	17	0	3	0	0	0	2	2	0	.176	.294	0
JOHNNY	ROMANO	1958	Chicago White Sox	AL	4	7	1	2	0	0	0	1	1	0	.286	.286	0
JOHNNY	ROMANO	1959	Chicago White Sox	AL	53	126	20	37	5	1	5	25	23	18	.294	.468	0
JOHNNY	ROMANO	1960	Cleveland Indians	AL	108	316	40	86	12	2	16	52	37	50	.272	.475	0
JOHNNY	ROMANO	1961	Cleveland Indians	AL	142	509	76	152	29	3	21	80	61	60	.299	.483	0
JOHNNY	ROMANO	1962	Cleveland Indians	AL	135	459	71	120	19	2	25	81	73	64	.261	.479	0
JOHNNY	ROMANO	1963	Cleveland Indians	AL	89	255	28	55	5	1	10	34	38	49	.216	.369	4
JOHNNY	ROMANO	1964	Cleveland Indians	AL	106	352	46	85	18	0	19	47	51	83	.241	.460	2
JOHNNY	ROMANO	1965	Chicago White Sox	AL	122	356	39	86	11	0	18	48	59	74	.242	.424	0

FIRST	LAST	YEAR	TEAM	LEAGUE	G	AB	R	H	2B	3B	HR	RBI	BB	SO	AVG	SLUG	SB
JOHNNY	ROMANO	1966	Chicago White Sox	AL	122	329	33	76	12	0	15	47	58	72	.231	.404	0
JOHNNY	ROMANO	1967	St. Louis Cardinals	NL	24	58	1	7	1	0	0	2	13	15	.121	.138	1
TOM	ROMANO	1987	Montreal Expos	NL	7	3	0	0	0	0	0	0	1		.000		0
BOB	ROSELLI	1955	Milwaukee Braves	NL	6	9	1	2	1	0	0	1	0	4	.222	.333	0
BOB	ROSELLI	1956	Milwaukee Braves	NL	4	2	0	1	0	0	0	0	1		.500		0
BOB	ROSELLI	1958	Milwaukee Braves	NL	1	1	0	0	0	0	0	0	0	1	.000		0
BOB	ROSELLI	1961	Chicago White Sox	AL	22	38	2	10	3	0	1	4	11	11	.263	.342	0
BOB	ROSELLI	1962	Chicago White Sox	AL	35	64	4	12	3	1	0	5	8	15	.188	.312	1
JOE	RULLO	1943	Philadelphia Athletics	AL	16	55	2	16	3	0	0	6	7	7	.291	.345	0
JOE	RULLO	1944	Philadelphia Athletics	AL	35	96	5	16	0	0	0	5	6	19	.167	.167	1
GENE	RYE	1931	Boston Red Sox	AL	17	39	3	7	0	1	0	1	6	5	.179	.179	0
F.P.	Santangelo	1995	Montreal Expos	NL	35	98	11	29	5	0	1	9	2	9	.296	.398	1
F.P.	Santangelo	1996	Montreal Expos	NL	152	393	54	109	20	5	7	56	49	61	.277	.407	5
F.P.	Santangelo	1997	Montreal Expos	NL	130	350	56	87	19	5	5	31	50	73	.249	.374	8
F.P.	Santangelo	1998	Montreal Expos	NL	122	383	53	82	18	3	4	23	44	72	.214	.292	7
F.P.	Santangelo	1999	San Francisco Giants	NL	113	254	49	66	17	2	3	26	53	54	.260	.386	12
F.P.	Santangelo	2000	Los Angeles Dodgers	NL	81	142	19	28	4	0	1	9	21	33	.197	.246	3
F.P.	Santangelo	2001	Oakland Athletics	AL	32	71	16	14	4	0	0	8	11	17	.197	.254	3
RON	SANTO	1960	Chicago Cubs	NL	95	347	44	87	24	2	9	44	31	44	.251	.409	0
RON	SANTO	1961	Chicago Cubs	NL	154	578	84	164	32	6	23	83	73	77	.284	.479	2
RON	SANTO	1962	Chicago Cubs	NL	162	604	44	137	20	4	17	83	65	94	.227	.358	4
RON	SANTO	1963	Chicago Cubs	NL	162	630	79	187	29	6	25	99	42	92	.297	.481	6
RON	SANTO	1964	Chicago Cubs	NL	161	592	94	185	33	13	30	114	86	96	.312	.564	3
RON	SANTO	1965	Chicago Cubs	NL	164	608	88	173	30	4	33	101	88	109	.285	.510	3
RON	SANTO	1966	Chicago Cubs	NL	155	561	93	175	21	8	30	94	95	78	.312	.558	4
RON	SANTO	1967	Chicago Cubs	NL	161	586	107	176	23	4	31	98	96	103	.300	.512	1
RON	SANTO	1968	Chicago Cubs	NL	162	577	86	142	17	3	26	98	96	106	.246	.421	3
RON	SANTO	1969	Chicago Cubs	NL	160	575	97	166	18	4	29	123	96	97	.289	.485	1
RON	SANTO	1970	Chicago Cubs	NL	154	555	83	148	30	4	26	114	92	108	.267	.476	2
RON	SANTO	1971	Chicago Cubs	NL	154	555	77	148	22	1	21	88	79	95	.267	.423	4
RON	SANTO	1972	Chicago Cubs	NL	133	464	68	140	25	5	17	74	69	75	.302	.487	1
RON	SANTO	1973	Chicago Cubs	NL	149	556	65	143	29	2	20	77	63	97	.267	.440	3
RON	SANTO	1974	Chicago White Sox	AL	117	375	29	83	12	1	5	41	37	72	.221	.299	0
BILL	SARNI	1951	St. Louis Cardinals	NL	36	86	7	15	1	0	0	2	9	13	.174	.186	1
BILL	SARNI	1952	St. Louis Cardinals	NL	3	5	0	1	0	0	0	0	0	1	.200	.200	0

FIRST	LAST	YEAR	TEAM	LEAGUE	G	AB	R	H	2B	3B	HR	RBI	BB	SO	AVG	SLUG	SB
BILL	SARNI	1954	St. Louis Cardinals	NL	123	380	40	114	18	4	9	70	25	42	.300	.439	3
BILL	SARNI	1955	St. Louis Cardinals	NL	107	325	32	83	15	2	3	34	27	33	.255	.342	1
BILL	SARNI	1956	New York Giants	NL	78	238	16	55	9	3	5	23	20	31	.231	.357	0
BILL	SARNI	1956	St. Louis Cardinals	NL	43	148	12	43	7	2	5	22	8	15	.291	.466	1
TOM	SATRIANO	1961	Los Angeles Angels	AL	35	96	15	19	5	1	1	8	12	16	.198	.302	2
TOM	SATRIANO	1962	Los Angeles Angels	AL	10	19	4	8	2	0	2	6	0	1	.421	.842	0
TOM	SATRIANO	1963	Los Angeles Angels	AL	23	50	1	9	1	0	0	2	9	10	.180	.200	0
TOM	SATRIANO	1964	Los Angeles Angels	AL	108	255	18	51	9	0	1	17	30	37	.200	.247	1
TOM	SATRIANO	1965	California Angels	AL	47	79	8	13	2	0	0	4	10	10	.165	.228	0
TOM	SATRIANO	1966	California Angels	AL	103	226	16	54	5	3	0	24	27	32	.239	.288	3
TOM	SATRIANO	1967	California Angels	AL	90	201	13	45	7	0	4	21	28	25	.224	.318	1
TOM	SATRIANO	1968	California Angels	AL	111	297	20	75	9	0	8	35	37	44	.253	.364	0
TOM	SATRIANO	1969	Boston Red Sox	AL	47	127	9	24	2	0	0	11	22	12	.189	.205	0
TOM	SATRIANO	1969	California Angels	AL	41	108	5	28	2	0	0	16	18	15	.259	.306	0
TOM	SATRIANO	1970	Boston Red Sox	AL	59	165	21	39	9	1	3	13	21	23	.236	.358	5
STEVE	SAX	1981	Los Angeles Dodgers	NL	31	119	15	33	2	0	2	9	7	14	.277	.345	5
STEVE	SAX	1982	Los Angeles Dodgers	NL	150	638	88	180	23	7	4	47	49	55	.282	.359	49
STEVE	SAX	1983	Los Angeles Dodgers	NL	155	623	94	175	18	5	5	41	58	73	.281	.350	56
STEVE	SAX	1984	Los Angeles Dodgers	NL	145	569	70	138	24	4	1	35	47	53	.243	.304	34
STEVE	SAX	1985	Los Angeles Dodgers	NL	136	488	62	136	8	4	6	42	54	43	.279	.318	27
STEVE	SAX	1986	Los Angeles Dodgers	NL	157	633	91	210	43	4	6	56	59	58	.332	.441	40
STEVE	SAX	1987	Los Angeles Dodgers	NL	157	610	84	171	22	7	6	46	44	61	.280	.369	37
STEVE	SAX	1988	Los Angeles Dodgers	NL	160	632	70	175	19	4	5	57	45	51	.277	.343	42
STEVE	SAX	1989	New York Yankees	AL	158	651	88	205	26	3	5	63	52	44	.315	.387	43
STEVE	SAX	1990	New York Yankees	AL	155	615	70	160	24	2	4	42	49	46	.260	.325	43
STEVE	SAX	1991	New York Yankees	AL	158	652	85	198	38	2	10	56	41	38	.304	.414	31
STEVE	SAX	1992	Chicago White Sox	AL	143	567	74	134	26	4	4	47	43	42	.236	.317	30
STEVE	SAX	1993	Chicago White Sox	AL	57	119	20	28	5	0	1	8	8	6	.235	.303	7
STEVE	SAX	1994	Oakland Athletics	AL	7	24	2	6	0	0	0	1	0	2	.250	.333	0
DAVE	SAX	1982	Los Angeles Dodgers	NL	2	8	0	0	0	0	0	0	0	0	.000		0
DAVE	SAX	1983	Los Angeles Dodgers	NL	7	3	2	0	0	0	0	1	0	0	.000		0
DAVE	SAX	1985	Boston Red Sox	AL	22	36	1	11	3	0	0	6	3	3	.306	.389	0
DAVE	SAX	1986	Boston Red Sox	AL	4	11	0	5	1	0	1	1	0	1	.455	.818	0
DAVE	SAX	1987	Boston Red Sox	AL	2		1	0	0	0	0	0	0	1	.000		0
JERRY	SCALA	1948	Chicago White Sox	AL	3	6	1	0	0	0	0	0	0	3	.000		0

FIRST	LAST	YEAR	TEAM	LEAGUE	G	AB	R	H	2B	3B	HR	RBI	BB	SO	AVG	SLUG	SB
JERRY	SCALA	1949	Chicago White Sox	AL	37	120	17	30	7	1	1	13	17	19	.250	.350	3
JERRY	SCALA	1950	Chicago White Sox	AL	40	67	8	13	2	1	0	6	10	10	.194	.254	0
SKEETER	SCALZI	1939	New York Giants	NL	11	18	3	6	0	0	0	0	3	2	.333	.333	1
JOHNNY	SCALZI	1931	Boston Braves	NL	2	1	1	0	0	0	0	0	0	1	.000		0
LES	SCARSELLA	1935	Cincinnati Reds	NL	6	10	4	2	1	0	0	0	3	1	.200	.300	0
LES	SCARSELLA	1936	Cincinnati Reds	NL	115	485	63	152	21	9	3	65	14	36	.313	.412	6
LES	SCARSELLA	1937	Cincinnati Reds	NL	110	329	35	81	11	4	3	34	17	26	.246	.331	5
LES	SCARSELLA	1939	Cincinnati Reds	NL	16	14	0	2	0	0	0	2	0	5	.143	.143	0
LES	SCARSELLA	1940	Boston Braves	NL	18	60	7	18	1	3	0	8	3	5	.300	.417	2
STEVE	SCARSONE	1992	Baltimore Orioles	AL	7	17	2	3	0	0	0	0	1	6	.176	.176	0
STEVE	SCARSONE	1992	Philadelphia Phillies	NL	7	13	1	2	0	0	0	0	1	6	.154	.154	0
STEVE	SCARSONE	1993	San Francisco Giants	NL	44	103	16	26	9	0	2	15	4	32	.252	.398	0
STEVE	SCARSONE	1994	San Francisco Giants	NL	52	103	21	28	8	0	2	13	10	20	.272	.408	0
STEVE	SCARSONE	1995	San Francisco Giants	NL	80	233	33	62	10	3	11	29	18	82	.266	.476	3
STEVE	SCARSONE	1996	San Francisco Giants	NL	105	283	28	62	12	1	5	23	25	91	.219	.322	2
STEVE	SCARSONE	1997	St. Louis Cardinals	NL	5	10	0	1	0	0	0	0	2	5	.100	.100	1
STEVE	SCARSONE	1999	Kansas City Royals	AL	46	68	8	14	5	0	1	8	9	24	.206	.279	1
MIKE	SCIOSCIA	1980	Los Angeles Dodgers	NL	54	134	8	34	5	1	1	8	12	9	.254	.328	1
MIKE	SCIOSCIA	1981	Los Angeles Dodgers	NL	93	290	27	80	10	0	2	29	36	18	.276	.331	0
MIKE	SCIOSCIA	1982	Los Angeles Dodgers	NL	129	365	31	80	11	1	5	38	44	31	.219	.296	2
MIKE	SCIOSCIA	1983	Los Angeles Dodgers	NL	12	35	3	11	3	0	0	7	5	2	.314	.486	0
MIKE	SCIOSCIA	1984	Los Angeles Dodgers	NL	114	341	29	93	18	0	5	38	52	26	.273	.370	2
MIKE	SCIOSCIA	1985	Los Angeles Dodgers	NL	141	429	47	127	26	3	7	53	77	21	.296	.420	3
MIKE	SCIOSCIA	1986	Los Angeles Dodgers	NL	122	374	36	94	18	1	5	26	62	23	.251	.345	3
MIKE	SCIOSCIA	1987	Los Angeles Dodgers	NL	142	461	44	122	26	1	6	38	55	23	.265	.364	7
MIKE	SCIOSCIA	1988	Los Angeles Dodgers	NL	130	408	29	105	18	0	3	35	38	31	.257	.324	0
MIKE	SCIOSCIA	1989	Los Angeles Dodgers	NL	133	408	40	102	16	0	10	44	52	29	.250	.363	0
MIKE	SCIOSCIA	1990	Los Angeles Dodgers	NL	135	435	46	115	25	0	12	66	55	31	.264	.405	4
MIKE	SCIOSCIA	1991	Los Angeles Dodgers	NL	119	345	39	91	16	2	8	40	47	32	.264	.391	4
MIKE	SCIOSCIA	1992	Los Angeles Dodgers	NL	117	348	19	77	6	3	3	24	32	31	.221	.282	3
SONNY	SENERCHIA	1952	Pittsburgh Pirates	NL	29	100	5	22	5	0	1	11	4	21	.220	.360	0
BILL	SERENA	1949	Chicago Cubs	NL	12	37	3	8	3	0	1	7	7	9	.216	.378	0
BILL	SERENA	1950	Chicago Cubs	NL	127	435	56	104	20	4	17	61	65	75	.239	.421	1
BILL	SERENA	1951	Chicago Cubs	NL	13	39	8	13	3	1	1	4	11	4	.333	.538	0
BILL	SERENA	1952	Chicago Cubs	NL	122	390	49	107	21	5	15	61	39	83	.274	.469	1

FIRST	LAST	YEAR	TEAM	LEAGUE	G	AB	R	H	2B	3B	HR	RBI	BB	SO	AVG	SLUG	SB
BILL	SERENA	1953	Chicago Cubs	NL	93	275	30	69	10	5	10	52	41	46	.251	.433	0
BILL	SERENA	1954	Chicago Cubs	NL	41	63	8	10	0	1	4	13	14	18	.159	.381	0
PAUL	SERNA	1981	Seattle Mariners	AL	30	94	11	24	2	0	4	9	3	11	.255	.404	2
PAUL	SERNA	1982	Seattle Mariners	AL	65	169	15	38	3	0	3	8	4	13	.225	.296	0
WALTER	SESSI	1941	St. Louis Cardinals	NL	5	13	2	0	0	0	0	0	1	2	.000		0
WALTER	SESSI	1946	St. Louis Cardinals	NL	15	14	2	2	0	0	1	2	0	4	.143	.357	0
DAVE	SILVESTRI	1992	New York Yankees	AL	7	13	3	4	1	0	1	1	0	3	.308	.615	0
DAVE	SILVESTRI	1993	New York Yankees	AL	12	21	4	6	1	0	1	4	5	3	.286	.476	0
DAVE	SILVESTRI	1994	New York Yankees	AL	17	18	1	2	0	0	0	2	4	9	.111	.111	0
DAVE	SILVESTRI	1995	Montreal Expos	NL	39	72	12	19	6	0	2	7	9	27	.264	.431	2
DAVE	SILVESTRI	1995	New York Yankees	AL	22	21	1	2	0	0	0	1	4	9	.095	.238	2
DAVE	SILVESTRI	1996	Montreal Expos	NL	86	162	16	33	4	0	1	17	34	41	.204	.247	2
DAVE	SILVESTRI	1997	Texas Rangers	AL	2	4	0	0	0	0	0	0	0	2	.000		0
DAVE	SILVESTRI	1998	Tampa Bay Devil Rays	AL	8	14	0	1	0	0	0	0	0	7	.071	.071	0
DAVE	SILVESTRI	1999	Anaheim Angels	AL	3	11	0	1	0	0	0	1	0	1	.091	.091	0
KEN	SILVESTRI	1939	Chicago White Sox	AL	28	75	6	13	3	0	2	5	6	13	.173	.293	0
KEN	SILVESTRI	1940	Chicago White Sox	AL	17	24	5	6	2	0	2	4	4	7	.250	.583	0
KEN	SILVESTRI	1941	New York Yankees	AL	13	40	6	10	5	0	1	6	7	6	.250	.450	0
KEN	SILVESTRI	1946	New York Yankees	AL	3	21	0	6	1	0	0	0	3	7	.286	.333	0
KEN	SILVESTRI	1947	New York Yankees	AL	4	10	1	2	0	0	0	1	2	2	.200	.200	0
KEN	SILVESTRI	1949	Philadelphia Phillies	NL	11	4	2	0	0	0	0	0	2	1	.000		0
KEN	SILVESTRI	1950	Philadelphia Phillies	NL	4	20	2	5	0	1	0	4	4	3	.250	.350	0
KEN	SILVESTRI	1951	Philadelphia Phillies	NL	12	9	4	2	0	0	0	2	3	4	.222	.222	0
MATT	SINATRO	1981	Atlanta Braves	NL	20	32	2	9	3	0	0	4	5	4	.281	.375	1
MATT	SINATRO	1982	Atlanta Braves	NL	37	81	10	11	2	0	1	5	4	9	.136	.198	0
MATT	SINATRO	1983	Atlanta Braves	NL	7	12	0	2	0	0	0	1	2	1	.167	.167	0
MATT	SINATRO	1984	Atlanta Braves	NL	2	4	0	0	0	0	0	0	0	1	.000		0
MATT	SINATRO	1987	Oakland Athletics	AL	6	3	1	0	0	0	0	0	1	3	.000		0
MATT	SINATRO	1988	Oakland Athletics	AL	10	9	2	3	2	0	0	4	4	1	.333	.556	0
MATT	SINATRO	1989	Detroit Tigers	AL	13	25	2	3	0	0	0	2	0	10	.120	.120	0
MATT	SINATRO	1990	Seattle Mariners	AL	30	50	7	15	1	0	0	5	1	5	.300	.320	0
MATT	SINATRO	1991	Seattle Mariners	AL	5	8	0	2	0	0	0	1	0	1	.250	.250	1
MATT	SINATRO	1992	Seattle Mariners	AL	18	28	0	3	0	1	0	0	4	3	.107	.107	0
SIBBY	SISTI	1939	Boston Braves	NL	63	215	19	49	7	1	1	11	12	38	.228	.284	4
SIBBY	SISTI	1940	Boston Braves	NL	123	459	73	115	19	5	6	34	36	64	.251	.353	4

FIRST	LAST	YEAR	TEAM	LEAGUE	G	AB	R	H	2B	3B	HR	RBI	BB	SO	AVG	SLUG	SB
SIBBY	SISTI	1941	Boston Braves	NL	140	541	72	140	24	3	1	45	38	76	.259	.320	7
SIBBY	SISTI	1942	Boston Braves	NL	129	407	50	86	11	4	4	35	45	55	.211	.287	5
SIBBY	SISTI	1946	Boston Braves	NL	1	0	0	0	0	0	0	0	0	0			0
SIBBY	SISTI	1947	Boston Braves	NL	56	153	22	43	8	0	0	15	20	17	.281	.373	2
SIBBY	SISTI	1948	Boston Braves	NL	83	221	30	54	6	2	2	21	31	34	.244	.290	0
SIBBY	SISTI	1949	Boston Braves	NL	101	268	39	69	12	0	5	22	34	42	.257	.358	1
SIBBY	SISTI	1950	Boston Braves	NL	69	105	21	18	3	1	2	11	16	19	.171	.276	
SIBBY	SISTI	1951	Boston Braves	NL	114	362	46	101	20	2	4	38	32	50	.279	.362	4
SIBBY	SISTI	1952	Boston Braves	NL	90	245	19	52	10	1	0	24	14	43	.212	.310	2
SIBBY	SISTI	1953	Milwaukee Braves	NL	38	23	8	5	1	0	0	4	5	0	.217	.261	0
SIBBY	SISTI	1954	Milwaukee Braves	NL	9	0	2	0	0	0	0	0	2	0			0
PAUL	SORRENTO	1989	Minnesota Twins	AL	14	21	2	5	0	0	0	1	5	4	.238	.238	0
PAUL	SORRENTO	1990	Minnesota Twins	AL	41	121	11	25	4	0	5	13	12	31	.207	.380	1
PAUL	SORRENTO	1991	Minnesota Twins	AL	26	47	6	12	2	1	4	13	4	11	.255	.553	0
PAUL	SORRENTO	1992	Cleveland Indians	AL	140	458	52	123	24	1	18	60	51	89	.269	.443	0
PAUL	SORRENTO	1993	Cleveland Indians	AL	148	463	75	119	26	1	18	65	58	121	.257	.434	3
PAUL	SORRENTO	1994	Cleveland Indians	AL	95	322	43	90	14	0	14	62	34	68	.280	.453	0
PAUL	SORRENTO	1995	Cleveland Indians	AL	104	323	50	76	14	1	25	79	51	71	.235	.511	1
PAUL	SORRENTO	1996	Seattle Mariners	AL	143	471	67	136	32	0	23	93	57	103	.289	.507	0
PAUL	SORRENTO	1997	Seattle Mariners	AL	146	457	68	123	19	1	31	80	51	112	.269	.514	0
PAUL	SORRENTO	1998	Tampa Bay Devil Rays	AL	137	435	40	98	27	0	17	57	54	133	.225	.405	2
PAUL	SORRENTO	1999	Tampa Bay Devil Rays	AL	99	294	40	69	14	1	11	42	49	101	.235	.401	1
ED	SPIEZIO	1964	St. Louis Cardinals	NL	12	12	0	4	0	0	0	0	0	0	.333	.333	0
ED	SPIEZIO	1965	St. Louis Cardinals	NL	10	18	0	3	0	1	0	5	1	4	.167	.167	0
ED	SPIEZIO	1966	St. Louis Cardinals	NL	26	73	4	16	5	0	2	10	5	11	.219	.397	1
ED	SPIEZIO	1967	St. Louis Cardinals	NL	55	105	9	22	2	0	3	10	7	18	.210	.314	2
ED	SPIEZIO	1968	San Diego Padres	NL	29	51	1	8	0	0	0	2	5	6	.157	.157	1
ED	SPIEZIO	1969	San Diego Padres	NL	121	355	29	83	9	0	13	43	38	64	.234	.369	1
ED	SPIEZIO	1970	San Diego Padres	NL	110	316	45	90	18	1	12	42	43	42	.285	.462	4
ED	SPIEZIO	1971	San Diego Padres	NL	97	308	16	71	10	1	7	36	22	50	.231	.338	6
ED	SPIEZIO	1972	Chicago White Sox	AL	74	277	20	66	10	0	2	22	13	43	.238	.303	0
ED	SPIEZIO	1972	San Diego Padres	NL	20	29	6	4	2	0	0	4	1	6	.138	.207	0
SCOTT	SPIEZIO	1996	Oakland Athletics	AL	9	29	6	9	2	0	2	8	4	6	.310	.586	0
SCOTT	SPIEZIO	1997	Oakland Athletics	AL	147	538	58	131	28	4	14	65	44	75	.243	.388	9
SCOTT	SPIEZIO	1998	Oakland Athletics	AL	114	406	54	105	19	1	9	50	44	56	.259	.377	1

FIRST	LAST	YEAR	LEAGUE	TEAM	G	AB	R	H	2B	3B	HR	RBI	BB	SO	AVG	SLUG	SB
SCOTT	SPIEZIO	1999	AL	Oakland Athletics	89	247	31	60	24	0	8	33	29	36	.243	.437	0
SCOTT	SPIEZIO	2000	AL	Anaheim Angels	123	297	47	72	11	2	17	49	40	56	.242	.465	1
SCOTT	SPIEZIO	2001	AL	Anaheim Angels	139	457	57	124	29	4	13	54	34	65	.271	.438	5
ANDY	SPOGNARDI	1932	AL	Boston Red Sox	17	34	9	10	1	0	0	1	6	6	.294	.324	0
JOHN	STEFERO	1983	AL	Baltimore Orioles	9	11	2	5	1	0	0	4	3	2	.455	.545	0
JOHN	STEFERO	1986	AL	Baltimore Orioles	52	120	14	28	0	0	2	13	16	25	.233	.300	0
JOHN	STEFERO	1987	NL	Montreal Expos	18	56	4	11	0	0	1	3	3	17	.196	.250	0
JOHN	TAMARGO	1976	NL	St. Louis Cardinals	10	10	2	3	0	0	0	1	0	2	.300	.300	0
JOHN	TAMARGO	1977	NL	St. Louis Cardinals	4	4	0	0	0	0	0	0	1	0	.000		0
JOHN	TAMARGO	1978	NL	San Francisco Giants	36	92	6	22	4	1	1	8	18	7	.239	.337	1
JOHN	TAMARGO	1978	NL	St. Louis Cardinals	6	6	0	0	0	0	0	0	0	2	.000		0
JOHN	TAMARGO	1979	NL	Montreal Expos	12	21	0	8	2	0	0	5	3	3	.381	.476	0
JOHN	TAMARGO	1979	NL	San Francisco Giants	30	60	7	12	3	0	2	6	4	8	.200	.350	0
JOHN	TAMARGO	1980	NL	Montreal Expos	37	51	4	14	3	0	1	13	6	5	.275	.392	0
GENE	TENACE	1969	AL	Oakland Athletics	16	38	1	6	0	0	1	2	1	15	.158	.237	0
GENE	TENACE	1970	AL	Oakland Athletics	38	105	19	32	6	0	7	20	23	30	.305	.562	0
GENE	TENACE	1971	AL	Oakland Athletics	65	179	26	49	7	0	7	25	29	34	.274	.430	2
GENE	TENACE	1972	AL	Oakland Athletics	82	227	22	51	5	3	5	32	24	42	.225	.339	2
GENE	TENACE	1973	AL	Oakland Athletics	160	510	83	132	18	2	24	84	101	94	.259	.443	2
GENE	TENACE	1974	AL	Oakland Athletics	158	484	71	102	17	1	26	73	110	105	.211	.411	2
GENE	TENACE	1975	AL	Oakland Athletics	158	498	83	127	17	0	29	87	106	127	.255	.464	7
GENE	TENACE	1976	AL	Oakland Athletics	128	417	64	104	19	1	22	66	81	91	.249	.458	5
GENE	TENACE	1977	NL	San Diego Padres	147	437	66	102	24	4	15	61	125	119	.233	.410	6
GENE	TENACE	1978	NL	San Diego Padres	142	401	60	90	18	4	16	61	101	98	.224	.409	2
GENE	TENACE	1979	NL	San Diego Padres	151	463	61	122	16	4	20	67	105	106	.263	.445	4
GENE	TENACE	1980	NL	San Diego Padres	133	316	46	70	11	1	17	50	92	63	.222	.424	4
GENE	TENACE	1981	NL	St. Louis Cardinals	58	129	26	30	7	0	5	22	38	26	.233	.403	0
GENE	TENACE	1982	NL	St. Louis Cardinals	66	124	18	32	9	0	7	18	36	31	.258	.500	1
GENE	TENACE	1983	NL	Pittsburgh Pirates	53	62	7	11	2	0	0	6	12	17	.177	.258	0
FRANK	TEPEDINO	1967	AL	New York Yankees	9	5	0	2	0	0	0	0	1	1	.400	.400	0
FRANK	TEPEDINO	1969	AL	New York Yankees	13	39	6	9	0	0	0	4	4	4	.231	.231	1
FRANK	TEPEDINO	1970	AL	New York Yankees	16	19	2	6	2	0	0	2	1	2	.316	.421	0
FRANK	TEPEDINO	1971	AL	Milwaukee Brewers	53	106	11	21	2	0	2	7	4	17	.198	.264	2
FRANK	TEPEDINO	1971	AL	New York Yankees	6	6	0	0	0	0	0	0	0	0	.000		0
FRANK	TEPEDINO	1972	AL	New York Yankees	8	8	0	0	0	0	0	0	0	1	.000		0

FIRST	LAST	YEAR	TEAM	LEAGUE	G	AB	R	H	2B	3B	HR	RBI	BB	SO	AVG	SLUG	SB
FRANK	TEPEDINO	1973	Atlanta Braves	NL	74	148	20	45	5	0	4	29	13	21	.304	.419	0
FRANK	TEPEDINO	1974	Atlanta Braves	NL	78	169	11	39	5	1	0	16	9	13	.231	.272	1
FRANK	TEPEDINO	1975	Atlanta Braves	NL	8	7	0	0	0	0	0	0	1	2	.000		0
NICK	TESTA	1958	San Francisco Giants	NL	1	0	0	0	0	0	0	0	0	0			1
FRANK	TORRE	1956	Milwaukee Braves	NL	111	159	17	41	6	0	5	16	11	4	.258	.296	0
FRANK	TORRE	1957	Milwaukee Braves	NL	129	364	46	99	19	5	5	40	29	19	.272	.393	1
FRANK	TORRE	1958	Milwaukee Braves	NL	138	372	41	115	22	5	6	55	42	14	.309	.444	2
FRANK	TORRE	1959	Milwaukee Braves	NL	115	263	23	60	15	1	1	33	35	12	.228	.304	2
FRANK	TORRE	1960	Philadelphia Phillies	NL	21	44	2	9	1	0	0	5	3	2	.205	.227	0
FRANK	TORRE	1962	Philadelphia Phillies	NL	108	168	13	52	8	2	0	20	24	6	.310	.381	1
FRANK	TORRE	1963	Philadelphia Phillies	NL	92	112	8	28	7	0	1	10	11	7	.250	.375	0
JOE	TORRE	1960	Milwaukee Braves	NL	2	2	0	1	0	0	0	0	2	1	.500	.500	0
JOE	TORRE	1961	Milwaukee Braves	NL	113	406	40	113	21	4	10	42	28	60	.278	.424	3
JOE	TORRE	1962	Milwaukee Braves	NL	80	220	23	62	8	1	5	26	24	24	.282	.395	1
JOE	TORRE	1963	Milwaukee Braves	NL	142	501	57	147	19	4	14	71	42	79	.293	.431	1
JOE	TORRE	1964	Milwaukee Braves	NL	154	601	87	193	36	5	20	109	36	67	.321	.498	2
JOE	TORRE	1965	Milwaukee Braves	NL	148	523	68	152	21	1	27	80	61	79	.291	.489	0
JOE	TORRE	1966	Atlanta Braves	NL	148	546	83	172	20	3	36	101	60	61	.315	.560	0
JOE	TORRE	1967	Atlanta Braves	NL	135	477	67	132	18	1	20	68	49	75	.277	.444	2
JOE	TORRE	1968	Atlanta Braves	NL	115	424	45	115	11	2	10	55	34	72	.271	.377	1
JOE	TORRE	1969	St. Louis Cardinals	NL	159	602	72	174	29	6	18	101	66	85	.289	.447	0
JOE	TORRE	1970	St. Louis Cardinals	NL	161	624	89	203	27	9	21	100	70	91	.325	.498	2
JOE	TORRE	1971	St. Louis Cardinals	NL	161	634	97	230	34	8	24	137	63	70	.363	.555	4
JOE	TORRE	1972	St. Louis Cardinals	NL	149	544	71	157	26	6	11	81	54	64	.289	.419	3
JOE	TORRE	1973	St. Louis Cardinals	NL	141	519	67	149	17	2	13	69	65	78	.287	.403	2
JOE	TORRE	1974	St. Louis Cardinals	NL	147	529	59	149	28	1	11	70	69	88	.282	.401	1
JOE	TORRE	1975	New York Mets	NL	114	361	33	89	16	3	6	35	35	55	.247	.357	0
JOE	TORRE	1976	New York Mets	NL	114	310	36	95	10	3	5	31	21	35	.306	.406	1
JOE	TORRE	1977	New York Mets	NL	26	51	2	9	3	0	1	9	2	10	.176	.294	0
BOBBY	VALENTINE	1969	Los Angeles Dodgers	NL	5	0	3	0	0	0	0	0	0	0			0
BOBBY	VALENTINE	1971	Los Angeles Dodgers	NL	101	281	32	70	10	2	1	25	15	20	.249	.310	5
BOBBY	VALENTINE	1972	Los Angeles Dodgers	NL	119	391	42	107	11	2	3	32	27	33	.274	.335	5
BOBBY	VALENTINE	1973	California Angels	AL	32	126	12	38	5	2	1	13	5	9	.302	.397	6
BOBBY	VALENTINE	1974	California Angels	AL	117	371	39	97	10	3	3	39	25	25	.261	.329	8
BOBBY	VALENTINE	1975	California Angels	AL	26	57	5	16	2	0	0	5	4	3	.281	.316	0

FIRST	LAST	YEAR	TEAM	LEAGUE	G	AB	R	H	2B	3B	HR	RBI	BB	SO	AVG	SLUG	SB
BOBBY	VALENTINE	1975	San Diego Padres	NL	7	15	1	2	0	0	1	1	4	0	.133	.333	1
BOBBY	VALENTINE	1976	San Diego Padres	NL	15	49	3	18	4	0	0	4	6	2	.367	.449	0
BOBBY	VALENTINE	1977	New York Mets	NL	42	83	8	11	1	0	1	3	6	9	.133	.181	0
BOBBY	VALENTINE	1977	San Diego Padres	NL	44	67	5	12	3	0	1	10	7	10	.179	.269	0
BOBBY	VALENTINE	1978	New York Mets	NL	69	160	17	43	7	0	1	18	19	18	.269	.331	1
BOBBY	VALENTINE	1979	Seattle Mariners	AL	62	98	9	27	6	0	0	7	22	5	.276	.337	1
ROBIN	VENTURA	1989	Chicago White Sox	AL	16	45	5	8	3	0	0	7	8	6	.178	.244	0
ROBIN	VENTURA	1990	Chicago White Sox	AL	150	493	48	123	17	1	5	54	55	53	.249	.318	1
ROBIN	VENTURA	1991	Chicago White Sox	AL	157	606	92	172	25	1	23	100	80	67	.284	.442	2
ROBIN	VENTURA	1992	Chicago White Sox	AL	157	592	85	167	38	1	16	93	93	71	.282	.431	2
ROBIN	VENTURA	1993	Chicago White Sox	AL	157	554	85	145	27	1	22	94	105	82	.262	.433	1
ROBIN	VENTURA	1994	Chicago White Sox	AL	109	401	57	113	15	1	18	78	61	69	.282	.459	3
ROBIN	VENTURA	1995	Chicago White Sox	AL	135	492	79	145	22	0	26	93	75	98	.295	.498	4
ROBIN	VENTURA	1996	Chicago White Sox	AL	158	586	96	168	31	2	34	105	78	81	.287	.520	1
ROBIN	VENTURA	1997	Chicago White Sox	AL	54	183	27	48	10	1	6	26	34	21	.262	.426	0
ROBIN	VENTURA	1998	Chicago White Sox	AL	161	590	84	155	31	4	21	91	79	111	.263	.456	1
ROBIN	VENTURA	1999	New York Mets	NL	161	588	88	177	38	0	32	120	74	109	.301	.529	1
ROBIN	VENTURA	2000	New York Mets	NL	141	469	61	109	23	0	24	84	75	91	.232	.439	3
ROBIN	VENTURA	2001	New York Mets	NL	142	456	70	108	20	0	21	61	88	101	.237	.419	2
FRANK	VERDI	1953	New York Yankees	AL	1	0	0	0	0	0	0	0	0	0			0
GEORGE	VICO	1948	Detroit Tigers	AL	144	521	50	139	23	9	8	58	39	39	.267	.392	2
GEORGE	VICO	1949	Detroit Tigers	AL	67	142	15	27	5	2	4	18	21	17	.190	.338	0
JOE	VITELLI	1944	Pittsburgh Pirates	NL	4	3	0	0	0	0	0	0	0	0	.000		0
JOE	VITELLI	1945	Pittsburgh Pirates	NL	1	0	1	0	0	0	0	0	0	0			0
JOE	VITIELLO	1995	Kansas City Royals	AL	53	130	13	33	4	0	7	21	8	25	.254	.446	0
JOE	VITIELLO	1996	Kansas City Royals	AL	85	257	29	62	15	1	8	40	38	69	.241	.401	2
JOE	VITIELLO	1997	Kansas City Royals	AL	51	130	11	31	6	0	5	18	14	37	.238	.400	0
JOE	VITIELLO	1998	Kansas City Royals	AL	3	7	4	1	0	0	0	0	1	2	.143	.143	0
JOE	VITIELLO	1999	Kansas City Royals	AL	13	41	7	6	1	0	1	4	2	9	.146	.244	0
JOE	VITIELLO	2000	San Diego Padres	NL	39	52	2	13	3	0	2	8	10	9	.250	.423	0
FRANK	ZUPO	1957	Baltimore Orioles	AL	10	12	1	1	0	0	0	0	1	4	.083	.083	0
FRANK	ZUPO	1958	Baltimore Orioles	AL	1	2	0	0	0	0	0	0	0	1	.000		0
FRANK	ZUPO	1961	Baltimore Orioles	AL	5	4	1	2	1	0	0	0	0	1	.500	.750	0
PAUL	ZUVELLA	1982	Atlanta Braves	NL	2	1	0	0	0	0	0	0	0	0	.000		0
PAUL	ZUVELLA	1983	Atlanta Braves	NL	3	5	0	0	0	0	0	0	2	1	.000		0

FIRST	LAST	YEAR	TEAM	LEAGUE	G	AB	R	H	2B	3B	HR	RBI	BB	SO	AVG	SLUG	SB
PAUL	ZUVELLA	1984	Atlanta Braves	NL	11	25	2	5	1	0	0	1	2	3	.200	.240	0
PAUL	ZUVELLA	1985	Atlanta Braves	NL	81	190	16	48	8	1	0	4	16	14	.253	.305	2
PAUL	ZUVELLA	1986	New York Yankees	AL	21	48	2	4	1	0	0	2	5	4	.083	.104	0
PAUL	ZUVELLA	1987	New York Yankees	AL	14	34	2	6	0	0	0	0	0	4	.176	.176	0
PAUL	ZUVELLA	1988	Cleveland Indians	AL	51	130	9	30	5	1	0	7	8	13	.231	.285	0
PAUL	ZUVELLA	1989	Cleveland Indians	AL	24	58	10	16	2	0	2	6	1	11	.276	.414	0
PAUL	ZUVELLA	1991	Kansas City Royals	AL	2	0	0	0	0	0	0	0	0	0			0

Italian American Player Totals

FIRST	LAST	G	AB	R	H	2B	3B	HR	RBI	BB	SO	AVG	SLUG	SB
ED	ABBATICCHIO	855	3044	355	772	99	43	11	324	289	16	.254	.325	142
JIM	ADDUCI	70	144	11	34	8	1	1	15	2	27	.236	.326	0
BOB	ALLIETTA	21	45	4	8	1	0		2	1	6	.178	.267	0
JOE	ALTOBELLI	166	257	27	54	8	3	5	28	23	42	.210	.323	3
JOEY	AMALFITANO	643	1715	248	418	67	19	9	123	185	224	.244	.321	19
JOHN	ANTONELLI	135	528	50	133	28	2	1	29	24	29	.252	.318	1
BILL	ANTONELLO	40	43	9	7	1	1	1	4	2	11	.163	.302	0
KEN	ASPROMONTE	475	1483	171	369	69	3	19	124	179	149	.249	.338	7
BOB	ASPROMONTE	1324	4369	386	1103	135	26	60	457	333	459	.252	.336	19
RICH	AURILIA	731	2555	350	724	129	11	98	354	209	375	.283	.458	13
STEVE	BALBONI	960	3120	351	714	127	11	181	495	273	856	.229	.451	1
MIKE	BALENTI	78	219	19	40	2	4	0	11	6	33	.183	.228	6
CHRIS	BANDO	498	1284	134	292	46	2	27	142	138	197	.227	.329	1
SAL	BANDO	2019	7060	982	1790	289	38	242	1039	1031	923	.254	.408	75
DICK	BARONE	3	6	0	0	0	0	0	0	0	1	.000		0
TONY	BARTIROME	124	355	32	78	10	3	0	16	26	37	.220	.265	3
MARK	BELANGER	2016	5784	676	1316	175	33	20	389	576	839	.228	.280	167
WAYNE	BELARDI	263	592	71	145	13	5	28	74	66	97	.242	.422	1
ZEKE	BELLA	52	92	10	18	2	1	1	9	10	16	.196	.272	0
JOHNNY	BERARDINO	912	3028	334	755	167	23	36	387	284	268	.249	.355	27
AUGIE	BERGAMO	174	496	86	151	23	5	5	63	78	44	.304	.401	0
DALE	BERRA	853	2553	236	603	109	9	49	278	210	422	.236	.344	32
YOGI	BERRA	2120	7555	1175	2150	321	49	358	1430	704	414	.285	.482	30
BUDDY	BIANCALANA	311	550	70	113	16	7	6	30	41	157	.205	.293	8
TOMMY	BIANCO	18	34	6	6	1	0	0	0	3	7	.176	.206	0
HANK	BIASATTI	21	24	6	2	2	0	0	2	8	5	.083		0
CRAIG	BIGGIO	1955	7383	1305	2149	437	46	180	811	913	1146	.291	.436	365
DANN	BILARDELLO	382	949	79	194	39	1	18	91	65	170	.204	.305	4
JOHN	BOCCABELLA	551	1462	117	320	56	5	26	148	96	246	.219	.317	3
SAL	BUTERA	359	801	63	182	24	3	8	76	86	85	.227	.295	0
PING	BODIE	1050	3670	393	1011	169	72	43	516	312	240	.275	.396	83
NINO	BONGIOVANNI	68	166	17	43	7	2	1	16	9	8	.259	.301	0
ZEKE	BONURA	917	3582	600	1099	232	29	119	704	404	180	.307	.487	19
RICK	BOSETTI	445	1543	172	385	70	8	17	133	79	188	.250	.338	50
JOHN	BOTTARINI	26	40	3	11	3	0	1	7	5	10	.275	.425	0

FIRST	LAST	G	AB	R	H	2B	3B	HR	RBI	BB	SO	AVG	SLUG	SB
LARRY	BOWA	2247	8418	987	2191	262	99	15	525	474	569	.260	.320	318
AL	BRANCATO	282	930	117	199	37	11	4	80	96	92	.214	.290	5
FRED	BRATSCHI	89	196	12	54	11	1	0	22	14	17	.276	.342	0
RICO	BROGNA	848	2958	379	795	176	13	106	458	227	655	.269	.445	32
JOE	BROVIA	21	18	0	2	0	0	0	4	1	6	.111	.111	0
PUTSY	CABALLERO	322	658	81	150	21	3	1	40	41	34	.228	.274	10
SAM	CALDERONE	91	141	16	41	5	0	1	25	7	13	.291	.348	0
HANK	CAMELLI	159	376	33	86	15	4	2	26	46	39	.229	.306	0
DOLPH	CAMILLI	1490	5553	936	1482	261	86	239	950	947	961	.277	.492	60
DOUG	CAMILLI	313	767	56	153	22	4	18	80	56	146	.199	.309	0
LOU	CAMILLI	107	151	7	22	4	0	0	3	13	23	.146	.172	0
KEN	CAMINITI	1760	6288	894	1710	348	17	239	983	727	1163	.272	.447	88
ROY	CAMPANELLA	1215	4205	627	1161	178	18	242	856	533	501	.276	.500	25
AL	CAMPANIS	7	20	3	2	0	0	0	0	4	5	.100	.100	0
GEORGE	CANALE	44	73	15	12	4	0	4	13	12	15	.164	.384	0
JOHN	CANGELOSI	1038	2004	328	501	73	15	12	134	358	322	.250	.319	154
JAY	CANIZARO	157	484	59	125	27	2	10	57	34	97	.258	.384	5
CHRIS	CANNIZZARO	740	1950	132	458	66	12	18	169	241	354	.235	.309	3
NICK	CAPRA	45	54	9	9	1	0	1	1	6	7	.167	.241	3
PAT	CAPRI	7	1	0	0	0	0	0	0	0	0	.000		0
MIKE	CARUSO	269	1052	141	292	28	10	7	90	34	74	.278	.343	34
JACK	CASSINI	8	0	3	0	0	0	0	0	0	0			0
JIM	CASTIGLIA	16	18	2	7	0	0	0	2	1	3	.389	.389	0
PETE	CASTIGLIONE	545	1670	205	426	62	11	24	150	103	126	.255	.349	10
JOHN	CASTINO	666	2320	293	646	86	34	41	249	177	298	.278	.398	22
VINCE	CASTINO	88	215	24	49	7	0	2	23	25	31	.228	.288	0
FRANK	CATALANOTTO	438	1270	198	382	78	9	38	159	102	186	.301	.466	27
PHIL	CAVARRETTA	2050	6754	990	1977	347	99	95	920	820	598	.293	.416	65
RICK	CERONE	1329	4069	393	998	190	15	59	436	320	450	.245	.343	6
DINO	CHIOZZA	2	0	1	0	0	0	0	0	0	0			0
LOU	CHIOZZA	616	2288	303	633	107	22	14	197	145	165	.277	.361	45
HARRY	CHITI	502	1495	135	356	49	9	41	179	115	242	.238	.365	4
ARCHI	CIANFROCCO	500	1276	136	308	59	7	34	185	80	360	.241	.379	16
LARRY	CIAFFONE	5	5	0	0	0	0	0	0	1	2	.000		0
JOE	CICERO	40	81	14	18	3	4	0	8	2	13	.222	.358	0

FIRST	LAST	G	AB	R	H	2B	3B	HR	RBI	BB	SO	AVG	SLUG	SB
GINO	CIMOLI	969	3054	370	808	133	48	44	321	221	474	.265	.383	21
FRANK	CIPRIANI	13	36	2	9	0	0	0	2	2	4	.250	.250	0
JEFF	CIRILLO	1084	3937	627	1224	265	19	94	570	440	507	.311	.459	47
JACK	CLARK	1994	6847	1118	1826	332	39	340	1180	1262	1441	.267	.476	77
ROCKY	COLAVITO	1841	6503	971	1730	283	21	374	1159	951	880	.266	.489	19
MICHAEL	COLANGELO	51	93	10	23	3	3	2	8	9	30	.247	.409	0
CHRIS	COLETTA	14	30	5	9	1	0	1	7	1	4	.300	.433	0
BOB	COLUCCIO	370	1095	141	241	38	15	26	114	128	202	.220	.353	33
TONY	CONIGLIARO	876	3221	464	849	139	23	166	516	287	629	.264	.476	20
BILLY	CONIGLIARO	347	1130	142	289	56	10	40	128	86	244	.256	.429	9
BILLY	CONSOLO	603	1178	158	260	51	11	9	83	161	297	.221	.289	9
DAN	COSTELLO	154	350	35	85	6	4	0	24	21	62	.243	.283	12
TIM	COSTO	43	134	16	30	7	0	3	14	9	23	.224	.343	0
CREEPY	CRESPI	264	911	125	240	32	4	4	88	90	102	.263	.321	8
DAVE	CRISCIONE	7	9	3	3	0	0	1	1	0	2	.333	.667	0
TONY	CRISCOLA	184	367	35	91	12	4	1	28	30	32	.248	.311	2
FRANKIE	CROSETTI	1683	6277	1006	1541	260	65	98	649	792	799	.245	.354	113
TONY	CUCCINELLO	1704	6184	730	1729	334	46	94	884	579	497	.280	.394	42
AL	CUCCINELLO	54	165	27	41	7	1	4	20	1	20	.248	.376	0
MARK	DALESANDRO	79	129	17	31	7	0	3	17	3	14	.240	.364	1
DOM	DALLESSANDRO	746	1945	242	520	110	23	22	303	310	150	.267	.381	16
FATS	DANTONIO	50	135	12	33	6	1	0	12	11	7	.244	.304	3
DOUG	DASCENZO	540	1225	156	287	42	10	5	90	103	117	.234	.297	49
DOUG	DeCINCES	1649	5809	778	1505	312	29	237	879	618	904	.259	.445	58
BOBBY	DelGRECO	731	1982	271	454	95	11	42	169	271	372	.229	.352	16
DAVE	DELLUCCI	355	819	103	232	40	15	17	111	74	195	.283	.431	7
JOE	DeMAESTRI	1121	3441	322	813	114	23	49	281	168	511	.236	.325	15
AL	DEMAREE	232	456	30	54	3	1	0	16	23	148	.118	.129	5
SAM	DENTE	745	2320	205	585	78	16	4	214	167	96	.252	.305	5
MARK	DEROSA	100	188	38	52	9	0	3	23	14	23	.277	.372	9
BUTTERCUP	DICKERSON	408	1762	302	500	84	34	4	127	48	51	.284	.377	2
JAY	DIFANI	4	3	0	1	1	0	0	0	0	2	.333	.667	0
MIKE	DIFELICE	352	1068	91	257	52	6	21	111	62	230	.241	.360	2
DOM	DiMAGGIO	1399	5640	1046	1680	308	57	87	618	750	571	.298	.419	100
JOE	DiMAGGIO	1736	6821	1390	2214	389	131	361	1537	790	369	.325	.579	30

FIRST	LAST	G	AB	R	H	2B	3B	HR	RBI	BB	SO	AVG	SLUG	SB
VINCE	DiMAGGIO	1110	3849	491	959	209	24	125	584	412	837	.249	.413	79
BOB	DiPIETRO	4	11	0	1	—	—	0	0	1	1	.091	.091	0
GARY	DiSARCINA	1086	3744	444	966	186	20	28	355	154	306	.258	.341	47
BENNY	DiSTEFANO	240	360	35	82	13	5	7	42	31	66	.228	.350	1
SAMMY	ESPOSITO	560	792	130	164	27	2	8	73	145	127	.207	.277	7
CARMEN	FANZONE	237	588	66	132	27	1	20	94	74	119	.224	.372	7
SAL	FASANO	252	668	89	144	27	0	30	95	51	188	.216	.391	3
ERNIE	FAZIO	141	274	37	50	10	4	2	8	33	85	.182	.270	2
JOE	FERGUSON	1013	3001	407	719	121	11	122	445	562	607	.240	.409	5
AL	FERRARA	574	1382	148	358	60	7	51	198	156	286	.259	.423	22
MIKE	FERRARO	162	500	28	116	18	2	2	30	23	61	.232	.288	0
NEIL	FIALA	5	5	1	1	0	0	0	—	0	2	.200	.200	0
MIKE	FIGGA	46	94	13	20	4	0	1	5	2	31	.213	.287	0
MIKE	FIORE	254	556	75	126	18	0	13	50	124	115	.227	.333	5
DAN	FIROVA	17	7	0	0	0	0	0	—	0	1	.000	—	0
KEVIN	FLORA	29	84	14	17	3	0	2	7	5	28	.202	.310	2
TIM	FOLI	1696	6047	576	1515	241	20	25	501	265	399	.251	.309	81
MATT	FRANCO	468	638	74	163	23	2	13	72	86	101	.255	.359	1
TITO	FRANCONA	1719	5121	650	1395	224	34	125	656	544	694	.272	.403	46
TERRY	FRANCONA	708	1731	163	474	74	6	16	143	65	119	.274	.351	12
HERMAN	FRANKS	188	403	35	80	18	2	3	43	57	37	.199	.275	2
JIM	FREGOSI	1902	6523	844	1726	264	78	151	706	715	1097	.265	.398	76
CARL	FURILLO	1806	6378	895	1910	324	56	192	1058	514	436	.299	.458	48
GARY	GAETTI	2507	8951	1130	2280	443	39	360	1341	634	1602	.255	.434	96
PHIL	GAGLIANO	702	1411	150	336	50	7	14	159	163	184	.238	.313	5
RALPH	GAGLIANO	1	0	0	0	0	0	0	0	0	0	—	—	0
MIKE	GALLEGO	1111	2931	374	700	111	12	42	282	326	465	.239	.328	24
JOE	GARAGIOLA	676	1872	198	481	82	16	42	255	267	173	.257	.385	5
DANNY	GARDELLA	169	543	74	145	12	3	24	85	57	68	.267	.433	2
AL	GARDELLA	16	26	2	2	0	0	0	1	4	3	.077	.077	0
ART	GARIBALDI	71	232	30	64	12	4	0	20	16	30	.276	.341	3
MIKE	GAZELLA	160	352	51	85	14	4	0	32	56	50	.241	.304	8
GEORGE	GENOVESE	3	1	1	0	0	0	0	0	0	0	.000	—	0
JIM	GENTILE	936	2922	434	759	113	6	179	549	475	663	.260	.486	3
SAM	GENTILE	8	4	1	1	1	0	0	0	1	0	.250	—	0

FIRST	LAST	G	AB	R	H	2B	3B	HR	RBI	BB	SO	AVG	SLUG	SB
JASON	GIAMBI	953	3398	601	1048	228	7	187	675	586	602	.308	.545	9
JEREMY	GIAMBI	336	977	146	266	53	3	27	149	146	220	.272	.416	0
RAY	GIANNELLI	18	35	2	5	1	0	0	0	8	13	.143	.171	1
JOE	GIANNINI	1	2	0	1	1	0	0	0	0		.500		0
AL	GIONFRIDDO	228	580	95	154	22	12	0	58	91	39	.266	.355	15
TOMMY	GIORDANO	11	40	6	7	2	0	2	5	5	6	.175	.375	0
ED	GIOVANOLA	218	301	41	65	5	4	1	19	44	49	.216	.269	4
JOE	GIRARDI	1171	3870	434	1044	176	25	35	408	260	568	.270	.355	43
TONY	GIULIANI	243	674	58	157	18	3	0	69	38	41	.233	.269	1
TONY	GLAVIANO	389	1008	191	259	55	6	24	108	208	173	.257	.395	11
TONY	GRAFFANINO	414	964	148	248	48	8	19	95	101	205	.257	.383	21
MICKEY	GRASSO	322	957	78	216	23	1	5	87	81	108	.226	.268	2
BEN	GUINTINI	5	7	0	0	0	0	0	0	0		.000		0
LOU	GUISTO	156	449	35	88	19	3	0	59	46	44	.196	.252	5
FRANKIE	GUSTINE	1261	4582	553	1214	222	47	38	480	369	427	.265	.359	60
PETE	INCAVIGLIA	1284	4233	546	1043	194	21	206	655	360	1277	.246	.448	33
PAUL	KONERKO	522	1843	268	519	101	5	84	306	163	271	.282	.479	3
JOE	LAFATA	127	256	31	54	3	2	5	34	24	42	.229	.322	2
MIKE	LAGA	188	423	39	84	18	0	16	55	22	115	.199	.355	1
RAY	LAMANNO	442	1408	122	355	57	5	18	150	118	151	.252	.338	2
RICK	LANCELLOTTI	36	65	4	11	2	0	2	11	2	18	.169	.292	0
FRANK	LaPORTE	1194	4212	501	1185	198	79	15	560	288	85	.281	.377	101
TONY	LaRUSSA	132	176	15	35	5	2	0	7	23	37	.199	.250	0
TOM	LASORDA	27	14	0	1	0	0	0	0	0	4	.071	.071	0
TONY	LAZZERI	1740	6297	986	1840	334	115	178	1191	869	864	.292	.467	148
JIM	LENTINE	95	205	23	54	9	1	1	20	31	38	.263	.332	3
DARIO	LODIGIANI	405	1564	142	355	71	7	16	156	141	86	.260	.358	12
PAUL	LODUCA	201	634	90	189	32	0	30	110	55	48	.298	.491	3
ERNIE	LOMBARDI	1853	5855	601	1792	277	27	190	990	430	262	.306	.460	8
PHIL	LOMBARDI	43	92	10	22	4	0	3	9	9	17	.239	.380	0
STEVE	LOMBARDOZZI	446	1264	153	294	61	12	20	107	131	206	.233	.347	13
MARK	LORETTA	710	2379	326	693	121	13	27	253	224	272	.291	.387	22
JAY	LOVIGLIO	46	52	17	10	0	0	0	4	3	6	.192	.192	5
JOE	LOVITTO	306	763	70	165	22	4	4	53	80	113	.216	.271	22
TOREY	LOVULLO	303	737	80	165	35	1	15	60	80	121	.224	.335	9

FIRST	LAST	G	AB	R	H	2B	3B	HR	RBI	BB	SO	AVG	SLUG	SB
JOHNNY	LUCADELLO	239	686	95	181	36	7	5	60	93	56	.264	.359	6
LEW	MALONE	133	367	28	74	11	7	1	28	28	60	.202	.278	8
FRANK	MALZONE	1441	5428	647	1486	239	21	133	728	337	434	.274	.399	14
GUS	MANCUSO	1460	4505	386	1194	197	16	53	543	418	264	.265	.351	8
FRANK	MANCUSO	337	1002	85	241	37	7	5	98	101	118	.241	.306	2
DON	MANNO	25	37	3	7	1	0	1	8	3	9	.189	.297	0
JEFF	MANTO	289	713	97	164	35	2	31	97	97	182	.230	.415	3
BILLY	MARTIN	1021	3419	425	877	137	28	64	333	188	355	.257	.369	34
JOHN	MARZANO	301	794	79	191	45	2	11	72	39	138	.241	.344	0
PHIL	MASI	1229	3468	420	917	164	31	47	417	410	311	.264	.370	45
GORDON	MASSA	8	17	2	7	1	0	0	3	4	5	.412	.471	0
CARMEN	MAURO	167	416	40	96	9	8	2	33	37	65	.231	.305	6
MEL	MAZZERA	207	507	75	136	22	8	10	66	45	71	.268	.402	2
LEE	MAZZILLI	1475	4124	571	1068	191	24	93	460	642	627	.259	.385	197
DUTCH	MELE	6	14	1	2	1	0	0	1	1		.143	.214	0
SAM	MELE	1046	3437	406	916	168	39	80	544	311	342	.267	.408	15
SKI	MELILLO	1377	5063	590	1316	210	64	22	548	327	306	.260	.340	69
JOE	MELLANA	4	7	1	2	0	0	0	2	0	1	.286	.286	0
RUDY	MEOLI	310	626	69	133	20	4	2	40	69	88	.212	.267	10
FRANK	MENECHINO	214	625	113	155	31	3	18	86	99	146	.245	.390	3
LOU	MERLONI	174	496	59	139	34	2	5	59	25	89	.280	.387	4
LENNIE	MERULLO	639	2071	191	497	92	8	6	152	136	174	.240	.301	38
MATT	MERULLO	223	496	37	116	17	2	7	59	32	69	.234	.319	0
MICKEY	MICELOTTA	17	7	2	0	0	0	0	0	1	1	.000	.000	0
DOUG	MIRABELLI	217	549	57	127	29	2	19	72	78	152	.231	.395	1
BOB	MOLINARO	401	803	106	212	25	2	14	90	65	57	.264	.375	46
BLAS	MONACO	17	13	2	2	0	1	0	2	1	3	.154	.308	0
ROSS	MOSCHITTO	110	36	13	6	0	0	1	3	1	14	.167	.250	0
CHAD	MOTTOLA	43	95	12	19	3	0	3	9	8	22	.200	.326	2
STEVE	NICOSIA	358	938	86	233	52	3	11	88	86	90	.248	.345	5
ERNIE	ORSATTI	701	2165	306	663	129	39	10	237	176	208	.306	.416	46
JOHN	ORSINO	332	1014	114	252	44	5	40	123	92	191	.249	.420	3
FRANK	ORTENZIO	9	25	1	7	2	0	1	6	2	6	.280	.480	0
JIM	PAGLIARONI	849	2465	269	622	98	7	90	326	330	494	.252	.407	4
MIKE	PAGLIARULO	1246	3901	462	942	206	18	134	505	343	785	.241	.407	18

FIRST	LAST	G	AB	R	H	2B	3B	HR	RBI	BB	SO	AVG	SLUG	SB
TOM	PAGNOZZI	927	2896	247	733	153	11	44	320	189	450	.253	.359	18
JOE	PALMISANO	19	44	5	10	2	0	0	4	6	3	.227	.273	0
TONY	PARISSE	10	21	0	3	0	0	0	1	2	3	.143	.143	0
DAN	PASQUA	905	2620	341	638	129	15	117	390	335	642	.244	.438	7
MIKE	PASQUELLA	2	2	1	1	0	0	0	0	0	1	.500	.500	0
BILL	PECOTA	698	1527	223	380	72	11	22	148	160	216	.249	.354	52
EDDIE	PELLAGRINI	563	1423	167	321	42	13	20	133	128	201	.226	.316	13
JOE	PEPITONE	1397	5097	606	1315	158	35	219	721	302	526	.258	.432	41
JACK	PERCONTE	433	1441	191	389	47	16	2	76	149	123	.270	.329	78
SAM	PERLOZZO	12	26	6	7	0	2	0	0	3	3	.269	.423	0
GENO	PETRALLI	809	1874	184	501	83	9	24	192	216	263	.267	.360	8
RICO	PETROCELLI	1553	5390	653	1352	237	22	210	773	661	926	.251	.420	10
JOE	PETTINI	188	344	38	70	5	2	1	20	33	53	.203	.238	10
MIKE	PIAZZA	1258	4638	782	1507	228	4	314	975	506	719	.325	.579	17
JOE	PIGNATANO	307	689	81	161	25	4	16	62	94	116	.234	.351	8
BABE	PINELLI	774	2617	327	723	101	33	5	298	182	162	.276	.346	71
JIM	PISONI	103	189	26	40	3	3	6	20	16	47	.212	.354	0
CHRIS	PITTARO	53	95	16	21	3	1	0	7	6	21	.221	.274	2
ROB	PICIOLO	730	1628	192	381	56	10	17	109	25	254	.234	.312	9
NICK	PICCIUTO	36	89	7	12	6	0	0	6	6	17	.135	.202	0
JOHNNY	PRAMESA	185	526	29	141	17	3	13	59	31	41	.268	.386	0
GEORGE	PUCCINELLI	187	607	109	172	40	3	19	102	78	92	.283	.453	3
FRANK	QUILICI	405	682	78	146	23	6	5	53	66	120	.214	.287	3
BOB	RAMAZZOTTI	346	851	86	196	22	9	4	53	45	107	.230	.291	15
BILL	RENNA	370	918	123	219	36	10	28	119	99	166	.239	.391	2
TONY	RENSA	200	514	71	134	26	5	7	65	57	54	.261	.372	5
DINO	RESTELLI	93	270	42	65	12	0	13	43	37	30	.241	.450	3
HARRY	RICONDA	243	765	83	189	44	11	4	70	61	91	.247	.349	13
JOHNNY	RIZZO	557	1842	268	497	90	16	61	289	200	197	.270	.435	7
PHIL	RIZZUTO	1661	5816	877	1588	239	62	38	563	651	398	.273	.355	149
MICKEY	ROCCO	440	1721	219	444	73	17	30	186	174	146	.258	.372	6
LOU	ROCHELLI	5	17	0	3	0	1	0	2	2	6	.176	.294	0
JOHNNY	ROMANO	905	2767	355	706	112	10	129	417	414	485	.255	.443	7
TOM	ROMANO	7	3	1	0	0	0	0	0	0	1	.000		0
BOB	ROSELLI	68	114	8	25	7	1	2	10	12	31	.219	.351	1

FIRST	LAST	G	AB	R	H	2B	3B	HR	RBI	BB	SO	AVG	SLUG	SB
JOE	RULLO	51	151	7	32	3	0	0	11	14	26	.212	.232	1
GENE	RYE	17	39	3	7	0	0	0	1	2	5	.179	.179	0
F.P.	Santangelo	665	1691	258	415	87	14	21	162	240	319	.245	.351	37
RON	SANTO	2243	8143	1138	2254	365	67	342	1331	1108	1343	.277	.464	35
BILL	SARNI	390	1182	107	311	50	11	22	151	89	135	.263	.380	6
TOM	SATRIANO	674	1623	130	365	53	5	21	157	214	225	.225	.303	7
STEVE	SAX	1769	6940	913	1949	278	47	54	550	556	584	.281	.358	444
DAVE	SCALA	37	60	3	16	4	0	1	8	3	5	.267	.383	0
JERRY	SCALA	80	193	26	43	9	2	1	19	27	32	.223	.306	3
SKEETER	SCALZI	11	18	3	6	0	0	0	0	3	2	.333	.333	1
JOHNNY	SCALZI	2	1	0	0	0	0	0	0	0	1	.000		0
LES	SCARSELLA	265	898	109	255	34	16	6	109	37	70	.284	.378	13
STEVE	SCARSONE	350	830	103	198	44	4	20	86	70	266	.239	.373	7
MIKE	SCIOSCIA	1441	4373	398	1131	198	12	68	446	567	307	.259	.356	29
SONNY	SENERCHIA	29	100	5	22	5	0	3	11	4	21	.220	.360	0
BILL	SERENA	408	1239	154	311	57	16	48	198	177	235	.251	.439	2
PAUL	SERNA	95	263	26	62	5	0	7	17	7	24	.236	.335	2
WALTER	SESSI	20	27	4	2	0	0	1	2	2	6	.074	.185	0
DAVE	SILVESTRI	181	336	42	68	12	3	6	36	56	96	.202	.310	4
KEN	SILVESTRI	102	203	26	44	11	1	5	25	31	41	.217	.355	0
MATT	SINATRO	140	252	20	48	6	1	1	21	17	35	.190	.234	2
SIBBY	SISTI	1016	2999	401	732	121	19	27	260	283	440	.244	.324	30
PAUL	SORRENTO	1093	3412	454	876	176	5	166	565	426	844	.257	.457	8
ED	SPIEZIO	554	1544	126	367	56	4	39	174	135	245	.238	.355	16
SCOTT	SPIEZIO	621	1974	253	501	113	11	63	259	195	292	.254	.418	16
ANDY	SPOGNARDI	17	34	9	10	1	1	0	1	6	6	.294	.324	0
JOHN	STEFERO	79	187	20	44	3	0	3	20	22	44	.235	.299	0
JOHN	TAMARGO	135	244	19	59	12	1	4	33	34	27	.242	.348	1
GENE	TENACE	1555	4390	653	1060	179	20	201	674	984	998	.241	.429	36
FRANK	TEPEDINO	265	507	50	122	13	1	6	58	33	61	.241	.306	4
NICK	TESTA	1	0	0	0	0	0	0	0	0	0			0
FRANK	TORRE	714	1482	150	404	78	15	13	179	155	64	.273	.372	4
JOE	TORRE	2209	7874	996	2342	344	59	252	1185	779	1094	.297	.452	23
BOBBY	VALENTINE	639	1698	176	441	59	9	12	157	140	134	.260	.326	27
ROBIN	VENTURA	1698	6055	877	1638	300	13	248	1006	905	960	.271	.437	21

FIRST	LAST	G	AB	R	H	2B	3B	HR	RBI	BB	SO	AVG	SLUG	SB
FRANK	VERDI	1	0	0	0	0	0	0	0	0	0			0
GEORGE	VICO	211	663	65	166	28	11	12	76	60	56	.250	.380	2
JOE	VITELLI	5	3	1	0	0	0	0	0	0	0	.000		0
JOE	VITIELLO	244	617	64	146	29	1	23	91	73	151	.237	.399	2
FRANK	ZUPO	16	18	3	3	1	0	0	0	2	6	.167	.222	0
PAUL	ZUVELLA	209	491	41	109	17	2	2	20	34	50	.222	.277	2

Italian American Pitchers Season by Season

KEY

w = won

l = lost

pct = percentage

g = games

gs = games started

cg = complete games

sh = shut outs

sv = saves

ip = innings pitched

h = hits

er = errors

bb = base on balls

k = strike outs

era = earned run average

FIRST	LAST	YEAR	TEAM	LEAGUE	W	L	PCT	G	GS	CG	SH	SV	IP	H	ER	BB	K	ERA
JOE	ALBANESE	1958	Washington Senators	AL	0	0		6	0	0	0	0	6	8	3	2	3	4.50
JOHNNY	ANTONELLI	1948	Boston Braves	NL	0	0		4	0	0	0	1	4	2	1	3	2	2.25
JOHNNY	ANTONELLI	1949	Boston Braves	NL	3	7	.300	22	10	3	1	0	96	99	38	42	48	3.56
JOHNNY	ANTONELLI	1950	Boston Braves	NL	2	3	.400	20	6	2	1	0	57 2/3	81	38	22	33	5.93
JOHNNY	ANTONELLI	1953	Milwaukee Braves	NL	12	12	.500	31	26	11	2	0	175 1/3	167	62	71	131	3.18
JOHNNY	ANTONELLI	1954	New York Giants	NL	21	7	.750	39	37	18	6	2	258 2/3	209	66	94	152	2.30
JOHNNY	ANTONELLI	1955	New York Giants	NL	14	16	.467	38	34	14	2	1	235 1/3	206	87	82	143	3.33
JOHNNY	ANTONELLI	1956	New York Giants	NL	20	13	.606	41	36	15	5	1	258 1/3	225	82	75	145	2.86
JOHNNY	ANTONELLI	1957	New York Giants	NL	12	18	.400	40	30	8	3	0	212 1/3	228	89	67	114	3.77
JOHNNY	ANTONELLI	1958	San Francisco Giants	NL	16	13	.552	41	34	13	4	3	241 2/3	216	88	87	143	3.28
JOHNNY	ANTONELLI	1959	San Francisco Giants	NL	19	10	.655	40	38	17	4	1	282	247	97	76	165	3.10
JOHNNY	ANTONELLI	1960	San Francisco Giants	NL	6	7	.462	41	10	1	1	11	112 1/3	106	47	47	57	3.77
JOHNNY	ANTONELLI	1961	Cleveland Indians	AL	0	4	.000	11	7	0	0	0	48	68	35	18	23	6.56
JOHNNY	ANTONELLI	1961	Milwaukee Braves	NL	1	0	1.000	9	2	0	0	0	10 2/3	16	9	3	8	7.59
GERRY	ARRIGO	1962	Minnesota Twins	AL	0	1	.000	7	0	0	0	0	9 2/3	3	11	10	6	10.24
GERRY	ARRIGO	1963	Minnesota Twins	AL	0	0		5	0	0	0	0	1	3	2	1	13	18.00
GERRY	ARRIGO	1964	Minnesota Twins	AL	1	2	.333	5	1	0	0	1	15 2/3	12	5	4	96	2.87
GERRY	ARRIGO	1965	Cincinnati Reds	NL	7	4	.636	41	12	2	1	0	105 1/3	97	45	45	43	3.84
GERRY	ARRIGO	1966	Cincinnati Reds	NL	2	4	.333	27	5	2	0	2	54	75	37	30	3	6.17
GERRY	ARRIGO	1966	New York Mets	NL	2	0	1.000	3	0	0	0	0	7 1/3	7	4	3	28	4.91
GERRY	ARRIGO	1967	Cincinnati Reds	NL	3	3	.500	17	5	0	0	0	43 1/3	47	18	16	56	3.74
GERRY	ARRIGO	1968	Cincinnati Reds	NL	6	6	.500	32	31	1	1	1	74	61	26	35	140	3.16
GERRY	ARRIGO	1969	Cincinnati Reds	NL	12	10	.545	36	31	5	1	0	205 1/3	181	76	77	35	3.33
GERRY	ARRIGO	1970	Chicago White Sox	AL	4	7	.364	20	16	1	0	0	91	89	42	61	12	4.15
TONY	BALSAMO	1962	Chicago Cubs	NL	0	1	.000	18	0	0	0	0	13 1/3	18	19	20	27	12.82
FRANK	BERTAINA	1964	Baltimore Orioles	AL	1	0	1.000	6	4	1	0	0	29 1/3	34	21	13	18	6.44
FRANK	BERTAINA	1965	Baltimore Orioles	AL	0	0		2	0	0	0	1	26	23	8	9	15	2.77
FRANK	BERTAINA	1966	Baltimore Orioles	AL	2	5	.286	16	0	0	0	0	6	9	4	4	5	6.00
FRANK	BERTAINA	1967	Baltimore Orioles	AL	1	1	.500	5	5	1	0	0	63 1/3	52	22	36	46	3.13
FRANK	BERTAINA	1969	Baltimore Orioles	AL	0	0		4	2	0	0	0	21 2/3	17	8	14	19	3.32
FRANK	BERTAINA	1970	St. Louis Cardinals	NL	1	2	.333	3	0	0	0	0	6	1	0	3	5	0.00
MIKE	BERTOTTI	1995	Chicago White Sox	AL	1	1	.500	8	4	0	0	0	31 1/3	36	11	15	27	3.16
MIKE	BERTOTTI	1996	Chicago White Sox	AL	2	0	1.000	15	2	0	0	0	14 1/3	23	20	11	15	12.56
MIKE	BERTOTTI	1997	Chicago White Sox	AL	0	0		5	5	0	0	0	28	28	16	20	19	5.14
MIKE	BERTOTTI	1997	Chicago White Sox	AL	0	0		9	0	0	0	0	3 2/3	9	3	2	4	7.36

FIRST	LAST	YEAR	TEAM	LEAGUE	W	L	PCT	G	GS	CG	SH	SV	IP	H	ER	BB	K	ER
EMIL	BILDILLI	1937	St. Louis Browns	AL	0	1	.000	4	1	0	0	0	8	12	9	3	2	10.12
EMIL	BILDILLI	1938	St. Louis Browns	AL	1	2	.333	5	3	2	0	0	21 2/3	33	17	11	11	7.06
EMIL	BILDILLI	1939	St. Louis Browns	AL	1	1	.500	2	2	2	0	0	19	21	7	6	8	3.32
EMIL	BILDILLI	1940	St. Louis Browns	AL	2	4	.333	28	11	3	0	1	97	113	60	52	32	5.57
EMIL	BILDILLI	1941	St. Louis Browns	AL	0	0		2	0	0	0	0	2 1/3	5	3	3	2	11.57
DAN	BOITANO	1978	Philadelphia Phillies	NL	0	0		1	0	0	0	0	6	0	0	1	0	0.00
DAN	BOITANO	1979	Milwaukee Brewers	AL	0	1		5	0	0	0	0	6	6	1	3	5	1.50
DAN	BOITANO	1980	Milwaukee Brewers	AL	0	1	.000	11	0	0	0	0	17 2/3	26	16	6	11	8.15
DAN	BOITANO	1981	New York Mets	NL	2	1	.667	15	0	0	0	0	16 1/3	21	10	5	8	5.51
DAN	BOITANO	1982	Texas Rangers	AL	0	0		19	0	0	0	0	30 1/3	33	18	13	28	5.34
CHRIS	BOSIO	1986	Milwaukee Brewers	AL	0	4	.000	10	4	0	0	0	34 2/3	41	27	13	29	7.01
CHRIS	BOSIO	1987	Milwaukee Brewers	AL	11	8	.579	46	19	2	1	2	170	187	99	50	150	5.24
CHRIS	BOSIO	1988	Milwaukee Brewers	AL	7	15	.318	38	22	9	1	6	182	190	68	38	84	3.36
CHRIS	BOSIO	1989	Milwaukee Brewers	AL	15	10	.600	33	33	8	2	0	234 2/3	225	77	48	173	2.95
CHRIS	BOSIO	1990	Milwaukee Brewers	AL	4	9	.308	20	20	4	1	0	132 2/3	131	59	38	76	4.00
CHRIS	BOSIO	1991	Milwaukee Brewers	AL	14	10	.583	32	32	5	1	0	204 2/3	187	74	58	117	3.25
CHRIS	BOSIO	1992	Milwaukee Brewers	AL	16	6	.727	33	33	4	2	0	231 1/3	223	93	44	120	3.62
CHRIS	BOSIO	1993	Seattle Mariners	AL	9	9	.500	29	24	3	1	1	164 1/3	138	63	59	119	3.45
CHRIS	BOSIO	1994	Seattle Mariners	AL	4	10	.286	19	19	4	0	0	125	137	60	40	67	4.32
CHRIS	BOSIO	1995	Seattle Mariners	AL	10	8	.556	31	31	4	0	0	170	211	93	69	85	4.92
CHRIS	BOSIO	1996	Seattle Mariners	AL	4	4	.500	18	9	0	0	0	60 2/3	72	40	24	39	5.93
RICKY	BOTTALICO	1994	Philadelphia Phillies	NL	0	0		3	0	0	0	1	3	3	0	1	3	0.00
RICKY	BOTTALICO	1995	Philadelphia Phillies	NL	5	3	.625	62	0	0	0	34	87 2/3	50	24	42	87	2.46
RICKY	BOTTALICO	1996	Philadelphia Phillies	NL	4	5	.444	61	0	0	0	34	67 2/3	47	24	23	74	3.19
RICKY	BOTTALICO	1997	Philadelphia Phillies	NL	2	5	.286	69	0	0	0	34	74	68	30	42	89	3.65
RICKY	BOTTALICO	1998	Philadelphia Phillies	NL	1	5	.167	39	0	0	0	6	43 1/3	54	31	25	27	6.44
RICKY	BOTTALICO	1999	St. Louis Cardinals	NL	3	7	.300	68	0	0	0	20	73 1/3	83	40	49	66	4.91
RICKY	BOTTALICO	2000	Kansas City Royals	AL	9	6	.600	62	0	0	0	16	72 2/3	65	39	41	56	4.83
RICKY	BOTTALICO	2001	Philadelphia Phillies	NL	3	4	.429	66	0	0	0	3	67	58	29	25	57	3.90
RALPH	BRANCA	1944	Brooklyn Dodgers	NL	0	2	.000	21	1	0	0	1	44 2/3	46	35	32	16	7.05
RALPH	BRANCA	1945	Brooklyn Dodgers	NL	5	6	.455	16	15	7	0	1	109 2/3	73	37	79	69	3.04
RALPH	BRANCA	1946	Brooklyn Dodgers	NL	3	1	.750	24	10	2	2	3	67 1/3	62	29	41	42	3.88
RALPH	BRANCA	1947	Brooklyn Dodgers	NL	21	12	.636	43	36	15	4	1	280	251	83	98	148	2.67
RALPH	BRANCA	1948	Brooklyn Dodgers	NL	14	9	.609	36	28	11	1	1	215 2/3	189	84	80	122	3.51
RALPH	BRANCA	1949	Brooklyn Dodgers	NL	13	5	.722	34	27	9	2	1	186 2/3	181	91	91	109	4.39

FIRST	LAST	YEAR	TEAM	LEAGUE	W	L	PCT	G	GS	CG	SH	SV	IP	H	ER	BB	K	ER
RALPH	BRANCA	1950	Brooklyn Dodgers	NL	7	9	.438	43	15	5	0	7	142	152	74	55	100	4.69
RALPH	BRANCA	1951	Brooklyn Dodgers	NL	13	12	.520	42	27	13	3	3	204	180	74	85	118	3.26
RALPH	BRANCA	1952	Brooklyn Dodgers	NL	4	2	.667	16	7	2	0	0	61	52	26	21	26	3.84
RALPH	BRANCA	1953	Brooklyn Dodgers	NL	0	0		7	0	0	0	0	11	15	12	5	5	9.82
RALPH	BRANCA	1953	Detroit Tigers	AL	4	7	.364	17	14	7	0	1	102	98	47	31	50	4.15
RALPH	BRANCA	1954	New York Yankees	AL	3	3	.500	5	5	0	0	0	45 1/3	63	29	30	15	5.76
RALPH	BRANCA	1956	Brooklyn Dodgers	NL	1	0	1.000	1	0	0	0	0	12 2/3	9	4	13	7	2.84
TONY	BRIZZOLARA	1979	Atlanta Braves	NL	6	9	.400	20	19	2	0	0	107 1/3	133	63	33	64	5.28
TONY	BRIZZOLARA	1983	Atlanta Braves	NL	1	0	1.000	14	0	0	0	0	20 1/3	22	8	6	17	3.54
TONY	BRIZZOLARA	1984	Atlanta Braves	NL	1	2	.333	10	4	0	0	0	29	33	17	13	17	5.28
JOHNNY	BROACA	1934	New York Yankees	AL	12	9	.571	26	24	13	2	0	177 1/3	203	82	65	74	4.16
JOHNNY	BROACA	1935	New York Yankees	AL	15	7	.682	29	27	14	1	0	201	199	80	79	78	3.58
JOHNNY	BROACA	1936	New York Yankees	AL	12	7	.632	37	27	12	2	3	206	235	97	66	84	4.24
JOHNNY	BROACA	1937	New York Yankees	AL	1	4	.200	7	6	3	0	0	44	58	23	17	9	4.70
JOHNNY	BROACA	1939	Cleveland Indians	AL	4	2	.667	22	2	0	0	3	46	53	24	28	13	4.70
ERNIE	BROGLIO	1959	St. Louis Cardinals	NL	7	12	.368	35	25	6	3	0	181 1/3	174	95	89	133	4.72
ERNIE	BROGLIO	1960	St. Louis Cardinals	NL	21	9	.700	52	24	9	3	0	226 1/3	172	69	100	188	2.74
ERNIE	BROGLIO	1961	St. Louis Cardinals	NL	9	12	.429	29	26	7	2	0	174 2/3	166	80	75	113	4.12
ERNIE	BROGLIO	1962	St. Louis Cardinals	NL	12	9	.571	34	30	11	4	0	222 1/3	193	74	93	132	3.00
ERNIE	BROGLIO	1963	St. Louis Cardinals	NL	18	8	.692	39	35	11	5	1	250	202	83	90	145	2.99
ERNIE	BROGLIO	1964	Chicago Cubs	NL	4	7	.364	18	16	3	1	1	100 1/3	111	45	30	46	4.04
ERNIE	BROGLIO	1964	St. Louis Cardinals	NL	3	5	.375	11	11	3	0	0	69 1/3	65	27	26	36	3.50
ERNIE	BROGLIO	1965	Chicago Cubs	NL	1	6	.143	11	6	0	0	0	50 2/3	63	39	46	22	6.93
ERNIE	BROGLIO	1966	Chicago Cubs	NL	2	6	.250	15	11	2	0	1	62 1/3	70	44	38	34	6.35
TOM	BRUNO	1976	Kansas City Royals	AL	1	0	1.000	12	0	0	0	0	17 1/3	20	13	9	11	6.75
TOM	BRUNO	1977	Toronto Blue Jays	AL	0	3	.000	12	0	0	0	1	18 1/3	30	16	13	9	7.85
TOM	BRUNO	1978	St. Louis Cardinals	NL	4	3	.571	18	3	0	0	0	49 2/3	38	11	17	33	1.99
TOM	BRUNO	1979	St. Louis Cardinals	NL	2	3	.400	27	1	0	0	0	38 1/3	37	18	22	27	4.23
LEON	CADORE	1915	Brooklyn Dodgers	NL	0	2	.000	7	2	0	0	0	21	28	13	8	12	5.57
LEON	CADORE	1916	Brooklyn Dodgers	NL	0	0		1	0	0	0	0	6	10	3	3	2	4.50
LEON	CADORE	1917	Brooklyn Dodgers	NL	13	13	.500	37	30	21	1	3	264	231	72	63	115	2.45
LEON	CADORE	1918	Brooklyn Dodgers	NL	1	0	1.000	2	2	1	1	0	17	6	1	2	5	0.53
LEON	CADORE	1919	Brooklyn Dodgers	NL	14	12	.538	35	27	16	3	0	250 2/3	228	66	39	94	2.37
LEON	CADORE	1920	Brooklyn Dodgers	NL	15	14	.517	35	30	16	4	0	254 1/3	256	74	56	79	2.62

FIRST	LAST	YEAR	TEAM	LEAGUE	W	L	PCT	G	GS	CG	SH	SV	IP	H	ER	BB	K	ER
LEON	CADORE	1921	Brooklyn Dodgers	NL	13	14	.481	35	30	12	1	0	211 2/3	243	98	46	79	4.17
LEON	CADORE	1922	Brooklyn Dodgers	NL	8	15	.348	29	21	13	0	0	190 1/3	224	92	57	49	4.35
LEON	CADORE	1923	Brooklyn Dodgers	NL	4	1	.800	8	4	3	0	0	36	39	13	13	5	3.25
LEON	CADORE	1923	Chicago White Sox	AL	0	1	.000	1	1	0	0	0	2 1/3	6	6	2	3	23.14
LEON	CADORE	1924	New York Giants	NL	0	0		2		0	0	0	3 1/3	2	0	3	2	0.00
FRED	CAMBRIA	1970	Pittsburgh Pirates	NL	1	2	.333	6	5	0	0	1	33 1/3	37	13	12	14	3.51
MILO	CANDINI	1943	Washington Senators	AL	11	7	.611	28	21	8	3	1	166	144	46	65	67	2.49
MILO	CANDINI	1944	Washington Senators	AL	6	7	.462	28	10	4	2	1	103	110	47	49	31	4.11
MILO	CANDINI	1946	Washington Senators	AL	2	0	1.000	9	0	0	0	1	212 1/3	15	5	4	6	2.08
MILO	CANDINI	1947	Washington Senators	AL	3	4	.429	38	2	0	0	3	87	96	50	35	31	5.17
MILO	CANDINI	1948	Washington Senators	AL	2	3	.400	35	4	1	0	1	94 1/3	96	54	63	23	5.15
MILO	CANDINI	1949	Washington Senators	AL	0	0		3	0	0	0	0	5 2/3	4	3	1		4.76
MILO	CANDINI	1950	Philadelphia Phillies	NL	1	0	1.000	18	0	0	0	0	30	32	9	15	10	2.70
MILO	CANDINI	1951	Philadelphia Phillies	NL	1	0	1.000	15	0	0	1	0	30	33	20	18	14	6.00
TOM	CANDIOTTI	1983	Milwaukee Brewers	AL	4	4	.500	10	8	2	0	0	55 2/3	62	20	16	21	3.23
TOM	CANDIOTTI	1984	Milwaukee Brewers	AL	2	2	.500	8	6	0	1	0	32 1/3	38	19	10	23	5.29
TOM	CANDIOTTI	1986	Cleveland Indians	AL	16	12	.571	36	34	17	3	0	252 1/3	234	100	106	167	3.57
TOM	CANDIOTTI	1987	Cleveland Indians	AL	7	18	.280	32	32	7	2	0	201 2/3	193	107	93	111	4.78
TOM	CANDIOTTI	1988	Cleveland Indians	AL	14	8	.636	31	31	11	1	0	216 2/3	225	79	53	137	3.28
TOM	CANDIOTTI	1989	Cleveland Indians	AL	13	10	.565	31	31	4	0	0	206	188	71	55	124	3.10
TOM	CANDIOTTI	1990	Cleveland Indians	AL	15	11	.577	31	29	3	1	0	202	207	82	55	128	3.65
TOM	CANDIOTTI	1991	Cleveland Indians	AL	7	6	.558	15	15	3	0	0	108 1/3	88	27	28	86	2.24
TOM	CANDIOTTI	1991	Toronto Blue Jays	AL	6	7	.462	19	19	3	0	0	129 2/3	114	43	45	81	2.98
TOM	CANDIOTTI	1992	Los Angeles Dodgers	NL	11	15	.423	32	30	6	2	0	203 2/3	177	68	63	152	3.00
TOM	CANDIOTTI	1993	Los Angeles Dodgers	NL	8	10	.444	33	32	2	0	0	213 2/3	192	74	71	155	3.12
TOM	CANDIOTTI	1994	Los Angeles Dodgers	NL	7	7	.500	23	22	5	0	0	153	149	70	54	102	4.12
TOM	CANDIOTTI	1995	Los Angeles Dodgers	NL	7	14	.333	30	30	1	1	0	190 1/3	187	74	58	141	3.50
TOM	CANDIOTTI	1996	Los Angeles Dodgers	NL	9	11	.450	28	27	1	0	0	152 1/3	172	76	43	79	4.49
TOM	CANDIOTTI	1997	Los Angeles Dodgers	NL	10	7	.588	41	18	3	0	0	135	128	54	40	89	3.60
TOM	CANDIOTTI	1998	Oakland Athletics	AL	11	16	.407	33	33	0	0	0	201	222	108	63	98	4.84
TOM	CANDIOTTI	1999	Cleveland Indians	AL	1	1	.500	7	2	0	0	1	14 2/3	19	18	7	11	11.05
TOM	CANDIOTTI	1999	Oakland Athletics	AL	3	5	.375	11	11	0	0	0	56 2/3	67	40	23	30	6.35
GEORGE	CAPPUZZELLO	1981	Detroit Tigers	AL	1	1	.500	18	3	0	0	0	33 2/3	28	13	18	19	3.48
GEORGE	CAPPUZZELLO	1982	Houston Astros	NL	0	1	.000	17	3	0	0	0	191 1/3	16	6	7	13	2.79
BUZZ	CAPRA	1971	New York Mets	NL	0	1	.000	3	0	0	0	0	5 1/3	3	5	5	6	8.44

FIRST	LAST	YEAR	TEAM	LEAGUE	W	L	PCT	G	GS	CG	SH	SV	IP	H	ER	BB	K	ER
BUZZ	CAPRA	1972	New York Mets	NL	3	2	.600	14	6	0	0	0	53	50	27	27	45	4.58
BUZZ	CAPRA	1973	New York Mets	NL	2	7	.222	24	0	0	0	4	42	35	18	28	35	3.86
BUZZ	CAPRA	1974	Atlanta Braves	NL	16	8	.667	39	27	11	5	1	217	163	55	84	137	2.28
BUZZ	CAPRA	1975	Atlanta Braves	NL	4	7	.364	12	12	5	0	0	78 1/3	77	37	28	35	4.25
BUZZ	CAPRA	1976	Atlanta Braves	NL	0	0	.000	5	0	0	0	0	9 1/3	9	9	6	4	8.68
BUZZ	CAPRA	1977	Atlanta Braves	NL	6	11	.353	45	16	0	2	1	139 1/3	142	83	80	100	5.36
JOE	CASCARELLA	1934	Philadelphia Athletics	AL	12	15	.444	42	22	9	0	0	194 1/3	214	101	104	71	4.68
JOE	CASCARELLA	1935	Boston Red Sox	AL	0	1	.000	6	4	0	2	0	17	25	13	11	9	6.88
JOE	CASCARELLA	1935	Philadelphia Athletics	AL	1	6	.143	9	3	1	0	0	32 1/3	29	19	22	15	5.29
JOE	CASCARELLA	1936	Boston Red Sox	AL	0	2	.000	10	1	0	0	0	20 2/3	27	16	9	7	6.97
JOE	CASCARELLA	1936	Washington Senators	AL	9	8	.529	22	16	7	1	1	139 1/3	147	63	54	34	4.07
JOE	CASCARELLA	1937	Cincinnati Reds	NL	1	2	.333	11	3	2	0	1	43 2/3	44	19	22	16	3.92
JOE	CASCARELLA	1937	Washington Senators	AL	0	5	.000	10	4	0	0	1	32 1/3	50	29	23	10	8.07
JOE	CASCARELLA	1938	Cincinnati Reds	NL	4	7	.364	33	1	1	0	4	61	66	31	22	30	4.57
ART	CECCARELLI	1955	Kansas City Athletics	AL	4	7	.364	31	16	3	1	0	123 2/3	123	73	71	68	5.31
ART	CECCARELLI	1956	Kansas City Athletics	AL	0	1	.000	3	2	0	0	0	10	13	8	4	2	7.20
ART	CECCARELLI	1957	Baltimore Orioles	AL	0	3	.000	20	8	0	0	0	58	62	29	31	30	4.50
ART	CECCARELLI	1959	Chicago Cubs	NL	5	5	.500	18	15	4	2	0	102	95	54	37	56	4.76
ART	CECCARELLI	1960	Chicago Cubs	NL	0	2	.000	7	1	0	0	0	13	16	8	4	10	5.54
JOHN	CERUTTI	1985	Toronto Blue Jays	AL	0	2	.000	4	1	0	0	0	6 2/3	10	4	4	5	5.40
JOHN	CERUTTI	1986	Toronto Blue Jays	AL	9	4	.692	34	20	2	1	1	145 1/3	150	67	47	89	4.15
JOHN	CERUTTI	1987	Toronto Blue Jays	AL	11	4	.733	44	21	2	0	0	151 1/3	144	74	59	92	4.40
JOHN	CERUTTI	1988	Toronto Blue Jays	AL	6	7	.462	46	12	2	0	1	123 2/3	120	43	42	65	3.13
JOHN	CERUTTI	1989	Toronto Blue Jays	AL	11	11	.500	33	31	3	1	0	205 1/3	214	70	53	69	3.07
JOHN	CERUTTI	1990	Toronto Blue Jays	AL	9	9	.500	30	23	0	0	2	140	162	74	49	49	4.76
JOHN	CERUTTI	1991	Detroit Tigers	AL	3	6	.333	38	8	1	0	0	88 2/3	94	45	37	29	4.57
ITALO	CHELINI	1935	Chicago White Sox	AL	0	1	.000	2	0	0	0	0	5	7	7	4	1	12.60
ITALO	CHELINI	1936	Chicago White Sox	AL	4	3	.571	18	6	5	0	0	83 2/3	100	46	30	16	4.95
ITALO	CHELINI	1937	Chicago White Sox	AL	1	2	.333	4	0	0	0	0	8 2/3	15	10	0	3	10.38
SCOTT	CHIAMPARINO	1990	Texas Rangers	AL	1	0	1.000	6	6	0	0	0	37 2/3	36	11	12	19	2.63
SCOTT	CHIAMPARINO	1991	Texas Rangers	AL	0	4	.000	5	5	0	0	0	22 1/3	26	10	12	8	4.03
SCOTT	CHIAMPARINO	1992	Texas Rangers	AL	1	1	.500	4	4	0	0	0	25 1/3	25	10	5	13	3.55
MARK	CIARDI	1987	Milwaukee Brewers	AL	0	2	.000	4	3	0	0	0	16 1/3	26	17	9	8	9.37
PETE	CIMINO	1965	Minnesota Twins	AL	0	0		1	0	0	0	0	1	0	0	0	0	0.00
PETE	CIMINO	1966	Minnesota Twins	AL	2	5	.286	35	0	0	0	4	64 2/3	53	21	30	57	2.92

FIRST	LAST	YEAR	TEAM	LEAGUE	W	L	PCT	G	GS	CG	SH	SV	IP	H	ER	BB	K	ER
PETE	CIMINO	1967	California Angels	AL	3	3	.500	46	1	0	0	1	88 1/3	73	32	31	80	3.26
PETE	CIMINO	1968	California Angels	AL	0	0		4	0	0	0	1	7	7	2	4	2	2.57
FRANK	CIMORELLI	1994	St. Louis Cardinals	NL	0	0		11	0	0	0	1	13 1/3	20	13	10	7	8.78
LOU	CIOLA	1943	Philadelphia Athletics	AL	1	3	.250	12	3	2	0	0	43 2/3	48	27	22	4	5.56
RALPH	CITARELLA	1983	St. Louis Cardinals	NL	0	0		6	0	0	0	0	11	8	2	3	4	1.64
RALPH	CITARELLA	1984	St. Louis Cardinals	NL	0	1	.000	10	2	0	0	0	22 1/3	20	9	7	15	3.63
RALPH	CITARELLA	1987	Chicago White Sox	AL	0	0		5	3	0	0	0	11	13	9	4	5	7.36
CHRIS	CODIROLI	1982	Oakland Athletics	AL	1	2	.333	3	3	0	0	0	16 2/3	16	8	4	9	4.32
CHRIS	CODIROLI	1983	Oakland Athletics	AL	12	12	.500	37	31	7	2	1	205 2/3	208	102	72	85	4.46
CHRIS	CODIROLI	1984	Oakland Athletics	AL	6	4	.600	28	14	1	0	0	89 1/3	111	58	34	44	5.84
CHRIS	CODIROLI	1985	Oakland Athletics	AL	14	14	.500	37	37	4	2	0	226	228	112	78	111	4.46
CHRIS	CODIROLI	1986	Oakland Athletics	AL	5	8	.385	16	16	1	0	0	91 2/3	91	41	38	43	4.03
CHRIS	CODIROLI	1987	Oakland Athletics	AL	0	2	.000	3	2	0	0	0	11 1/3	12	11	8	4	8.74
CHRIS	CODIROLI	1988	Cleveland Indians	AL	0	4	.000	14	2	0	0	1	19 1/3	32	20	10	12	9.31
CHRIS	CODIROLI	1990	Kansas City Royals	AL	0	1	.000	6	2	0	0	0	10 1/3	13	11	17	8	9.58
HENRY	COPPOLA	1935	Washington Senators	AL	3	4	.429	19	5	2	1	0	59 1/3	72	39	29	19	5.92
HENRY	COPPOLA	1936	Washington Senators	AL	0	0		6	1	0	0	1	14	17	7	12	7	4.50
JIM	CORSI	1988	Oakland Athletics	AL	0	1	.000	11	0	0	0	0	21 1/3	20	9	6	10	3.80
JIM	CORSI	1989	Oakland Athletics	AL	1	2	.333	22	0	0	0	0	38 1/3	26	8	10	21	1.88
JIM	CORSI	1991	Houston Astros	NL	0	5	.000	47	0	0	0	0	77 2/3	76	32	23	53	3.71
JIM	CORSI	1992	Oakland Athletics	AL	4	2	.667	32	0	0	0	0	44	44	7	18	19	1.43
JIM	CORSI	1993	Florida Marlins	NL	0	2	.000	15	0	0	0	0	20 1/3	28	15	10	7	6.64
JIM	CORSI	1995	Oakland Athletics	AL	2	4	.333	38	0	0	0	2	45	51	11	26	26	2.20
JIM	CORSI	1996	Oakland Athletics	AL	6	0	1.000	57	0	0	0	3	73 2/3	71	33	34	43	4.03
JIM	CORSI	1997	Boston Red Sox	AL	5	3	.625	52	0	0	0	2	57 2/3	56	22	21	40	3.43
JIM	CORSI	1998	Boston Red Sox	AL	3	2	.600	59	0	0	0	2	66	58	19	23	49	2.59
JIM	CORSI	1999	Baltimore Orioles	AL	0	1	.000	13	0	0	0	0	13 1/3	15	4	1	8	2.70
JIM	CORSI	1999	Boston Red Sox	AL	1	2	.333	23	0	0	0	0	24	25	14	19	14	5.25
LEO	CRISTANTE	1951	Philadelphia Phillies	NL	1	1	.500	10	1	0	0	0	22	28	12	9	6	4.91
LEO	CRISTANTE	1955	Detroit Tigers	AL	0	1	.000	20	1	0	0	0	36 2/3	37	13	14	9	3.19
COOKIE	CUCCURULLO	1943	Pittsburgh Pirates	NL	0	0		1	0	0	0	4	7	10	5	3	3	6.43
COOKIE	CUCCURULLO	1944	Pittsburgh Pirates	NL	2	1	.667	32	1	0	0	1	106 1/3	110	48	44	51	4.06
COOKIE	CUCCURULLO	1945	Pittsburgh Pirates	NL	1	3	.250	29	4	0	0	0	56 2/3	68	33	34	17	5.24
John	D'Acquisto	1973	San Francisco Giants	NL	1	1	.500	7	3	1	1	0	27 2/3	23	11	19	29	3.58
John	D'Acquisto	1974	San Francisco Giants	NL	12	14	.462	38	36	5	1	0	215	182	90	124	167	3.77

FIRST	LAST	YEAR	TEAM	LEAGUE	W	L	PCT	G	GS	CG	SH	SV	IP	H	ER	BB	K	ERA
John	D'Acquisto	1975	San Francisco Giants	NL	2	4	.333	10	6	0	0	0	28	29	32	34	22	10.29
John	D'Acquisto	1976	San Francisco Giants	NL	3	8	.273	28	19	0	0	0	106	93	63	102	53	5.35
John	D'Acquisto	1977	San Diego Padres	NL	1	2	.333	17	12	0	0	0	44	49	34	47	45	6.95
John	D'Acquisto	1977	St. Louis Cardinals	NL	0	0		3	2	0	0	0	8 1/3	5	4	10	9	4.32
John	D'Acquisto	1978	San Diego Padres	NL	4	3	.571	45	3	0	1	10	93	60	22	56	104	2.13
John	D'Acquisto	1979	San Diego Padres	NL	9	13	.409	51	11	1	0	2	133 2/3	140	73	86	97	4.92
John	D'Acquisto	1980	Montreal Expos	NL	0	2	.000	11	0	0	0	2	20 2/3	14	5	9	15	2.18
John	D'Acquisto	1980	San Diego Padres	NL	2	3	.400	39	0	0	0	1	67	67	28	36	44	3.76
John	D'Acquisto	1981	California Angels	AL	0	0		6	5	0	0	0	19 1/3	26	23	12	8	10.71
John	D'Acquisto	1982	Oakland Athletics	AL	2	4	.333	11	5	2	0	0	17	20	10	9	7	5.29
PETE	DAGLIA	1932	Chicago White Sox	AL	0	0		12	0	0	0	0	50	67	32	20	16	5.76
Jeff	D'Amico	1996	Milwaukee Brewers	AL	6	6	.500	17	17	1	1	0	86	88	52	31	53	5.44
Jeff	D'Amico	1997	Milwaukee Brewers	AL	9	7	.562	23	23	1	0	0	135 2/3	139	71	43	94	4.71
Jeff	D'Amico	1999	Milwaukee Brewers	AL	0	0		1	0	0	0	0	1	1	0	0	1	0.00
Jeff	D'Amico	2000	Milwaukee Brewers	NL	12	7	.632	23	23	1	1	0	162 1/3	143	48	46	101	2.66
FRANK	DASSO	1945	Cincinnati Reds	NL	4	5	.444	16	12	6	1	0	95 2/3	89	39	53	39	3.67
FRANK	DASSO	1946	Cincinnati Reds	NL	0	0		2	0	1	0	0	1	2	3	2	1	27.00
RICH	DeLUCIA	1990	Seattle Mariners	AL	1	2	.333	5	5	0	0	0	36	30	8	9	20	2.00
RICH	DeLUCIA	1991	Seattle Mariners	AL	12	13	.480	32	31	1	0	1	182	176	103	78	98	5.09
RICH	DeLUCIA	1992	Seattle Mariners	AL	3	6	.333	30	11	0	0	0	83 2/3	100	51	35	66	5.49
RICH	DeLUCIA	1993	Seattle Mariners	AL	3	6	.333	30	1	0	0	0	42 2/3	46	22	23	48	4.64
RICH	DeLUCIA	1994	Cincinnati Reds	NL	0	0		8	0	0	0	0	10 2/3	9	5	5	15	4.22
RICH	DeLUCIA	1995	St. Louis Cardinals	NL	8	7	.533	56	0	0	0	3	82 1/3	63	31	36	76	3.39
RICH	DeLUCIA	1996	San Francisco Giants	NL	3	6	.333	56	0	0	0	0	61 2/3	62	40	31	55	5.84
RICH	DeLUCIA	1997	Anaheim Angels	AL	6	4	.600	33	0	0	0	3	42 1/3	29	17	27	42	3.61
RICH	DeLUCIA	1997	San Francisco Giants	NL	0	0		3	0	0	0	0	1 2/3	6	2	0	2	10.80
RICH	DeLUCIA	1998	Anaheim Angels	AL	2	6	.250	61	0	0	0	1	71 2/3	56	34	46	73	4.27
RICH	DeLUCIA	1999	Cleveland Indians	AL	0	1	.000	6	0	0	0	0	9 1/3	13	7	9	7	6.75
DON	DeMOLA	1974	Montreal Expos	NL	1	0	1.000	25	0	0	0	0	57 2/3	46	20	21	47	3.12
DON	DeMOLA	1975	Montreal Expos	NL	4	7	.364	60	0	0	0	1	97 2/3	92	45	42	63	4.15
TOM	DETTORE	1973	Pittsburgh Pirates	NL	0	1	.000	12	0	0	0	0	22 2/3	33	15	14	13	5.96
TOM	DETTORE	1974	Chicago Cubs	NL	3	5	.375	16	4	0	0	0	64 2/3	64	30	31	43	4.18
TOM	DETTORE	1975	Chicago Cubs	NL	5	4	.556	36	9	1	0	0	85 1/3	88	51	31	46	5.38
TOM	DETTORE	1976	Chicago Cubs	NL	0	1	.000	4	1	0	0	0	7	11	8	2	4	10.29
JACK	DiLAURO	1969	New York Mets	NL	1	4	.200	23	4	0	0	1	63 2/3	50	17	18	27	2.40

FIRST	LAST	YEAR	TEAM	LEAGUE	W	L	PCT	G	GS	CG	SH	SV	IP	H	ER	BB	K	ERA
JACK	DiLAURO	1970	Houston Astros	NL	1	3	.250	42	0	0	0	3	33 2/3	34	16	17	23	4.28
FRANK	DiPINO	1981	Milwaukee Brewers	AL	0	0		2	0	0	0	0	2 1/3	0	0	3	3	0.00
FRANK	DiPINO	1982	Houston Astros	NL	2	2	.500	6	6	0	0	0	28 1/3	32	19	11	25	6.04
FRANK	DiPINO	1983	Houston Astros	NL	3	4	.429	53	0	0	0	20	71 1/3	52	21	20	67	2.65
FRANK	DiPINO	1984	Houston Astros	NL	4	9	.308	57	0	0	0	14	75 1/3	74	28	36	65	3.35
FRANK	DiPINO	1985	Houston Astros	NL	3	7	.300	54	0	0	0	6	76	69	34	43	49	4.03
FRANK	DiPINO	1986	Chicago Cubs	NL	2	4	.333	30	0	0	0	6	40	47	23	14	43	5.17
FRANK	DiPINO	1986	Houston Astros	NL	1	3	.250	31	0	0	0	3	40 1/3	27	16	16	27	3.57
FRANK	DiPINO	1987	Chicago Cubs	NL	3	3	.500	69	0	0	0	4	80	75	28	34	61	3.15
FRANK	DiPINO	1988	Chicago Cubs	NL	2	3	.400	63	0	0	0	6	90 1/3	102	50	32	69	4.98
FRANK	DiPINO	1989	St. Louis Cardinals	NL	9	0	1.000	67	0	0	0	6	88 1/3	73	24	20	44	2.45
FRANK	DiPINO	1990	St. Louis Cardinals	NL	5	2	.714	62	0	0	0	3	81	92	41	31	49	4.56
FRANK	DiPINO	1992	St. Louis Cardinals	NL	0	1		9	0	0	0	0	11	9	2	3	8	1.64
FRANK	DiPINO	1993	Kansas City Royals	AL	1	1	.500	11	0	0	0	1	15 2/3	9	12	6	5	6.89
RON	DiORIO	1973	Philadelphia Phillies	NL	0	0		23	0	0	0	0	19 1/3	18	5	6	11	2.33
RON	DiORIO	1974	Philadelphia Phillies	NL	0	0		2	0	0	0	0	1	2	2	1	0	18.00
JERRY	DiPOTO	1993	Cleveland Indians	AL	4	4	.500	46	0	0	0	11	56 1/3	57	15	30	41	2.40
JERRY	DiPOTO	1994	Cleveland Indians	AL	0	0		7	0	0	0	0	15 2/3	26	14	10	9	8.04
JERRY	DiPOTO	1995	New York Mets	NL	4	6	.400	58	0	0	0	2	78 2/3	77	33	29	49	3.78
JERRY	DiPOTO	1996	New York Mets	NL	7	2	.778	57	0	0	0	0	77 1/3	91	36	45	52	4.19
JERRY	DiPOTO	1997	Colorado Rockies	NL	5	3	.625	74	0	0	0	16	95 2/3	108	50	33	74	4.70
JERRY	DiPOTO	1998	Colorado Rockies	NL	3	4	.429	68	0	0	0	19	71 1/3	61	28	25	49	3.53
JERRY	DiPOTO	1999	Colorado Rockies	NL	4	5	.444	63	0	0	0	1	86 2/3	91	41	44	69	4.26
JERRY	DiPOTO	2000	Colorado Rockies	NL	0	0		17	0	0	0	1	13 2/3	16	6	5	9	3.95
DICK	DRAGO	1969	Kansas City Royals	AL	11	13	.458	41	26	10	2	1	200 2/3	190	84	65	108	3.77
DICK	DRAGO	1970	Kansas City Royals	AL	9	15	.375	35	34	7	1	0	240	239	100	72	127	3.75
DICK	DRAGO	1971	Kansas City Royals	AL	17	11	.607	35	34	15	4	0	241 1/3	251	80	46	109	2.98
DICK	DRAGO	1972	Kansas City Royals	AL	12	17	.414	34	33	11	2	0	239 1/3	230	80	51	135	3.01
DICK	DRAGO	1973	Kansas City Royals	AL	12	14	.462	37	33	8	1	0	212 2/3	252	100	76	98	4.23
DICK	DRAGO	1974	Boston Red Sox	AL	7	10	.412	33	18	0	0	3	175 2/3	165	68	56	90	3.48
DICK	DRAGO	1975	Boston Red Sox	AL	2	2	.500	40	0	0	0	15	72 2/3	69	31	51	43	3.84
DICK	DRAGO	1976	California Angels	AL	7	8	.467	43	0	0	0	6	79 1/3	80	39	31	43	4.42
DICK	DRAGO	1977	Baltimore Orioles	AL	6	3	.667	36	0	0	0	3	39 2/3	49	16	15	20	3.63
DICK	DRAGO	1977	California Angels	AL	0	1	.000	13	0	0	0	2	21	22	7	3	15	3.00
DICK	DRAGO	1978	Boston Red Sox	AL	4	4	.500	37	1	0	0	7	77 1/3	71	26	32	42	3.03

FIRST	LAST	YEAR	TEAM	LEAGUE	W	L	PCT	G	GS	CG	SH	SV	IP	H	ER	BB	K	ER
DICK	DRAGO	1979	Boston Red Sox	AL	10	6	.625	53	1	0	0	13	89	85	30	21	67	3.03
DICK	DRAGO	1980	Boston Red Sox	AL	7	7	.500	43	7	0	0	3	132 2/3	127	61	44	63	4.14
DICK	DRAGO	1981	Seattle Mariners	AL	4	6	.400	39	0	0	0	5	53 2/3	71	33	15	27	5.53
DAVE	DRAVECKY	1982	San Diego Padres	NL	5	3	.625	31	10	0	1	2	105	86	30	33	59	2.57
DAVE	DRAVECKY	1983	San Diego Padres	NL	14	10	.583	28	28	9	1	0	183 2/3	181	73	44	74	3.58
DAVE	DRAVECKY	1984	San Diego Padres	NL	9	8	.529	50	14	3	2	8	156 2/3	125	51	51	71	2.93
DAVE	DRAVECKY	1985	San Diego Padres	NL	13	11	.542	34	31	7	2	0	214 2/3	200	70	57	105	2.93
DAVE	DRAVECKY	1986	San Diego Padres	NL	9	11	.450	26	26	3	1	0	161 1/3	149	55	54	87	3.07
DAVE	DRAVECKY	1987	San Diego Padres	NL	3	7	.300	18	10	1	0	0	79	71	33	31	60	3.76
DAVE	DRAVECKY	1987	San Francisco Giants	NL	7	5	.583	18	18	4	3	0	112 1/3	115	40	33	78	3.20
DAVE	DRAVECKY	1988	San Francisco Giants	NL	2	2	.500	7	7	0	0	0	37	33	13	8	19	3.16
DAVE	DRAVECKY	1989	San Francisco Giants	NL	2	0	1.000	2	2	0	0	0	13	8	5	4	5	3.46
JIM	DUFFALO	1961	San Francisco Giants	NL	5	1	.833	24	4	1	0	1	61 2/3	59	29	32	37	4.23
JIM	DUFFALO	1962	San Francisco Giants	NL	1	2	.333	24	2	0	0	0	42	42	17	23	29	3.64
JIM	DUFFALO	1963	San Francisco Giants	NL	4	2	.667	34	5	0	0	2	75 1/3	56	24	37	55	2.87
JIM	DUFFALO	1964	San Francisco Giants	NL	5	1	.833	35	3	0	0	3	74	57	24	31	55	2.92
JIM	DUFFALO	1965	Cincinnati Reds	NL	0	1	.000	22	0	0	0	0	44 1/3	33	17	30	34	3.45
JIM	DUFFALO	1965	San Francisco Giants	NL	0	0	.000	2	0	0	0	0	0 1/3	1	1	2	0	27.00
FRANK	EUFEMIA	1985	Minnesota Twins	AL	4	2	.667	39	0	0	0	2	61 2/3	56	26	21	30	3.79
PETE	FALCONE	1975	San Francisco Giants	NL	12	11	.522	39	32	3	1	0	190	171	88	111	131	4.17
PETE	FALCONE	1976	San Francisco Giants	NL	12	16	.429	32	32	9	2	0	212	173	76	93	138	3.23
PETE	FALCONE	1977	St. Louis Cardinals	NL	4	8	.333	27	22	2	0	1	124	130	75	61	75	5.44
PETE	FALCONE	1978	St. Louis Cardinals	NL	2	7	.222	19	14	2	0	2	75	94	48	48	28	5.76
PETE	FALCONE	1979	New York Mets	NL	6	14	.300	31	31	0	1	0	184	194	85	76	113	4.16
PETE	FALCONE	1980	New York Mets	NL	7	10	.412	37	23	1	1	1	157 1/3	163	79	58	109	4.52
PETE	FALCONE	1981	New York Mets	NL	5	3	.625	35	9	3	1	1	95 1/3	84	27	36	56	2.55
PETE	FALCONE	1982	New York Mets	NL	8	10	.444	40	23	2	0	2	171	159	73	71	101	3.84
PETE	FALCONE	1983	Atlanta Braves	NL	9	4	.692	33	15	2	1	2	106 2/3	102	43	60	59	3.63
PETE	FALCONE	1984	Atlanta Braves	NL	5	7	.417	35	16	2	0	2	120	115	55	57	55	4.12
JEFF	FASSERO	1991	Montreal Expos	NL	2	5	.286	51	0	0	0	8	55 1/3	39	15	17	42	2.44
JEFF	FASSERO	1992	Montreal Expos	NL	8	7	.533	70	0	0	0	1	85 2/3	81	27	34	63	2.84
JEFF	FASSERO	1993	Montreal Expos	NL	12	5	.706	56	15	0	0	1	149 2/3	119	38	54	140	2.29
JEFF	FASSERO	1994	Montreal Expos	NL	8	6	.571	21	21	1	0	0	138 2/3	119	46	40	119	2.99
JEFF	FASSERO	1995	Montreal Expos	NL	13	14	.481	30	30	1	1	0	189	207	91	74	164	4.33
JEFF	FASSERO	1996	Montreal Expos	NL	15	11	.577	34	34	5	1	0	231 2/3	217	85	55	222	3.30

FIRST	LAST	YEAR	TEAM	LEAGUE	W	L	PCT	G	GS	CG	SH	SV	IP	H	ER	BB	K	ER
JEFF	FASSERO	1997	Seattle Mariners	AL	16	9	.640	35	35	2	1	0	234 1/3	226	94	84	189	3.61
JEFF	FASSERO	1998	Seattle Mariners	AL	13	12	.520	32	32	7	0	0	224 2/3	223	99	66	176	3.97
JEFF	FASSERO	1999	Seattle Mariners	AL	4	14	.222	30	24	0	0	0	139	188	114	73	101	7.38
JEFF	FASSERO	1999	Texas Rangers	AL	1	0	1.000	7	3	0	0	0	17 1/3	20	11	10	13	5.71
JEFF	FASSERO	2000	Boston Red Sox	AL	8	8	.500	38	23	0	0	0	130	153	69	50	97	4.78
JEFF	FASSERO	2001	Chicago Cubs	NL	4	4	.500	82	0	0	0	12	73 2/3	66	28	23	79	3.42
DON	FERRARESE	1955	Baltimore Orioles	AL	0	0		6	0	0	0	2	9	8	3	11	5	3.00
DON	FERRARESE	1956	Baltimore Orioles	AL	4	10	.286	36	14	3	1	0	102	86	57	64	81	5.03
DON	FERRARESE	1957	Baltimore Orioles	AL	1	1	.500	6	2	0	0	2	19	14	10	12	13	4.74
DON	FERRARESE	1958	Cleveland Indians	AL	3	4	.429	28	10	2	0	1	94 2/3	91	39	46	62	3.71
DON	FERRARESE	1959	Cleveland Indians	AL	5	3	.625	15	10	4	0	0	76	58	27	51	45	3.20
DON	FERRARESE	1960	Chicago White Sox	AL	0	0	.000	5	0	0	0	1	4	8	8	9	4	18.00
DON	FERRARESE	1961	Philadelphia Phillies	NL	5	12	.294	42	14	3	1	0	138 2/3	120	58	68	89	3.76
DON	FERRARESE	1962	Philadelphia Phillies	NL	0	0	.000	5	0	0	0	0	6 2/3	9	6	3	6	8.10
DON	FERRARESE	1962	St. Louis Cardinals	NL	1	4	.200	38	0	0	0	1	56 2/3	55	17	31	45	2.70
BILL	FERRAZZI	1935	Philadelphia Athletics	AL	1	2	.333	3	2	1	0	0	7	7	4	5	0	5.14
TIM	FORTUGNO	1992	California Angels	AL	1	1	.500	14	5	1	1	1	41 2/3	37	24	19	31	5.18
TIM	FORTUGNO	1994	Cincinnati Reds	NL	1	0	1.000	25	0	0	0	0	30	32	14	14	29	4.20
TIM	FORTUGNO	1995	Chicago White Sox	AL	1	3	.250	57	0	0	0	0	38 2/3	30	24	19	24	5.59
JOHN	FRANCO	1984	Cincinnati Reds	NL	6	2	.750	54	0	0	0	4	79 1/3	74	23	36	55	2.61
JOHN	FRANCO	1985	Cincinnati Reds	NL	12	3	.800	67	0	0	0	12	99	83	24	40	61	2.18
JOHN	FRANCO	1986	Cincinnati Reds	NL	6	6	.500	74	0	0	0	29	101	90	33	44	84	2.94
JOHN	FRANCO	1987	Cincinnati Reds	NL	8	5	.615	68	0	0	0	32	82	76	23	27	61	2.52
JOHN	FRANCO	1988	Cincinnati Reds	NL	6	6	.500	70	0	0	0	39	86	60	15	27	46	1.57
JOHN	FRANCO	1989	Cincinnati Reds	NL	4	8	.333	60	0	0	0	32	80 2/3	77	28	36	60	3.12
JOHN	FRANCO	1990	New York Mets	NL	5	3	.625	55	0	0	0	33	67 2/3	66	19	21	56	2.53
JOHN	FRANCO	1991	New York Mets	NL	5	9	.357	52	0	0	0	30	55 1/3	61	18	18	45	2.93
JOHN	FRANCO	1992	New York Mets	NL	6	2	.750	31	0	0	0	15	33	24	6	11	20	1.64
JOHN	FRANCO	1993	New York Mets	NL	4	3	.571	35	0	0	0	10	36 1/3	46	21	19	29	5.20
JOHN	FRANCO	1994	New York Mets	NL	1	4	.200	47	0	0	0	30	50	47	15	19	42	2.70
JOHN	FRANCO	1995	New York Mets	NL	5	3	.625	48	0	0	0	29	51 2/3	48	14	17	41	2.44
JOHN	FRANCO	1996	New York Mets	NL	4	3	.571	51	0	0	0	28	54	54	11	21	48	1.83
JOHN	FRANCO	1997	New York Mets	NL	5	3	.625	59	0	0	0	36	60	49	17	20	53	2.55
JOHN	FRANCO	1998	New York Mets	NL	0	8	.000	61	0	0	0	38	64 2/3	66	26	29	59	3.62
JOHN	FRANCO	1999	New York Mets	NL	0	2	.000	46	0	0	0	19	40 2/3	40	13	19	41	2.88

FIRST	LAST	YEAR	TEAM	LEAGUE	W	L	PCT	G	GS	CG	SH	SV	IP	H	ER	BB	K	ER
JOHN	FRANCO	2000	New York Mets	NL	5	4	.556	62	0	0	0	4	55 2/3	46	21	26	56	3.40
JOHN	FRANCO	2001	New York Mets	NL	6	2	.750	58	0	0	0	2	53 1/3	55	24	19	50	4.05
JOHN	FRASCATORE	1994	St. Louis Cardinals	NL	0	1	.000	1	1	0	0	0	3 1/3	7	6	2	2	16.20
JOHN	FRASCATORE	1995	St. Louis Cardinals	NL	5	2	.714	59	4	0	0	0	32 2/3	39	16	16	21	4.41
JOHN	FRASCATORE	1997	St. Louis Cardinals	NL	3	4	.429	69	0	0	0	0	80	74	22	33	58	2.48
JOHN	FRASCATORE	1998	St. Louis Cardinals	NL	1	4	.200	26	0	0	0	0	95 2/3	95	44	36	49	4.14
JOHN	FRASCATORE	1999	Arizona Diamondbacks	NL	7	1	.875	33	0	0	0	1	33	31	15	12	15	4.09
JOHN	FRASCATORE	1999	Toronto Blue Jays	AL	2	4	.333	60	0	0	0	0	37	42	14	9	22	3.41
JOHN	FRASCATORE	2000	Toronto Blue Jays	AL	1	0	1.000	57	0	0	0	0	73	87	44	33	30	5.42
JOHN	FRASCATORE	2001	Toronto Blue Jays	AL	1	0	1.000	14	0	0	0	0	16 1/3	16	4	4	9	2.20
MARION	FRICANO	1952	Philadelphia Athletics	AL	1	0	1.000	2	0	0	0	0	5	5	1	1	0	1.80
MARION	FRICANO	1953	Philadelphia Athletics	AL	9	12	.429	39	23	10	0	1	211	206	91	90	67	3.88
MARION	FRICANO	1954	Philadelphia Athletics	AL	5	11	.312	37	20	4	0	0	151 2/3	163	87	64	43	5.16
MARION	FRICANO	1955	Kansas City Athletics	AL	0	0		10	0	0	0	0	20	19	7	9	5	3.15
DANNY	FRISELLA	1967	New York Mets	NL	1	6	.143	14	11	0	0	0	74	68	28	33	51	3.41
DANNY	FRISELLA	1968	New York Mets	NL	2	4	.333	19	4	0	0	2	50 2/3	53	22	17	47	3.91
DANNY	FRISELLA	1969	New York Mets	NL	0	0		3	1	0	0	0	4 2/3	8	4	3	5	7.71
DANNY	FRISELLA	1970	New York Mets	NL	8	3	.727	30	0	0	0	1	65 2/3	49	22	34	54	3.02
DANNY	FRISELLA	1971	New York Mets	NL	8	5	.615	53	0	0	0	12	90 2/3	76	20	30	93	1.99
DANNY	FRISELLA	1972	New York Mets	NL	5	8	.385	39	0	0	0	9	67 1/3	63	25	20	46	3.34
DANNY	FRISELLA	1973	Atlanta Braves	NL	1	2	.333	42	0	0	0	8	45	40	21	23	27	4.20
DANNY	FRISELLA	1974	Atlanta Braves	NL	3	4	.429	56	0	0	0	6	41 2/3	37	24	28	27	5.18
DANNY	FRISELLA	1975	San Diego Padres	NL	1	6	.143	65	0	0	0	6	97 2/3	86	34	51	67	3.13
DANNY	FRISELLA	1976	Milwaukee Brewers	AL	5	2	.714	32	0	0	0	9	49 1/3	30	15	34	43	2.74
DANNY	FRISELLA	1976	St. Louis Cardinals	NL	0	0		18	0	0	0	1	22 2/3	19	10	13	11	3.97
BOB	GALASSO	1977	Seattle Mariners	AL	0	6	.000	11	7	0	0	0	35	57	35	8	21	9.00
BOB	GALASSO	1979	Milwaukee Brewers	AL	3	1	.750	31	1	0	0	3	51 1/3	64	25	26	28	4.38
BOB	GALASSO	1981	Seattle Mariners	AL	1	1	.500	13	0	0	0	1	31 2/3	32	17	13	14	4.83
BOB	GARIBALDI	1962	San Francisco Giants	NL	0	0		9	0	0	0	0	12 1/3	13	7	5	9	5.11
BOB	GARIBALDI	1963	San Francisco Giants	NL	0	1	.000	4	0	0	0	0	8	8	1	4	4	1.12
BOB	GARIBALDI	1966	San Francisco Giants	NL	0	0		1	0	0	0	0	1	0	0	1	0	0.00
BOB	GARIBALDI	1969	San Francisco Giants	NL	0	0		3	0	0	0	0	5	6	1	2	1	1.80
WILLIE	GARONI	1899	New York Giants	NL	0	1	.000	1	1	1	0	0	10	12	5	2	2	4.50
DAVE	GIUSTI	1962	Houston Colt. 45s	NL	2	3	.400	22	5	0	0	0	73 2/3	82	46	30	43	5.62
DAVE	GIUSTI	1964	Houston Colt. 45s	NL	0	0		8	0	0	0	0	25 2/3	24	9	8	16	3.16

FIRST	LAST	YEAR	TEAM	LEAGUE	W	L	PCT	G	GS	CG	SH	SV	IP	H	ER	BB	K	ER
DAVE	GIUSTI	1965	Houston Colt. 45s	NL	8	7	.533	38	13	4	1	3	131 1/3	132	63	46	92	4.32
DAVE	GIUSTI	1966	Houston Astros	NL	15	14	.517	34	33	9	4	0	210	215	98	54	131	4.20
DAVE	GIUSTI	1967	Houston Astros	NL	11	15	.423	37	33	8	1	1	221 2/3	231	103	58	157	4.18
DAVE	GIUSTI	1968	Houston Astros	NL	11	14	.440	37	34	12	1	0	251	226	89	67	186	3.19
DAVE	GIUSTI	1969	St. Louis Cardinals	NL	3	7	.300	22	12	2	2	0	99 2/3	96	40	37	62	3.61
DAVE	GIUSTI	1970	Pittsburgh Pirates	NL	9	3	.750	66	1	2	0	26	103	98	35	39	85	3.06
DAVE	GIUSTI	1971	Pittsburgh Pirates	NL	5	6	.455	58	0	0	0	30	86	79	28	31	55	2.93
DAVE	GIUSTI	1972	Pittsburgh Pirates	NL	7	4	.636	54	0	0	0	22	74 2/3	59	16	20	54	1.93
DAVE	GIUSTI	1973	Pittsburgh Pirates	NL	9	2	.818	67	0	0	0	20	98 2/3	89	26	37	64	2.37
DAVE	GIUSTI	1974	Pittsburgh Pirates	NL	7	5	.583	64	2	0	0	12	105 2/3	101	39	40	53	3.32
DAVE	GIUSTI	1975	Pittsburgh Pirates	NL	5	4	.556	61	0	0	0	17	91 2/3	79	30	42	38	2.95
DAVE	GIUSTI	1976	Pittsburgh Pirates	NL	5	4	.556	40	0	0	0	6	58 1/3	59	28	27	24	4.32
DAVE	GIUSTI	1977	Chicago Cubs	NL	2	2	.000	20	0	0	0	1	25 1/3	30	17	14	15	6.04
DAVE	GIUSTI	1977	Oakland Athletics	AL	3	3	.500	40	0	0	0	6	60 1/3	54	20	20	28	2.98
GUIDO	GRILLI	1966	Boston Red Sox	AL	0	1	.000	6	0	0	0	0	4 2/3	5	4	9	4	7.71
GUIDO	GRILLI	1966	Kansas City Athletics	AL	0	0	.000	16	0	0	0	0	15 2/3	19	12	11	8	6.89
STEVE	GRILLI	1975	Detroit Tigers	AL	0	0		3	0	0	0	0	6 2/3	3	1	6	5	1.35
STEVE	GRILLI	1976	Detroit Tigers	AL	3	1	.750	36	0	0	0	3	66	63	34	41	36	4.64
STEVE	GRILLI	1977	Detroit Tigers	AL	1	2	.333	30	2	0	0	0	72 2/3	71	39	49	49	4.83
STEVE	GRILLI	1979	Toronto Blue Jays	AL	0	0		1	0	0	0	0	2 1/3	1	0	0	1	0.00
FRANK	LaCORTE	1975	Atlanta Braves	NL	0	3	.000	3	2	0	0	0	13 2/3	13	8	6	10	5.27
FRANK	LaCORTE	1976	Atlanta Braves	NL	3	12	.200	19	17	1	0	0	105 1/3	97	55	53	79	4.70
FRANK	LaCORTE	1977	Atlanta Braves	NL	1	8	.111	14	7	0	0	0	57	67	48	29	28	11.68
FRANK	LaCORTE	1978	Atlanta Braves	NL	0	1	.000	2	2	0	0	0	14 2/3	9	6	4	7	3.68
FRANK	LaCORTE	1979	Atlanta Braves	NL	0	0		6	3	0	0	0	8 1/3	9	7	5	6	7.56
FRANK	LaCORTE	1979	Houston Astros	NL	1	2	.333	12	0	0	0	11	27	21	15	10	24	5.00
FRANK	LaCORTE	1980	Houston Astros	NL	8	5	.615	55	0	0	0	5	83	61	26	43	66	2.82
FRANK	LaCORTE	1981	Houston Astros	NL	4	2	.667	37	0	0	0	7	42	41	17	21	40	3.64
FRANK	LaCORTE	1982	Houston Astros	NL	1	5	.167	55	0	0	0	3	76 1/3	71	38	46	51	4.48
FRANK	LaCORTE	1983	Houston Astros	NL	4	4	.500	57	1	0	0	3	53 1/3	35	30	28	48	5.06
FRANK	LaCORTE	1984	California Angels	AL	2	2	.333	13	1	0	0	0	29 1/3	33	23	13	13	7.06
AL	LaMACCHIA	1943	St. Louis Browns	AL	0	0		1	0	0	0	0	4	9	5	2	2	11.25
AL	LaMACCHIA	1945	St. Louis Browns	AL	2	0	1.000	5	0	0	0	0	9	6	2	3	2	2.00
AL	LaMACCHIA	1946	St. Louis Browns	AL	0	0		8	0	0	0	0	15	17	10	7	3	6.00
AL	LaMACCHIA	1946	Washington Senators	AL	0	1	.000	2	0	0	0	0	2 2/3	6	5	2	0	16.88

FIRST	LAST	YEAR	TEAM	LEAGUE	W	L	PCT	G	GS	CG	SH	SV	IP	H	ER	BB	K	ER
FRANK	LaMANNA	1940	Boston Braves	NL	1	0	1.000	5	1	1	0	0	13 1/3	13	7	8	3	4.72
FRANK	LaMANNA	1941	Boston Braves	NL	5	4	.556	35	4	1	0	1	72 2/3	77	43	56	23	5.33
FRANK	LaMANNA	1942	Boston Braves	NL	0	1	.000	5	0	0	0	0	6 2/3	5	4	3	2	5.40
WALT	LANFRANCONI	1941	Chicago Cubs	NL	0	1	.000	2	1	0	0	0	6	7	2	2	1	3.00
WALT	LANFRANCONI	1947	Boston Braves	NL	4	4	.500	36	4	1	0	1	64	65	21	27	18	2.95
TOM	LASORDA	1954	Brooklyn Dodgers	NL	0	0		4	0	0	0	0	9	8	5	5	4	5.00
TOM	LASORDA	1955	Brooklyn Dodgers	NL	0	0		4	1	0	0	0	4	5	6	6	4	13.50
TOM	LASORDA	1956	Kansas City Athletics	AL	0	4	.000	18	5	0	0	0	45 1/3	40	31	45	28	6.15
MARK	LEMONGELLO	1976	Houston Astros	NL	3	1	.750	34	4	0	0	0	29	26	9	7	9	2.79
MARK	LEMONGELLO	1977	Houston Astros	NL	9	14	.391	34	30	5	0	0	214 2/3	237	83	52	83	3.48
MARK	LEMONGELLO	1978	Houston Astros	NL	9	14	.391	33	30	5	1	1	210 1/3	204	92	66	77	3.94
MARK	LEMONGELLO	1979	Toronto Blue Jays	AL	1	9	.100	18	10	2	0	0	83	97	58	34	40	6.29
ANGELO	LIPETRI	1956	Philadelphia Phillies	NL	0	0		6	0	0	0	0	11	7	4	3	8	3.27
ANGELO	LIPETRI	1958	Philadelphia Phillies	NL	0	0		4	0	0	0	0	4	6	5	0	1	11.25
VIC	LOMBARDI	1945	Brooklyn Dodgers	NL	10	11	.476	38	24	9	2	4	203 2/3	195	75	86	64	3.31
VIC	LOMBARDI	1946	Brooklyn Dodgers	NL	13	10	.565	41	25	13	2	3	193	170	62	84	60	2.89
VIC	LOMBARDI	1947	Brooklyn Dodgers	NL	12	11	.522	33	20	7	3	3	174 2/3	156	58	65	72	2.99
VIC	LOMBARDI	1948	Pittsburgh Pirates	NL	10	9	.526	38	17	9	0	4	163	156	67	67	54	3.70
VIC	LOMBARDI	1949	Pittsburgh Pirates	NL	5	5	.500	34	12	4	0	1	134	149	68	68	64	4.57
VIC	LOMBARDI	1950	Pittsburgh Pirates	NL	0	5	.000	39	2	0	0	1	76 1/3	93	56	48	26	6.60
LOU	LOMBARDO	1948	New York Giants	NL	0	0		2	0	0	0	0	5 1/3	5	4	5	8	6.75
RALPH	LUMENTI	1957	Washington Senators	AL	0	1	.000	3	2	0	0	0	9 1/3	9	7	5	8	6.75
RALPH	LUMENTI	1958	Washington Senators	AL	1	2	.333	8	4	0	0	0	21	21	20	36	20	8.57
RALPH	LUMENTI	1959	Washington Senators	AL	0	0		2	0	0	0	0	3	2	0	1	2	0.00
SAL	MAGLIE	1945	New York Giants	NL	5	4	.556	13	10	7	3	0	84 1/3	72	22	22	32	2.35
SAL	MAGLIE	1950	New York Giants	NL	18	4	.818	47	16	12	5	1	206	169	62	86	96	2.71
SAL	MAGLIE	1951	New York Giants	NL	23	6	.793	42	37	22	3	4	298	254	97	86	146	2.93
SAL	MAGLIE	1952	New York Giants	NL	18	8	.692	35	31	12	5	0	216	199	70	75	112	2.92
SAL	MAGLIE	1953	New York Giants	NL	8	9	.471	27	24	9	3	2	145 1/3	158	67	47	80	4.15
SAL	MAGLIE	1954	New York Giants	NL	14	6	.700	34	32	9	1	2	218 1/3	222	79	70	117	3.26
SAL	MAGLIE	1955	Cleveland Indians	AL	0	2	.000	10	2	0	0	2	25 2/3	26	11	7	11	3.86
SAL	MAGLIE	1955	New York Giants	NL	9	5	.643	23	21	6	3	0	129 2/3	142	54	48	71	3.75
SAL	MAGLIE	1956	Brooklyn Dodgers	NL	13	5	.722	28	26	9	0	0	191	154	61	52	108	2.87
SAL	MAGLIE	1956	Cleveland Indians	AL	0	0		2	0	0	0	0	5	6	2	2	2	3.60
SAL	MAGLIE	1957	Brooklyn Dodgers	NL	6	6	.500	19	17	4	1	1	101 1/3	94	33	26	50	2.93

FIRST	LAST	YEAR	TEAM	LEAGUE	W	L	PCT	G	GS	CG	SH	SV	IP	H	ER	BB	K	ER
SAL	MAGLIE	1957	New York Yankees	AL	2	0	1.000	6	3	1	1	3	26	22	5	7	9	1.73
SAL	MAGLIE	1958	New York Yankees	AL	1	1	.500	7	3	0	0	0	23 1/3	27	12	9	7	4.63
SAL	MAGLIE	1958	St. Louis Cardinals	NL	2	6	.250	10	10	2	0	0	53	46	28	25	21	4.75
MIKE	MAGNANTE	1991	Kansas City Royals	AL	0	1	.000	38	0	0	0	0	55	55	15	23	42	2.45
MIKE	MAGNANTE	1992	Kansas City Royals	AL	4	9	.308	44	12	0	0	0	89 1/3	115	49	35	31	4.94
MIKE	MAGNANTE	1993	Kansas City Royals	AL	1	2	.333	7	6	0	0	0	51 1/3	37	16	11	16	4.08
MIKE	MAGNANTE	1994	Kansas City Royals	AL	2	3	.400	36	1	0	0	0	47	55	24	16	21	4.60
MIKE	MAGNANTE	1995	Kansas City Royals	AL	2	2	.500	28	0	0	0	0	44 2/3	45	21	16	28	4.23
MIKE	MAGNANTE	1996	Kansas City Royals	AL	2	2	.500	38	1	0	0	0	54	58	34	24	32	5.67
MIKE	MAGNANTE	1997	Houston Astros	NL	3	1	.750	40	0	0	0	1	47 2/3	39	12	11	43	2.27
MIKE	MAGNANTE	1998	Houston Astros	NL	4	7	.364	48	0	0	0	2	51 2/3	56	28	26	39	4.88
MIKE	MAGNANTE	1999	Anaheim Angels	AL	5	2	.714	53	0	0	0	0	69 1/3	68	26	29	44	3.38
MIKE	MAGNANTE	2000	Oakland Athletics	AL	1	1	.500	55	0	0	0	0	39 2/3	50	19	19	17	4.31
MIKE	MAGNANTE	2001	Oakland Athletics	AL	3	1	.750	65	0	0	0	0	55 1/3	50	17	13	23	2.77
PETE	MAGRINI	1966	Boston Red Sox	AL	0	1	.000	3	1	0	0	0	7 1/3	8	8	8	3	9.82
JOE	MARGONERI	1956	New York Giants	NL	6	6	.500	23	13	2	0	0	91 2/3	88	40	49	49	3.93
JOE	MARGONERI	1957	New York Giants	NL	1	1	.500	13	2	0	0	0	34 1/3	44	20	21	18	5.24
LOU	MARONE	1969	Pittsburgh Pirates	NL	1	1	.500	29	0	0	0	0	35 1/3	24	10	13	25	2.55
LOU	MARONE	1970	Pittsburgh Pirates	NL	0	0	—	1	0	0	0	0	2 1/3	2	1	0	0	3.86
JOE	MARTINA	1924	Washington Senators	AL	6	8	.429	24	13	8	0	0	125 1/3	129	65	56	57	4.67
WEDO	MARTINI	1935	Philadelphia Athletics	AL	0	2	.000	3	2	0	0	0	6 1/3	8	12	11	1	17.05
RALPH	MAURIELLO	1958	Los Angeles Dodgers	NL	1	1	.500	3	2	0	0	0	11 2/3	10	6	8	11	4.63
MIKE	MEOLA	1933	Boston Red Sox	AL	0	0	—	3	1	0	0	1	2 1/3	5	6	2	1	23.14
MIKE	MEOLA	1936	Boston Red Sox	AL	0	2	.000	6	3	0	0	0	21 1/3	29	13	10	8	5.48
MIKE	MEOLA	1936	St. Louis Browns	AL	0	1	.000	9	0	0	0	0	19 1/3	29	20	13	6	9.31
DAN	MICELI	1993	Pittsburgh Pirates	NL	0	1	.000	9	0	0	0	0	5 1/3	6	3	3	4	5.06
DAN	MICELI	1994	Pittsburgh Pirates	NL	2	1	.667	28	0	0	0	2	27 1/3	28	18	11	27	5.93
DAN	MICELI	1995	Pittsburgh Pirates	NL	4	4	.500	58	0	0	0	21	58	61	30	28	56	4.66
DAN	MICELI	1996	Pittsburgh Pirates	NL	2	10	.167	44	0	0	0	3	85 2/3	99	55	45	66	5.78
DAN	MICELI	1997	Detroit Tigers	AL	3	2	.600	71	0	0	0	2	82 2/3	77	46	38	79	5.01
DAN	MICELI	1998	San Diego Padres	NL	10	5	.667	67	0	0	0	2	72 2/3	64	26	27	70	3.22
DAN	MICELI	1999	San Diego Padres	NL	4	5	.444	66	0	0	0	1	68 2/3	67	34	36	59	4.46
DAN	MICELI	2000	Florida Marlins	NL	6	4	.600	45	0	0	0	0	48 2/3	45	23	18	40	4.25
DAN	MICELI	2001	Colorado Rockies	NL	2	0	1.000	22	0	0	0	1	20 1/3	18	5	5	17	2.21
DAN	MICELI	2001	Florida Marlins	NL	0	5	.000	29	0	0	0	0	24 2/3	29	19	11	31	6.93

FIRST	LAST	YEAR	TEAM	LEAGUE	W	L	PCT	G	GS	CG	SH	SV	IP	H	ER	BB	K	ER
SAM	MILITELLO	1992	New York Yankees	AL	3	3	.500	9	9	0	0	0	60	43	23	32	42	3.45
SAM	MILITELLO	1993	New York Yankees	AL	1	1	.500	3	2	0	0	0	9 1/3	10	7	7	5	6.75
CRAIG	MINETTO	1978	Oakland Athletics	AL	0	0		4	1	0	0	0	12	13	5	7	3	3.75
CRAIG	MINETTO	1979	Oakland Athletics	AL	1	5	.167	36	13	0	0	0	118 1/3	131	73	58	64	5.55
CRAIG	MINETTO	1980	Oakland Athletics	AL	0	2	.000	7	1	0	0	0	8	11	7	3	5	7.88
CRAIG	MINETTO	1981	Oakland Athletics	AL	0	0		8	0	0	0	1	6 2/3	7	2	4	4	2.70
STEVE	MINGORI	1970	Cleveland Indians	AL	1	0	1.000	21	0	0	0	1	20 1/3	17	6	12	16	2.66
STEVE	MINGORI	1971	Cleveland Indians	AL	1	2	.333	54	0	0	0	4	56 2/3	31	9	24	45	1.43
STEVE	MINGORI	1972	Cleveland Indians	AL	0	6	.000	41	0	0	0	10	57	67	25	36	47	3.95
STEVE	MINGORI	1973	Cleveland Indians	AL	0	0		5	0	0	0	0	11 2/3	10	8	10	4	6.17
STEVE	MINGORI	1973	Kansas City Royals	AL	3	3	.500	19	0	0	0	1	56 1/3	59	19	23	46	3.04
STEVE	MINGORI	1974	Kansas City Royals	AL	2	3	.400	36	0	0	0	2	67 1/3	53	21	23	43	2.81
STEVE	MINGORI	1975	Kansas City Royals	AL	0	3	.000	36	0	0	0	2	50 1/3	42	14	20	25	2.50
STEVE	MINGORI	1976	Kansas City Royals	AL	5	5	.500	55	0	0	0	10	85 1/3	73	22	25	38	2.32
STEVE	MINGORI	1977	Kansas City Royals	AL	2	4	.333	43	0	0	0	4	64	59	22	19	19	3.09
STEVE	MINGORI	1978	Kansas City Royals	AL	1	4	.200	45	0	0	0	7	69	69	21	16	28	2.74
STEVE	MINGORI	1979	Kansas City Royals	AL	3	3	.500	30	1	0	0	0	46 2/3	69	30	17	18	5.79
GINO	MINUTELLI	1990	Cincinnati Reds	NL	0	0		2	0	0	0	0	1	0	1	2	0	9.00
GINO	MINUTELLI	1991	Cincinnati Reds	NL	0	2	.000	16	3	0	0	0	25 1/3	30	17	18	21	6.04
GINO	MINUTELLI	1993	San Francisco Giants	NL	0	1	.000	9	0	0	0	1	14 1/3	7	6	15	10	3.77
PAUL	MIRABELLA	1978	Texas Rangers	AL	3	2	.600	10	4	0	0	0	28	30	18	17	23	5.79
PAUL	MIRABELLA	1979	New York Yankees	AL	0	2	.000	10	0	0	0	0	14 1/3	16	14	10	4	8.79
PAUL	MIRABELLA	1980	Toronto Blue Jays	AL	5	12	.294	33	22	3	0	0	130 2/3	151	63	66	53	4.34
PAUL	MIRABELLA	1981	Toronto Blue Jays	AL	0	0		8	1	0	0	3	14 2/3	20	12	7	9	7.36
PAUL	MIRABELLA	1982	Texas Rangers	AL	2	2	.500	40	0	0	0	0	50 2/3	46	27	22	29	4.80
PAUL	MIRABELLA	1983	Baltimore Orioles	AL	0	0		3	2	0	0	3	9 2/3	9	6	7	4	5.59
PAUL	MIRABELLA	1984	Seattle Mariners	AL	2	5	.286	52	1	0	0	0	68	74	33	32	41	4.37
PAUL	MIRABELLA	1985	Seattle Mariners	AL	0	0		10	0	0	0	3	13 2/3	9	2	4	8	1.32
PAUL	MIRABELLA	1986	Seattle Mariners	AL	0	0		8	0	0	0	0	6 1/3	13	6	3	6	8.53
PAUL	MIRABELLA	1987	Milwaukee Brewers	AL	2	1	.667	29	0	0	0	2	29 1/3	30	16	16	14	4.91
PAUL	MIRABELLA	1988	Milwaukee Brewers	AL	2	2	.500	38	0	0	0	4	60	44	11	21	33	1.65
PAUL	MIRABELLA	1989	Milwaukee Brewers	AL	0	0		13	0	0	0	0	15 1/3	18	13	7	6	7.63
PAUL	MIRABELLA	1990	Milwaukee Brewers	AL	4	2	.667	44	2	0	0	0	59	66	26	27	28	3.97
JOHN	MONTEFUSCO	1974	San Francisco Giants	NL	3	2	.600	7	5	1	0	0	39 1/3	41	21	19	34	4.81
JOHN	MONTEFUSCO	1975	San Francisco Giants	NL	15	9	.625	35	34	10	4	0	243 2/3	210	78	86	215	2.88

FIRST	LAST	YEAR	TEAM	LEAGUE	W	L	PCT	G	GS	CG	SH	SV	IP	H	ER	BB	K	ER
JOHN	MONTEFUSCO	1976	San Francisco Giants	NL	16	14	.533	57	36	11	6	0	253 1/3	224	80	74	172	2.84
JOHN	MONTEFUSCO	1977	San Francisco Giants	NL	7	12	.368	26	25	4	0	0	157 1/3	170	61	46	110	3.49
JOHN	MONTEFUSCO	1978	San Francisco Giants	NL	11	9	.550	36	36	3	0	0	238 2/3	233	101	68	177	3.81
JOHN	MONTEFUSCO	1979	San Francisco Giants	NL	3	8	.273	22	22	1	0	0	137	145	60	51	76	3.94
JOHN	MONTEFUSCO	1980	San Francisco Giants	NL	4	8	.333	22	17	0	0	1	113 1/3	120	55	39	85	4.37
JOHN	MONTEFUSCO	1981	Atlanta Braves	NL	2	3	.400	26	9	0	0	0	77 1/3	75	30	27	34	3.49
JOHN	MONTEFUSCO	1982	San Diego Padres	NL	10	11	.476	32	32	1	0	0	184 1/3	177	82	41	83	4.00
JOHN	MONTEFUSCO	1983	New York Yankees	AL	5	0	1.000	6	6	0	0	0	38	39	14	10	15	3.32
JOHN	MONTEFUSCO	1983	San Diego Padres	NL	9	4	.692	31	10	1	0	4	95 1/3	94	35	32	52	3.30
JOHN	MONTEFUSCO	1984	New York Yankees	AL	5	3	.625	11	11	0	0	0	55 1/3	55	22	13	23	3.58
JOHN	MONTEFUSCO	1985	New York Yankees	AL	0	0		3	1	0	0	0	7	12	8	2	2	10.29
JOHN	MONTEFUSCO	1986	New York Yankees	AL	0	0		4	0	0	0	0	12 1/3	9	3	5	2	2.19
RICH	MONTELEONE	1987	Seattle Mariners	AL	0	0		3	0	0	0	0	7	10	5	4	2	6.43
RICH	MONTELEONE	1988	California Angels	AL	0	0		3	0	0	0	0	4 1/3	4	0	1	3	0.00
RICH	MONTELEONE	1989	California Angels	AL	2	2	.500	24	0	0	0	0	39 2/3	39	14	13	27	3.18
RICH	MONTELEONE	1990	New York Yankees	AL	0	1	.000	5	0	0	0	0	7 1/3	8	5	2	8	6.14
RICH	MONTELEONE	1991	New York Yankees	AL	3	1	.750	26	0	0	0	0	47	42	19	19	34	3.64
RICH	MONTELEONE	1992	New York Yankees	AL	7	3	.700	47	0	0	0	0	92 2/3	82	34	27	62	3.30
RICH	MONTELEONE	1993	New York Yankees	AL	7	4	.636	42	0	0	0	0	85 2/3	85	47	35	50	4.94
RICH	MONTELEONE	1994	San Francisco Giants	NL	4	3	.571	39	0	0	0	0	45 1/3	43	16	13	16	3.18
RICH	MONTELEONE	1995	California Angels	AL	1	0	1.000	9	0	0	0	0	9	8	2	3	5	2.00
RICH	MONTELEONE	1996	California Angels	AL	0	3	.000	12	0	0	0	0	15 1/3	23	10	2	5	5.87
DAN	MOROGIELLO	1983	Baltimore Orioles	AL	0	1	.000	22	0	0	0	0	37 2/3	39	10	10	15	2.39
DON	MOSSI	1954	Cleveland Indians	AL	6	1	.857	40	5	2	0	7	93	56	20	39	55	1.94
DON	MOSSI	1955	Cleveland Indians	AL	4	3	.571	57	1	0	0	9	81 2/3	81	22	18	69	2.42
DON	MOSSI	1956	Cleveland Indians	AL	6	5	.545	48	3	0	0	11	87 2/3	79	35	33	59	3.59
DON	MOSSI	1957	Cleveland Indians	AL	11	10	.524	36	22	6	1	2	159	165	73	57	97	4.13
DON	MOSSI	1958	Cleveland Indians	AL	7	8	.467	43	5	0	1	3	101 2/3	106	44	30	55	3.90
DON	MOSSI	1959	Detroit Tigers	AL	17	9	.654	34	30	15	3	0	228	210	85	49	125	3.36
DON	MOSSI	1960	Detroit Tigers	AL	9	8	.529	23	22	9	2	1	158 1/3	158	61	32	69	3.47
DON	MOSSI	1961	Detroit Tigers	AL	15	7	.682	35	34	12	1	1	240 1/3	237	79	47	137	2.96
DON	MOSSI	1962	Detroit Tigers	AL	11	13	.458	35	27	8	1	2	180 1/3	195	84	36	121	4.19
DON	MOSSI	1963	Detroit Tigers	AL	7	7	.500	24	16	3	0	2	122 2/3	110	51	17	68	3.74
DON	MOSSI	1964	Chicago White Sox	AL	3	1	.750	34	0	0	0	7	40	57	13	7	36	2.92
DON	MOSSI	1965	Kansas City Athletics	AL	5	8	.385	51	0	0	0	7	51 1/3	59	23	20	41	3.74

FIRST	LAST	YEAR	TEAM	LEAGUE	W	L	PCT	G	GS	CG	SH	SV	IP	H	ER	BB	K	ER
MIKE	MUSSINA	1991	Baltimore Orioles	AL	4	5	.444	12	12	2	0	0	87 2/3	77	28	21	52	2.87
MIKE	MUSSINA	1992	Baltimore Orioles	AL	18	5	.783	32	32	8	4	0	241	212	68	48	130	2.54
MIKE	MUSSINA	1993	Baltimore Orioles	AL	14	6	.700	25	25	3	2	0	167 2/3	163	83	44	117	4.46
MIKE	MUSSINA	1994	Baltimore Orioles	AL	16	5	.762	24	24	3	0	0	176 1/3	163	60	42	99	3.06
MIKE	MUSSINA	1995	Baltimore Orioles	AL	19	9	.679	32	32	7	4	0	221 2/3	187	81	50	158	3.29
MIKE	MUSSINA	1996	Baltimore Orioles	AL	19	11	.633	36	36	4	1	0	243 1/3	264	130	69	204	4.81
MIKE	MUSSINA	1997	Baltimore Orioles	AL	15	8	.652	33	33	4	2	0	224 2/3	197	80	54	208	3.20
MIKE	MUSSINA	1998	Baltimore Orioles	AL	13	10	.565	29	29	4	0	0	206 1/3	189	80	41	175	3.49
MIKE	MUSSINA	1999	Baltimore Orioles	AL	18	7	.720	31	31	4	1	0	203 1/3	207	79	52	172	3.50
MIKE	MUSSINA	2000	Baltimore Orioles	AL	11	15	.423	34	34	6	3	0	237 2/3	236	100	46	210	3.79
MIKE	MUSSINA	2001	New York Yankees	AL	17	11	.607	34	34	4	3	0	228 2/3	202	80	42	214	3.15
JOHN	PACELLA	1977	New York Mets	NL	0	0		3	0	0	0	0	4	2	0	2	1	0.00
JOHN	PACELLA	1979	New York Mets	NL	0	2	.000	4	3	0	0	0	161 1/3	16	8	4	12	4.41
JOHN	PACELLA	1980	New York Mets	NL	3	4	.429	32	15	0	0	2	84	89	48	59	68	5.14
JOHN	PACELLA	1982	Minnesota Twins	AL	1	2	.333	21	1	0	0	0	51 2/3	61	42	37	20	7.32
JOHN	PACELLA	1982	New York Yankees	AL	0	1	.000	3	1	0	0	0	10	13	8	9	2	7.20
JOHN	PACELLA	1984	Baltimore Orioles	AL	0	0		6	0	0	0	0	14 2/3	15	11	9	8	6.75
JOHN	PACELLA	1986	Detroit Tigers	AL	0	0		5	0	0	0	1	11	10	5	13	5	4.09
PAT	PACILLO	1987	Cincinnati Reds	NL	3	3	.500	12	7	0	0	0	39 2/3	41	27	19	23	6.13
PAT	PACILLO	1988	Cincinnati Reds	NL	1	0	1.000	6	6	0	0	0	10 2/3	14	6	4	11	5.06
JOHN	PAPA	1961	Baltimore Orioles	AL	0	0		2	0	0	0	0	1	3	2	3	3	18.00
JOHN	PAPA	1962	Baltimore Orioles	AL	0	0		1	0	0	0	0	1	3	3	1	0	27.00
FRANK	PASTORE	1979	Cincinnati Reds	NL	6	7	.462	30	9	2	1	0	95 1/3	102	45	23	63	4.25
FRANK	PASTORE	1980	Cincinnati Reds	NL	13	7	.650	27	27	9	2	0	184 2/3	161	67	42	110	3.27
FRANK	PASTORE	1981	Cincinnati Reds	NL	4	9	.308	22	22	2	1	0	132	125	59	35	81	4.02
FRANK	PASTORE	1982	Cincinnati Reds	NL	8	13	.381	31	29	3	2	0	188 1/3	210	83	57	94	3.97
FRANK	PASTORE	1983	Cincinnati Reds	NL	9	12	.429	36	29	4	1	0	184 1/3	207	100	64	93	4.88
FRANK	PASTORE	1984	Cincinnati Reds	NL	3	8	.273	24	16	1	0	0	98 1/3	110	71	40	53	6.50
FRANK	PASTORE	1985	Cincinnati Reds	NL	2	1	.667	17	6	0	0	0	54	60	23	16	29	3.83
FRANK	PASTORE	1986	Minnesota Twins	AL	3	1	.750	33	1	0	0	2	49 1/3	54	22	24	18	4.01
CARL	PAVANO	1998	Montreal Expos	NL	6	9	.400	24	23	0	0	0	134 2/3	130	63	43	83	4.21
CARL	PAVANO	1999	Montreal Expos	NL	6	8	.429	19	18	1	1	0	104	117	65	35	70	5.62
CARL	PAVANO	2000	Montreal Expos	NL	8	4	.667	15	15	0	0	0	97	89	33	34	64	3.06
CARL	PAVANO	2001	Montreal Expos	NL	1	6	.143	8	8	0	0	0	42 2/3	59	30	16	36	6.33
BILL	PERTICA	1918	Boston Red Sox	AL	0	0		1	0	0	0	0	3	3	1	0	1	3.00

FIRST	LAST	YEAR	TEAM	LEAGUE	W	L	PCT	G	GS	CG	SH	SV	IP	H	ER	BB	K	ER
BILL	PERTICA	1921	St. Louis Cardinals	NL	14	10	.583	38	31	15	2	2	208 1/3	212	78	70	67	3.37
BILL	PERTICA	1922	St. Louis Cardinals	NL	8	8	.500	34	14	2	0	0	117 1/3	153	77	65	30	5.91
BILL	PERTICA	1923	St. Louis Cardinals	NL	0	0		1	1	0	0	0	2 1/3	2	1	3	0	3.86
PRETZEL	PEZZULLO	1935	Philadelphia Phillies	NL	3	5	.375	41	7	2	0	1	84 1/3	115	60	45	24	6.40
PRETZEL	PEZZULLO	1936	Philadelphia Phillies	NL	0	0		2	0	0	0	0	2	2	1	6	0	4.50
MARIO	PICONE	1947	New York Giants	NL	0	1	.000	2	1	0	0	0	7	10	6	2	1	7.71
MARIO	PICONE	1952	New York Giants	NL	0	0		2	0	0	0	0	9	11	7	5	3	7.00
MARIO	PICONE	1954	Cincinnati Reds	NL	0	0	.000	4	1	0	0	0	10 1/3	9	7	7	1	6.10
MARIO	PICONE	1954	New York Giants	NL	0	0		5	0	0	0	0	13 2/3	13	8	11	6	5.27
MARINO	PIERETTI	1945	Washington Senators	AL	14	13	.519	44	27	14	3	2	233 1/3	235	86	91	66	3.32
MARINO	PIERETTI	1946	Washington Senators	AL	2	2	.500	30	2	1	0	0	62	70	41	40	20	5.95
MARINO	PIERETTI	1947	Washington Senators	AL	2	4	.333	23	10	2	0	0	83 1/3	97	39	47	32	4.21
MARINO	PIERETTI	1948	Chicago White Sox	AL	8	10	.444	21	18	4	0	1	120	117	66	52	28	4.95
MARINO	PIERETTI	1948	Washington Senators	AL	0	0	.000	8	0	0	0	0	11 2/3	18	14	7	6	10.80
MARINO	PIERETTI	1949	Chicago White Sox	AL	4	6	.400	39	9	0	0	4	116	131	71	54	25	5.51
MARINO	PIERETTI	1950	Cleveland Indians	AL	0	1	.000	29	1	0	0	1	47 1/3	45	22	30	11	4.18
AL	PIEROTTI	1920	Boston Braves	NL	1	1	.500	6	2	0	0	0	25	23	8	9	12	2.88
AL	PIEROTTI	1921	Boston Braves	NL	0	1	.000	2	0	0	0	0	1 2/3	3	4	3	1	21.60
BILL	PIERRO	1950	Pittsburgh Pirates	NL	0	2	.000	12	3	0	0	0	29	33	34	28	13	10.55
MARC	PISCIOTTA	1997	Chicago Cubs	NL	3	1	.750	24	0	0	0	0	28 1/3	20	10	16	21	3.18
MARC	PISCIOTTA	1998	Chicago Cubs	NL	1	2	.333	43	0	0	0	0	44	44	20	32	31	4.09
MARC	PISCIOTTA	1999	Kansas City Royals	AL	0	2	.000	8	0	0	0	0	8 1/3	9	8	10	3	8.64
LOU	POLLI	1932	St. Louis Browns	AL	0	0		5	0	0	0	0	6 2/3	13	4	5	5	5.40
LOU	POLLI	1944	New York Giants	NL	0	2	.000	19	1	0	0	3	35 2/3	42	18	20	6	4.54
JOHN	POLONI	1977	Texas Rangers	AL	1	0	1.000	2	1	0	0	0	7	8	5	1	5	6.43
CHARLIE	PULEO	1981	New York Mets	NL	0	0		4	1	0	0	0	13 1/3	8	0	8	8	0.00
CHARLIE	PULEO	1982	New York Mets	NL	9	9	.500	36	24	1	1	1	171	179	85	90	98	4.47
CHARLIE	PULEO	1983	Cincinnati Reds	NL	6	12	.333	27	24	1	0	0	143 2/3	145	78	91	71	4.89
CHARLIE	PULEO	1984	Cincinnati Reds	NL	1	2	.333	4	4	0	0	0	22	27	14	15	6	5.73
CHARLIE	PULEO	1986	Atlanta Braves	NL	1	2	.333	5	3	1	0	0	24 1/3	13	8	12	18	2.96
CHARLIE	PULEO	1987	Atlanta Braves	NL	6	8	.429	35	16	0	0	0	123 1/3	122	58	40	99	4.23
CHARLIE	PULEO	1988	Atlanta Braves	NL	5	5	.500	53	3	0	0	3	106 1/3	101	41	47	70	3.47
CHARLIE	PULEO	1989	Atlanta Braves	NL	1	1	.500	15	0	0	0	0	29	26	15	16	17	4.66
AL	RAFFO	1969	Philadelphia Phillies	NL	1	3	.250	45	0	0	0	1	72 1/3	81	33	25	38	4.11
BRADY	RAGGIO	1997	St. Louis Cardinals	NL	1	2	.333	15	4	0	0	0	31 1/3	44	24	16	21	6.89

FIRST	LAST	YEAR	TEAM	LEAGUE	W	L	PCT	G	GS	CG	SH	SV	IP	H	ER	BB	K	ER
BRADY	RAGGIO	1998	St. Louis Cardinals	NL	1	1	.500	4	1	0	0	0	7	22	12	3	3	15.43
VIC	RASCHI	1946	New York Yankees	AL	2	0	1.000	2	2	2	0	0	16	14	7	5	11	3.94
VIC	RASCHI	1947	New York Yankees	AL	7	2	.778	15	14	6	1	1	104 2/3	89	45	38	51	3.87
VIC	RASCHI	1948	New York Yankees	AL	19	8	.704	36	31	18	6	0	222 2/3	208	95	74	124	3.84
VIC	RASCHI	1949	New York Yankees	AL	21	10	.677	38	37	21	3	1	274 2/3	247	102	138	124	3.34
VIC	RASCHI	1950	New York Yankees	AL	21	8	.724	33	32	17	2	1	256 2/3	232	114	116	155	4.00
VIC	RASCHI	1951	New York Yankees	AL	21	10	.677	35	34	15	2	0	258 1/3	233	94	103	164	3.27
VIC	RASCHI	1952	New York Yankees	AL	16	6	.727	31	31	13	4	1	223	174	69	91	127	2.78
VIC	RASCHI	1953	New York Yankees	AL	13	6	.684	28	26	7	4	0	181	150	67	55	76	3.33
VIC	RASCHI	1954	St. Louis Cardinals	NL	8	9	.471	30	29	6	2	0	179	182	94	71	73	4.73
VIC	RASCHI	1955	Kansas City Athletics	AL	4	6	.400	20	18	1	0	0	101 1/3	132	61	35	38	5.42
VIC	RASCHI	1955	St. Louis Cardinals	NL	0	1	.000	1	1	0	0	0	1 2/3	5	4	1	1	21.60
BARRY	RAZIANO	1973	Kansas City Royals	AL	0	0		2	0	0	0	1	8 1/3	6	5	8	0	5.40
BARRY	RAZIANO	1974	California Angels	AL	0	2	.333	13	0	0	0	2	16 2/3	15	12	8	9	6.48
XAVIER	RESCIGNO	1943	Pittsburgh Pirates	NL	6	9	.400	37	14	5	1	2	132 2/3	125	44	45	41	2.98
XAVIER	RESCIGNO	1944	Pittsburgh Pirates	NL	10	8	.556	48	6	2	0	5	124	146	60	34	45	4.35
XAVIER	RESCIGNO	1945	Pittsburgh Pirates	NL	3	5	.375	44	1	0	0	9	78 2/3	95	50	34	29	5.72
FRANK	RICCELLI	1976	San Francisco Giants	NL	1	0	.500	4	3	0	0	0	16	16	10	5	11	5.62
FRANK	RICCELLI	1978	Houston Astros	NL	0	0		2	0	0	0	0	3	1	0	0	1	0.00
FRANK	RICCELLI	1979	Houston Astros	NL	2	2	.500	11	2	0	0	0	22	22	10	18	20	4.09
CHUCK	RICCI	1995	Philadelphia Phillies	NL	1	0	1.000	7	0	0	0	0	10	9	2	3	9	1.80
DAVE	RIGHETTI	1979	New York Yankees	AL	0	4	.000	3	3	0	0	0	17 1/3	10	7	10	13	3.63
DAVE	RIGHETTI	1981	New York Yankees	AL	8	4	.667	15	15	2	2	0	105 1/3	75	24	38	89	2.05
DAVE	RIGHETTI	1982	New York Yankees	AL	11	10	.524	33	27	4	0	1	183	155	77	108	163	3.79
DAVE	RIGHETTI	1983	New York Yankees	AL	14	8	.636	31	31	7	2	0	217	194	83	67	169	3.44
DAVE	RIGHETTI	1984	New York Yankees	AL	5	6	.455	64	0	0	0	31	96 1/3	79	25	37	90	2.34
DAVE	RIGHETTI	1985	New York Yankees	AL	12	7	.632	74	0	0	0	29	107	96	33	45	92	2.78
DAVE	RIGHETTI	1986	New York Yankees	AL	8	8	.500	74	0	0	0	46	106 2/3	88	29	35	83	2.45
DAVE	RIGHETTI	1987	New York Yankees	AL	8	6	.571	60	0	0	0	31	95	95	37	44	77	3.51
DAVE	RIGHETTI	1988	New York Yankees	AL	5	4	.556	60	0	0	0	25	87	86	34	37	70	3.52
DAVE	RIGHETTI	1989	New York Yankees	AL	2	6	.250	55	0	0	0	25	69	73	23	26	51	3.00
DAVE	RIGHETTI	1990	New York Yankees	AL	1	7	.500	53	0	0	0	36	53	48	21	28	43	3.57
DAVE	RIGHETTI	1991	San Francisco Giants	NL	2	7	.222	61	0	0	0	24	71 2/3	64	27	26	51	3.39
DAVE	RIGHETTI	1992	San Francisco Giants	NL	2	7	.222	54	4	0	0	3	78 1/3	79	44	36	47	5.06
DAVE	RIGHETTI	1993	San Francisco Giants	NL	1	1	.500	51	0	0	0	1	47 1/3	58	30	17	31	5.70

FIRST	LAST	YEAR	TEAM	LEAGUE	W	L	PCT	G	GS	CG	SH	SV	IP	H	ER	BB	K	ER
DAVE	RIGHETTI	1994	Oakland Athletics	AL	0	0		7	0	0	0	0	7	13	13	9	4	16.71
DAVE	RIGHETTI	1994	Toronto Blue Jays	AL	0	1	.000	13	0	0	0	0	13 1/3	9	10	10	10	6.75
DAVE	RIGHETTI	1995	Chicago White Sox	AL	3	2	.600	10	9	0	0	0	49 1/3	65	23	18	29	4.20
TODD	RIZZO	1998	Chicago White Sox	AL	0	0		9	0	0	0	0	6 2/3	12	10	6	3	13.50
TODD	RIZZO	1999	Chicago White Sox	AL	0	2	.000	3	0	0	0	0	1 1/3	4	1	3	1	6.75
JOE	ROSSELLI	1995	San Francisco Giants	NL	2	1	.667	9	5	0	0	0	30	39	29	20	7	8.70
FRANK	ROSSO	1944	New York Giants	NL	0	0		2	0	0	0	2	4	11	4	3	1	9.00
MARIUS	RUSSO	1939	New York Yankees	AL	8	3	.727	21	11	9	2	2	116	86	31	41	55	2.41
MARIUS	RUSSO	1940	New York Yankees	AL	14	8	.636	30	24	15	2	1	189 1/3	181	69	55	87	3.28
MARIUS	RUSSO	1941	New York Yankees	AL	14	10	.583	28	27	17	3	0	209 2/3	195	72	87	105	3.09
MARIUS	RUSSO	1942	New York Yankees	AL	4	1	.800	9	5	2	1	0	45 1/3	41	14	14	15	2.78
MARIUS	RUSSO	1943	New York Yankees	AL	5	10	.333	24	14	5	1	1	101 2/3	89	42	45	42	3.72
MARIUS	RUSSO	1946	New York Yankees	AL	0	2	.000	8	3	1	0	0	18 2/3	26	9	11	7	4.34
JOE	SAMBITO	1976	Houston Astros	NL	3	2	.600	20	4	1	1	1	53 1/3	45	21	14	26	3.54
JOE	SAMBITO	1977	Houston Astros	NL	5	5	.500	54	1	0	0	7	89	77	23	24	67	2.33
JOE	SAMBITO	1978	Houston Astros	NL	4	9	.308	62	0	0	0	11	88	85	30	32	96	3.07
JOE	SAMBITO	1979	Houston Astros	NL	8	7	.533	63	0	0	0	22	91 1/3	80	18	23	83	1.77
JOE	SAMBITO	1980	Houston Astros	NL	8	4	.667	64	0	0	0	17	90 1/3	65	22	22	75	2.19
JOE	SAMBITO	1981	Houston Astros	NL	5	5	.500	49	0	0	0	10	63 2/3	43	13	22	41	1.84
JOE	SAMBITO	1982	Houston Astros	NL	0	0		9	0	0	0	4	12 2/3	7	1	2	7	0.71
JOE	SAMBITO	1984	Houston Astros	NL	0	0		32	0	0	0	0	47 2/3	39	16	16	26	3.02
JOE	SAMBITO	1985	New York Mets	NL	0	0	1.000	8	0	0	0	0	10 2/3	21	15	8	3	12.66
JOE	SAMBITO	1986	Boston Red Sox	AL	2	0	.250	53	0	0	0	12	44 2/3	54	24	16	30	4.84
JOE	SAMBITO	1987	Boston Red Sox	AL	2	6	.000	47	0	0	0	0	37 2/3	46	29	16	35	6.93
AL	SANTORINI	1968	Atlanta Braves	NL	0	1		1	1	0	1	0	3	4	0	0	0	0.00
AL	SANTORINI	1969	San Diego Padres	NL	8	14	.364	32	30	2	2	0	184 2/3	194	81	73	111	3.95
AL	SANTORINI	1970	San Diego Padres	NL	1	8	.111	21	12	0	0	1	75 2/3	91	51	43	41	6.07
AL	SANTORINI	1971	San Diego Padres	NL	0	2	.000	18	3	0	0	0	38 1/3	43	16	11	21	3.76
AL	SANTORINI	1971	St. Louis Cardinals	NL	0	2	.000	19	5	0	0	2	49 2/3	51	21	19	21	3.81
AL	SANTORINI	1972	St. Louis Cardinals	NL	8	11	.421	30	19	3	3	0	133 2/3	136	61	46	72	4.11
CALVIN	SCHIRALDI	1984	New York Mets	NL	0	2	.000	6	3	0	0	0	8 1/3	14	5	2	2	5.40
CALVIN	SCHIRALDI	1985	New York Mets	NL	0	1	.000	5	3	0	0	0	17 1/3	20	11	10	16	5.71
CALVIN	SCHIRALDI	1985	New York Mets	NL	2	1	.667	10	4	0	0	0	26 1/3	43	26	11	21	8.89
CALVIN	SCHIRALDI	1986	Boston Red Sox	AL	4	2	.667	25	0	0	0	9	51	36	8	15	55	1.41
CALVIN	SCHIRALDI	1987	Boston Red Sox	AL	8	5	.615	62	1	0	0	6	83 2/3	75	41	40	93	4.41

FIRST	LAST	YEAR	TEAM	LEAGUE	W	L	PCT	G	GS	CG	SH	SV	IP	H	ER	BB	K	ER
CALVIN	SCHIRALDI	1988	Chicago Cubs	NL	9	13	.409	29	27	2	0	1	166 1/3	166	81	63	140	4.38
CALVIN	SCHIRALDI	1989	Chicago Cubs	NL	3	6	.333	54	0	0	0	4	78 2/3	60	33	50	54	3.78
CALVIN	SCHIRALDI	1989	San Diego Padres	NL	3	1	.750	5	4	0	0	0	21 1/3	12	6	13	17	2.53
CALVIN	SCHIRALDI	1990	San Diego Padres	NL	3	8	.273	42	8	0	0	0	104	105	51	60	74	4.41
CALVIN	SCHIRALDI	1991	Texas Rangers	AL	0	1	.000	3	0	0	0	0	4 2/3	5	6	5	1	11.57
FRANK	SEMINARA	1992	San Diego Padres	NL	9	4	.692	19	18	0	0	0	100 1/3	98	41	46	61	3.68
FRANK	SEMINARA	1993	San Diego Padres	NL	3	3	.500	18	7	0	0	0	46 1/3	53	23	21	22	4.47
FRANK	SEMINARA	1994	New York Mets	NL	0	2	.000	10	1	0	0	0	17	20	11	8	7	5.82
DAN	SERAFINI	1996	Minnesota Twins	AL	0	1	.000	1	1	0	0	0	4 1/3	7	5	2	1	10.38
DAN	SERAFINI	1997	Minnesota Twins	AL	2	1	.667	6	4	1	0	0	26 1/3	27	10	11	15	3.42
DAN	SERAFINI	1998	Minnesota Twins	AL	7	4	.636	28	9	0	0	0	75	95	54	29	46	6.48
DAN	SERAFINI	1999	Chicago Cubs	NL	3	2	.600	42	4	0	0	1	62 1/3	86	48	32	17	6.93
DAN	SERAFINI	2000	Pittsburgh Pirates	NL	2	5	.286	11	11	0	0	0	62 1/3	70	34	26	32	4.91
DAN	SERAFINI	2000	San Diego Padres	NL	0	0		3	3	0	0	0	3	9	6	2	3	18.00
AL	SIMA	1950	Washington Senators	AL	4	5	.444	17	9	1	0	0	77	89	41	26	23	4.79
AL	SIMA	1951	Washington Senators	AL	3	7	.300	18	8	1	0	0	77	79	41	41	26	4.79
AL	SIMA	1953	Washington Senators	AL	2	3	.400	31	5	1	0	1	68 1/3	63	26	31	25	3.42
AL	SIMA	1954	Chicago White Sox	AL	0	1	.000	5	1	0	0	1	7	11	4	2	1	5.14
AL	SIMA	1954	Philadelphia Athletics	AL	2	5	.286	29	7	0	0	2	79 1/3	101	46	32	36	5.22
JOHN	SMOLTZ	1988	Atlanta Braves	NL	2	7	.222	12	12	0	0	0	64	74	39	33	37	5.48
JOHN	SMOLTZ	1989	Atlanta Braves	NL	12	11	.522	29	29	5	2	0	208	160	68	72	168	2.94
JOHN	SMOLTZ	1990	Atlanta Braves	NL	14	11	.560	34	34	6	2	0	231 1/3	206	99	90	170	3.85
JOHN	SMOLTZ	1991	Atlanta Braves	NL	14	13	.519	36	36	5	2	0	229 2/3	206	97	77	148	3.80
JOHN	SMOLTZ	1992	Atlanta Braves	NL	15	12	.556	35	35	9	3	0	246 2/3	206	78	80	215	2.85
JOHN	SMOLTZ	1993	Atlanta Braves	NL	15	11	.577	35	35	3	1	0	243 2/3	208	98	100	208	3.62
JOHN	SMOLTZ	1994	Atlanta Braves	NL	6	10	.375	21	21	1	0	0	134 2/3	120	62	48	113	4.14
JOHN	SMOLTZ	1995	Atlanta Braves	NL	12	7	.632	29	28	2	1	0	192 2/3	166	68	72	193	3.18
JOHN	SMOLTZ	1996	Atlanta Braves	NL	24	8	.750	35	35	6	2	0	253 2/3	199	83	55	276	2.94
JOHN	SMOLTZ	1997	Atlanta Braves	NL	15	12	.556	35	35	7	2	0	256	234	86	63	241	3.02
JOHN	SMOLTZ	1998	Atlanta Braves	NL	17	3	.850	26	26	2	1	0	167 2/3	145	54	44	173	2.90
JOHN	SMOLTZ	1999	Atlanta Braves	NL	11	8	.579	29	29	1	0	0	186 1/3	168	66	40	156	3.19
JOHN	SMOLTZ	2001	Atlanta Braves	NL	3	3	.600	36	5	0	0	10	59	53	22	10	57	3.36
JOE	SPARMA	1964	Detroit Tigers	AL	5	6	.455	21	11	3	2	0	84	62	28	45	71	3.00
JOE	SPARMA	1965	Detroit Tigers	AL	13	8	.619	30	28	6	6	0	167	142	59	75	127	3.18
JOE	SPARMA	1966	Detroit Tigers	AL	2	7	.222	29	13	0	0	0	91 2/3	103	54	52	61	5.30

FIRST	LAST	YEAR	TEAM	LEAGUE	W	L	PCT	G	GS	CG	SH	SV	IP	H	ER	BB	K	ER
JOE	SPARMA	1967	Detroit Tigers	AL	16	9	.640	37	37	11	5	0	217 2/3	186	91	85	153	3.76
JOE	SPARMA	1968	Detroit Tigers	AL	10	10	.500	34	31	7	1	0	182 1/3	169	75	77	110	3.70
JOE	SPARMA	1969	Detroit Tigers	AL	6	8	.429	23	16	3	2	0	92 2/3	78	49	77	41	4.76
JOE	SPARMA	1970	Montreal Expos	NL	0	4	.000	9	6	1	0	0	29 1/3	34	23	25	23	7.06
TOM	URBANI	1993	St. Louis Cardinals	NL	1	3	.250	18	9	0	0	0	62	73	32	26	33	4.65
TOM	URBANI	1994	St. Louis Cardinals	NL	3	7	.300	20	10	0	0	0	80 1/3	98	46	21	43	5.15
TOM	URBANI	1995	St. Louis Cardinals	NL	3	5	.375	24	13	0	0	0	82 2/3	99	34	21	52	3.70
TOM	URBANI	1996	Detroit Tigers	AL	2	2	.500	16	2	0	0	0	23 2/3	31	22	14	20	8.37
TOM	URBANI	1996	St. Louis Cardinals	NL	1	0	1.000	3	2	0	0	0	11 2/3	15	10	4	1	7.71
VITO	VALENTINETTI	1954	Chicago White Sox	AL	0	0	—	1	0	0	0	1	1	4	6	2	1	54.00
VITO	VALENTINETTI	1956	Chicago Cubs	NL	6	4	.600	42	2	0	0	1	95 1/3	84	40	36	26	3.78
VITO	VALENTINETTI	1957	Chicago Cubs	NL	0	2	.000	9	0	0	0	2	12	12	3	7	8	2.25
VITO	VALENTINETTI	1957	Cleveland Indians	AL	2	2	.500	11	2	0	0	0	23 2/3	26	13	13	10	4.94
VITO	VALENTINETTI	1958	Detroit Tigers	AL	1	0	1.000	15	0	0	0	2	18 2/3	18	7	5	7	3.38
VITO	VALENTINETTI	1958	Washington Senators	AL	4	6	.400	23	10	2	0	0	95 2/3	106	54	49	33	5.08
VITO	VALENTINETTI	1959	Washington Senators	AL	0	2	.000	7	1	0	0	1	10 2/3	16	12	10	7	10.12
RON	VILLONE	1995	San Diego Padres	NL	2	1	.667	19	0	0	0	0	25 2/3	24	12	11	37	4.21
RON	VILLONE	1995	Seattle Mariners	AL	0	2	.000	19	0	0	0	1	19 1/3	20	17	23	26	7.91
RON	VILLONE	1996	Milwaukee Brewers	AL	0	0	—	23	0	0	0	2	24 2/3	14	9	18	19	3.28
RON	VILLONE	1996	San Diego Padres	NL	1	1	.500	21	0	0	0	0	18 1/3	17	6	7	19	2.95
RON	VILLONE	1997	Milwaukee Brewers	AL	0	0	—	50	0	0	0	0	52 2/3	54	20	36	40	3.42
RON	VILLONE	1998	Cleveland Indians	AL	0	0	—	25	0	0	0	2	27	30	18	22	15	6.00
RON	VILLONE	1999	Cincinnati Reds	NL	9	7	.562	29	22	2	0	0	142 2/3	114	67	73	97	4.23
RON	VILLONE	2000	Cincinnati Reds	NL	10	10	.500	35	23	0	0	0	141	154	85	78	77	5.43
RON	VILLONE	2001	Colorado Rockies	NL	1	3	.250	22	6	0	0	0	46 2/3	56	33	29	48	6.36
RON	VILLONE	2001	Houston Astros	NL	5	7	.417	31	6	0	1	0	68	77	42	24	65	5.56
FRANK	VIOLA	1982	Minnesota Twins	AL	4	10	.286	22	22	3	0	0	126	152	73	38	84	5.21
FRANK	VIOLA	1983	Minnesota Twins	AL	7	15	.318	35	34	4	0	0	210	242	128	92	127	5.49
FRANK	VIOLA	1984	Minnesota Twins	AL	18	12	.600	35	35	10	4	0	257 2/3	225	92	73	149	3.21
FRANK	VIOLA	1985	Minnesota Twins	AL	18	14	.562	36	36	9	0	0	250 2/3	262	114	68	135	4.09
FRANK	VIOLA	1986	Minnesota Twins	AL	16	13	.552	37	37	7	1	0	245 2/3	257	123	83	191	4.51
FRANK	VIOLA	1987	Minnesota Twins	AL	17	10	.630	36	36	7	1	0	251 2/3	230	81	66	197	2.90
FRANK	VIOLA	1988	Minnesota Twins	AL	24	7	.774	35	35	7	2	0	255 1/3	236	75	54	193	2.64
FRANK	VIOLA	1989	Minnesota Twins	AL	8	12	.400	24	24	7	1	0	175 2/3	171	74	47	138	3.79
FRANK	VIOLA	1989	New York Mets	NL	5	5	.500	12	12	2	0	0	85 1/3	75	32	27	73	3.38

FIRST	LAST	YEAR	TEAM	LEAGUE	W	L	PCT	G	GS	CG	SH	SV	IP	H	ER	BB	K	ER
FRANK	VIOLA	1990	New York Mets	NL	20	12	.625	35	35	7	3	0	249 2/3	227	74	60	182	2.67
FRANK	VIOLA	1991	New York Mets	NL	13	15	.464	35	35	3	0	0	231 1/3	259	102	54	132	3.97
FRANK	VIOLA	1992	Boston Red Sox	AL	13	12	.520	35	35	6	1	0	238	214	91	89	121	3.44
FRANK	VIOLA	1993	Boston Red Sox	AL	11	8	.579	29	29	2	1	0	183 2/3	180	64	72	91	3.14
FRANK	VIOLA	1994	Boston Red Sox	AL	1	1	.500	6	6	0	0	0	31	34	16	17	9	4.65
FRANK	VIOLA	1995	Cincinnati Reds	NL	0	1	.000	3	3	0	0	0	14 1/3	20	10	3	4	6.28
FRANK	VIOLA	1996	Toronto Blue Jays	AL	1	3	.250	6	6	0	0	0	30 1/3	43	26	21	18	7.71
JOE	VITELLI	1944	Pittsburgh Pirates	NL	0	0		4	0	0	0	2	7	5	2	7	2	2.57
DOM	ZANNI	1958	San Francisco Giants	NL	1	0	1.000	1	0	0	0	0	4	7	1	1	3	2.25
DOM	ZANNI	1959	San Francisco Giants	NL	0	0		9	0	0	0	0	11	12	8	8	11	6.55
DOM	ZANNI	1961	San Francisco Giants	NL	1	0	1.000	8	0	0	0	0	13 2/3	13	6	12	11	3.95
DOM	ZANNI	1962	Chicago White Sox	AL	6	5	.545	44	2	0	0	5	86 1/3	67	36	31	66	3.75
DOM	ZANNI	1963	Chicago White Sox	AL	0	0		5	0	0	0	0	4 1/3	5	4	4	2	8.31
DOM	ZANNI	1963	Cincinnati Reds	NL	1	1	.500	31	1	0	0	5	43	39	20	21	40	4.19
DOM	ZANNI	1965	Cincinnati Reds	NL	0	0		8	0	0	0	0	13 1/3	7	2	5	10	1.35
DOM	ZANNI	1966	Cincinnati Reds	NL	0	0		5	0	0	1	0	7 1/3	5	0	3	5	0.00
BARRY	ZITO	2000	Oakland Athletics	AL	7	4	.636	14	14	1	1	0	92 2/3	64	28	45	78	2.72
BARRY	ZITO	2001	Oakland Athletics	AL	17	8	.680	35	35	3	2	0	214 1/3	184	83	80	205	3.49

Italian American Pitcher Totals

FIRST	LAST	W	L	PCT	G	GS	CG	SH	SV	IP	H	ER	BB	K	ERA	BATS	THROWS
JOE	ALBANESE	0	0		6	0	0	0	0	6	8	3	2	3	4.50	R	R
JOHNNY	ANTONELLI	126	110	.534	377	268	102	25	21	1992 1/3	1870	739	687	1162	3.34	L	L
GERRY	ARRIGO	35	40	.467	194	80	9	3	4	620	605	285	291	433	4.14	L	L
TONY	BALSAMO	0	1	.000	18	0	0	0	0	29 1/3	34	21	20	27	6.44	R	R
FRANK	BERTAINA	19	29	.396	99	66	6	5	0	413	399	176	214	280	3.84	L	L
MIKE	BERTOTTI	3	1	.750	28	6	0	0	0	46	60	39	33	38	7.63	L	L
EMIL	BILDILLI	4	8	.333	41	17	7	0	1	148	184	96	75	55	5.84	R	R
DAN	BOITANO	2	2	.500	51	0	0	0	0	71 1/3	86	45	28	52	5.68	R	R
CHRIS	BOSIO	94	93	.503	309	246	39	9	9	1710	1742	753	481	1059	3.96	R	R
RICKY	BOTTALICO	27	35	.435	430	0	0	0	114	488 2/3	428	217	248	459	4.00	L	R
RALPH	BRANCA	88	68	.564	322	188	71	12	19	1484	1372	625	663	829	3.79	R	R
TONY	BRIZZOLARA	8	11	.421	44	23	2	0	3	156 2/3	188	88	52	98	5.06	R	R
JOHNNY	BROACA	44	29	.603	121	86	42	4	1	674 1/3	748	306	255	258	4.08	R	R
ERNIE	BROGLIO	77	74	.510	259	184	52	18	2	1337 1/3	1216	556	587	849	3.74	R	R
TOM	BRUNO	7	7	.500	69	4	0	0	1	123 2/3	125	58	61	80	4.22	R	R
LEON	CADORE	68	72	.486	192	147	83	10	3	1257 1/3	1273	438	289	445	3.14	R	R
FRED	CAMBRIA	1	2	.333	6	5	0	0	0	33 1/3	37	13	12	14	3.51	R	R
MILO	CANDINI	26	21	.553	174	37	13	5	8	537 2/3	530	234	250	183	3.92	R	R
TOM	CANDIOTTI	151	164	.479	451	410	68	11	0	2725	2662	1130	883	1735	3.73	R	R
GEORGE	CAPPUZZELLO	1	2	.333	35	3	0	0	1	53	44	19	25	32	3.23	L	L
BUZZ	CAPRA	31	37	.456	142	61	16	5	5	544 1/3	479	234	258	362	3.87	R	R
JOE	CASCARELLA	27	48	.360	143	54	20	3	8	540 2/3	602	291	267	192	4.84	R	R
ART	CECCARELLI	9	18	.333	79	42	8	2	0	306 2/3	309	172	147	166	5.05	L	L
JOHN	CERUTTI	49	43	.533	229	116	8	2	4	861	894	377	291	398	3.94	L	L
ITALO	CHELINI	4	4	.500	24	6	5	0	0	97 1/3	122	63	34	20	5.83	L	L
SCOTT	CHIAMPARINO	2	6	.250	15	15	0	0	0	85 1/3	87	31	29	40	3.27	R	R
MARK	CIARDI	1	1	.500	4	3	0	0	0	16 1/3	26	17	9	8	9.37	R	R
PETE	CIMINO	5	8	.385	86	1	0	0	5	161	133	55	65	139	3.07	R	R
FRANK	CIMORELLI	0	0		11	0	0	0	0	13 1/3	20	13	10	1	8.78	R	R
LOU	CIOLA	1	3	.250	12	3	2	0	0	43 2/3	48	27	22	7	5.56	R	R
RALPH	CITARELLA	0	1	.000	21	2	0	0	3	44 1/3	41	20	14	28	4.06	R	R
CHRIS	CODIROLI	38	47	.447	144	108	13	2	1	670 1/3	711	363	261	312	4.87	R	R
HENRY	COPPOLA	3	4	.429	25	5	2	1	1	73 1/3	89	46	41	21	5.65	R	R
JIM	CORSI	22	24	.478	369	1	0	0	7	481 1/3	450	174	191	290	3.25	R	R
LEO	CRISTANTE	1	2	.333	30	2	0	0	0	58 2/3	65	25	23	15	3.84	R	R

FIRST	LAST	W	L	PCT	G	GS	CG	SH	SV	IP	H	ER	BB	K	ERA	BATS	THROWS
COOKIE	CUCCURULLO	3	5	.375	62	9	0	0	5	170	188	86	81	51	4.55	L	L
John	D'Acquisto	34	51	.400	266	92	7	2	15	779 2/3	708	395	544	600	4.56	R	R
PETE	DAGLIA	2	4	.333	12	5	2	2	0	50	67	32	20	16	5.76	R	R
Jeff	D'Amico	27	20	.574	64	63	2	2	0	385	571	171	120	.249	4.00	R	R
FRANK	DASSO	4	5	.444	18	12	6	0	0	96 2/3	91	42	55	40	3.91	R	R
RICH	DeLUCIA	38	51	.427	320	49	1	0	7	624	590	320	299	502	4.62	R	R
DON	DeMOLA	5	7	.417	85	0	0	0	1	155 1/3	138	65	63	110	3.77	R	R
TOM	DETTORE	8	11	.421	68	15	1	0	0	179 2/3	196	104	78	106	5.21	L	R
JACK	DiLAURO	2	7	.222	65	4	0	0	4	91 1/3	84	33	35	50	3.05	B	L
FRANK	DiPINO	35	38	.479	514	6	0	0	56	700	673	298	269	515	3.83	L	L
RON	DIORIO	0	0	.000	25	0	0	0	1	20 1/3	20	7	7	11	3.10	R	R
JERRY	DIPOTO	27	24	.529	390	0	0	0	49	495 1/3	527	223	221	352	4.05	R	R
DICK	DRAGO	108	117	.480	519	189	62	10	58	1875	1901	755	558	987	3.62	R	R
DAVE	DRAVECKY	64	57	.529	226	146	28	9	10	1062 2/3	968	370	315	558	3.13	L	L
JIM	DUFFALO	15	8	.652	141	14	2	0	6	297 2/3	248	112	155	210	3.39	R	R
FRANK	EUFEMIA	4	2	.667	39	0	0	0	2	61 2/3	56	26	21	30	3.79	R	R
PETE	FALCONE	70	90	.438	325	217	25	7	7	1435 1/3	1385	649	671	865	4.07	L	L
JEFF	FASSERO	104	95	.523	486	217	17	2	22	1669	1658	717	580	1405	3.87	L	L
DON	FERRARESE	19	36	.345	183	50	12	2	5	506 2/3	449	225	295	350	4.00	R	L
BILL	FERRAZZI	1	2	.333	3	2	1	0	0	7	7	4	5	0	5.14	R	R
TIM	FORTUGNO	3	4	.429	76	5	0	1	1	110 1/3	99	62	52	84	5.06	L	L
JOHN	FRANCO	88	76	.537	998	0	0	0	422	1150 1/3	1062	351	449	907	2.75	L	L
JOHN	FRASCATORE	20	17	.541	274	5	0	0	26	371	391	165	145	206	4.00	R	R
MARION	FRICANO	15	23	.395	88	43	14	0	1	387 2/3	393	186	164	115	4.32	R	R
DANNY	FRISELLA	34	40	.459	351	17	0	0	57	609 1/3	529	225	286	471	3.32	R	R
BOB	GALASSO	4	8	.333	55	8	0	0	4	118	153	77	47	63	5.87	R	R
BOB	GARIBALDI	0	2	.000	15	1	0	0	2	26 1/3	28	9	11	14	3.08	L	R
WILLIE	GARONI	0	1	.000	3	1	1	0	0	10	12	5	2	2	4.50	R	R
DAVE	GIUSTI	100	93	.518	668	133	35	9	145	1716 2/3	1654	687	570	1103	3.60	R	R
GUIDO	GRILLI	0	2	.000	22	0	0	0	1	20 1/3	24	16	20	12	7.08	L	L
STEVE	GRILLI	4	3	.571	70	0	0	0	3	147 2/3	138	74	96	91	4.51	R	R
FRANK	LaCORTE	23	44	.343	253	32	1	0	26	490	457	273	258	372	5.01	R	R
AL	LaMACCHIA	2	2	.500	16	1	0	0	0	30 2/3	38	22	14	7	6.46	R	R
FRANK	LaMANNA	6	5	.545	45	5	0	0	1	92 2/3	95	54	67	28	5.24	R	R
WALT	LANFRANCONI	4	5	.444	38	5	1	0	1	70	72	23	29	19	2.96	R	R

FIRST	LAST	W	L	PCT	G	GS	CG	SH	SV	IP	H	ER	BB	K	ERA	BATS	THROWS
TOM	LASORDA	0	4	.000	26	6	0	1	1	58 1/3	53	42	56	37	6.48	L	L
MARK	LEMONGELLO	22	38	.367	89	74	17		1	537	564	242	159	209	4.06	R	R
ANGELO	LIPETRI	0	0		10	0	0		0	15	13	9	3	9	5.40	R	R
VIC	LOMBARDI	50	51	.495	223	100	42	5	16	944 2/3	919	386	418	340	3.68	L	L
LOU	LOMBARDO	0	0		2	0	0		0	5 1/3	5	4	5	0	6.75	L	L
RALPH	LUMENTI	1	3	.250	13	6	0	0	0	33 1/3	32	27	42	30	7.29	R	L
SAL	MAGLIE	119	62	.657	303	232	93	25	14	1723	1591	603	562	862	3.15	R	R
MIKE	MAGNANTE	26	30	.464	452	19	0	0	3	589	628	261	223	336	3.99	L	L
PETE	MAGRINI	0	1	.000	3	1	0	0	0	7 1/3	8	8	8	3	9.82	R	R
JOE	MARGONERI	7	7	.500	36	15	3	0	0	126	132	60	70	67	4.29	L	L
LOU	MARONE	1	1	.500	30	0	0	0	0	37 2/3	26	11	13	25	2.63	L	L
JOE	MARTINA	6	8	.429	24	13	8	0	0	125 1/3	129	65	56	57	4.67	R	R
WEDO	MARTINI	0	2	.000	3	2	0	0	0	6 1/3	8	12	11	1	17.05	R	R
RALPH	MAURIELLO	1	1	.500	3	2	0	0	0	11 2/3	10	6	8	11	4.63	L	L
MIKE	MEOLA	0	3	.000	18	3	1	0	1	43	63	39	25	15	8.16	R	R
DAN	MICELI	33	36	.478	439	9	0	0	32	494	494	259	222	449	4.72	R	R
SAM	MILITELLO	4	4	.500	12	11	0	0	0	69 1/3	55	30	39	47	3.89	R	R
CRAIG	MINETTO	1	7	.125	55	15	0	0	1	145	162	87	72	76	5.40	L	L
STEVE	MINGORI	18	33	.353	385	2	0	0	42	584 2/3	544	197	225	329	3.03	L	L
GINO	MINUTELLI	0	3	.000	27	3	0	0	0	40 2/3	37	24	35	31	5.31	L	L
PAUL	MIRABELLA	19	29	.396	298	33	3	1	13	499 2/3	526	247	239	258	4.45	L	L
JOHN	MONTEFUSCO	90	83	.520	298	244	32	11	5	1652 1/3	1604	650	513	1081	3.54	R	R
RICH	MONTELEONE	24	17	.585	210	0	0	0	0	353 1/3	344	152	119	212	3.87	R	R
DAN	MOROGIELLO	0	0	.000	22	0	0	0	1	37 2/3	39	10	10	15	2.39	L	L
DON	MOSSI	101	80	.558	460	165	55	8	50	1548	1493	590	385	932	3.43	R	L
MIKE	MUSSINA	164	92	.641	322	322	49	18	0	2238 1/3	2097	869	509	1749	3.49	R	R
JOHN	PACELLA	4	10	.286	74	21	0	0	3	191 2/3	206	122	133	116	5.73	R	R
PAT	PACILLO	4	3	.571	18	7	0	0	0	50 1/3	55	33	23	34	5.90	R	R
JOHN	PAPA	0	0		3	0	0	0	0	2	5	5	4	3	22.50	R	R
FRANK	PASTORE	48	58	.453	220	139	22	7	6	986 1/3	1029	470	301	541	4.29	R	R
CARL	PAVANO	21	27	.438	66	64	1	1	0	378 1/3	395	191	128	255	4.54	R	R
BILL	PERTICA	22	18	.550	74	46	17	2	2	331	370	157	138	98	4.27	R	R
PRETZEL	PEZZULLO	3	5	.375	42	7	2	0	1	86 1/3	116	61	51	24	6.36	L	L
MARIO	PICONE	0	2	.000	13	3	0	0	0	40	43	28	25	11	6.30	R	R
MARINO	PIERETTI	30	38	.441	194	68	21	4	8	673 2/3	713	339	321	188	4.53	R	R

FIRST	LAST	W	L	PCT	G	GS	CG	SH	SV	IP	H	ER	BB	K	ERA	BATS	THROWS
AL	PIEROTTI	1	2	.333	8	2	2	0	0	26 2/3	26	12	12	13	4.05	R	R
BILL	PIERRO	0	5	.000	12	3	0	0	0	29	33	34	28	13	10.55	R	R
MARC	PISCIOTTA	4	5	.444	75	0	0	0	0	80 2/3	73	38	58	55	4.24	R	R
LOU	POLLI	0	2	.000	24	1	0	0	3	42 1/3	55	22	23	11	4.68	R	R
JOHN	POLONI	1	0	1.000	2	1	0	0	0	7	8	5	1	5	6.43	L	L
CHARLIE	PULEO	29	39	.426	180	76	3	1	2	633	621	299	319	387	4.25	R	R
AL	RAFFO	1	3	.250	45	0	0	0	1	72 1/3	81	33	25	38	4.11	R	R
BRADY	RAGGIO	2	3	.400	19	5	0	0	0	38 1/3	66	36	19	24	8.45	R	R
VIC	RASCHI	132	66	.667	269	255	106	26	3	1819	1666	752	727	944	3.72	R	R
BARRY	RAZIANO	1	2	.333	15	0	0	0	1	21 2/3	21	15	9	9	6.23	B	R
XAVIER	RESCIGNO	19	22	.463	129	21	7	0	16	335 1/3	366	154	113	115	4.13	R	R
FRANK	RICCELLI	3	3	.500	17	5	0	0	0	41	39	20	23	32	4.39	L	L
CHUCK	RICCI	1	0	1.000	7	0	0	0	0	10	9	2	3	9	1.80	R	R
DAVE	RIGHETTI	82	79	.509	718	89	13	2	252	1403 2/3	1287	540	591	1112	3.46	L	L
TODD	RIZZO	0	2	.000	12	0	0	0	0	8	16	11	9	5	12.38	R	L
JOE	ROSSELLI	2	1	.667	9	5	0	0	0	30	39	29	20	7	8.70	L	L
FRANK	ROSSO	0	0		2	0	0	0	0	4	11	4	3	1	9.00	R	R
MARIUS	RUSSO	45	34	.570	120	84	48	6	5	680 2/3	618	237	255	311	3.13	L	L
JOE	SAMBITO	37	38	.493	461	5	1	1	84	629	562	212	195	489	3.03	L	L
AL	SANTORINI	17	38	.309	127	70	5	4	3	493 1/3	533	235	194	268	4.29	R	R
CALVIN	SCHIRALDI	32	39	.451	235	47	2	0	21	553 1/3	522	263	267	471	4.28	R	R
FRANK	SEMINARA	12	9	.571	47	26	0	0	0	163 2/3	171	75	75	90	4.12	R	R
DAN	SERAFINI	14	13	.519	91	29	1	0	1	231 1/3	294	157	102	114	6.06	B	L
AL	SIMA	11	21	.344	100	30	4	0	4	308 2/3	343	158	132	111	4.61	R	R
JOHN	SMOLTZ	160	116	.580	392	361	47	14	10	2473 1/3	2435	920	784	2155	3.34	R	R
JOE	SPARMA	52	52	.500	183	142	31	10	0	864 2/3	774	379	436	586	3.94	R	R
TOM	URBANI	10	17	.370	81	36	0	0	0	260 1/3	316	144	86	149	4.98	L	L
VITO	VALENTINETTI	13	14	.481	108	15	3	0	3	257	266	135	122	94	4.73	R	R
RON	VILLONE	29	31	.483	274	57	2	0	5	566	560	309	321	443	4.91	L	L
FRANK	VIOLA	176	150	.540	421	420	74	16	0	2836 1/3	2827	1175	864	1844	3.73	L	L
JOE	VITELLI	0	0		4	0	0	0	0	7	5	2	7	2	2.57	R	R
DOM	ZANNI	9	6	.600	111	3	0	0	10	183	155	77	85	148	3.79	R	R
BARRY	ZITO	24	12	.667	49	49	4	3	0	307	248	111	125	283	3.25	L	L